THE STRUGGLE FOR WESTERN SAHARA

Erik Jensen's impressive diplomatic career, which involved postings and missions around the world from New York, Geneva and London to Bahrain, Pakistan and Bangladesh, East Timor, Nigeria, Chad and Western Sahara, culminated in his appointment as an Under-Secretary-General of the United Nations. He holds degrees from Oxford and Harvard and honorary doctorates from Connecticut and Seoul and has been a Senior Associate Member of St Antony's, Oxford, Visiting Fellow at the LSE and Warburg Professor in International Relations at Simmons College/University, Boston.

He has written several books including *The Iban and their Religion; Under the Sun* (as Erik Jay); *Western Sahara: Anatomy of a Stalemate*; *Where Hornbills Fly* and, most recently, his acclaimed memoir *Alien Aloft*. He was an original Fellow of the Borneo Research Council and is a Fellow of the Royal Geographical Society and sometime Member of the Royal Insititute of International Affairs.

Front cover: 'Saharan sheikh' from an original oil painting by Erik Jensen

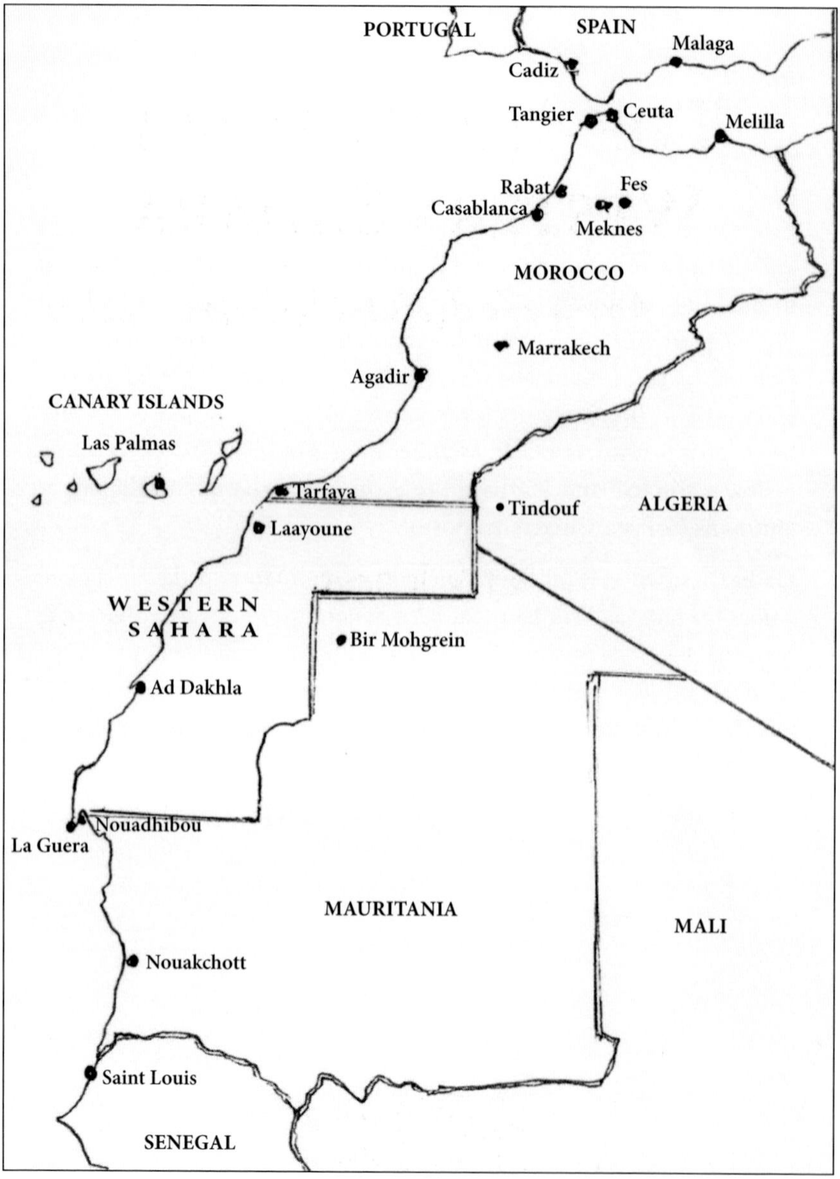
PORTUGAL
SPAIN
Malaga
Cadiz
Tangier
Ceuta
Melilla
Rabat
Fes
Casablanca
Meknes
MOROCCO
Marrakech
Agadir
CANARY ISLANDS
Las Palmas
Tarfaya
Tindouf
ALGERIA
Laayoune
WESTERN SAHARA
Bir Mohgrein
Ad Dakhla
Nouadhibou
La Guera
MAURITANIA
MALI
Nouakchott
Saint Louis
SENEGAL

The Struggle for Western Sahara

Africa's Last Colony

Erik Jensen

ELSP

Published in 2022 by
ELSP

Origination by Ex Libris Press
www.ex-librisbooks.co.uk

Typeset in 10.5/14 point Minion Pro

Printed and bound in the UK by
CPI Group (UK) Ltd, Croydon, CR0 4YY

ISBN 9781912020218

CONTENTS

Michael Willis of St Antony's College, Oxford, Director of the Middle East Centre, writes:

'It is a great book. I will certainly be putting it on the reading list for my students here at Oxford. Erik Jensen's book provides the reader with a front row seat on the lengthy and often complex diplomatic negotiations that sought to resolve one of the longest running and still continuing territorial disputes in the world today. As the senior UN diplomat in Western Sahara in the 1990s, Jensen is able to provide a valuable and more neutral perspective on a dispute that continues to arouse fierce passions five decades on from its first eruption in the 1970s. Replete with fascinating detail and personal insights, Jensen's book is essential reading for anyone who wants to understand the conflict over the Western Sahara, why it endures and, crucially, how it might be finally resolved.'

Some reviews of Erik Jensen's book Where Hornbills Fly published in 2010:

'I have just read a lovely book about the Iban … which anyone who has travelled to Borneo would love … With apparent total recall, reminiscent of Paddy Leigh Fermor's *Time of Gifts,* he evokes the wonderful life of the 'ulu', which is sadly largely forgotten today. I recommend it to all who know Borneo already and to those who will understand so much more of what is left if they read it before they go.'

Robin Hanbury-Tenison, *Traveller*, April 2011

'A vivid narrative of the ups and downs of community development … the sheer power of Jensen's prose draws the reader into the rain-forest world of the Ibans … this is a must-read for those interested in the hard realities of the development experience in tropical socieites and for those with a commitment to an applied and engaged anthropology.'

Victor T. King, *Asian Affairs,* Nov. 2011

'It's as freshly written as if he were remembering yesterday, full of the incongruous, arresting details … that bring a book to life.'

Mick Herron, *Geographical,* March 2011

'a sage and enthralling account … deserves to be read in toto both as the testimony of a remarkable pioneer and as a testament to an easily maligned people.'

John Keay, *Literary Review,* December 2010

Prologue

King Hassan II wanted history to remember him as the Moroccan realm's reunifier. His father, the liberator, had achieved independence from the French protectorate and the Spanish. Hassan would recover the colonial vestiges remaining and restore glory to his ancient dynasty.

Moroccans are a proud people, recalling with special pride their greatness when the sultan commanded obeisance from southern Spain to the river Senegal. They resented when European powers nibbled at the coast then encroached inland till the whole country came under foreign domination: Spanish enclaves, French and Spanish protectorates and Tangier internationally administered.

Hassan's negotiation with Spain achieved restitution of Spanish colonial possessions in southern Morocco but the vast desert of Spanish Sahara eluded him. An International Court of Justice opinion failed to endorse Morocco's claim but empowered Hassan to launch the 'Green March'. Three hundred and fifty thousand Moroccans, waving national flags and the Koran, marched peacefully across the frontier to reclaim the territory. The people's support was overwhelming; Hassan became personally popular. Within weeks the Madrid Accords divided administration of Spanish Sahara between Morocco and Mauritania. Hassan deployed troops and established an administering presence. He counted on international recognition in due course.

Sahrawi tribes in southern Morocco had welcomed absorption into the realm. Western Sahara responded differently. Support there was, also opposition. The Frente Polisario, a Sahrawi movement founded to campaign for independence from Spain, resisted aggressively. Polisario units battled Moroccan forces until superior weaponry forced their retreat eastward. Algerian soldiers arriving to help were defeated. By year's end Polisario, accompanied by some 50,000 Sahrawis, had found refuge in southern Algeria. A day after Spain took final leave of the territory in February 1976 Polisario declared Western Sahara an independent state and raised the flag of the Sahrawi Arab Democratic Republic in the desert. The SADR was officially recognized by Algeria.

For Morocco the enemy was Algeria: Polisario an Algerian proxy, reliant on Algerian material, political and diplomatic support. Algeria was as determined to frustrate Hassan's ambition to incorporate Western Sahara into the kingdom as he to realize it. Armed Polisario incursions deep into Moroccan areas, a costly embarrassment, were eventually countered by the building of a defensive wall the length of the territory. The Cold War, with Algeria close to the Soviets and Morocco in the western camp, froze attempts at mediation. When Algeria masterminded admission of SADR as a member state of the Organisation of African Unity Morocco left. Morocco awaited regime change in Algeria; Algiers expected Moroccan monarchical rule to implode.

The fall of the Berlin wall and United Nations success in tackling hitherto insoluble conflicts led attention to Western Sahara. The UN secretary-general developed a settlement plan. In 1991 the plan, to be implemented with the parties' voluntary cooperation and without a predetermined outcome unlike other major operations, was approved by the Security Council. Council members were seemingly unaware of both sides' reservations. Secretary-General Perez de Cuellar may have envisaged mediating a political compromise before the end of his mandate. He reached a cease-fire agreement but modification of the original plan in the very month he retired did little to improve its prospects.

The settlement plan pointed to a referendum with the choice between independence and integration with Morocco. The contentious issue: who should vote. Polisario adhered rigidly to a Spanish 1974 census, Morocco demanded a much more inclusive electoral roll. The plan, as belatedly modified, admitted some not included in the census and recognized oral testimony. Hassan assured Moroccans of a 'confirmatory' referendum, underwritten by Driss Basri, his minister of interior, who (in later years) proudly claimed that he controlled the levers necessary to ensure massive support for attachment to the kingdom.[1]

Hassan's goal was never in doubt: Western Sahara was Moroccan Sahara. He parried interference during the Cold War and from a divided OAU but the UN Security Council was different. The UN would not be party to a fraudulent process, nor could it be easily manipulated. Morocco craved respect as a nation seen to abide by Council decisions in conformity with international law, but Hassan refused to relinquish control. He deployed tactics as circumstances dictated, stalling, diverting, buying time. At the critical juncture when the Council seemed poised to endorse a solution for which Hassan was unready Morocco exploited all means to block it. Not long afterwards Hassan died and Mohammed VI was able to declare the settlement plan lapsed.

Two further peace plans failed, being accepted by one side or the other but not both. The conflict became a war of attrition. The Security Council called for a politically negotiated solution depriving Polisario of its preferred option. Morocco, relaxed, allowed time to serve its interests in Western Sahara as the population evolved while, in an unstable Algeria, the Polisario leadership aged. In 2016, the secretary-general Ban Ki-Moon, on a visit to the Polisario camps, referred to Western Sahara as 'occupied'. Morocco was outraged and following mass demonstrations expelled the civilian component of the UN mission. In April 2017 secretary-general Gutteres released a report calling for a new dynamic and spirit: for the parties to negotiate without preconditions, explore ways to self-determination, for Algeria and Mauritinia to be involved. The Security Council underwrote his determination to resolve the conflict.

1

Secret meeting

In 1996 on a perfect summer's evening I walked from the Palais des Nations down towards the lake of Geneva. Ancient cedars asserted their dignity, specimen trees flaunted singular foliage, shrubs flowered, a peacock screeched. This was August, holiday month. Geneva brimmed with expensively dressed tourists. I was there for a different reason.

Just before leaving the Palais, shortly after six o'clock, I finally reached Bachir by telephone. Thank god. He had not been in Algiers at 3.30, as planned, when an Arabic speaker answered the phone. I knew enough Arabic to grasp that Bachir had yet to arrive. Half an hour later I called back. In halting French this time I was urged to try again in a couple of hours. Then he was there. He had come through the door, he said, at precisely that moment. Plane problems: instead of flying in the early hours it was after noon before they could take off from their encampment in the southern desert. No problem, though, with onward flight plans, seats on Air Algerie were confirmed. Of course, scheduled departures from Algiers were frequently delayed, but he would definitely be coming, '*inshallah*', as agreed. He would call in the morning to confirm their precise departure time. Later he telephoned to suggest the meeting proposed for six o'clock the following evening be postponed to seven, just in case. Almost as an afterthought he mentioned that he and his two counsellors had no hotel booking and could I please organise somewhere for them to stay.

Mustapha Bachir Sayed, known as Bachir, was the spokesman and effective leader internationally of the *Frente Popular para la Libercion de Seguia el-Hamra y Rio de Oro*, the Polisario Front independence movement formed from Sahrawi tribes initially to expel Spanish colonialists and subsequently against Morocco's armed presence in Western Sahara. For three years I had known him. A man of charm and ability, and formidable champion of his people's cause. We came as close to friendliness as should be when one is trying to mediate between adversaries at war. War it was. Two of Africa's most serious armies continued to face each other along a thousand mile front – even as armed engagement evolved into warfare by other means. The UN Security Council achieved a cease-fire but the settlement plan to resolve the conflict, deeply flawed, and dependent on voluntary cooperation, showed little prospect of being fully implemented. Bachir told me, when he began to trust me, that the only hope lay in direct talks between Polisario and Morocco at the highest level, anything less being pointless in that society.

The Moroccans refused to believe that the Polisario would respect discretion. They could never commit their king or crown prince to an exercise that might be twisted into political recognition of Polisario and its self-proclaimed sovereign state. Eventually, after three years' negotiating, Morocco's strong man, Driss Basri, Minister of Interior, and the kingdom's most powerful personage under King Hassan II, paid me his finest compliment: he took my word. He agreed, with the king's authority, to meet in person with Bachir as preliminary to an encounter at the highest level. Confidentiality was paramount, the merest inkling in diplomatic circles, let alone the media, and all would be denied. A weekend in Geneva at the height of summer, full of tourists, many Arabic, offered ideal cover. That was why I was there.

That Friday I inspected the Hotel des Bergues, arguably establishment Geneva's preferred hotel, to ensure that Basri had his suite and that a suitably discreet conference room stood ready. The manager's comportment underlined that Geneva was all too often the site for secret politicking. Geneva in August was heavily booked but late that evening, after the conversation with Bachir, I did obtain reservations for him plus two at the Hotel President. It was a Morton's fork of anything more down-market with the reaction 'Who do you think we are?' or too fancy and 'What do you take us for?' I could convincingly maintain that this was the only suitable hotel with a vacancy.

The following morning, Saturday, I waited in my infinitely more modest hotel room for notice that a plane of the king's flight would be arriving with Morocco's Minister of Interior and that Bachir had left on Air Algerie. At ten a.m. the phone rang. The Polisario representative in Algiers informed me that Bachir had departed for the airport but take-off was two hours delayed. Two hours posed no problem, he would still be landing before Basri was due, and in ample time for the six o'clock, now seven o'clock, meeting. The representative promised to call again to confirm departure. When next he called, take-off had been further postponed: the flight would now be three hours late in leaving. He did not call again. I tried phoning airport enquiries. Recorded messages in English, French and German – then a live woman came on line.

All she could tell me was that the flight had not yet taken off from Algiers. A two hour delay, then three, yes, but the flight was still expected. We began speaking so often that she recognised my voice. She became genuinely helpful. No confirmation of departure had been received when three hours were up – 'but they have been known to forget to do so promptly.' More uncertainty, then, at long last, she confirmed that Air Algerie was air borne and predicted to land in Switzerland around 6.30. I thanked her profusely. Relief swept over me. I had taken a risk. At first news of the three-hour delay there would have been time to alert Basri before his leaving Rabat. I decided against. If I tried explaining to Basri that Bachir was delayed he would put all manner of interpretation on it, and wait. And by the time Bachir did arrive, because I remained convinced that he was in good faith and would come, it might prove impossible to reconfigure flights and meeting arrangements. Both would see themselves as having been stood up by the other. The critical element of trust, so laboriously built up, would be lost.

A telephone call announced Basri's arrival, slightly ahead of schedule, and I was being asked whether Bachir had landed when we were cut off. Then Bachir came on the phone. The sense of relief that swept over me on hearing of Air Algerie en route evaporated instantly. 'Where are you?' I asked, how could he suddenly be in Geneva? He was in Algiers, he said. My heart sank. 'But I have just heard that the plane has taken off.' 'I know,' he said,' but we couldn't get seats.' They had checked in at the airport, he explained, then when an extended delay was announced they left for a meeting and returned at the appointed hour to find boarding completed, the plane full. Basri is already here, I told him, ready to meet you this evening. 'Yes,' he said, 'I'm going to come. There is a flight to Lyon in the early morning. We could catch that and drive from there.'

I did not bother to speculate about possible delays. Without a second's doubt I knew that Basri would never compromise, before nightfall he would be on his special plane back to Rabat. I saw the imminent collapse of years' work, squandering the trust placed in me and my word by two powerful, self-important men who rarely trusted anyone.

'Can't the Algerian government provide an aircraft?' Bachir was dubious. Perhaps I could help, if I were to call the foreign minister, use my influence, that would make a difference. He gave me a selection of telephone numbers for the Algerian Ministry of Foreign Affairs. I despaired, by now it was nearly six-thirty on a Saturday evening in summer. The first two numbers rang and rang, the special 'permanence' did not reply. With little hope I tried the ministry head, the secretary-general's direct line. A secretary answered. I gave my name. Said it was most urgent, I needed to speak to M. Bendjama. She put me through. When I told Bendjama how relieved I was to find him in the office on a Saturday he reminded me curtly that Muslims had Friday off. Fortunately I had advised the Algerian foreign ministry in general of my plans: the Polisario would not have dared proceed if Algeria objected. Basri, I explained, was already in Geneva while Bachir had missed the flight from Algiers. Bendjama had been briefed. Could he please, please help? Not that easy, he said, but he would do what he could.

While I was trying to reach the foreign ministry there had been one incoming call, which I chose to ignore. It could only be Basri insisting on confirmation of Bachir's arrival. Then the phone rang again. Basri himself. Where was Bachir? On his way, I believed, there had been flight delays, but he was coming. The first meeting would have to be postponed to the morning. Basri insisted on seeing me as a matter of urgency: he had things to discuss. Of course, I said, then thought it best to await news from Algiers. It came just as I began to feel I could wait no longer. A ministry spokesman confirmed that an Algerian government aircraft had been cleared for take-off and was estimated to land in Geneva around nine-thirty.

Basri, having showered, lay bare-chested on his king-size bed to receive me. What had happened to Bachir? It all went to show that you could not really trust the Polisario. But he had just bathed and was uncharacteristically relaxed. I suspected he already had intelligence as to what had transpired, the Moroccans had multiple sources of information. I provided no detail, said nothing about the Air Algerie flight, but confirmed that Bachir and counsellors were in the air. The initial meeting I suggested for ten-thirty in the morning. Why not ten, or even earlier? Basri asked, then relented. As soon as Bachir landed would I please call him or his adviser Governor Azmi – whatever the hour, he added.

I left for the President hotel to brief Bachir on arrival. As well that I did because the reservations had been cancelled, no one having appeared by nine o'clock. I reconfirmed minutes before a couple presented themselves to enquire whether by any chance a cancelled room had become available only to be told that there was no vacancy. Airport information had nothing on private flights and my enquiries 'friend' had left. By ten o'clock I became nervous and prevailed upon the hotel receptionist to use her contacts at the airport to discover whether a special flight from Algiers had landed. I waited; she consulted. She spoke to one person then another, before explaining that no private flights were permitted to land in Geneva after a certain hour; an incoming aircraft had indeed been diverted, to Lyon. I had no idea whether Bachir and company had the necessary visa to enter France or currency or how long it would take overland or how to reach them. All I could do was hope and wait.

I waited in the spacious hotel lounge. A party of Latin Americans danced the Macarena with enthusiasm. I made a drink last a long, long time. Around midnight the Macarena dancers dispersed, an hour later bar service closed. It was almost two when a dishevelled Bachir with his exhausted counsellors finally appeared. They had taken a taxi, he said, from Lyon, and were extremely tired. They looked it. Before they stumbled up to bed I explained that the meeting with Basri had been rescheduled for ten-thirty; I would be there in the morning to escort them. Then I tried reaching Governor Azmi but his number did not answer according to the operator who put me straight through to Basri, who sounded asleep, not pleased to be woken.

Sunday morning dawned bright and beautiful. On waking I telephoned Bachir, apparently still sleeping, to remind him of the ten-thirty appointment, and offered to collect him. Azmi, when I called to reconfirm arrangements, insisted that he had been in his room all evening watching television and the hotel was talking nonsense, but, yes, Basri had mentioned my message about Bachir – and the hour. At the President hotel Bachir was ready, in good spirits; he introduced his younger brother and the Polisario representative from Brussels, both accompanying him as counsellors. I might have preferred walking along the lakeside but suggested a taxi, in the cab we could talk. It was necessary to respect Basri's reaction to yesterday's uncertainty and the repeated postponement. I counted on Bachir making a special effort to foster a positive atmosphere and focus on agreeing a specific place and date for the top-level meeting, and not to try for more. On arriving at the Hotel des Bergues Bachir asked if I would settle the fare since he had no Swiss francs.

Les Bergues exuded elegance, understated opulence, tranquillity. Few people were about. Azmi arrived with an invitation to Basri's suite and Bachir accepted – although in preliminary discussion he had insisted on neutral ground. Upstairs, Basri was in the corridor to greet Bachir and welcomed him with an Arabic kiss on both cheeks. I was 'presented' as everyone's friend, '*ami de tous*.' Basri escorted Bachir into the salon followed by his counsellors and Azmi. I nodded and left, it had been a rigid Moroccan condition that any negotiation take place without an outside presence.

This preliminary meeting was to launch the encounter that my predecessor had striven for and two UN secretaries-general had laboured, unsuccessfully, to achieve. It offered the prospect of negotiating a settlement to Africa's long outstanding post-colonial conflict, more than twenty years warfare and the protracted distress of a hundred thousand or more refugees.

Not sure what to do I wandered across the Pont du Mont Blanc into Geneva old town. Passing a church where a service was beginning I prayed, I do not know to whom, before walking down to the Place Molard and its restaurants. I was ravenous, having hardly eaten all day before. Brunch over, I ventured back to Les Bergues. My intention was to find Azmi for news of progress. On the steps I heard someone call 'Monsieur Jensen' and turned to see Bachir hurrying towards me, smiling broadly, such a climate of confidence was achieved that he had left his briefcase behind. As he spoke his brother emerged with it. Together we walked beside the lake to the President hotel. The meeting had opened, he told me, with the traditional politenesses before they began talking seriously. He had found Basri courteous, well-informed and reasonably open-minded. A good atmosphere prevailed throughout. The main encounter would likely be with the king, possibly within the week. Morocco continued to insist that the UN not be directly implicated though he Bachir was determined that I should be fully apprised of all proceedings, waiting in the wings for whatever walk-on part prove warranted.

Later Azmi called. He sounded cheerful, told me that they had all had lunch together, had they known where to find me I would have been included; the mood had been positively convivial. He invited me to meet Basri. By the time I reached Les Bergues Basri was already on the point of leaving for the airport, his expansive Smalto cabin trunk, labelled 'wanted on voyage', stood up-ended, packed for dispatch together with much other luggage, his valet and, I believe, personal doctor. He had changed into another sharp suit, only the fly still undone, which he realised half way through the briefing.

Basri was disposed to be generous with his time – take-off could wait – and concerned that I be well informed. If his account was selective, it did not sound so. The atmosphere had been good, he reiterated, even warm. One earlier encounter, years before, when Bachir became over-excited, had been written off, nothing remotely similar arose on this occasion. Without delving deep into substance they had covered important ground. No need to speak only of 'dialogue', Basri said, that taboo could be put aside, Morocco was prepared to 'negotiate'. In accepting the UN Security Council plan Morocco had effectively recognised the Polisario as the 'other party'. He was not preoccupied with diplomatic niceties, he wished to be pragmatic – pragmatic a word he repeated several times. Independence, of course, was not subject to discussion. He remained adamant that Morocco would have the votes in an eventual referendum but was willing to seek a solution now, after twenty years conflict, the king was open to that. The alternative meant abandoning Polisario to humanitarian aid, arms suppliers and whatever support they could muster for the next two or three centuries. If that was what they wanted. Integration could be discussed as regionalism with autonomy in whatever interpretation. Polisario's dignity would be fully respected, he insisted; they had fought for their cause honourably, as soldiers; civilians had not been abused and no action degraded their code of honour.

Basri was confident that the king would agree to a meeting at the highest level. He made ready to report to His Majesty, who would decide.

2

Forming of Hassan

HIS MAJESTY KING HASSAN II had come to the throne unexpectedly when his father died following minor surgery. A young man in his twenties translated from playboy prince into ruler he felt challenged by his father's legacy. Mohammed V endured humiliation under the French and exile, but with dignity survived to see Morocco independent of France and Spain's protectorate to his people's enthusiastic acclaim. His place in history as the Liberator was assured.

Independence, however, as proclaimed by the leader of Istiqlal, the independence party, would be complete only when all the lands once forming part of Greater Morocco were restored to the throne. 'So long as Tangier is not liberated from its international statute, so long as the Spanish deserts of the south, the Sahara from Tindouf to Atar and the Algerian-Moroccan borderlands are not liberated from their trusteeship, our independence will remain incomplete and our first duty will be to carry on action to liberate the country and to unify it.'[1]

Moroccan claims were buttressed by their concept of sovereignty. Sovereignty derived less from ownership or territorial rights: it was rooted in allegiance. The *beiya* oath of loyalty to the sultan as spiritual and temporal head equated to nationality. The challenge to unify an independent Morocco meant asserting the sultan's rule throughout government controlled lands (*Bled-el-Makhzen*) and also the 'lands of dissidence' (*Bled-el-Siba*), where the *beiya* was honoured, as well as recovering foreign colonial holdings. Mohammed V, unable to countenance the monarchy outdistanced in patriotic fervour by Istiqlal, made Greater Morocco his official cause.

Two enclaves on the Mediterranean, Ceuta and Melilla, together with the Chafferine (Zafferine) islands, remained Spanish, as they had been for centuries,[2] but in the south Spain was pressured into surrendering its colonial holding round Tarfaya. It refused to relinquish its right to Sidi Ifni underwritten in perpetuity by an 1860 Treaty of Peace and Amity. And there could be no question of abandoning Spanish Sahara. On a visit to the Draa valley in far southern Morocco King Mohammed pledged to recover all that 'by the evidence of history and the will of the inhabitants belongs of right to our kingdom'.[3]

If his father had his undisputed place as 'liberator', Hassan would be the 'unifier'. His first act was to assert territorial claims along the disputed Moroccan-Algerian border, barely twelve months after Algeria, following eight tortuous years of bloody fighting, had wrested independence from France. Hassan visited Algiers, where Ben Bella, newly president, asked for time to restore his mauled country and to establish institutions before discussing frontiers. But in late summer border incidents offered a pretext for action. Morocco's Forces Armees Royales (FAR) invaded. The Algerians retook two towns only to lose them again. Ben Bella ordered general mobilisation. His troops attacked into Morocco while Moroccan forces advanced towards Tindouf until diplomatic pressure from the United States and France enabled the Organisation of African Unity (OAU) to mediate. Hassan and Ben Bella were persuaded to agree a cease-fire.[4]

The outcome, far from heroic, did nothing to boost Hassan's standing at home, where Istiqlal's left wing campaigned for a constitutional monarchy within a genuinely democratic system. But the constitution, revised, named the monarchy constitutional without depriving the king of divine right. As commander of the faithful, supreme chief of the army, with the government nominated by him and a judiciary subject to his ultimate authority, this hardly represented curtailment of the king's absolute power. Hassan stood firm in the face of pervasive dissatisfaction aggravated by economic decline. Recession affected all save the privileged class. By 1965 a third of the population lived in urban areas and Casablanca had three hundred thousand unemployed. Unrest spilled out from the ever-burgeoning shanty towns. Chaos was only brought under control by a machine-gunning helicopter, which flew along the avenues till everyone still living had been dispersed. Hundreds were killed, possibly thousands.

To boost the depressed national mood the king proclaimed Morocco on the cusp of a most important moment in its history. Expectations rose. Before incredulity greeted publication of the text of another constitution: no concession to democratic rule, the king's absolute power actually reinforced: parliamentary immunity was withdrawn and no challenge to the monarchic principle or Muslim religion permitted. The leading parties, outraged, ignored their differences and called for rejection. The interior minister still announced the proposed constitution adopted by 98.85 percent of those who voted, with participation at 93 percent.

Spain, meanwhile, under mounting pressure at the United Nations, had agreed to bilateral talks with Morocco about Sidi Ifni. General Franco, convinced that the enclave served no further economic or strategic purpose, consented and in January 1969 Spain signed the Treaty of Fez. Six months later Ifni came under Moroccan administration. Hassan was gratified that Sahrawi tribes living in the area welcomed integration into Morocco. Though the recovery of Sidi Ifni failed to generate widespread acclaim or significantly bolster Hassan's standing in the eyes of his people it did boost his hopes for negotiating a solution to the Saharan dispute. Hassan had been urging Franco to discuss the Sahara, threatening 'to inject the virus of self-determination'[5] if he refused. In 1971 Hassan visited Madrid to propose a deal: guarantees for Spain's strategic interests in the region, cooperative economic measures on land, in mining and at sea, even provision for bases. Franco rejected the offer as tantamount to suicide.[6]

Hassan liked celebrating his birthday in style. In 1971 guests received the royal command to the seaside palace at Skhirat. Hospitality was lavish: the choicest food in superabundance, with champagne and whiskey discreetly available. At just after two o'clock shots sounded, fireworks thought some, then more shots as troops charged in shooting wildly, killing and wounding; a hundred died, including the Belgian ambassador, ministers and eminent guests. The soldiers' leader, M'Hamed Abadou, astonishingly, abandoned the assassination of Hassan, rushed into Rabat to take control, which allowed the king to reassert himself. Next day Hassan, addressing the Moroccan people, dismissed this 'underdeveloped' coup attempt by imbeciles.[7] The perpetrators were executed – and the price of sugar was reduced.

A year later, having celebrated his birthday slightly less lavishly, Hassan chose to holiday in France. When entering Moroccan air space on the return six fighter aircraft attacked taking out two of his Boeing's three reactors. The plane plummeted a thousand metres before the pilot succeeded in stabilising for an emergency landing. The king fought to reassure him till they reached Rabat. No explosion. Hassan, only somewhat dishevelled, reviewed a guard of honour briskly before entering the *salon d'honneur*. As king and party made to depart fighter aircraft flew low and strafed, killing eight and wounding fifty. Hassan commandeered a car that was not an official vehicle, took the wheel and drove away from Rabat, while fighters bombarded the royal palace. From

Skhirat, secured by loyal troops, the king reclaimed his authority.

Responsibility for the coup was traced to Oufkir, general, minister of defence and interior, on whom Hassan had bestowed ever greater power, privilege and friendship, the man he most trusted. Confronted by Hassan with undeniable evidence, Oufkir shot himself – it was claimed.[8] The next day, the national news agency reported the general's suicide and King Hassan addressed the nation. He announced his decision to eliminate the office of minister of defence and all military ranks at major-general and above. After two coups and near death Hassan's obsession with loyalty was hardly surprising nor his determination to win the affection of his people.

3

Masterstroke and its aftermath

SPAIN, STILL UNDER PRESSURE at the United Nations, while accepting in principle to prepare for the ending of colonial rule in Spanish Sahara, planned a status to safeguard Spanish interests. From being at best a prestige asset with useful fishing rights the discovery and exploitation of high-grade phosphate rock had given the territory value.

A Sahrawi resistance movement to Spanish rule, the *Mouvement de Resistance des Hommes Bleus*, petered out in 1973 within a year of its founding. The same year, also in Rabat, Sahrawi students formed the Frente Polisario. It evolved rapidly as a political force. Disturbances in the territory and mounting pressure, internal and external, induced Spain to offer domestic autonomy. A population census was undertaken in 1974. To foster a political climate favourable to themselves the Spanish authorised a party, which, despite being called 'revolutionary' and 'progressive', was committed to modernising on conservative lines and to preserving special relations with Spain. The *Partido de la Union Nacional Saharaoui*, PUNS, was registered in February 1975.[1]

In May of 1975 Spain, having previously refused permission outright, acquiesced in the UN (Decolonisation) Committee of 24 dispatching a mission. The day before the mission was due troops muntinied.[2] Mass demonstrations greeted its arrival in Laayoune. Enthusiasm for Polisario took the Spanish authorities by surprise and the lack of support for PUNS; the PUNS leader, Khalihenna Ould Rachid, left for Morocco to swear allegiance to King Hassan. The UN secretary-general visited the region[3] but his attempt to convene a four-way conference failed.

With Spain seemingly poised to surrender sovereignty and rumoured to intend transferring power to Polisario, Hassan acted. To Franco he stressed that 'this territory belongs to me'.[4] Successful retrocession of Sidi Ifni had reinforced his conviction that the people of the Saharan south would welcome absorption into the kingdom. Counting on arguments of history and the principle of territorial integrity, he urged a joint approach to the International Court of Justice for a non-binding advisory opinion. Spain refused. The Moroccans then persuaded the UN to sanction an approach to the Court by Morocco and Mauritania.[5] Hassan could hardly wait for the advisory opinion to be delivered, on 16 October. His decision already made, he instantly hailed the opinion, as sufficient authority to vindicate the Moroccan claim and unleashed a 'spontaneous' mass movement to recover Morocco's Saharan territory.

The Court's opinion was more ambivalent than Hassan claimed. Legal ties of allegiance between the Sultan of Morocco and some of the tribes living in the territory were recognised, as with the 'Mauritanian entity'. 'On the other hand, the Court's conclusion is that the materials and information presented to it do not establish any tie of territorial sovereignty' and the Court upheld 'the principle of self-determination through free and genuine expression of the will of the peoples of the Territory'.[6] Hassan's interpretation, according to an eminent international lawyer, was worthy of Alice in Wonderland.[7]

For more than a month Hassan had, in strictest secrecy, been preparing a plan. On 20 August, the eve of his annual address commemorating the Sultan's departure in exile, Hassan awoke in the middle of the night with a brilliant idea.[8] He imagined a huge throng marching peacefully. Next day he convoked three confidants, made them swear to divulge nothing, and began working to mobilise 350,000 Moroccans, equivalent to the number born annually. When the march was proclaimed publicly the response was overwhelming – we could have had a million or two, Hassan maintained. Participants were selected by quota, ten percent women, some pregnant; eleven babies were born during the march.

For Spain the timing was awful. General Franco, aged 82, lay in a coma after a series of heart attacks having but recently recovered from serious phlebitis. The Spanish military, resolutely opposed to Moroccan demands, had means to resist but some eighteen thousand Spaniards living in Morocco, Ceuta and Melilla were a concern. Spain asked Hassan to postpone the march. After first claiming that as impossible, he revised the date to 28 October, and again to early November. By then a confidential deal had been reached for a ten-kilometre demilitarised zone that would permit the marchers to enter the territory before withdrawing.[9] Spain still demanded the Security Council to insist, not merely request, that Morocco desist from the march. Hassan rejected further conciliatory efforts as overtaken by events and, on 5 November, launched the Green March.

The king warned the marchers, as they gathered at Tarfaya north of the frontier, of danger from landmines, from armoured vehicles and artillery fire. He knew the risk but counted on the Spanish military, disciplined troops, refusing to shoot unarmed civilians. His confidence was based on the secret understanding that Moroccans would cross the border but halt at less than ten kilometres. It was still a gamble – not merely of Spanish discipline but to maintain order, supply and control 350,000 persons from all walks of life, and ensure their orderly withdrawal. In Moroccan eyes this vast assembly of unarmed civilians, brandishing the Koran and waving Moroccan flags, marching over the border before facing Mecca to give thanks to the Almighty, was made of heroes, victoriously reclaiming territory of their ancient sultanate.

The Green March, named after the holy colour of Islam, took its place in history. More particularly in Moroccan mythology. It showed a defiant monarch able to mobilise support on a massive scale, confront an historic imperial power and resist international pressure while achieving peacefully the objective. Hassan had freed the last great colonial holding in the sultanate's sphere. He had risen to expectation as king, commander of the faithful and heir to Mohammed V. His people loved him.

Hassan had confidence in France not undermining Moroccan interests and in his alliance with the United States, as anti-communist in the enduring cold war, sympathetic to NATO and almost the only Arab leader willing to deal with Israel. An American assistant secretary of state twice visited Rabat and the US president's trusted emissary, General Vernon Walters, flew to Madrid. Henry Kissinger, US secretary of state, who had also been in Morocco, alarmed at the prospect of an Algerian dominated mini-state, said that he would 'not allow another Angola on the east flank of the Atlantic Ocean'.[10] The government of Spain accepted to hand over administration of the Sahara, two-thirds to Morocco, the remainder to Mauritania. With Franco on his deathbed, the Madrid Accords, concluded on 14 November, formally ceded administration of the territory, with Spain committed to withdraw by the end of February following.[11] The Saharan population's views, as expressed through the Djemaa, general assembly of tribal leaders, would be respected.. By the end of November Hassan declared the Saharan file closed.

The UN general assembly was not convinced. On 10 December 1976 it adopted two resolutions. The one, ignoring the Madrid Accords, called on Spain to take all necessary measures so that the people of Spanish Sahara might exercise fully and freely their inalienable right to self-determinaton.[12] The other took note of the Madrid tripartite agreement and endorsed steps to ensure respect for the freely expressed aspirations of 'all the Saharan populations originating in the Territory' who 'will be able to exercise their inalienable right to self-determination through free consultations organized with the assistance of a representative of the United Nations appointed by the Secretary-General'.[13]

Algeria deplored the Security Council failing to prevent the march and dismissed the assembly's divided verdict. President Boumediennne taunted Hassan: 'I am not like Christ. I will not offer my cheek for a second blow. I shall respond to the utmost of my ability'[14] when Moroccan forces were immediately deployed across the northern two thirds of the territory. The Red Cross reported some forty thousand Sahrawis leaving towns and settlements to flee eastwards, and at Amgala, 180 kilometres from the Algerian border, Algerian soldiers were ordered 'to assist'. Moroccan troops retaliated, killing or capturing ninety-nine Algerians. Boumedienne withdrew. Hassan blamed Algeria when three weeks later Polisario was accused of 'massacring' Moroccan soldiers. Morocco is alleged to have deployed air power, even napalm, at Guelta Zemmour and Oum Dreyga where Sahrawis were grouping. Before the end of the year 50,000 refugees, according to the UN High Commissioner for Refugees, had fled to southern Algeria.[15]

Under the Madrid agreement the views of the Saharan population were to be expressed through the Djemaa, general assembly of tribal leaders. Of the 102 members convoked in special session on 29 November only 32 came; 67 members were reported as having voted the previous day, alongside Polisario at Guelta Zemmour, to dissolve their assembly. The UN secretary-general dispatched a senior Swedish diplomat, who concluded, after a visit, that genuine consultation was not possible.[16] Another Djemaa, convoked on 26 February, with 57 tribal leaders attending, voted unanimously to approve decolonisation of the territory and its 'reintegration' with Morocco and Mauritania. Although Spain refused to recognise this as the 'popular consultation' foreseen, that same 26 February, two days ahead of schedule, it completed the evacuation of civilians, exhumation of Christian corpses, shipment of animals from the zoo and departed.

Twenty-four hours later the Polisario's Provisional Sahrawi National Council, meeting at the desert oasis of Bir Lahlou, raised its flag and declared the Western Sahara an independent state: the Sahrawi Arab Democratic Republic, the SADR, better known as RASD, its French acronym. The new state-to-be was recognised by Madagascar the day following. When Algeria officially recognised the SADR, Morocco broke off diplomatic relations.[17]

Polisario turned on Morocco. Polisario forces benefited from ancestral familiarity with desert warfare, specific knowledge of the terrain and powerful motivation. They were supported by Algeria and well armed, principally by Libya. The razzia, the daring raid perpetrated over long distances when the raiding party vanished afterwards into the same desert vastness from which it had emerged, was Sahrawi tribal tradition. Polisario attacked Moroccan units successfully and ambushed convoys, which embarrassed the kingdom and sapped morale. Raids multiplied not only into Western Sahara, where Polisario units sabotaged the invaluable phosphate conveyor belt and attacked vessels off-shore, but into southern Morocco. Most dramatic was an attack on the town of Tan-Tan where Morocco's regional governor came close to being captured.[18] This was more than embarrassing. Polisario, lacking air power, might be unable to hold territory but Morocco seemed incapable of preventing deep incursions even into an undisputed region. Reinforcement helped, greater desert fighting experience and the leadership of Dlimi, who had proven himself in charge of Green March logistics. Ahmed Dlimi, Oufkir's successor as royal man of confidence and given responsibility for the Western Sahara campaign, rose to the challenge. He succeeded in reversing earlier defeats and eventually reoccupied all former Spanish garrisons and settlements.

Moroccan control was buttressed by construction of a massive defensive sandwall, the berm. Rumour attributed this to Israeli advice. Whatever the source it worked. The initial defensive wall curtained off the 'useful' triangle, with phosphate extraction, in the northern corner; it was ultimately extended under Dlimi's orders the length of the territory, more than two thousand kilometres long. The wall, with strong points, fortified posts manned by well-armed military, defended by minefields and equipped with listening devices, might be breached but blocked earlier hit and run tactics. It was set back from the border, permitting hot pursuit. Polisario referred to the empty strip as 'liberated territory' but it was effectively no-man's land.

Polisario moved against Mauritania, where armed forces and defence offered less contest. Polisario fighting units, disciplined and experienced, had the advantage of initiative, drive and weaponry supplied by Libya and Algeria. An incursion took them within fifty miles of Nouakchott, the capital. They lobbed shells into the presidential compound at the next assault. During the engagement Polisario's brilliant, handsome and charismatic leader was killed: shot through the head. In war people die differently but a shot through the head gave rise to suspicion that El-Ouali Mustapha Sayed was not killed by enemy fire. His independent spirit may have alarmed the Algerians; his successor proved more beholden to them.

French air forces, under a defence agreement, were invoked to save Mauritania from capitulating to Polisario. But the government fell in July 1978, ousted in a military coup. The usurping regime signed a peace accord, relinquished its claim to the southern third of Western Sahara, and withdrew. Some thought that Polisario would overrun that part, Spain's former colony of Villa Cisneros, make this their country. Before anything was done Morocco advanced with military force and established its administration throughout the territory. That placed Morocco where Mauritania most feared, peering over the non-existent garden fence, and a potential threat to iron ore mining near the border at Zouerate, which accounted for eighty-five percent of Mauritanian exports.

The prevailing Cold War militated against great power involvement. The US and France were sympathetic to Morocco; the Soviet Union, though backing Algeria, was a major purchaser of Moroccan phosphate for its fertiliser industry with little wish to create problems. King Hassan presumably hoped that Morocco's presence would morph into established fact, allowing international law to recognise the territory's integration into the kingdom. Algeria was adamant that should not happen. Polisario, militarily stalled by the defensive wall, fought on politically with Algerian material and diplomatic support. The OAU provided an arena and following events in Mauritania became more energetically engaged with calls to talk. Hassan refused to recognise Polisario as a negotiating partner – 'Morocco will only negotiate with its equals, with recognized states'[19] – and Algeria refused to negotiate on behalf of Polisario. Following its 'Committee of Wisemen's' failed mediation, the OAU proceeded to call for a ceasefire and the holding of a free and fair referendum giving the Sahrawi people the right to choose between independence and the status quo.[20] Twelve months later came moves to admit the SADR as an OAU member state.

Hassan acted to retrieve the initiative, to forestall Polisario's graduation to statehood. At the OAU summit in Nairobi in 1981 he announced that he would accept a 'controlled referendum whose modalities would give justice simultaneously to the objectives of ...the Committee of Wisemen and to Morocco's conviction regarding the legitimacy of its rights.'[21] Back home he interpreted the referendum as confirmatory and identified the interested parties as Morocco, Algeria and Mauritania. His foreign minister clarified that Polisario was not officially classed as a liberation movement and the so-called SADR not recognised as a state and the king could only negotiate with recognised states. Algeria, angered by Hassan's intransigence, lobbied for SADR's admission to full state membership of the OAU. At the 1982 pre-summit meeting when pressure mounted for SADR to be admitted Morocco and eighteen other member states walked out; the summit itself was aborted.

Saudi Arabia tried helping. King Fahd brought Hassan together with Algeria's new president, Chadli Bendjedid. Hassan was purported to have said: 'Leave me the stamp and the flag (the symbols of sovereignty), all else is negotiable'.[22] But expectations were disappointed, nothing emerged from a follow-up secret meeting between senior Moroccans and three Polisario leaders. Instead, like the conjuror he enjoyed being, Hassan astounded observers with a crafty move, he accepted Khaddafi's invitation for political union. Pending negotiation as to how this be implemented there was one immediate implication: Libya was stopped from arming Polisario. A confident Hassan told the UN general assembly in the autumn that Morocco was ready to hold a referendum, under conditions for a just, fair and true consultation. The UN general assembly still called for direct negotiations. At the next OAU summit SADR was elected to membership of the organisation through a procedure suspiciously stage-managed. Outraged, Morocco left the OAU of which it had been a founder member.

The Non-Aligned Movement voted for direct negotiations and yet again the UN general assembly, echoing the OAU, urged direct negotiations, a cease-fire and a referendum. King Fahd of Saudi Arabia mediated a second encounter between Hassan and Bendjidid. Fahd himself was present, his powers of persuasion enhanced by the Saudi's $1 billion a year purportedly contributed to Morocco. If results fell short of expectation the meeting improved relations sufficiently to permit an exchange of prisoners-of-war, and a year later diplomatic ties were re-established between Morocco and Algeria. The resumption of diplomatic relations was thought linked to a solution for Western Sahara though this was not explicit in the communiqué. Improved relations between Morocco and Algeria were welcomed throughout the region and beyond, and vaguely assumed as detrimental to the Sahrawi cause. King Hassan, in an interview, spoke of Sahrawis being granted autonomy as Moroccans; he rejected independence. The Saudis intervened in a final effort to further the process but nothing came of a secret meeting at Ta'ef.

More than ten years after the Green March and ten years of intermittent fighting the cold war's ending enabled the Security Council to function. The blustery wind of change blowing around the world after the fall of the Berlin wall cleared many obstacles to compromise. Entrenched conflicts in southwest Africa, Cambodia, central America and elsewhere became amenable to solution. The expulsion of the Iraqi invader from Kuwait showed the international community acting with force, decisively, and united. In that climate where all looked possible, on 11 August 1988, the UN secretary-general presented Morocco and Polisario with a joint UN-OAU plan for a cease-fire and referendum: proposals for a just and definitive solution of the question of Western Sahara, to enable the people of Western Sahara, in the exercise of their right to self-determination, to choose between independence and integration with Morocco.[23] Both sides informed the secretary-general of their agreement in principle on 30 August while 'making comments and observations'. Javier Perez de Cuellar, the secretary-general, submitted the outline proposals to the Security Council together with the parties' agreement in principle, but not their reservations.[24] On 20 September the Council approved the plan.

When the UN general assembly adopted a resolution that November calling for direct negotiations Morocco dismissed it as at variance with the secretary-general's initiative. But while refusing to 'negotiate' the king agreed to meet Sahrawis, including Polisario representatives, for 'discussion'.[25] On 4 and 5 January 1989 Hassan received in Marrakech a Sahrawi delegation comprising Bachir Mustapha Sayed, brother of El-Ouali, Mahfoud Ali Beiba and Brahim Ghali; they carried a signed and sealed mandate to negotiate as SADR plenipotentiaries. The king told the Sahrawis, according to Polisario, that 'despite all the investments I have made in the territory, I haven't succeeded in winning your hearts. There has been too much bloodshed, we need to put an end to this conflict'.[26] He did not wish to leave a 'time-bomb' for his son, the crown prince. But there was no agreement on autonomy, which the Polisario delegation had wanted to discuss. Afterwards Hassan announced that he had received 'Moroccans who have gone astray … in the hope that they would be put back on the right path. Never were they received as members of the so-called Polisario'. Western Sahara was Moroccan territory and we 'will not give an inch'.[27] He promised that when the Sahrawi nationalists 'have reintegrated their homeland, they would benefit from the regionalisation plan which has been envisaged.'[28] Polisario was severely criticised by Morocco for abusing the meeting to imply a degree of political recognition.

That March, when the Maghreb Arab Union of Algeria, Libya, Mauritania, Morocco and Tunisia was inaugurated without the SADR, Polisario abrogated the unilateral cease-fire declared only a month before. Hassan rejected further talks as superfluous: there was nothing to negotiate because Western Sahara was Moroccan territory. Fighting resumed.

In elaborating his outline plan the UN secretary-general had entrusted a member of his immediate staff with responsibility for detailed proposals. The staff member negotiated with the Moroccans and Polisario separately, in confidence. Even the UN High Level Task Force for Western Sahara was not fully briefed, a fact much resented by more than one of its members,[29] and neither Task Force nor Security Council was made aware of the reservations both sides expressed.

The implementation plan presented to the Council in June 1990[30] provided for a cease-fire, establishing an electoral roll, phased troop withdrawal and confinement, repatriation of refugees, and the holding of a referendum. Determining those eligible to vote was treated as technical: persons included in the Spanish census of 1974 after review and updating by experts. The parties' acceptance was assured according to the secretary-general, and in approving his report the Council called on them to cooperate fully. Morocco countered with a fiercely critical twelve-page letter addressed personally to Perez de Cuellar. The letter made no effort to conceal the king's frustration that his reservations had been ignored before broaching security issues, law and order, administrative responsibilities, the armed forces and focusing on the 'exaggeratedly optimistic' proposals for establishing the electoral roll and the time this would require. A paragraph spelled out specifically the 'problem of taking into account … Saharans who sought refuge in Morocco when the Territory was under Spanish domination'. When, after almost three months, the letter had not been communicated to the Security Council Morocco issued the contents as a press release.[31] Polisario had also reacted to the plan presented to the Council. Their comments too remained confidential until after the Moroccan press release when the Polisario office issued them in New York.[32] For Polisario the Spanish census of 1974 provided the 'only and unique basis for the preparation of the electoral lists'. Updating meant simply to correct the spelling of names and delete persons deceased. It was essential that the UN ensure against an influx of 'foreign population'.

Though the fault line was manifest both secretary-general and well-informed Council members chose to ignore arguments undermining the parties' 'agreement in principle', perhaps believing that it would be 'all right on the night', that international pressures would prevail. Conceivably. More plausibly, the restoration of diplomatic ties between Algeria and Morocco and the king's meeting with Polisario in Marrakech gave cause for optimism. A negotiated deal might be in the offing, which could be endorsed in an act of self-determination. The secretary-general's term of office was nearing the end and there are hints that he had an undeclared agenda and 'was hoping that, before the end of his mandate, he could mediate a political deal based on enhanced autonomy for Western Sahara within the kingdom of Morocco' providing the proposition on which the Sahrawis could vote in a referendum.[33] In his memoirs he states: 'I was never convinced that independence promised the best future for the inhabitants of the Western Sahara.'[34]

The secretary-general moved the settlement plan into the mainstream of UN politics in April 1991 with a second report to the Council.[35] Together with an action plan and timetable, he elaborated on how to determine those qualified to vote. The 1974 census remained the baseline, to be up-dated by an identification commission; applications would also be considered from Western Saharans omitted from the Spanish census. Tribal chiefs, sheikhs, would assist the commission. Perez de Cuellar admitted that his proposals involved compromise; they did not meet all concerns. The Security Council in approving the settlement plan expressed support for a UN mission (to be known as Minurso, the French acronym for *Mission des Nations Unies pour l'Organisation du Referendum au Sahara Occidental*) and called on the parties to cooperate fully in implementing the plan. Neither Morocco nor Polisario chose to add publicly to their original agreement in principle or to subtract from reservations already expressed. Nothing was signed.[36]

Hopes were quickly dashed by renewed hostilities, fighting and aerial bombardment. In the interest of peace Perez de Cuellar decided to divorce the cease-fire from other steps in the plan and have it come into effect on 6 September. This decoupled a major incentive and allowed the timetable to unravel. Both sides concurred though 'notwithstanding the parties' earlier acceptance … substantial areas of difference remained'.[37] King Hassan warned that he would not allow regular deployment of Minurso until the issue of voter eligibility had been settled. At the same time Morocco submitted the names of 120,000 potential voters additional to the 73,497 Saharans in the 1974 census. That month 170,000 persons were reported as moving to Western Sahara to 'facilitate' their identification by the UN. In a submission to the Council in December 1991, just before his retirement, the secretary-general conceded that the plan was already in jeopardy. Lack of progress was 'largely due to the complexity of the identification process, whose purpose is to establish the list of those who would vote in the referendum.' The 'indispensable climate of confidence' was not helped by news that a number of persons, claimed to belong to Western Sahara, had been moved into the territory: a violation of the spirit if not the letter of the plan, according to critics[38] – and the secretary-general's second special representative chose to leave.

Whether Perez de Cuellar bowed to Moroccan pressure (press reports claimed that he was being appointed to the board of a Moroccan holding company, Omnium Nord Africa, which he denied), or was influenced by interested powers or his adviser,[39] he chose that moment, two weeks before retiring, to conclude a valedictory report to the Council with a bombshell.[40] The Spanish census of 1974 could not constitute the entire list of those qualified to vote. This followed from the Saharans' nomadic way of life ignoring national borders, people fleeing colonialism and conflict as well as individuals leaving the territory for personal and economic reasons, for education and medical treatment. He presented criteria justifying eligibility far exceeding what Polisario deemed acceptable. Saharans in Western Sahara during the census but not counted were admissible together with members of their immediate family; also children of a Saharan born in the territory, and any Saharan who had lived in the territory prior to 1975 for six years consecutively or twelve intermittently. Those in the census had (Spanish) documentation, few others did. The identification commission would rely on oral testimony, true to Sahrawi tradition, and tribal expertise, in particular the sheikhs and notables, to identify those qualified to vote. Morocco argued that the one-generation limit was unduly restrictive; Polisario rejected every attempt to exceed the census listing.

The Security Council was confused. Eligibility to vote was obviously critical. No census was perfect and it had been intimated that the voters' list might be augmented by an additional 10,000 or so. But the further 120,000 produced by Morocco raised a major problem. The US assistant secretary of state for international organisation affairs, John Bolton, described Perez de Cuellar's proposition as 'simply unacceptable'; the 'new criteria did not match our understanding of what the parties had previously agreed. Indeed, our understanding … was that the parties themselves, or at least one of the parties, were not going to agree to what the Secretary-General had come up with.'[41] If the US chose not to reject Perez de Cuellar's report it was because they relied on his input in the days remaining to bring to successful resolution the crises in Nicaragua and El Salvador. 'It will come as no surprise that within the US government's deliberations on which priority we felt was higher, Central America won'[42] and it was one or the other. In consequence, the Security Council simply 'welcomed' the secretary-general's report, not 'endorsing' the recommendations or approving the voter criteria. The 'welcoming' resolution[43] was adopted on New Year's Eve, Perez de Cuellar's last official day in office.

His successor, as secretary-general, was Boutros Boutros-Ghali, from

Egypt. He took advantage of the Security Council being convoked for the first time at the level of heads of state and government in January 1992 to promote an 'Agenda for Peace'. President George Bush was expected, benignly overseeing a newer world order, and, among others, King Hassan of Morocco, Morocco having been elected to a two-year non-permanent seat on the Council. Hassan, on this first occasion that I saw him, was fastidiously dressed in traditional Moroccan style; he understood theatre and always attached importance to appearance – his own and others'.

Western Sahara was not on the official agenda but would be discussed informally. Boutros-Ghali, as a former Egyptian minister, was familiar with the conflict's background and history and he shared Perez de Cuellar's assumption that Morocco would not accept a vote in favour of independence. He contemplated asking the Council to renegotiate the settlement plan, and to apply pressure thought of appointing an American as his special representative. General Vernon Walters was rumoured, but was unable or unwilling to agree. King Hassan approved the nomination of Washington's good friend, Sahabzada Yaqub-Khan. Yaqub-Khan was a patrician Pakistani, who had risen to the rank of Lieutenant-General and served as Governor of East Pakistan prior to secession; he had been ambassador in Paris and Moscow as well as Washington before becoming foreign minister.[44]

The cease-fire was holding, despite some violations, and after shipment obstacles and delays to transport had eventually been resolved, military observers were given access to monitor the situation. All else was deadlocked. Boutros-Ghali reported to the Council in February, May, August, October and December 1992 but had no progress to report. Yaqub-Khan was unable to make any headway with the plan; it had not even been possible to hold a consultative meeting of tribal chiefs. In January 1993 the secretary-general reiterated that disagreements on fundamental issues persisted. After suggesting that the Council might wish to consider alternatives, he proposed three options: continuation and intensification of talks; implementation of the settlement plan even with one party alone; adoption of an alternative approach.[45] The Council was divided. France sympathised with Morocco's idea of holding a referendum with the party that was willing; others rejected a one-sided referendum as meaningless, dismissed by the US as 'slam-dunk'. The few well briefed among Council members, aware of the obstacles, inclined towards an alternative approach without specifying what this could be. The majority, confused by ill-delineated geography, convoluted interpretations of history and the arcane intricacies of Sahrawi tribal structure and distribution, plumped for the classical UN remedy, piously intoning a self-determination referendum, at least give it a further try. In March 1993 the Council adopted resolution 809 blithely inviting the parties to resolve their differences regarding voter eligibility.[46] The secretary-general was to proceed with preparations for a referendum and to commence voter registration starting with the updated lists of the 1974 census.

4

Western Sahara

When appointed to the mission I admit to knowing only superficially of Western Sahara, the fighting and plight of refugees. What I then learned was part gossip and entirely depressing. The previous deputy had departed under a cloud. It seemed that every senior person assigned to Western Sahara left in unhappy circumstances. The settlement plan was entirely deadlocked; the secretary-general's special representative had been unable to achieve any opening, even the revised list, up-dating the 1974 census eluded him. The latest Security Council resolution was intended to stimulate action that many knew as unrealistic, though my briefing made no specific mention of the parties' differences, differences in the Council or doubts about financing. Had the secretary-general been in New York he might have shared his pessimistic assessment but he was travelling. I benefited from few clear instructions beyond the sense that expectations were minimal.

Sahabzada Yaqub-Khan received me courteously. He embodied the Pakistani aristocrat in manner and dress. And as he turned he presented a profile uncannily like an image published in anthropology's mischievous youth when human character was deduced from the animals people resembled: he the tawny owl – not only its outline but the owl's reputation for wisdom and for not sharing its thoughts. Yaqub-Khan assured me, in impeccable old school English, the best of his range of languages, that he fully approved of my appointment. He would continue to handle the politics, out of New York, he explained; he had by now concluded that a solution outside the plan's parameters offered the only hope – although he did not tell me this. I was to administer the mission in the region, be responsible for all 'technical' aspects of the plan, principally identifying voters. I would be based in Laayoune, 'capital' of Western Sahara. He wished me well.

Of two under-secretaries-general for political affairs one dealt with African issues. The newly-appointed James Jonah from Sierra Leone was bright, highly-educated and very ambitious, and, as one critic said, 'carrying a lot of sail for one so young.'[1] He and Yaqub-Khan were not on speaking terms. Jonah advised me to give Yaqub-Khan a wide berth and concentrate on the substantive work of the mission, as spelled out in the latest Security Council resolution. The Council had emphasised the primary importance of launching the identification process, which was what the Secretary-General expected of me. Jonah was confident this could be achieved by keeping politics out. I departed New York with copies of relevant resolutions and a bundle of reports to read – and try to read between the lines.

Royal Air Maroc delivered me overnight to Casablanca Mohammed V airport. I was received directly off the aircraft by a delegation of three. M. Alaoui of Foreign Affairs introduced himself and marched beside me along the nobble-floored corridors entirely vacant at that hour of the morning. Another took my bag until he identified a minion to carry it behind us to the magnificent salon VIP, dominated by a life-size portrait of Hassan II. His Excellency Governor Azmi removed the cheroot he had been smoking and advanced to greet me, on behalf of the minister of interior he welcomed me to Morocco. Would I like mint tea? and summoned the servant waiting with a tray. We could leave for Rabat as soon as I wished.

Casablanca hovered distantly at first: a silhouette of modern buildings thrusting upwards proclaimed Morocco's burgeoning hub of commerce, its business metropolis, its aspiring New York. Flanking the well-mannered and litterless road ran an un-graffitied wall, high enough to block whatever lay behind. Only as we filtered off onto the Rabat motorway did a slight rise afford a glimpse of cardboard packing in an ocean of corrugated iron roofing, abob with satellite dishes. This vast shanty-town accommodated many thousand Moroccans who had migrated from impoverished rural areas in search of work and livelihood, with few succeeding. Governor Azmi, sitting beside me, relit a cheroot; he asked whether I minded his smoking. Of course not, I said, as I always did, if someone was civil enough to ask. We made small talk. Had I had a comfortable flight? Did I get some sleep? Where was my family? And I enquired after his. My first visit to Morocco? he asked when I said what a fine new motorway this was. Yes, I said, and turned to admire the landscape glowing in the early sun. I saw the surrounding countryside and hamlets like a background scene long familiar from Christmas cards. A parched river-course cracked the open land. Vegetation was sparse, with no hedges and few trees. Shepherds lay minding their sheep or watched, a goatherd struggled to control his flock as it dispersed, a cowherd led home lowing oxen, and by rough farm buildings a peasant woman drew water from the well.

At the Rabat Hyatt hotel I was ushered to a sumptuous suite. Flowers abounded, beautifully arranged. Moroccan pastries, in little pyramids, insisted on being eaten – Azmi picked an almond paste '*corne de gazelle*' while showing me round. Beyond the bedroom was a marble Jacuzzi reminding me of what I most wanted after the overnight flight: to wash and change. The minister of interior, Monsieur le Ministre, Driss Basri, would receive me later in the day, Azmi said, meanwhile, Moulay Ali Skalli, former Moroccan ambassador at Geneva and New York, was deputed to entertain me. I had known Ali Skalli in both Geneva and New York; more white haired than I remembered but with the same twinkle in his grey circled eyes. Over lunch we talked, he had nothing of substance to convey. He took me to see the Mohammed V mausoleum, Hassan's lavish display of filial piety, past the royal palace to the ancient Andalusian walled garden abutting the fortified citadel that commanded the estuary whence Barbary corsairs once infamously embarked to raid coastal shipping. Twice a discreet official appeared to announce that the appointment with Basri had been briefly postponed.

The ministry of interior was architecturally unpretentious in ex-colonial buildings. I was invited to wait for a minute in an office, smallish and modestly furnished. Behind a padded door the minister remained in conference with other ministers but would be with me momentarily. His executive assistant shook my hand firmly, a younger man, elegant in Parisian style. He asked whether I had I ever visited Morocco before. No, I said, but I had been made familiar with things Moroccan by my colleague Joseph Verner Reed, who had served as US ambassador in Rabat and loved the country. Did he know him? Of course, of course, Ambassador Reed was very well known in Morocco. But to have been introduced by him to Morocco was unfortunate –pause for effect – because he was so hopelessly biased. With that he turned to answer a ringing phone and holding the mouthpiece at a slight distance spoke crisply with executive precision in a compound of Arabic and impeccable French. The minister would be pleased to receive me.

I walked through the door as if appearing on stage. A barrage of lights, floodlights, footlights, flashlights blinded me, I barely distinguished the sharp faced, publicly grinning man who gave me his hand, then holding mine in a staged handshake presented his fixed-smile to the surrounding press corps. While cameramen continued clicking and filming, lighting adjusters reangling their beam and assorted extras shuffling cables, Driss Basri, minister of interior and trusted counsellor of His Majesty King Hassan II, crossed the floor then invited me to be seated in a voluminous leather chair near his own, slightly higher, seat. He launched into a set piece speech, on the need to implement all relevant UN resolutions without specifying which they were. His tone was didactic, hectoring. He punctuated each clause with an emphatic '*Monsieur le President*', my title in French as chairman of the identification commission, and faced the cameras. I was not expected to ignore that he was also minister for information. Morocco, he declaimed, was an ancient kingdom with a proud history, it sought only what was right. When in walked a gentleman, presented as the minister of health, Basri added that the humanitarian aspect also mattered; families would be reunited once no longer sequestered by the Polisario. And he waved the media out.

The substantive meeting, if that is what it was, followed. It was succinct. To Basri Morocco's case lay beyond refutation, with the collapse of Spanish imperialism His Majesty only wanted to re-establish historical frontiers and honour the commitment of Sahrawis, whose sheikhs had sworn fealty. Conflict was engineered by Algeria. Algeria – though Moroccans had fought alongside Algerians in their war of independence – exploited Polisario to embarrass Morocco, to achieve hegemony throughout the region, and because Algeria coveted access to the Atlantic via a client mini-state. Were that to happen Morocco would be an island, cut off from Africa. There were no 'ifs' and 'buts'; no comment expected, as he paused to pick vitilego-dried skin from his lip. I thanked him for the reception, the arrangements made, and assured him that my appointment was an earnest of the UN secretary-general's determination to implement the resolutions of the Security Council. The Council was concerned that in two years there had been little movement in reconciling the parties' conflicting views about voter qualification. My immediate task, as mandated by the Council, was to start identifying as potential voters those included in the Spanish census. Later I learned that Basri abhorred all reference to 'parties' meaning Morocco and Polisario; for him the other 'party' was Algeria. And he rejected categorically any suggestion that those in the Spanish census should have priority. With a smile, a smile of tempered steel, he said 'Yes, yes,' as one humouring an innocent. 'Of course, we cannot possibly deprive of the right to vote those whose early commitment to the anti-colonial struggle against Spain had them excluded from the census. It is inconceivable that those who campaigned for their country should not be allowed to participate in determining its future.'

Dlimi, killed in a road accident, had replaced Oufkir, shot, as the state's most powerful officer under the king. That power had since been bestowed on Basri. Unlike his predecessors he had neither military connections nor political base of his own. Loyalty was paramount and Hassan rewarded Basri's immutable loyalty with increasing wealth, prestige and might. In addition to interior administration he controlled policing, security and public information, whatever the Moroccan people were supposed to know. Next morning I read what he had released to '*Le Matin*', the official newspaper. Any resemblance to what I had said was marginal.

If Basri was the king's man of confidence, Governor Mohammed Azmi was Basri's. Azmi enjoyed the minister's bounty and repaid with devoted service. An intelligent man with a remarkable memory, and who knew more about Sahrawis than anyone in Rabat. At an early age he had been made governor of Tan-Tan province in southern Morocco, a region inhabited by Sahrawi tribes. His wife was Sahrawi. He liked Sahrawis and their ways – though he preferred to forget the raid when he narrowly escaped capture by Polisario. Now a senior governor he had been appointed Morocco's representative on matters concerning the UN mission in Western Sahara. We became friendly and from him I learned much, but if I expected helpful indiscretions I was mistaken. His commitment to Basri and the king and the king's policy was never, for a second, open to question. I remember, when we knew each other better, his emotional, almost violent, reaction at my urging Morocco to show some flexibility. 'For you this is a mission. For us this is a matter of life and death. It is everything.'

Returning from the ministry Azmi confirmed what Basri had told me. Indeed, all those I spoke to before leaving Rabat said much the same. Morocco, ancient kingdom with a proud history, had an identity and a distinct culture embracing the diversity of the sultan's realm. Morocco's unity lay in allegiance to the sovereign. King Hassan, like the long line of sultans who preceded him, was 'Commander of the Faithful', a descendant of the prophet, both religious leader and political. Mohammed V had successfully recovered ancestral lands from French dominion and more, Hassan would liberate the remnants of Spain's west African empire, including the great expanse of sometime Spanish, Moroccan Sahara. Algeria had contrived the conflict. Algerian leaders were suspicious of monarchy, they resented Morocco's place in the post cold war world and were embarrassed by failings of their own socialist system. Aspiring to international standing they exploited automatic support for 'liberation movements' such as Polisario. And Polisario, Azmi insisted, could no longer be called a liberation movement; it had been: against Spain. A diplomat warned me that it was a criminal offence to question the king's policy on Western Sahara.

On the flight to Laayoune the Atlas mountains, glittering snow-bright, were ranged on our left while the Atlantic ocean rolled in to the right. We landed halfway at Agadir, some five hundred miles south of Rabat. Inland lay Marrakech, bridging the divide between the caravanned deserts of the south and more fertile lands and ports to the north. The city prospered following its foundation in 1062 by the mighty Yusuf ibn Tashfin, whose reach was to stretch from the southern deserts to southern Spain. In the seventeenth century the first Alaouite sultan took power, his successor, Moulay Ismail, consolidated control of all Morocco and mounted desert expeditions to enforce at least nominal sovereignty over the wider region: Morocco at its zenith. The Alaouite dynasty survived despite foreign incursion and occupation, revolt and regional uprising, and palace coups, as recently as the attempts on Hassan's life.

After Agadir, the landscape became more desiccated toward the Draa valley, the defining geographical feature. Beyond stretched desert: parched land in every direction, scratched only here and there by a watercourse, a wadi. We overflew Ifni and Tan-Tan. From the plane I saw nothing bar occasional glimpses of a narrow road sneaking along the coastline till Tarfaya passed below. Here it was that thousands assembled for the Green March into Spanish Sahara to reclaim the territory for Morocco and realise King Hassan's dream of recapturing the Alaouite sultanate's ancient grandeur.

The airport in Laayoune, where we landed, was to my surprise fully equipped to handle large passenger planes as well as military aircraft. I was escorted to a VIP room adorned with the customary royal portrait, offered mint tea, introduced to UN staff and local dignitaries, before driving to the hotel Parador, where senior mission members were accommodated. The acting force commander saluting me was a Belgian brigadier-general. He had arrived some months earlier following the Canadian Major-General Roy's unhappy departure at the same time as my predecessor as assistant secretary-general, the latter accused of complicity with Morocco and the former suspected of inappropriate sympathy for Polisario; their dislike was mutual and intense, creating ugly division within the mission. Van Baelen was a soldier's soldier, kept fit, rode, played tennis most days, and in turbulent military aircraft insulated himself with pulp fiction in Flemish. His briefing of me was non-political, concise. An estimated 90,000 armed men were deployed on the Moroccan side and up to 10,000 with Polisario though figures varied. To monitor the cease-fire from both sides of the wall ten desert team-sites accommodated UN military observers.

In addition to the military, including a Swiss medical unit under command of a colonel, the mission had three components. The civil police commissioner was a German. The Tunisian chief administrative officer came from the secretariat, someone I already knew as an experienced admin man who understood in-house procedures, and had the asset of speaking fluent French and his native Arabic as well as English. Chairman, or, in French, President, of the Identification Commission was me. I was responsible for implementing this core aspect of the settlement plan in addition to heading the mission overall in the region and dealing with the parties.

The parties, according to the UN Security Council, were Morocco and the Polisario Front, with neighbours, Algeria and Mauritania, recognised as 'interested' countries. Polisario supporters lived in refugee camps, as exiles in southern Algeria. For my first visit I flew in one of the mission's solid, economical and uncomfortable ex-Soviet helicopters. The newly appointed police commissioner Reimann wished to escort me, and, to save flying hours, we dropped General van Baelen on an inspection tour at Smara, before Morocco's fortified line. To the north no-mans-land bulged and Polisario claimed a former oasis settlement, Bir Lahlou, as their address for official pronouncements. We saw nothing but mile upon mile of lifeless rocky desert. Reimann, fascinated by the emptiness, stared through a porthole. 'What, what,' he asked, baffled, confused, 'are they fighting about?'

Extraordinary to think that this had been fertile savannah. Petroglyphs bore testimony to an inhabited world two to three millennia ago. Giraffes, rhinoceros, wild cattle, elephants, even hippopotamus, and antelopes, long extinct, survived in rock-graven images. On the walls of cave shelters human figures hunted and cavorted. The Bafur people vanished, probably southwards, as with a changing climate the desert expanded to deprive plants, animals and humans of the means to exist. Centuries later Berber nomads ventured in. The introduction of the camel, thought to have happened in the first century of our era, revolutionised desert living. This remarkable animal, uniquely adapted, could survive in extreme heat without drinking for five days and for weeks in cooler weather. As beast of burden it was able to carry great loads, three hundred pounds or more, over prolonged distances. Its milk was exceptionally nutritious, protein rich and almost fat-free, and the female gave twelve pints a day or nearly twice as much after bearing young. Camel hair and hide served for tent cloth and leather, and the meat could be eaten. The camel rendered possible the trans-Saharan caravan routes and trade bringing marginal prosperity for hundreds of years.[2]

Arab Bedouin tribes began invading the Maghreb in the eleventh century and in the thirteenth Bedouin Arabs penetrated the Sahara. A group of tribes, the Beni Hassan, purportedly originating in the Yemen, dominated. The Beni Hassan were warrior people with marked hierarchy within and between tribes. Social stratification descended from warrior to artisan, craftsman and bard, to slave – black African slaves being acquired through war or purchase. They spoke Hassaniya, closer to literary Arabic than the dialect of others in the region. They dressed distinctively, the men wore the '*drah*', a voluminous outer garment usually blue, and a turban, the women dressed in the '*malhaffah*', a length of flimsy coloured material draped, and constantly redraped, about the body and over the head. The Beni Hassan way of life was adapted to desert living, as was their observance of Islam: they were zealous in devotion to prayer but washed with sand not water, and being without mosque buidings improvised an alignment of stones.[3]

In constant search of pasturage for their camel herds and goats they tracked any cloud cover in hope of rainfall – were often referred to as children of the clouds '*les enfants des nuages*'.[4] They roamed over thousands of miles, the camel enabling a sparse population to survive. Caravans navigating the great ocean of desert were raided for valuables, gold, ivory and slaves, and essentials like sugar, tea and especially salt – or to extract protection money. The area dominated by Beni Hassan tribes expanded, they ventured north towards the Draa, where some settled, all across the northern half of present day Mauritania, into south-western Algeria, as well as what became Spanish Sahara. Except for the Atlantic Ocean in the west the region lacked natural borders, nothing obstructed a tribe's wandering apart from those more powerful. The Beni Hassan were not identified by locality, by land they occupied or places they lived, identity derived from tribal affiliation. The most successful tribes dominated a habitual circuit: the Reguibat a huge swathe from the Seguia-el-Hamra southwards, and so prospered that the tribe became two tribes, Reguibat Sahel and Reguibat Charg. The Oulad Delim was paramount in the southwest. Across the territory lived too the Arosien, Ait Lahsen, Izerguien and Oulad Tidrarin, and Chorfa descended from the prophet. In southern Morocco the Ait Baamran, Tekna, Ait Ousa were also Hassaniya tribes as were others in Mauritania. All were Beni Hassan, Sahrawi, this identity only loosely modified by acts of allegiance or overlaid by modern notions of nationality.

Tindouf, our destination, an important oasis in the trans-Saharan caravan trade, had been overwhelmed by an Reguibat force in 1895. In 1934 the French made it a base for colonial operations and it retained a Foreign Legion aura. The helicopter, cleared for landing, descended noisily to an impressive airfield, the airport mattered strategically to the Algerian military and was correspondingly well-surfaced. Dust-sheet covered MIGs stood parked at the perimeter. A UN military observer was later to tell me that in an earlier advisory incarnation he had visited Tindouf airfield and seen elaborate underground installations, hangars, launch pads, even a rest and recreation centre. Of that nothing was visible as I emerged from the helicopter, hot, wind-swept and half-deafened, to be greeted by an official of the Algerian government and taken in hand by our senior UN military observer in Tindouf, a Russian colonel. Beyond the town a tarmaced road led to the UN base, former Algerian army barracks, with doors and shutters painted UN blue. That was until I realised that most doors and store-blinds in and around Tindouf were the same blue, which complemented the omnipresent ochre of buildings and sand.

Nothing blue coloured the landscape beyond. Ochre everywhere, a greyish ochre. Even the sky was glazed ochre with sand dust, in every direction I saw only sand, rocky sand, stony outcrops and sand mixed with stone, no pristine rolling dunes, no camels, just hard ground. '*Hammada*' they called this stony desert in Arabic, and preferred to avoid it. In the distance, as we drove towards the Polisario encampment, appeared a vast lake. The mirage quivered and flickered in the heat haze. We were running late, I mentioned to the colonel. Before departure he had wanted to confirm to headquarters my arrival and planned movements and the signals officer encountered lengthy delay in transmitting by cryptofax, that and landing in Smara had cost us an hour. Polisario were not clock conscious, the colonel assured me, as we passed a desultory checkpoint. On raised ground in the middle distance stood Polisario's official reception centre at Rabouni, an assortment of baked earth buildings, yellow and reddish ochre.

Between high mud walls a passage led towards a screened opening. Behind the screen a room was furnished with settees and a large, rectangular coffee table. Against one wall stood a bookcase stacked with a television set, there were no books. An air-conditioning unit rattling aggressively helped temper the increasingly oppressive heat and harsh dry wind. Mustapha Bachir Sayed, Polisario's official number two, their spokesman to the wider world, brother of their charismatic founder who had been killed fighting for the cause, made an entry. He was dressed in combat fatigues, his hair desert ruffled. It was usual, he said, greeting me a little formally, for a meeting of such importance to take place on time, he hoped no accident had caused our lateness. I apologised profusely and explained that we had experienced some technical hitches and were pleased to have arrived incident free. Bachir smiled.

Bachir, when he relaxes into a smile and with his eyes smiling has considerable charm. He expounded the Polisario position at length, sounding reasonable, calmly presenting the weaker side's case. They looked, he said, to the international community, the UN, to ensure their right: for the Sahrawi people to decide their own future. In substance there was nothing new, when Bachir spoke of the Sahrawis I knew he meant those included in the Spanish census, that had been the core of the original settlement proposals, he said, only modified at Morocco's insistence that the census omitted many Sahrawis. How to identify these and how many there could conceivably be was a challenge and the bone of contention. All those bussed in by Morocco during the 'second green march' were an outrage, an insult, Bachir repeated, to the UN and international opinion, these people had nothing to do with Western Sahara. Knowing that they considered my predecessors guilty of bias I emphasised my determination to be scrupulously fair. Since this was an introductory visit, a presenting of personal credentials, I said no more. I liked Bachir well enough at this our first meeting and hoped he would reciprocate sufficiently for us to work together, his half embrace was encouraging when I left to meet tribal leaders.

From the only surfaced road we branched off into the desert. No sign-posts, no natural features offered a bearing. Criss-crossing wheel-marks like interwoven snake tracks confounded any sense of direction. The colonel had previously served in other deserts and drove, dustily, at speed. Anything slower and the corrugated surface made sitting spine-shatteringly painful. Best not to follow in the dust wake of another vehicle, he explained, as we ventured across a markerless expanse of stony sand until finding ourselves doubled back to where we had been. A battered Land Rover assigned as Polisario escort emerged from a fog of sand-dust. We trailed in its slip-stream for a mile or more till beyond another rise appeared in a hollow Wilaya El-Aiun.

The Sahrawi refugees were grouped in four camps named after the principal places in Western Sahara: El-Aiun, Smara, Dakhla and Ausserd (for Boujdour). For seventeen years the people had been living in tent cloth settlements – white for temporary and black camel hair for permanent and these were whitish, deliberately provisional because the leadership wanted no enduring ties to this inhospitable, unproductive rocky desert – without camel herds, flocks of sheep, much less, agriculture. Goats survived on miscellaneous waste and wrapping material from relief supplies. They foraged sporadically in the outskirts through which we approached. The camp itself was astonishingly clean and orderly. Children – there were numbers of them – played in open spaces. They waved cheerfully in response to my wave, and smiled. A few women were about. I saw no men, or only old men.

The venerable seniors in the tent to which I was guided were elders, sheikhs of their tribal sub-group. In Sahrawi society each tribe was divided into 'fractions' and each 'fraction' into 'sub-fractions' with its sheikh. Subfractions were composed of '*ahel*', extended family groups, but 'sub-fraction' was the key entity. The sheikhs took seriously their position and valued the status it afforded. In trying to forge a modern, Western Saharan national identity, the Polisario leadership sought to transcend tribal loyalty by deliberately mixing refugees in the four main camps, marginalising the sheikhs' role. But the proposed referendum and identification of eligible voters restored power to the sheikhs since only they had authority to testify who belonged and thus be entitled to vote. The sheikhs assembled in the spacious tent greeted me solemnly.

All were classically dressed: black turban, tied or untied, over an expansive flowing blue robe. The blue, giving Sahrawis their soubriquet 'blue men' (*Les hommes bleus*), had provided the first independence movement its name. With a theatrical gesture each sheikh cast his robe back over the shoulders and pronounced his name. Some embraced me. Having greeted the sheikhs I sat back and admired the tent walls entirely lined with rugs and the floor carpeted. We reclined on low rug-covered cushions while tea was prepared with intricate ceremony: quantities of sugar and multiple pourings from kettle to glass to container to kettle to glass – raised high for maximum visual effect and to create froth, then offered, Sahrawi style, very strong, very sweet and very hot. No air circulated in the stifling heat.

Formal pronouncements followed, the formality emphasised by consecutive interpretation. The most revered sheikh, as spokesman, said he had been a member of the Spanish Cortes, the parliament, before leaving to fight for independence. Several elderly sheikhs spoke, fluently, at considerable length, saying much the same like the repetitive chorus in a Greek play: only those included in the Spanish census had the right to vote in a referendum on the future of the territory. One sheikh, younger than the others, had recently succeeded his late father; he alone had anything in writing, he manifestly deferred to the elders' oral wisdom, and re-endorsed the Spanish census of 1974 as the touchstone and 'bible' – his word – of Polisario, not subject to amendment. I assured the tribal leaders that I had noted what they said. When the sheikhs filed out through the tent-flap to prostrate themselves in evening prayer, low dining-tables were brought in.

For this 'banquet' by Polisario standards tables were set with glasses of water and orangeade with spoons, knives and forks laid should anyone not use fingers to eat – the colonel and I. Soup was served, noisily consumed, then a salad of tomato, cucumber and onion, and roast goat. The goat was especially tender, said one who spoke some Spanish-sounding French, although that was not my impression. The sheikhs relished it all, for refugees the concluding pastry and fruit were further exceptional indulgence.

The return drive to base was reckless and very uncomfortable but we arrived. On next morning's flight back to Laayoune, despite heat, noise and being rattled by vibration, I had occasion to reflect on assumptions made in the Spanish census, to which Polisario clung and which Morocco rejected as partial. The 'interested' countries, Algeria and Mauritania, were unlikely to offer guidance but I needed to know how they assessed the situation, and to present my credentials.

For regional travel the mission disposed of Antonov fixed-wing aircraft, Soviet now Russian military transport and troop carriers; a competitive Russian tender had induced the UN contracts committee to accept their bid. The planes had collapsible metal jump-seats down both sides with webbing, no lavatory and, other than the pilot's hatch, no door. Below the tail-plane a ramp descended, designed for vehicles rather than personnel. Albeit slow the Antonov was reputed to be safe. The crews were Romanian, later Ukrainian; none spoke much English and they had neither French nor Arabic.

Movement control prepared a detailed flight plan with the necessary clearance for my flight to Algiers. At Algiers airport I bumped down the ramp to be received in style by representatives of the presidency, protocol and foreign affairs. Formalities were expeditiously handled and the chief of protocol accompanied me into a large Mercedes. In front was a security vehicle, another behind, four motorcycle outriders completed the escort. Door closed, we shot off at high speed like an acceleration test. On the motorway into town we drove on the wrong side of the road against the traffic, our motorcycle outriders waving aside oncoming vehicles. It was safer, the chief of protocol insisted. Algeria was in an unofficial state of civil war, ambushes frequent and killing an everyday event, with international personages targets amenable to publicity. Ever since military leaders had intervened to annul an election that Islamists were projected to win, the country had been at war with itself. The press was reined in to curb damage to the national image; more than one courageous journalist had been eliminated. The situation was improving, it was already much improved, the chief of protocol assured me as we slowed down to leave the motorway.

A winding road between walls led to the government guest-house. We were nearly there and back on the right side of the road, the outriders had branched off, when a car came at us and everyone stood on the brakes – including those not driving. The oncoming car collided with the security vehicle in front; my Mercedes bumped them gently and the vehicle behind bruised us. Miraculously, no one was seriously hurt, and it was not an ambush. We entered an expansive compound with a villa and hotel for government guests. The hotel, overlooking the bay of Algiers, enjoyed a fine view of the surrounding town, the sea glittered beyond the built-up sweep stretching sickle-shaped from one reach to the other. Commanding all rose the martyrs' memorial, an enduring reminder of the fight with France, a mighty structure in modern materials not unlike an outsize three-pronged inverted clothes peg. I left to call on the foreign minister.

Less charming was the town at close quarters. Dirty, poorly maintained, and at every corner groups of men standing, aimlessly, just standing. Unemployment approached fifty per cent among the young. Shades of Camus – it felt threatening, nothing was said or done, no demonstration or gesture against our large official car, but frustration and menace were in the air. From the narrow, hilly streets near the hotel with high walls guarding what had once been prosperous French expatriate villas, having negotiated less salubrious districts, we passed security barriers to reach the ministry. The minister received me, in beautiful French, with great courtesy. We chatted about New York and people he knew at the UN, where he had been posted. He was pleased that the issue of Western Sahara was being seriously addressed; it should not be allowed to drift. Algeria was profoundly committed to the principle of self-determination, that was what mattered: the indisputable right of the Sahrawi people to determine their own future. His government welcomed my appointment and looked to me for genuine impartiality. The latest Security Council resolution was unambivalent: quite obviously the Spanish census had to be the basis for an electoral roll. He looked forward to meeting me again after I had become familiar with the detail. The message was evident: Algeria championed a principled stance supporting Polisario to ensure that Morocco not bulldoze through its own solution.

The final courtesy call was on Mauritania. I was programmed to fly direct to Nouakchott from Algiers, eight hours by Antonov. I stood ready next morning for early departure only to be told that we had no clearance for take-off. UN movement control had been emphatic that all clearances were received for my flight through restricted zones in southern Algeria and parts of Mauritania. Delay threatened to disrupt the overflight times authorised. The problem arose from the airport authorities' inability to give change when an unforeseen $3 charge was levied, and the pilot's inability to communicate in French. We left late and strong headwind compounded the delay.

Two hours behind schedule the Antonov began its descent towards Nouakchott. It had been snowing, so it appeared through the peephole of a window. The ground, buildings and the occasional tree were powdered, at closer range snowy whiteness turned to the pallid off-white of blowing sand, sand everywhere and over everything. Sand coloured cloud suffused the landing zone as we touched down. The stern ramp rumbled mechanically into place. Dressed like a guard of honour at its base stood the reception party. The president's personal representative, head of the foreign ministry, chief of protocol and more, they were all waiting. I saw them as I tightened my tie and staggered, after eight uncomfortable hours on a jump-seat, dishevelled, parched, and desperate for a pee, onto the sloping ramp. Francophone west Africa expected visiting dignitaries to wear a suit and tie and appropriate shoes. My leather soles slipped on the metal ramp's steep incline, rather than fall ignominiously I jumped the last few feet and wobbled to an undignified landing before the president's representative. A guard saluted. As soon as we had shaken hands I led the way more briskly than usual to the VIP reception area and found a lavatory.

Mauritanian men not dressed like Frenchmen wore the same traditional clothes as the Sahrawi and they spoke the same Hassaniya Arabic. All who passed were brown, lean, sinewy men of the desert, their women though, when I encountered them, the women of the privileged class, were voluminous. Exuberantly rounded bodies were female beauty priorities, which they went to extraordinary lengths in achieving, French style had yet to penetrate the world of women in Mauritania. In other ways also Mauritania remained isolated, it had only abolished slavery as recently as 1980, and that on paper, many former slaves opting to remain with their 'owner' having nowhere else, no alternative means of support or prospect of employment. Mining iron ore and off-shore fishery sustained the economy but offered little to most people. Extensive in area but thinly populated, Mauritania was, like many African territories, a colonial construct. Sahrawi tribes lived in the northern part of the country and historically dominated black Africans further south. The border between this formerly French possession and Spanish Sahara followed imperially ruled straight lines, except for an odd corner incorporating the iron ore deposits.

The coup, change of government and withdrawal from Western Sahara left the presidency chastened. Mauritania recognised Polisario, having little choice, but respected Morocco's dominant position and looked warily towards Algeria.

For the audience I was driven to the presidential palace, an ordinary colonial villa enhanced by a spacious reception chamber and defended by sand-coated soldiers. The president, enthroned in an outsize ornate chair, presided at one end before two rows, empty but for the foreign ministry head and myself – opposite each other. He spoke little and softly, noisy air-conditioning making him hard to hear. He nodded when I summarised the recent Security Council resolution. Mauritania was not a party to the dispute, President Mamouya Ould Taya insisted, whatever was agreed by Morocco and Polisario to resolve their dispute over Western Sahara was acceptable to Mauritania.

The courtesy calls were useful in that I met the individuals with whom I had to deal. I wanted to believe these were people I could work with, the chemistry adequate for building trust, but as I was to warn my successor five years later, however brilliant you may be in assessing others, they have also to assess you, your judgment, to decide whether you are a man of your word and, equally important, whether you can deliver, which in the UN context could not always be taken for granted.

The UN representative carries a purely symbolic stick and has no carrots to offer. International approbation was desirable but its opposite, condemnation in the court of world opinion, not greatly dreaded, sanctions were not on the cards. The Security Council resolutions were to be implemented with the voluntary cooperation of the parties, despite their expressed reservations. On the key issue, the electoral roll, their views were diametrically opposed. Polisario was adamant that the eventual voters' list be derived from the Spanish census, and Algeria backed them; Morocco had no intention of limiting voters to the Spanish census, dismissed as a politically motivated, imperial exercise, which excluded thousands of genuine Sahrawis, outside Western Sahara as traditional nomads, for education, commercial interests, or campaigning against Spanish colonialism. Entitlement to vote in a referendum needed to encompass *jus sanquinis* not merely *jus solis*, Sahrawis even if not listed as West Saharans. If theoretically feasible, and it might not be, it would take time to extract compromise or concession.

Impartial books were hard to find but I persevered in trying to grasp the structure and dispersion of Sahrawi society. Some tribes were indubitably based in the territory, though they too had members elsewhere, some lived mainly but not exclusively outside Western Sahara, some astride the frontier, the census also included groupings, not actual tribes. For census purposes individuals were listed in eighty-eight sub-fractions – with challenging Arabic nomenclature, triple-barrelled names differently transliterated. Our immediate mandate was to revise the list of persons in the census, omitting individuals who had died and adding those born since. Even that engendered strong reactions.

5

Minurso

A MESSAGE FROM BACHIR requested my return as soon as convenient. We flew into the heat drawn by centripetal force towards the eye of the sun. The Antonov sealed us in a cocoon of stifling temperature. It passed 50 degrees, I felt claustrophobic, as, through the tiny porthole, I watched the heat hazed desert wobble. The general stayed closeted with his paperback. No one spoke.

At Tindouf, when we landed, it was equally hot. I waited impatiently until Majid, returned from representing Polisario in New York pending assignment to their 'embassy' in Sweden, came. Talks, he announced pompously, would be political and with me alone, those accompanying me, the general, police commissioner and others, were invited to lunch following the meeting. He directed me into his ancient Land Rover and we drove off. 'Was my secretary French?' I replied that she was but her function was to take notes. Majid referred to unfortunate past experience, they did not trust the French. If they felt strongly, I said, she need not be present but I preferred, for my own benefit, to have a record. When we reached the mud complex the secretary jumped from the vehicle following and traipsed after us through the warren of spaces into the same room where I had my original meeting with Bachir. Bachir, already there and wearing a tie, greeted me in a friendly way. There was little introductory chit-chat. No one mentioned the secretary.

Bachir insisted that we ought to be beginning work on those in the '74 census, as the resolution specified, identifying those eligible to vote. How could Morocco claim that the majority of the Sahrawi population was outside the territory during the census? Never in history, whatever the nomadic wanderings, had that been so, except perhaps now, now that the majority of undisputed Sahrawis was there in refugee camps! Yes, there were indeed Sahrawi tribes in southern Morocco, the Tekna for instance and the Ait Ousa, and in Mauritania, but these did not belong, were not rooted in Western Sahara. Just because one or two of their number happened to be included in the census that must not open the door to an entire tribe. Then there was the Rif, which lay a thousand miles north of the Sahara and had been a Spanish protectorate, several Rifains were in the census having come south to serve in the army or during the phosphate boom, but that could not possibly justify giving a vote to the vast Rif region. 'We do not need their marijuana,' he interrupted himself, with a smile. The tribe was too encompassing an entity, the sub-fraction it was that counted, arguably even the '*ahel*' or extended family group. Only individuals belonging to a sub-fraction '*implantée*' – grounded, rooted, established – in the territory qualified, the sheikhs could say for certain which they were.

The sheikhs had to be involved from the outset. Bachir repeated: with the sheikhs or nothing. But even this was not straightforward since recognition of valid sheikhs was disputed. Yaqub-Khan had earlier tried to assemble the sheikhs on neutral ground in Geneva: an equal number presented by Morocco and by Polisario. The sheikhs arrived, but never met, Morocco's list included 'sheikhs' that Polisario sheikhs refused to recognise: notables elected or appointed after 1976, under Moroccan jurisdiction and beholden to Morocco. The failed encounter ruined hope that tribal elders between themselves would resolve a difference between the two sides. Whatever I suggested, and our discussion continued for an hour or more, Bachir restated over and over again that we should be beginning with persons in the '74 census and only the sheikhs could identify those qualified to vote and the sheikhs had to be involved from the outset.

Majid rose as Bachir finished and led me – and secretary – through the heat barrier across a hundred yards of gravely desert separating the hill-top buildings from a rectangular compound. The compound, walled in red ochre rammed earth, served as official Polisario reception centre with an open expanse for parade ground and traditional entertainment, cubicles along both sides and at the far end provided visitors' accommodation. I was escorted to a room sparsely cushioned to find the police commissioner and general, hot and losing patience. Bachir entered at the same moment with other Polisario dignitaries, greeted everybody affably and invited us to table in the adjoining chamber. Bachir placed me to his right; on my other side sat the Polisario head of security, a man of few words, dressed in uniform without badges, markings or insignia. Beyond him was the general, in a genial effort to engage van Baelen in conversation, Bachir lent forward: '*Comment vont les troupes*? (How are the troops?)' What troops? replied the general gruffly. Bachir, confused, seemed uncertain how to respond. 'They are officers,' van Baelen stated. Bachir resumed soft-spoken conversation with me, only now did he reveal the true reason for meeting urgently: an encounter between Morocco and Polisario. He had not wanted to mention this in the presence of Majid or anyone. The UN secretary-general proposed a date in mid July, the place Laayoune. Yaqub-Khan had not communicated anything, but I had learnt that in diplomatic intercourse it is best to feign knowledge without revealing what you know, or do not know, or cannot share. I nodded. Bachir was saying he had not been to El-Aiun in eighteen years. The level had yet to be agreed; if 'ministerial' he would be coming.

Tindouf airport was thick with heat, heat in the Antonov suffocating. For over forty minutes we sat, numbed and wretched, while the crew tried ineffectively to start an engine that refused to ignite. Fuel evaporates at that temperature before igniting, at each attempt a small explosion closed the engine. And we endured. Finally, finally, with the help of a pathetic little hand-held fire-extinguishing pump a crewman squirted enough cooling liquid on the propeller to spark revolving engines for take-off and the flight to Laayoune.

On my return the phone rang. Governor Azmi. He had been unable to locate me, had I been doing some tourism? The minister wished to meet with me. Basri was planning a visit to Laayoune; Azmi would be coming on ahead, the following day before noon. He arrived together with a university professor, a Sahrawi, whose brother, Azmi said, was on the other side, at the hotel the governor of Smara waited, also a Sahrawi committed to Morocco. Basri was expected the next morning by special flight accompanied by ten ministers and senior officials for a conference on regional resources. I mentioned the July meeting, Azmi said this was for discussion with the minister.

In the morning I called, expecting Azmi up and ready, to hear a sleepy '*allo*.' The special flight, postponed, not expected till evening, the conference had been rescheduled. A mission member with regional experience said 'Welcome to Morocco', rescheduling a fact of life. Basri's arrival was again postponed. After another twenty-four hours a special flight touched down delivering to what they insisted on calling Morocco's southern region the Prime Minister, Basri and eight lesser ministerial colleagues. Azmi asked that I remain available, his assistant adding helpfully that after lunch was the most likely time for a meeting. Around two-thirty a call informed me that I was to be joined by the force commander and the chief administrative officer. Minutes later the general knocked with military vigour, our chief of administration had better instincts and waited. It was late afternoon when we were invited, with utmost haste, to join Basri at the provincial governor's residence, formerly that of the Spanish commander-in-chief.

In both reception rooms a large number of evidently important people were finishing a traditional Moroccan banquet. I was squeezed between the governors of Smara and Boujdour. Then the media waters broke disgorging into the room a shoal of reporters, television cameramen and microphones on long stick-holders. Basri took the floor, he delivered a crisp, tightly worded statement on identification, all requests for registration, whether from persons in the '74 census or not, would have to be received by the identification commission from the very beginning. With a microphone abruptly thrust at my face, I mentioned the Security Council decision to start with persons in the '74 census. How could you possibly exclude, Basri declaimed for the benefit of a wider audience, Sahrawis, patriots, who had campaigned against colonialism and for that very reason were out of the territory in 1974 and therefore not included in the census? The present governor of Smara happened to be in the census, but the governor of Boujdour –and he gesticulated first towards one, then the other – had been an anti-colonial activist and was not included. How could you conceivably exclude such a person? I restated our mandate to start with the '74 census. You will have to receive all applications from the outset, retorted Basri. I agreed that from a practical point of view we could hardly prohibit individuals from submitting their names and suggested that the commission process those from the '74 census pending further agreement. Moroccan television covered Basri in full. The national press, days later, attributed to me a highly selective extract, in quotation marks, of what I had said.

As I was leaving Basri mentioned the mid-July meeting; Morocco pledged full support, he looked forward to seeing me in Rabat beforehand. Azmi said he would call to confirm and departed together with Basri and entourage. Next day I was invited to fly north with my senior advisors: the force commander and chief administrative officer. And the civil police commissioner? No. I suspect they had forgotten. He was slighted when it emerged we were to be presented to King Hassan. On arrival in Rabat, Azmi, like Hermes, messenger of the gods, produced the summons from on high, an outsize envelope elegantly hand inscribed and containing a large gold-bevel-edged card with proudly raised printing in Arabic one side and French the other. Prior to the palace we were to call on Basri.

Basri's mansion, his principal residence in the capital, was a flamboyant expression of opulence. It straddled the grounds of a park with immaculate lawns, swimming-pool, and a pool-house not unlike the Petit Trianon. The villa's interior, with European drawing-room and salon Maroccain both on the grand scale, dazzled with gold leaf, a cut-plaster ceiling had been gilded like much of the furniture and *objets d'art,* lilies gilded to overawe. Magnificent elephant tusks, gold mounted, presented arms before an antechamber where, framed in heavy silver, multiple photographs, most signed or dedicated, displayed the king, Basri with the king, with the crown prince, with both princes. Basri made an entrance, he greeted me, then the others, before introducing a distinguished French lawyer, who had completed a major work on Moroccan constitutional law to be presented in homage to the king, and announced that the king's birthday reception, to which we were honoured with an invitation, was next day.

The following morning a nervous Azmi escorted us past multiple check-points and, within the palace confines, through a maze of halls and chambers packed with courtiers, officers in full-dress uniform and waiting guests. Our identities were verified and royal command cards inspected. From a large, densely crowded salon we were ushered through scrupulously monitored doors into an airy reception room, elegantly furnished in French style with Moroccan accents. Select members of the diplomatic corps and privileged guests sipped mint tea and spoke in subdued voices. Noiselessly parade doors swung open and one by one we advanced into the presence. Basri, in control,

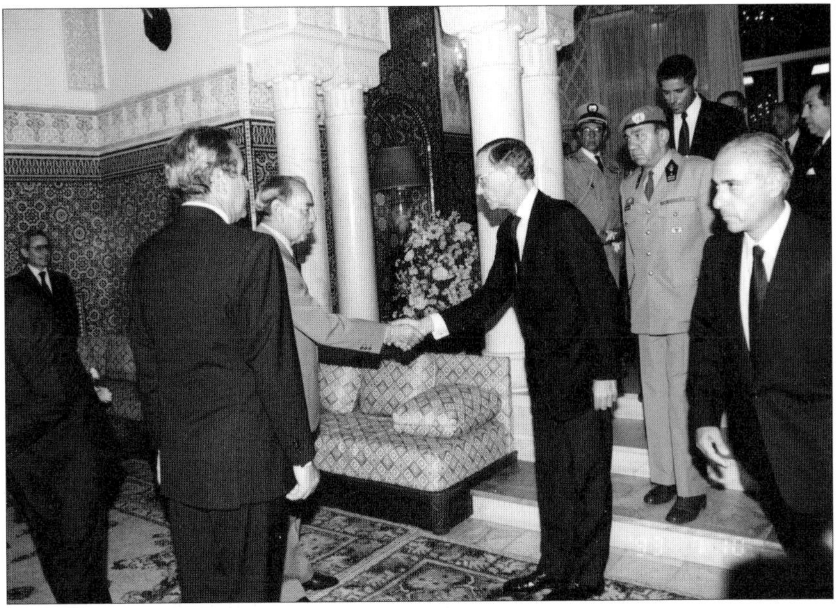

Received by King Hassan II with a handshake

bowed obsequiously low and kissed the king's hand before presenting me to His Majesty, the king gave me his hand to shake. Photographs taken, we descended to the gardens leaving others to the kissing of hands. A band played, fountains sparkled. Raked gravel paths, bordered with blossoming shrubs, clipped trees and brightly coloured flowers, bisected lawns, which were dressed with marquees, carpet-lined, and set with tables and chairs. Morocco's upper crust, the Makhzen, dark suited, uniformed or in traditional dress, promenaded, met, conversed in pairs and small groups, and indulged. Being a Moroccan occasion there were no women present. The few foreigners, diplomats longing for a glass of wine were disappointed, unlike the past only fruit juices flowed.

The United States ambassador, and the British and French, when we were introduced, wanted to know about the rumoured talks. I confirmed the date as set for 15 July and that both Morocco and Polisario would be sending delegations to Laayoune, that was all I knew. I had been informed of this and of Yaqub-Khan's arrival.

As senior UN representative in Laayoune I was to greet delegations. Polisario landed first. They had flown in a UN Antonov and descended unceremoniously down the rear ramp, I received them on the tarmac and in UN vehicles drove them direct to the hotel. The Moroccan delegation, advisors and staff emerged from a special 737 flight and surged to the VIP lounge to be welcomed by the Governor of Laayoune and served mint tea before their cavalcade rolled into town. The delegation was an issue, how constituted and who would lead it. Members of the Royal Consultative Council for Sahrawi Affairs were expected to be part but the leader, as understood by Polisario, was to be Ahmed Snoussi, Morocco's ambassador and permanent representative at the UN, who enjoyed the king's confidence, and was not a Sahrawi. On that assumption Bachir came as head of the Polisario team.

The delegation was not the first contentious issue, where to meet proved divisive. Morocco proposed a government building; Polisario refused. The compromise, which pleased Polisario and Morocco reluctantly accepted, was to open proceedings at UN headquarters, where we disposed of a modest conference room. The Polisario delegation eyed the Moroccans suspiciously. Sahrawis who had opted to side with Morocco and one or two who had switched allegiance from Polisario, made up the Moroccan team alongside Snoussi and Azmi. The two delegations settled on opposite sides of the table. Yaqub-Khan, at one end, read a message from the secretary-general, this was interpreted consecutively from French into Arabic, extending the formalities just long enough, given the hour, for Yaqub-Khan to propose adjournment till after lunch. Before breaking, both sides wished to make brief statements. The Moroccan delegation was given the floor.

Not Snoussi but Biadillah spoke. Dr Biadillah was a Sahrawi, had been a Polisario sympathiser when young, and almost exactly opposite, with the Polisario delegation, sat his brother. No twins were more alike, only clothing told them apart. No sooner had Biadillah begun speaking, apparently head of delegation, than Polisario reacted, they talked excitedly to each other, believed themselves deceived, tricked. Bachir, his colour rising, eyes flashing, afterwards accused Yaqub-Khan of having deliberately misled him. Yaqub-Khan, who had been in Paris, sick, denied it; 'possibly' and 'will' could have been garbled, Snoussi claimed to have informed the secretary-general's assistant correctly. The meeting broke up leaving Yaqub-Khan to mediate the next move.

Another meeting-space proved impossible to arrange. Polisario wanted only meetings at UN headquarters, Morocco disagreed. One proposal was to alternate between UN premises and a conference room at the hotel. The conference room at the Parador hotel, eminently suitable in most respects, displayed, like other public spaces, enlarged photographs of King Hassan. To the management I hinted that the portraits might benefit from cleaning. No. For Moroccans royal portraits were sacrosanct, this was a society where the slightest whisper of *lèse majesté* had consequences.[1] Morocco, after magnanimously conceding to open at UN premises, refused to budge. In Moroccan eyes the fact that Polisario had come to Laayoune implied knowing acceptance of Moroccan flags flying and royal portraits adorning the walls. But Polisario would not countenance sitting beneath the king's authoritarian gaze. When Yaqub-Khan failed to convince Bachir that he had not been inveigled to Laayoune under false pretences Polisario announced their departure for the following morning. Late that evening, a call from the US and American pressure persuaded Bachir to stay a little longer. But where to meet?

The Parador hotel had an extensive lounge, charmingly bisected by a rill dribbling from a fountain-head. The royal portrait was at one end. Beyond the rivulet at the other end a well-painted mural depicted an encampment with Sahrawis making music; fortunately nothing made explicit that this was a scene from the 'Green March'. Polisario accepted to foregather beyond the stream, since this was separate from the 'room' where the king's picture presided. Snoussi read out loud a message from King Hassan welcoming 'Moroccans' back into the fold, hence the designation of fellow Sahrawis on the Royal Consultative Council on Sahrawi Affairs to convey the invitation. Polisario rejected that interpretation out of hand, no way were they errant subjects of the Moroccan king, much less delinquent children as implied. The Sahrawi Arab Democratic Republic was recognised as a member state of the Organisation of African Unity and by some eighty countries worldwide. They would expect to deal with the ministry for foreign affairs, with genuine Moroccans, Moroccans who had power, and most emphatically not with traitors to the Sahrawi cause and turncoats.

Luncheon followed, in the circumstances surprisingly relaxed. Some were related by blood or marriage, had friends in common and personal news to exchange, the only dividend. Yaqub-Khan said that Laayoune constituted an 'extraordinary step', I was not convinced. Progress on the ground was needed to foster genuine interaction, perhaps less ambitious but more real. I escorted Bachir and delegation to the airport and bade them officially farewell. Azmi was livid that evening, outraged because someone in the last car had scattered a paper trail of tiny Polisario flags as they drove through town: 'Children!'

6

Voter registration

THE MISSION'S CIVILIAN COMPONENT was now largely in place. Identification commission members, registration officers, interpreters, administrative and secretarial personnel had been employed. As well as English most spoke French and Arabic, or at least French. Whereas UN missions had originally been staffed by persons on secondment, as I had been for several assignments, the surge in UN peace-keeping and long-term operations made that impossible, personnel had to be recruited.

Interpreters explored the peculiarities of regional usage and specialised vocabulary. Registration officers practised the skills envisaged, not least familiarising themselves with Sahrawi tribal structure and nomenclature. The gamut of eighty-eight sub-fractions was daunting, their names even for Arabists a challenge, for non Arabic-speakers personal as well as sub-fraction names were hard to pronounce and difficult to remember, the problem compounded by Sahrawi names being differently transliterated in French, Spanish and English lists, 'h' being 'j' in Spanish transliteration, 'w' 'ou' in French.

The identification commission members – they preferred being 'commissioners' – met daily with me to develop procedures for identifying those qualified to vote. No precedent existed: every step to be devised from scratch. One thing was glaringly obvious: the process was anything but technical, both sides saw it as political and at the core of their interests. Whatever we proposed had to convince and prove voluntarily acceptable to both Morocco and Polisario. Step one, up-dating the 1974 census lists, the revised list, eased once the parties' fear of fraudulent substitutions had been allayed, little else was straightforward, what gratified one usually offended the other. Identification had to involve sheikhs from both sides, and both would expect to be present as observers; the OAU had to be represented. It was going to be cumbersome, transport would be an issue, accommodation and not least security – Morocco and Polisario were at war. We studied lists of Sahrawi tribes and sub-fractions to decide how best to convoke applicants and where, and tackled a tentative time-table.

An application form had first to be drafted for completion by all claiming a right to vote, reflecting the revised criteria presented by Perez de Cuellar on the eve of retirement: these added to those in the '74 census persons who had been 'inadvertently' omitted with immediate family, could claim to have lived in the territory and children of persons born in the territory, if identified by tribal leaders. Polisario stayed intransigent: only the census listing was not subject to debate – or manipulation. It was conceivable, and the Spanish authorities admitted as much, that a few Sahrawis had been overlooked in that vast desert area, but there could be no new categories. Polisario predictably argued for limiting questions to the 1974 census, there must be no other questions on the form, Morocco, of course, insisted that the census could not stand alone. Polisario wanted information regarding tribal appurtenance to include details of '*ahel*' family membership while Morocco was equally insistent that only tribe and sub-fraction applied. Language was another issue: Arabic, naturally, together with French, said Morocco, which Polisario rejected in favour of Spanish. They disputed how to distribute forms and complete them in an illiterate society.

Every suggestion was hotly contested by one side or the other as we struggled towards compromise. The questions were adroitly arranged, those census-related appeared on the front, all others on the reverse ('We will only look at the front', Polisario said), '*ahel*' was placed beside 'sub-fraction' (irrelevant said Morocco; should be a separate entry said Polisario). Airport immigration cards suggested how to accommodate Arabic, which reads from right to left, together with a left to right European language, it was agreed to produce one version with French and another with Spanish. I dispatched faxes and advised New York. Polisario, anxious to proceed, concurred; Morocco hesitated. Before final approval by the minister, Azmi now said, options had to be discussed with the governor of Laayoune province.

Zemrag the governor was an old school patriot who had campaigned for independence and rejoiced to see both Frenchmen and Spaniards evicted. He politely offered tea before affirming that he resented profoundly the notion of a referendum, the Sahara was historically and in every way part of Morocco, a referendum uncalled for-Moroccans competed to outbid each other in patriotic fervour. I pointed out, gently, that not only were we mandated by the UN Security Council but by the decision of His Majesty the King who himself proposed a referendum. The governor deflected this with derogatory remarks about the UN and the Security Council, then astonished us by insinuating that the king's act was near treasonable; Azmi looked away. The governor had just received the proposed form, he said, he needed time for study, he had reservations, he promised to call as soon as he had examined the text.

When a message came suggesting the Monday following Azmi said he would gone. Decisions could be finalised only by Azmi with the governor's involvement and by the governor in Azmi's presence; they had fortunately abandoned the idea first mooted that all four Saharan provincial governors take part. Azmi departed Sunday, the following morning Zemrag telephoned about meeting in Rabat and seemed mildly surprised that I was not already en route. Basri had convoked him jointly with Azmi to iron out problems, I would be there presumably, minutes later came the summons from Rabat. I was pleased that events were evolving and that Basri would be giving direction to his governors. Zemrag, strangely, was not at the airport, I imagined he had left by a special flight. Azmi, at the terminal in Casablanca, was less than his ebullient self, but welcoming, confirmed appointment with Basri. I asked after Zemrag. 'The fool!' said Azmi, ' He's old and he's ill. He's been exploiting respect and sympathy for too long, he has lost his touch.'

The meeting with Basri was rescheduled for the following afternoon. Basri's workday had a pattern: golf in the morning accompanied by select ministers and others for discreet talk between holes, then to the palace, other appointments followed in both time and importance. Around three o'clock Azmi conducted me to the ministry, I was calmly tightening my tie when a phone rang. Azmi, instantly tense, as only in dealings with Basri and, of course, the king. said we had to rush, the meeting with Basri was at the '*plage*'. The *plage* was where privileged citizens of Rabat had seaside cottages. Of all Basri's properties that I entered this was the least pretentious. We approached through a small walled garden equipped with an ordinary striped deckchair and telephones on either side, inside the house was decorated with greatly enlarged photographs of Basri in assorted encounters with the king and royal princes, pride of place given to Basri, on a yacht, smiling radiantly beside His Majesty. Basri entered in person, Azmi withdrew to a corner, and Basri, having greeted me, began eating. I said it was a pleasure to meet him in such relaxed surroundings and to find him smiling. 'That's my nature,' he said, 'to be smilingly optimistic.'Between mouthfuls he bombarded me with questions requiring snap answers. The draft application form and schedule had already been given him, I said, 'You faxed it,' he corrected, 'after first sending it to New

York.' It rankled that before he had it Snoussi had seen the text at the UN. I paused. If the wording was agreed, I would order printing and have the forms ready for distribution. For the launch Basri proposed coming in person to Laayoune. He finished eating and drinking, left the room to respond to an urgent call.

To one side was a distinguished looking man. He introduced himself: Driss Slaoui. I knew who he was, he had been Morocco's ambassador at the UN and returned to become councillor to the king. Slaoui asked whether I saw any point in striving for direct talks now that identification looked set to begin. I said my hope was that one might reinforce the other, that identification would propel the parties toward meaningful talks. He was about to comment when Basri returned and said goodbye. Had he actually accepted the text I asked Azmi as we drove back to Rabat. 'You heard.'

From Rabat I passed instructions to print the form and drafted a covering letter for Basri and Bachir in virtually identical language, Azmi concurred when I translated it. No confirmation came from Basri about the launch. Bachir wanted action, but for Morocco to act too. Neither Basri nor Azmi responded to telephone calls, another meeting in Rabat might be necessary, Azmi said when finally I tracked him down.

At the airport he seemed almost offended. '*Il faut pas se precipiter*,' he insisted, 'must not be in a rush.' I smiled wanly. He said this was August, when people were on holiday, but crucially for the minister and staff and why they had been difficult to reach, this was the culminating moment before dedication of Casablanca's new mosque, le grand mosque Hassan II, I really had to understand that for Morocco and His Majesty this was of overarching significance. I enquired whether we could expect to start after the inauguration. 'Yes, yes,' he said, then, almost as an afterthought, he mentioned a problem they had with the application form. I thought Basri had agreed, and the Moroccan UN mission raised no objection, the secretary-general expected the process to begin. It was a minor difficulty, Azmi said, but it mattered to Morocco, Basri had instructed two or three principals in the ministry to recheck the form meticulously. What was the precise problem? I asked. Azmi did not have his papers, I offered to produce mine, not here, not now, he said, after the inauguration.

The grand mosque Hassan II, second largest mosque in the world, was consecrated with due pomp and circumstance on the eve of the prophet's birthday. Hassan, not only king but descendant of the prophet and spiritual leader of his people, exploited the consecration to bless his reign and vision.

Heads of state, ambassadors and Muslim dignitaries from far and wide arrived to pay respect in the vast, luminous space of this magnificent edifice cantilevered out over the Atlantic ocean. Organisational, logistical and security arrangements must have been a nightmare and it was a wonder that Basri had given any more thought to our form. After two days I tried telephoning Azmi on his office number, at home and on his mobile, to no avail, an engaged signal, an answering machine and a servant who spoke no French. Then he called to explain that the minister's mother had died, her death was unexpected and the minister was deeply attached to his mother. All appointments cancelled, none would be made for at least three or four days.

Laayoune was sand-encrusted, engulfed in a sandstorm. Residue, grey, gritty, coated the hotel grounds, wind-driven sand nestled in crevices, bringing August to a cheerless end. Now September and high time to act, Bachir, increasingly impatient, wanted a start date, but for Morocco to begin simultaneously, which was impossible while Basri cavilled. Although Morocco did not distance itself publicly from the Security Council decision to take first those in the '74 census, it had become obvious that Basri had no intention of starting until the additional categories were explicitly accepted, he stalled, comfortable with the thought that Polisario, exasperated, might abandon the plan.

That Arafat had been received by King Hassan the day after inauguration of the grand mosque and that Morocco had provided an aircraft to fly Arafat from Tunis to Washington, was widely known, the king had long played a role as the one Arab leader willing also to deal with the Israelis – which the Americans valued. On 13 September 1993 a signature and handshake promised mutual recognition and the prospect of a safer future for Israelis and Palestinians. Some thought these developments gave hope for the Sahara: dialogue leading to mutually acceptable compromise, others imagined an independent Palestinian state the model for Sahrawi independence: the RASD flag inspired by the PLO's was no coincidence.

That was the news when I flew to Tindouf. I was to meet Bachir at the isolated 'chicken farm', which was emerging from a mirage shimmering over the stony flats when a message rumbled on the driver's radio. Bachir had been in an accident, we should return to the UN base. My Polisario escort knew nothing, he asked to be dropped off, would find transport somehow or walk, but I insisted on taking him to Rabouni; we could hardly leave him wandering over open desert in searing heat. Emhamed Kheddad appeared as we drove into the courtyard, surprised, but pleasant enough when I jumped out to greet him. He had been with Bachir on a previous visit, rarely speaking but well-informed and to the point. The American colonel called him a fanatic, he was patently committed, but intelligent, quick to understand, and articulate in response, with facts at his fingertips, his French and English were fluent, in addition to Spanish and Arabic. I suspected he could prove tough, he smiled much less than Bachir.

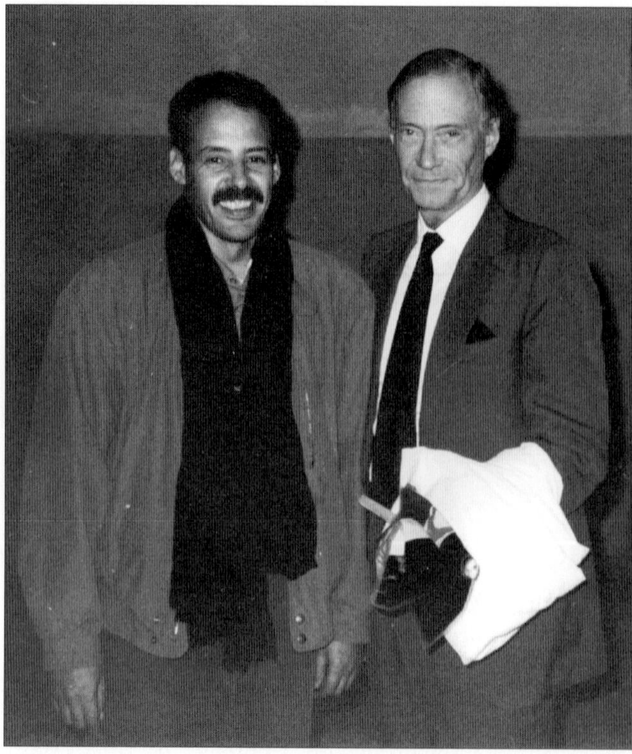

With Emhamed Kheddad in the POLISARIO camps

Bachir's accident, no, it had not been a driving accident, was not serious, Kheddad wished to assure me, an injury at work – work unspecified. Kheddad was to collect him from the hospital, we could meet at Rabouni around 3.30. When Bachir arrived, lightly bandaged: '*rien de grave* – nothing serious', I explained the difficulty with the Moroccans. He knew, the Moroccans would procrastinate, they would raise every obstacle to a referendum other than the one they chose. The additional criteria were absurd, opening floodgates to hundreds of thousand Moroccan voters, who were definitely not Sahrawis, their sheikhs would impose whatever was desired. the notion that sheikhs on the Moroccan side could be trusted to bear unbiased witness was ridiculous. The sheikhs, with few exceptions, could be corrupted, Bachir said. 'Even yours?' 'Well, we don't have the means; Morocco has plenty of money.'[1] Perhaps what we needed was an Oslo agreement, I suggested. Dialogue yes, said Bachir, he favoured dialogue but with the king or crown prince, in Morocco only the king and his son had power to compromise, talk with anyone else was play-acting. He refused categorically to negotiate with men in Sahrawi dress: it was an insult being asked to deal with traitors, he hoped not to encounter turncoats at whatever Yaqub-Khan might be planning next.

When I heard that Yaqub-Khan intended convening the parties in New York I advised against. New York, during the General Assembly, would heighten political tension, both sides tempted to seek plaudits from friends in the gallery. The date, twice postponed, was set for 25 October at Polisario's insistence on the presence in New York of the responsible US desk officer. 25 October had been the day discussed with the Moroccans to finalise public announcement of the application process and plans to distribute forms, assuming that the application form was agreed. Azmi, included in the delegation for New York, telephoned from Casablanca just before take-off to say that I was bound to understand this inevitable adjustment.

The event was a fiasco. Polisario was adamant in refusing to talk to 'turncoats' on the Moroccan delegation, the two sides never met, no communiqué was possible. Bachir told me that the confidence he expressed in my efforts risked being undermined by Yaqub-Khan's aborted talks in New York. Bone of contention was Omar Hadrami, Hadrami had been in the Polisario leadership and held powerful office before defecting to Morocco, he and Brahim Hakim, Polisario's successful 'foreign minister' were the most conspicuous personalities to have switched allegiance, stars in the Moroccan view and traitors to Polisario. I encountered Hadrami on his return from New York, on the failed meeting he had nothing to say but he had advice to give: the solution lay in convincing the Sahrawis detained in the camps that their only viable future was within a broad Moroccan framework: 'What do we have but our desert?'

On the same flight with the Moroccan delegation came Yaqub-Khan. I accompanied him to the luxurious villa placed at his disposal; 'it belongs to one of the royal princesses,' he told me, the Moroccans cosseted and pampered Yaqub-Khan like a pedigree racehorse, of delicate and sensitive disposition, but capable, with grooming, of delivering a trophy in the big race. At the villa, surrounded by pastry and whiskies in comprehensive variety, I reminded him of our pedestrian concern: to launch identification. It was crucial to obtain Morocco's formal agreement and the decision might lie with the king, an audience, I knew, was planned.

Snoussi accompanied Yaqub-Khan to the palace, the two returning very cheerful. Much banter over lunch, Snoussi flattered Yaqub-Khan on the brilliance of his diplomacy, Yaqub-Khan returned the compliment. Snoussi told anecdotes, nothing of substance was said. Only after Snoussi left did I extract from Yaqub-Khan an inkling of what had taken place, discussion had focussed on the breakdown of direct talks, the king expressing his conviction that further talks would be of little avail given Polisario's attitude, identification was not mentioned.

Snoussi was back: to discuss a proposed timetable, Yaqub-Khan deflected this to me as 'technical.'Some fine-tuning of specific dates was needed, for the launch I reasserted 'During the week of 1 November' not 'Saturday 6 November', as the anniversary of the 'Green March' would have provoked Polisario fury; another date was changed by a day. From further questions I deduced that Snoussi realised how preliminary analysis of applications could provide an indication of eventual votes, all conceivable measures, I assured him, were in place to protect information received. Snoussi reverted to their demand that everyone be given similar treatment with equal respect for all criteria from the outset. I restated my compromise to enable us to start: prior to identification applications had to be processed, any person believing himself eligible was permitted to apply but we would process those not included in the '74 census only after agreement on interpretation of the criteria.

Snoussi announced next day that the king would receive Yaqub-Khan a second time. Yaqub-Khan, nervous and tense, had questions about the timetable and relevant Security Council resolution, including what was said about the 1974 census. I gave him the text, in English and in French, reminding him that our mandate was to 'begin' with persons in the '74 census, but 'beginning' need not halt us. The king's accord was essential to launch the process, I emphasised as strongly as I dared the imperative to obtain royal approval.

Yaqub-Khan and Snoussi returned beaming, His Majesty had given his blessing. After lunch Yaqub-Khan elaborated, the king, while accepting the programme of work proposed, insisted on one condition, there should be no processing of any applications until the revised criteria were agreed. Yaqub-Khan thought this entirely reasonable, how would it be possible, he asked rhetorically, to process any application until the criteria had been finally settled? I suggested an analogy, people at a consulate applying for visas do not receive identical treatment, some are accorded visas immediately, others have to wait pending prior checks. Yaqub-Khan merely restated that he considered the king's position entirely reasonable and had expressed concurrence. That could mean months before real action, I said, a delay that would please neither the Americans nor the Council.

At 8 o'clock that evening we were asked to the ministry of interior. In Basri's outer office the chef de cabinet detached Yaqub-Khan, who was saying that he wished a few personal words with the minister to express condolence on the death of his mother. Snoussi and I remained in the anteroom. Half an hour passed, not all devoted to sympathy, I was sure, since Basri spared minimal time for such, and when we were ushered in it was obvious that discussion had already happened. Yaqub-Khan summarised, referring to the king's position, which, he repeated, seemed entirely reasonable, indeed, he did not see how it was possible to proceed otherwise. Basri insisted that Morocco stood by its commitments and the commitment made to me. There could, of course, be no processing until application of the criteria was fully agreed, until then no forms would be passed to the UN. Morocco, Basri said, would be responsible for ensuring that the forms were completed before giving them to us. I pointed out that according to the plan it was for individuals to complete and return the forms and that the UN should be involved. Basri turned this aside with a smile and Yaqub-Khan, smiling contentedly, said he saw no problem and was confident that such minor technical issues could be resolved. Basri summed up adding that if by January there was no accord on interpretation of the criteria Morocco would destroy all application forms. Yaqub-Khan nodded and rose to leave, Basri said '*Tafadel*' and the meeting broke up.

The visit to Polisario had another flavour. The misbegotten encounter in New York undermined respect for Yaqub-Khan, nor had Bachir forgotten Laayoune. Polisario behaviour was correct but lack of trust infused the atmosphere. Discussion circled round the same issues, the same arguments, the same objections: whether a sub-fraction 'belonged to the territory', how the new criteria could be rigorously and impartially applied, who would guarantee proceedings as truly free and fair? Yaqub-Khan did not always hear, he conceded that his hearing was better on one side than the other. The Polisario remained unmoved when he departed.

Yaqub-Khan was depressed. No success on the political front and he had little faith in any other approach, he admitted candidly, when we met in New York, to being 'fed up'; several times he mentioned an 'elegant exit'.[2] He had sounded the Americans about a referendum on one side only, Morocco was willing, but Washington's ambassador in New York said that the US was not able to support a one-sided referendum – 'What kind of referendum would that be?' Yaqub-Khan was tempted to report to the secretary-general and the Security Council that all an honest broker could do to reconcile differences had been done, given the intransigence of the parties, in particular Polisario's continuing rejection of the revised criteria, the representative's role was at an end. Yaqub-Khan could then depart, if not covered in glory at least with honour, admired for his patience and respected for realistic judgment.

Two days later the mood changed. Yaqub-Khan's appointment had been extended, I learnt from an assistant. He announced a wish to revisit the region, 'to show the flag,' he wished to travel soon. The revised lists were, at last, being made public, to coincide I proposed 'next week.' Too soon, he preferred the end of the month. Christmas, I pointed out, 'My dear Erik (he called me Erik selectively), these are Muslim countries that do not celebrate Christmas.' That I did know, but the UN observed official holidays in late December so international staff would be absent. In that case, he said, January: if not the first week, no later than the second.

Back in Laayoune, after weeks of toothache, my remaining wisdom tooth was extracted. The relief was no greater than my relief that the application form seemed to have been tacitly agreed with no specific objection from Morocco, that we had succeeded in publishing the census lists revised, with both sides accepting, to omit persons deceased and include those born, and were on the cusp of announcing officially the launch of identification. I published the date at which applicants had to be eighteen years of age, 31 December 1993.

Polisario invited me formally to spend some days with them, to balance, they said, the time I passed in Morocco. I was received as royally as refugee conditions permitted, with apparent warmth, shown the war museum of captured 'enemy' weaponry as evidence of military prowess, then schools and modest enterprises, before visiting the camps. Abandoned shipping containers, rusted, sand-blasted, their once garish paintwork bleached out, emphasised the length of time the refugees had depended on aid. Serious meetings culminated in a banquet attended by the entire government, their 'president' presiding. Abdel-Aziz delivered a speech, he repeated their bitterness at Yaqub-Khan and paid tribute to my efforts, which inspired a glimmer of optimism. When Bachir queried how the identification commission could assess Morocco's hundreds of thousands of would-be Sahrawis, I said the sheikhs – and to me it was self-evident that both sides would have their sheikh present – would confirm, or not, a candidate's Sahrawi identity. Burden of proof lay with the candidate, it was not for the commission to prove a claim invalid, I did not see how it could be otherwise.

I was back in Laayoune when, after midnight on 30 December, came an urgent summons to call the secretary-general's chief of staff, it was two in the morning before I had a line to New York. The secretary-general wished me to convey personally to Abdel-Aziz a proposal to meet in Geneva on 15 January; Yaqub-Khan was not being informed, I was told. I arranged flights to Tindouf only to find that Abdel-Aziz had departed for Dakhla camp. Dakhla, least accessible of the Polisario encampments, involved hours of cross-desert trekking, I commandeered a helicopter. Sand dusted by the rotor I was rushed to an improvised parade ground, on a reviewing stand Abdel-Aziz took the salute as Polisario troops marched past. The men were correctly uniformed, dressed for inspection, assorted footwear apart, women, in uniform, more aggressive-looking, asserted their soldierly determination as no way inferior, militia units followed – Dad's army – up to a thousand on parade, I estimated. Assembled for the army sports competition I was told while ushered to a tent for lunch with Bachir before meeting Abdel-Aziz. Abdel-Aziz noted the secretary-general's invitation and hoped to be able to accept, he would have liked to know whether Morocco would be represented and by whom. I could not tell him, I only knew that the encounter was strictly confidential.

Like Laayoune and New York it failed, though not for the same reason. Boutros, aware of Polisario sensitivity, convoked a Moroccan of convincing authority. King Hassan mandated General Khadiri, who was personally close and enjoyed his confidence. Boutros chose a hotel outside Geneva itself, for discretion, where he planned to coax the two sides together, but Abdel-Aziz was unwilling to meet with Khadiri, Khadiri was not at his level, if not the king then the crown prince. Boutros told me later he suspected a more subtle objection: Khadiri it was who negotiated the defection of Brahim Hakim and Abdel-Aziz might not have dared expose himself. Whatever the true reason the planned face-to-face encounter never took place.

Equally non-productive was Yaqub-Khan's last visit to Tindouf. The Polisario with elegance snubbed him, they designed a programme as for a distinguished tourist. He was met and accompanied by the charming 'minister of interior', Abdel-Kader, whose mandate precluded talk of the settlement plan and peace-keeping, at lunch Abdel-Kader was host, afterwards came visits to the war museum, a War on Want agricultural project and tour of Smara camp. Having been shown a kindergarten and a primary school we were conducted to a huge tent and served tea: the ritual consumed time: pouring, re-pouring, the three glasses, sweet as love, strong as friendship, bitter as death, served in sequence. Traditional entertainment followed, a troupe of women made music, sang, ululated, for what seemed hours. The typed programme had an item on political talks '*Entretiens politiques*' preceding official dinner, we waited. After more waiting we were escorted to a room, a school-room, with tables laid. Abdel-Aziz eventually arrived, no political discussion, only desultory conversation while we ate, and no speeches.[3] Immediately afterwards we dispersed.

Yaqub-Khan's exit drew nearer by the day. His disenchantment with the settlement plan was no secret, he was now arguing that every avenue had been explored, every effort made to obtain the parties' agreement to the criteria and their interpretation, and the will lacked, in the circumstances, it was realistic and responsible, for a statesman, to be decisive, show courage and close the dossier. The budget was already a problem, the Americans increasingly reluctant to contribute to open-ended peace-keeping. Abdel-Aziz travelled to the US, expressed Polisario's loss of confidence in Yaqub-Khan to the secretary-general while counting on the UN referendum and Washington's support. Morocco vehemently resented Polisario criticising Yaqub-Khan, an eminent personality, sympathetic to Morocco, yes, for good reason, who could not be considered guilty of undue bias, his responsibilities were always correctly handled. Why should Polisario call the shots? No reason for Yaqub-Khan to go just because Polisario did not like him, Morocco demanded that his name remain as special representative even as his staff was reassigned and office dismantled and he flew back to Pakistan. For Boutros-Ghali's own political calculations, the name, only, would stay attached to the mission.

Thus I became head of mission while continuing as chairman of the identification commission. I asked to meet Bachir to review the situation now that the Spanish census lists revised to omit persons no longer living and adding those who had not been eighteen at the time had been made public. A cryptic enquiry came as to who would accompany me, I proposed a *tête-à-tête* meeting, was there a problem with that? Only after a delay was it confirmed. But Bachir was in the alleyway as I entered the compound. The new Russian colonel – whose boisterous smart salute and 'Colonel Gerasimov reporting, Sir!' always cheered – a less-ranked military observer, a police officer and two from the identification commission, were escorted elsewhere. Bachir invited me to be seated at a table laid for luncheon with a bottle of Algerian wine, the only time I saw wine with Polisario. When I declined, with many thanks,

Bachir called for beer, which I accepted, he never drank. He was saying that he wondered whether Abdel-Aziz trip to Geneva had been worth it. Boutros-Ghali had listened, without comment or obvious reaction, before proposing that Abdel-Aziz meet, in secret, the Moroccan palace head of security, Bachir asked whether a general as head of security, even if he enjoyed the king's confidence, could commit his country. If President Abdel-Aziz were to deal with the Moroccan side it should be with the king, and it ought to be in presence of the UN, the last thing Polisario wanted was to become ensnared in a Moroccan conspiracy. The Moroccan ideal was a burning house with just one door through which all were compelled to rush. If Morocco continued acting injudiciously, Bachir warned, it would face the same turmoil as Algeria, extreme poverty among many ensuring that. Morocco, as the island of stability and relative prosperity it claimed to be, would vanish, even the Americans would be unable to sustain it.

The Americans still upheld the plan, I said; they would not accept a one-sided referendum, but they were impatient, we needed to act. Of course, it was all too easy to block progress. Polisario wanted progress, Bachir replied, they really did, in accordance with the plan. He agreed that a solution might be possible. At which moment Kheddad entered. They did not wish UN withdrawal, he maintained, after Bachir had summarised our exchange, but they were a people whose pride would rather honour and dignity than have them submit to injustice and fraudulent manipulation. Three hours focused discussion followed, only after yet more rounds of sweetened mint tea, did Bachir begin to yawn. Throughout the mood was excellent, the dialogue genuine dialogue, as if for the first time we desired a solution. The nub identification: sheikhs had to be present as well as representatives of both sides, with OAU observers, and the UN in charge, without question. The completion of application forms was less important in itself, for the Moroccan authorities to lend applicants a hand was not sinister; most Sahrawis were illiterate and needed help, the truth would out when applicants came to be identified. Bachir and Kheddad said the application process was happening in El-Aiun camp, expansion to the other camps depended on parallel action in the territory. That I rejected as unrealistic, on the other side eighty-five per cent of the population lived in Laayoune; the towns Smara, Boujdour and Dakhla had fewer inhabitants. They accepted. When Morocco did likewise, they would submit completed forms, they would also provide all relevant information computer-ready and in Spanish once certain that identification would start in accordance with the plan.

Bachir conceded the Spanish census of 1974 as imperfect but it was the only yardstick. He sketched a map to show Sahrawi tribes ranged across the region: into Mauritania, Algeria as well as southern Morocco, the Tekna federation and the Ait Ousa he confirmed as Sahrawi tribes but Morocco based, they were not West Saharans, the Ait Baamran straddled the border, some were West Saharans. The determining entity was the sub-fraction, large sub-fractions even had certain extended family units '*ahel*' in and others out, that was why Polisario had insisted on '*ahel*' appearing on the form. Only Western Saharans had the right to vote, Western Saharans were those who belonged not just to a Sahrawi tribe but to a sub-fraction, indeed an '*ahel*', of the territory; what Morocco proposed was a farce. As we talked Bachir completed the sketch: imperial maps had ruler straight lines with Spanish Sahara missing a chunk in the lower right hand corner, at Zouerate, where the iron ore was; the French carved it out for their colony – Bachir, with a deprecating smile, said France had more clout than Spain. Kheddad enumerated the eighty-eight census sub-fractions, and, one by one, he and Bachir showed me where each belonged in tribal context on the map. The seven great tribes posed less problems; the challenge was how to cope with the three composite tribal groupings, which for census purposes the Spanish treated like tribes: 'Northern tribes', 'Coastal and southern tribes' and 'Chorfa.' Persons listed by name were acceptable but must not be allowed to open the floodgates for hundreds of thousands of northerners. Surely the identification commission could handle that, I thought. Bachir and Kheddad wanted to be convinced. On another issue Bachir asked that the commission not overlook the genuine West Saharans who had taken refuge elsewhere, principally in Mauritania. We reviewed identification procedures and I came away confident that progress was possible.

Back in Laayoune Azmi ferreted for information about Geneva, and about Tindouf. Polisario was holding things up, he said, but he refused to commit regarding the timetable before stating categorically that once the criteria were agreed, Morocco was sure to provide all completed forms promptly. Personnel were being trained and arrangements put in hand to open registration centres beyond Laayoune, in Smara, Boujdour and Dakhla. But what about Polisario? He took some convincing that they were organised to provide computerised information, their numbers more modest and all grouped in four camps – a more accessible situation than that on the Moroccan side. How could it really be, I asked, that, according to Morocco, so many more West Saharans were excluded than included in the census? They were nomads, he said emphatically, and Spain ignored deliberately those opposed to its policies. Many evaded census-takers for fear of taxes, military conscription, or whatever, tribal feuding drove out some, not to forget those actively confronting the colonial regime, others left in search of business opportunities – what was there in Spanish Sahara? – and education: virtually all Polisario's leaders were omitted from the census because away studying – in Morocco. Colonel Cuevas, the Spanish official responsible for the census, himself claimed that at least thirty per cent were not included (I heard Cuevas say perhaps ten).

For Polisario, I told Azmi, launching the plan and starting identification was what mattered. They are the ones holding it up, he repeated. As well as moving ahead with the plan they were in favour of high-level talks. Discretion was critical, Azmi said, did I realise they leaked the meeting with Boutros-Ghali through the Algerian press, even mentioning me as emissary? Talks should not be twisted into propaganda, the only hope was for Polisario to learn that lesson, and be clear about the subject. A degree of autonomy, I ventured, having heard Bachir speak of linking independence with interdependence. Azmi mumbled, autonomy was a flexible concept, whatever the king might be willing to concede.

7

Official launch

A JOINT COMMUNIQUÉ, signed by Basri and myself on 12 January 1994, was, at long last, issued. Basri contested the text I proposed but eventually came to terms with phrasing pared down from official UN language. We informed all Sahrawis believing themselves qualified to vote, aged 18 or over on 31 December 1993, that the process leading to identification of voters was launched. Over his name the minister of interior and information invited applicants to complete forms at offices 'across all prefectures and provinces of the kingdom as well as embassies and consulates abroad'. Basri also announced the opening of as many registration offices as needed, while installing new governors in Dakhla and Smara, he emphasised Morocco's commitment to the referendum.

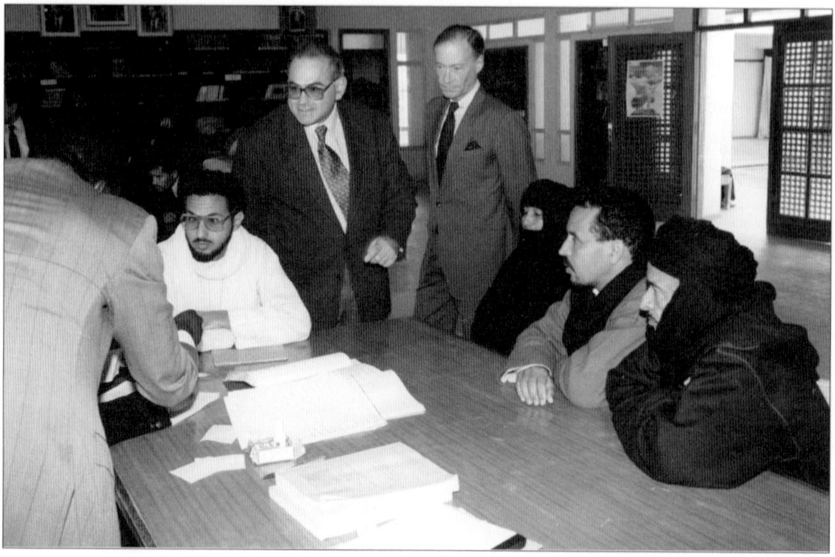

Registration of prospective voters begins

In New York some suspected Morocco of scheming to forge ahead as if criteria and their interpretation were agreed, and if Polisario failed to comply, Morocco could walk away, head held high, to do as it wished. A report of the secretary-general, on 10 March, reflecting the suspicions, faced the Council with a choice. The first option was to proceed with holding a referendum regardless of the cooperation of one party or the other. The second was for the identification commission to work for a prescribed time while trying to obtain the cooperation of both parties, the Council to review progress at the end of the prescribed period. The third would have the Council conclude that the cooperaton of both parties could not be obtained and decide that Minurso be phased out, though perhaps leaving military observers.[1]

Polisario threatened renewed hostilities if the UN withdrew, Morocco opposed leaving only military cease-fire observers, which would create 'another Cyprus'. Of the permanent members, America, Britain and France were unwilling to abandon ship. The British ambassador in Rabat told me London did not favour ending political activity including registration, the one positive achievement. The Council voted for option two: our work should continue – for a time.

Application forms were now available throughout the territory and in the refugee camps; the plan specified wherever Sahrawis lived '*en nombre*', in significant numbers, and some were in the Canary islands, in mainland Spain and in Cuba, but the largest concentration was in Mauritania. The Mauritanian president would, I knew, be reluctant to find his country drawn into a fringe of the dispute. I hoped for understanding when I flew to Nouakchott, it would concentrate minds, I believed, if the visit was brief, so arranged to fly in the morning and immediately after the audience return to Laayoune – albeit more Antonov hours than comfortable. Ould Taya received me *tête à tête*, graciously, as quietly spoken as before. I briefed him on progress to date, an application form had been agreed by both parties and distributed, forms were already being completed in the camps as well as in the territory. It would please the president, I knew, that we had made a start with both sides participating, to implement the plan we had also to receive applications from Sahrawis living in Mauritania. Ould Taya looked uneasy, he feared less this provoke unrest, lead to friction, any disturbance in Nouakchott might spiral out of control. He regretted … I promised him that applications would be invited in the border towns, Nouadhibou on the coast and Zouerate in the north, not in Nouakchott. He reflected, his government could in no way be involved. Of course not, I assured him, and any staff would be UN employees. He said he would think it over. I thanked him for his comprehension, his wish to see the settlement plan implemented, a commission member and registration officer could be dispatched to discuss modalities. I expressed appreciation again before leaving.

Basri's violent reaction when the meeting was reported, as successful, surpassed what I had feared. That he might remonstrate, yes, but he was bitter, seriously angry, accused me of exceeding my mandate. Where the plan spoke of Sahrawis living '*en nombre*' outside the territory it referred only to the refugee camps, nothing else. He threatened, he promised, if I persevered, to have the secretary-general remove me. Out.

Bachir congratulated me warmly on my achievement in Mauritania. Press reports, including major agencies, had carried news, it was a significant step. Kheddad was sure that at least five thousand Sahrawis, of those in the census, were living in Mauritania; with others, uncensored, it could come to twice that number. They were delighted. Mauritania's initial reluctance had been due to French pressure, Bachir said. I thought it was prompted more by fear of Morocco, and mentioned that Basri wanted me dismissed and the Moroccan foreign minister together with their ambassador in New York had criticised me to the secretary-general for going to Nouakchott: why had I gone – what had Mauritania to do with this process? .

Basri, who had been out of the country, asked to meet me on his return and proposed an afternoon appointment in Marrakech. Hours hard driving delivered me to the lush countryside round Marrakech and news that the appointment was postponed to nine o'clock. At 9.30 Azmi telephoned that the minister, just emerged from a ministerial gathering at the palace, was exhausted and suggested 8.30 the following morning. By 9 a.m. I was on the verge of returning to Laayoune, where business awaited me, having said that I would be pleased to return when the minister was able to give me a firm appointment when Basri eclipsed me. With a friendly gesture he drew me into an elevator before the door closed, in sweater and tartan trews he was on his way to play golf. Azmi, tense as a schoolboy in the headmaster's study, bustled me out at street level and into Basri's car. Seated in front beside the driver, Basri skimmed newspaper clippings, rather pointedly ignoring an Amnesty International insert in Le Figaro flagged for his attention. The royal golf course was immaculate, beautiful with morning freshness and birdsong. 'We have forty-five minutes,' Basri stated as we moved to the first green, 'say whatever you have to say,' though he did the talking. He teed off, drawing deferential applause from the ministers in train and dignitaries who trailed after. Between drives we walked and he talked, immune to advisers and listening walls, not a word about Mauritania, instead more registration centres, Morocco was moving ahead, would make the process irreversible. He wanted to know when Polisario were going to accept the criteria and their interpretation, as mandated by the Security Council, of course, all applicants had to be identified, the census served purely Spanish ends. Despite Polisario blocking, Morocco was determined to proceed. Another drive, to his satisfaction, and as we left the green he turned and in his most dogmatic manner said: 'You realise that Morocco will never abandon the Sahara.' Within the week seven new registration centres around Laayoune were announced and several more in Smara, Boujdour and Dakhla.

'It's no secret that Morocco's working on scuttling the referendum,' Kheddad was saying before my call on Abdel-Aziz. 'This is a case of a big country versus a little country, we need respect for our sovereignty, recognition that we exist. Compromise can be dangerous, look at the compromises we have made – where did they get us? We cannot gamble with our people's lives and future after all they have lost and suffered. Dialogue is essential, Morocco claims it won't meet Polisario because we will make propaganda of it. We can keep it confidential. We could work together.' It was regrettable that the Security Council resolution did not call for dialogue. Abdel-Aziz had little to add when he received me in the presidential bunker with its roof ingeniously constructed like a trampoline to bounce away bombs.

Meeting with Bachir afterwards was harder. Polisario wanted a credible referendum, a referendum not for the whole Maghreb but for Western Saharans to decide their future. Only after the settlement plan had been agreed were new criteria introduced to admit parents, children, other relatives and those claiming sometime residence or to have been omitted during census-taking. How could that be proven? Perez de Cuellar had not the time for so minor an issue – for him, Yaqub-Khan never mastered the dossier. Oral testimony was a mockery, Morocco had created hundreds of sheikhs, in Moroccan government pay, to do Morocco's bidding, who did not know the applicants' personal history or appurtenance. Bachir would never accept what was illegitimate and unjust to the rights of his people. When would oral testimony be valid? What would be the role of observers and OAU representatives? Beyond identification loomed more problems: what proof could the UN obtain that Morocco would withdraw its troops? Could we be sure that refugees would be permitted to return freely, not confined to Basri dictated ghettoes? How would the international community guarantee the long-term right to independence if the Sahrawis so decided? We want an end to this Calvary that our people have endured too long. He stopped.

Outside in a doll-sized desert garden the light was going; a few bright stars pricked the sky. The moon rose, larger and larger, to show filmy cloud floating dreamily in the distance. Clouds and rain never reach this far, Bachir said, Morocco and the Atlas mountains stop them. We talked of his children, they merited a future, then of his grandfather, buried at Smara; and his father, who died in Mauritania. Like his brother they were Ulad Mousa, he said, changing tone. Yes, I said, Thalat – their sub-fraction, he smiled at my knowing.

By then I knew the sub-fractions and that the majority was not disputed, most also had sheikhs surviving from the 1973 election. The identification commission would admit only documents issued prior to Spain's withdrawal, such as identity card or residence permit; I had already approached the Spanish government for relevant records. (Yes, said Bachir, Spain had comprehensive listings.) Oral testimony was complicated, I agreed. We would summon candidates for identification by sub-fraction with two sheikhs of that sub-fraction one from each side, the sheikhs would be asked to confirm personal identity: that name and individual corresponded, which would screen out impostors. It was then for the sheikhs to evaluate any claim under the revised criteria for persons not census-listed, the sheikhs, the real sheikhs, surely, were men of honour – and would be taking an oath on the Koran. The postulant had to convince the commission; it was not for the commission to prove a claim invalid. I genuinely believed that commission members' integrity could be trusted and throughout the proceedings both Morocco and Polisario were to be represented by official observers, as was the OAU. I urged him to have confidence, to believe me.

Bachir responded with questions. When Kheddad joined us they asked me to elaborate, mainly, to repeat. They wanted assurance that Polisario's sheikh would be present, that he could not be overruled by a Moroccan sheikh. To start with the undisputed sub-fractions seemed sensible. The 'tribes of the north' grouping was another matter, they saw no way of coming to terms with that. Other questions: where would their observers stay? What provision was there for their security? How about the OAU? Then, in detail, we again reviewed the entire process.

Polisario could not be expected, having consistently rejected Perez de Cuellar's 31 December criteria, simply to say they now accepted them. They could express acceptance of resolution 907, I suggested, with the criteria implicit, by agreeing formally to implement the Security Council resolution endorsing the secretary-general's recommendation to proceed on the basis of his compromise proposal.[2] It was late, very late, when Bachir asked that we meet again in the morning, he needed to think and to consult.

The consultations cannot have been straightforward, Bachir looked harried when I saw him again. He asked for clarification of various points, already discussed, before reiterating their rejection of northern tribes. Then, as if risking life and reputation, said 'Yes,' they accepted, given my assurances, for identification to begin as mandated by resolution 907. It was for me, with creative ambiguity if needed, to find the diplomatic wording. Minutes later I was conducted to another room where an Algerian journalist waited, this was news. Night was falling when I touched down back in Laayoune exhausted, but elated, elated enough to take lively part in a sixtieth birthday celebration for a senior staff member obliged to retire at the end of the month.

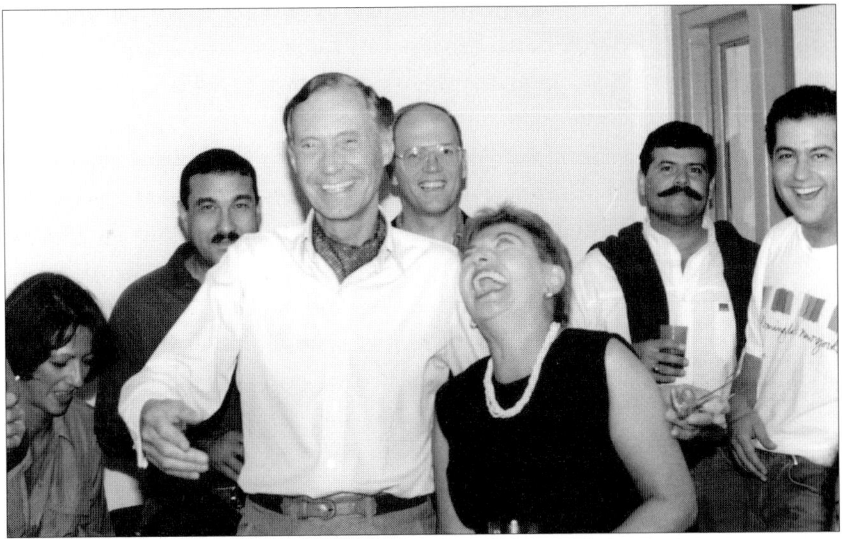

The evening I returned having negotiated POLISARIO's agreement. which coincided with the mission retirement party for Regine Kovitch

I had now to formulate a letter with near identical wording to both sides: to confirm in writing Polisario's agreement and convey to Morocco that this indicated acceptance of the revised criteria. I wrote, using formal language, in French, that I had the honour to refer to resolution 907 adopted by the Security Council on 29 March 1994. In operative paragraph 4 of that resolution the Council approved the course of action described in paragraph 25 of the secretary-general's report of 10 March. I expressed appreciation for commitment to implement the Council's decision and requested submission of applications to the identification commission by mid-May. Both letters were dated 27 April and dispatched also by fax.

Morocco did not react. World attention was on South Africa's post-apartheid elections where Azmi was among the international observers, I left a message to welcome him home asking that he call urgently. He did to say how tired he was, and what was the rush. 'You shouldn't be in such a hurry,' he repeated, Morocco would honour its commitments. 'We shall hand forms over when Polisario officially accept the criteria and their interpretation, not before. That's what the resolution called for.' Then suggested giving us five thousand for every one from Polisario. And what were Polisario doing? They had not accepted the criteria, Morocco would do nothing till they did. Azmi raised his voice: 'You remember what Monsieur le Ministre told Yaqub-Khan.' Polisario has accepted to proceed in accordance with resolution 907, I told him, as confirmed in my letter to Basri. What is that supposed to mean?' He was off his guard, I guessed that Azmi had yet to digest correspondence accumulated in his absence. I said we should talk again, very soon.

I telephoned New York, our Western Sahara desk officer. She checked with Morocco's permanent mission, which confirmed commitment to proceed. But conversation with Azmi after the weekend proved as inconclusive as before, he had still to talk to the minister. Same next day. I offered to fly to Rabat. A visit would require preparation, he said, as would an appointment with the minister. The old story: one side agrees, with full publicity fanfare, to a secretary-general's recommendation, or a decision of the Security Council because convinced the other will not. Nothing advances – which is what Morocco may want, without the opprobrium of not respecting international opinion. Basri, who had embraced almost enthusiastically 907's second option – failing the first – with talk of irreversible action, counted on Polisario rejecting, with Polisario, left in a negative light, ceding the field to Morocco for what it pleased. Polisario, by agreeing to act on the Security Council resolution upset the apple cart. The implicit acceptance of the revised criteria confused Morocco. Their analysts wondered what Polisario planned, always assuming that what benefited one side disadvantaged the other.

The following morning I reached Azmi in Rabat, he had still to see the minister, gave no clue as to whether Basri was travelling, had other priority commitments or was simply stalling, searching for language to disguise a policy shift. Hopeful that ambassador Snoussi in New York might help, I telephoned. He confirmed, reconfirmed Morocco as committed to moving ahead, the ambassador would cable Rabat requesting the palace to ensure prompt action with the king's backing. A day later Azmi was in Laayoune. No reference to any correspondence, he began brusquely that if I opened application offices in Mauritania, Morocco would close their centres. Then, had Polisario filled in forms? Yes, I said. The UN form? Yes. Morocco would hand over completed forms when Polisario did – in the same quantity. The usual dance. (A commissioner, who was Norwegian, suggested that Western Sahara served as model for Edvard Munch's 'The Scream'.) Azmi resumed his tirade against my intention to work in Mauritania, Why? He wanted to know. Because, as he knew perfectly well, the settlement plan called for application arrangements wherever Sahrawis lived '*en nombre*'; 'It refers to the camps. Besides, Sahrawis are all over,' he said,' even Beijing. You should open in China.' Fine, I said. Not just Mauritania, he repeated, before complimenting me on persistence in a tone that charged me with driving Morocco into commitments, against their interest.

Azmi still claimed never to have seen a Polisario letter accepting the criteria. Bachir's letter might simply be acknowledging mine. Was it stated that Polisario agreed to the criteria and resolution 907? This was a condition, as M. le Ministre had said. It was difficult to believe Azmi had not had sight of all related correspondence, it was not secret. I showed him photocopies of my exchange of letters with Bachir and that to Basri, identical in essence.

Morocco was opening more reception offices, Azmi asserted next day, making twenty-two within the week, in Laayoune, Smara, Dakhla and Boujdour, even a mobile office. They wanted to reach everyone. Then he reverted to Mauritania. I said a team had left earlier that day for Zouerate to handle applications. Azmi fulminated, then fulminated about Bachir; they had intelligence that he was active in the area armed with a communication satellite. Our activity was not designed to provoke, I insisted, I had promised the Mauritanian president that it would be low key. Azmi, unconvinced, stopped. What about the completed forms, I asked, when could we expect to begin processing? He parried with Polisario, as usual. This was becoming absurd, I said, a circular argument. Let's meet near Smara: me atop the berm, the wall, receiving simultaneously, with one hand from Polisario and the other from Morocco. At least he smiled. It had to be in Laayoune, our official seat. All right, I said, I will have Polisario give me three thousand completed forms on Monday if you promise to hand over an equivalent batch on Tuesday. It was a gamble. Polisario could raise obstacles, although they had been saying they had the forms and wished to start provided Morocco did too. Azmi, who had hinted at waiting till after the feast, the Eid, might try wriggling out of precise commitment. Well, will you? He responded with a great hand-slapping handshake. I went to arrange for Tindouf.

A worrying dispatch awaited me. Kheddad had left an urgent message. But the message that he had a message was garbled, barely intelligible. I could not get a line and when, eventually, I did, it went dead. For an hour and a half the process repeated itself. It was next day before we established communication: everything said to be in hand for three thousand forms. That Sunday evening Azmi came close to taunting me. What had Polisario really agreed? This was not a game, I said. He tensed. I said: 'You promised to give me your completed forms on Tuesday after Polisario have given me theirs. What time on Tuesday? I fly tomorrow early to Tindouf.' He said: 'I'll see you in the evening after you return, then we can decide,' in a tone of voice expecting to claim they failed to deliver. 'Bachir is in Mauritania, you know.' ' I know.' 'Then who will you speak to?' 'I'll see tomorrow.'

Tindouf airfield emerged from a sand filmy mirage. Colonel Gerasimov was there to greet me, and our commission staff together with the Algerian government representative. The colonel saluted smartly, as always, but the only one smiling was the Algerian official. When I enquired after the forms: were they ready, signed, the answer was an embarrassed 'no.' The computer had failed. Kheddad had been working till four in the morning, sleepless, desperate to rescue the operation. 'They really want to comply,' Raouf, our computer expert, insisted, 'they really do.' There had been a computer malfunction, key data lost without backup and no way of recovering lost memory quickly. Nor was their system UN compatible so Raouf had been unable to supplement their resources. They planned to present me the one hundred and thirty printed as a trial run. I imagined Azmi's expression.

The preceding night I had a sense of foreboding that Polisario might produce three thousand applications correctly presented in UN format, but unsigned. Azmi would be sure to ask. Pointless to be economical with the truth or evasive because, from his sources, he would know. He would smile an overbearing 'I knew it' smile, imply that I was party to a trick, relieving him of any obligation to honour his part of the bargain. But this was worse. Kheddad arrived, looking depressed and haggard, if he had not been up all night it was a convincing performance, I believed him. Unfortunately, it would look as if I had been duped, my credibility decimated. What could he say? He assured me of their good faith, reiterated their commitment and promised me the applications within the week, that was how long it would take to repair equipment, restore lost data and print. Lunch was distinctly subdued, tasting of failure. Afterwards, in the presence of some twenty sheikhs and dignitaries, I took formal receipt of a parcel containing one hundred and thirty application forms and departed.

In Laayoune Azmi awaited my return. With a supercilious smile but crowing less than I anticipated he greeted me. I admitted to having a lesser number of forms, sure he already knew; they always did, less than two hundred, I said, keeping it vague. He would not be giving me his three thousand, I feared, but our staff, now in place, needed experience in deciphering applications and transliteration, if he could give me six hundred forms, a figure reflecting the difference in numbers, it would help train our teams, and move the process forward. You take my jokes seriously, he said, when I reminded him of his earlier threat to deliver five forms for every one from Polisario, all right, he would produce six hundred.

It was late when I saw him again. After a disappointing day with twice two and a half hours in a small plane and rattling over corrugated desert tracks I was desperately tired. What time tomorrow – for the forms? I said and made to go. 'Monsieur le Ministre wants to meet you urgently.' The minister had always insisted on parallel action by Polisario, Azmi said, and Polisario had been devious. That simply was not true, I said. He accused me of treating Morocco just like Polisario, a serious state like a few scattered … Calmly but decisively I reaffirmed our UN position: Morocco was a member state with every privilege that implied, Polisario an independence movement, but both recognised as 'parties' to the conflict. '*Ces petits conards*' he said. Tired though I was, I slept badly.

Basri relished machine-gun interrogation. Polisario, what was their commitment? Yes, a letter acknowledging mine, he knew. Not just an acknowledgment, I said. He wanted to check resolution 907, particularly operative paragraph four, precisely what it implied. And the report of the secretary-general and timetable. The timetable he attributed to me, although it derived from a Council decision. And the criteria he re-examined. I had with me all relevant documents, in French, for him to scrutinize – something he must have done multiple times already. 'Well,' he said, tone changed, 'Morocco meets all its obligations.' Not quite, I said, since they were already to have handed over more application forms. 'What has Polisario done?' he asked. I told him. He dismissed computer malfunction as a childish excuse. Then announced they would give me thirty thousand next day, next day was a public holiday, Azmi interjected. 'Monday' Basri decided, even though Azmi said the feast would not be over till Tuesday. 'You will have the rest – the two hundred thousand – on the first of June, as the timetable dictates'. 'Actually that's not the date,' I said. 'No matter. You will have them by June first.' Meanwhile, he wished to meet me again.

The customary circus ensued. An early appointment, cancelled, rescheduled, brought forward, postponed because the minister was summoned to the palace. I called New York where the Advisory Committee on Administrative and Budgetary Questions was in session with the US increasingly reluctant to approve peace-keeping costs and doubtful about our prospects: 'Why don't they just reach a political settlement?' But Moroccan diplomats at the UN supported my efforts and attributed feet-dragging to the ministry of interior: vested interests, people whose position, power and disposable funds benefited. Azmi, when I hinted at Moroccans perpetuating the current stalemate, denied it roundly, at least for those in official positions, then conceded that some private individuals, and businessmen, stood to profit. The meeting with Basri was finally confirmed for the following morning, at his residence.

An idyllic day. The garden a delight as I was led past shrubbery and specimen trees, round the pool to the pool-house, only slightly less ornate than the mansion. Basri and another man were about to embark on a full five-course Moroccan breakfast: harira soup, dates, brochette, yoghurt and fruit juice with bread and pastry. He invited me to join them. Having breakfasted already I declined but accepted a glass of orange juice. At that moment several others arrived. One, the secretary-general for information, I recognised, another was introduced as director-general of MAP, the Moroccan Press Agency. Basri interrupted noisy eating to comment, for benefit of his officials, on current world affairs, before reverting to the application form: he wanted assurance that the formulation of questions complied with the criteria. They did, I told him, Azmi nodded. Basri wiped his mouth before abruptly switching tone, almost snarling he harangued me for going to Mauritania. Sounds of approval from those present. Basri glanced at his information secretary-general and news agency head: there has to be a press release to say that application processing has begun.

His words verbatim became the draft, without reflecting any point made by me. A thoroughly unpleasant exchange followed. I argued tooth and nail that if the text were to be jointly attributed, which he wanted, then it had to take my views into account. Every drafting suggestion provoked a negative retort. A simple phrase about Mauritania unleashed a barrage, did I know that the Mauritanian prime minister had publicly supported Polisario's idea for an international conference? Claimed they were bending to UN urging. Basri accused me of bringing pressure, of acting without authority, and, unlike Yaqub-Khan, exceeding my mandate, it was for me to put brakes on Mauritania: 'You stop them – or we stop,' he said, 'and insist on your termination.' Reverting to the press release Basri assailed me for being querulous about 'fact'. Eventually, eventually, with modified, neutral language we compromised. Next morning *Le Matin* front page carried Basri's original version and my photograph.

At my hotel a message waited, the minister for foreign affairs, Filali, wished to see me at the earliest opportunity. Filali was, and looked, a Fez aristocrat, his son married into the royal family, he enjoyed the king's confidence. His misfortune was to have fallen asleep while driving to jog after an overnight flight, physically crippled, he hobbled, courtesy intact, to receive me. Politely he wondered why I was not working more closely with Foreign Affairs. I followed Morocco's wishes, I thought, their designated channel of communication. He nodded. Would I be kind enough to review developments since resolution 907? Of course. I summarised the session with Bachir in Tindouf, when Polisario accepted the terms of the resolution, and concluded, with my recent encounters with Basri – sanitised. At criticism about Mauritania he expressed surprise, he had come direct from the palace, he said, His Majesty had said nothing about Mauritania. The king was fully committed to what I had initiated and had asked Filali to convey his support. It was time for me to be received in private audience by His Majesty, the minister continued, he would arrange the appointment. He knew that I was due to visit Algiers, on my return?

In Algiers security guards packed a vehicle ahead and one behind. Motorcycle outriders again flagged on-coming cars aside as we hurtled at speed along the wrong lane into town. The minister's representative, who accompanied me in the official Mercedes, was friendly, open, and when I asked about the situation, assured me that life in Algiers was no more dangerous than in New York, where he had been posted, arguably less so because victims were targeted. The UN resident representative had also come to receive me – partly for security reasons, he was equipped with a bulletproof vest such as he was instructed to wear: I required special clearance from the SG's security co-ordinator; without that I was no longer insured for loss of life or limb. The representative had spoken to the co-ordinator and was hopeful that in these exceptional circumstances coverage could be implemented retroactively, the UN security rating placed Algiers in the penultimate class, short of evacuation, his own secretary had gone after receiving death threats. Almost all Europeans, who could leave, had left, of thousands an estimated four hundred remained which made it still more dangerous, by rendering highly visible those who stayed. Forty had been killed in the last two years, three Russians had just been murdered in an ambush together with many of their escort, ironic because they were en route for the airport to depart the country. Ambassadors, those still there, drove in bulletproof cars. Algerian ministers were cannier, they opted for a battered old car with security detail in another and travelled on side roads, a Mercedes and outriders signalled importance. He was still explaining as our imposing official car approached the government's elegant residence/ hotel overlooking the Bay of Algiers.

Motorcycle outriders with imperious gestures waved away traffic when they escorted me next morning to the foreign ministry. Behind a UN flag flapping I was a very identifiable target, but arrived without incident at a modern, purpose built edifice to spend an hour with the secretary-general of the ministry, Mohammed Hanneche. He began by paying homage – the word he used – for the manner in which I was conducting the mission. Algeria had been following my comportment closely and praised my competence and impartiality, Yaqub-Khan, unfortunately, had not been impartial. In a climate of near total mistrust I was to be congratulated on the degree of trust I had established both sides. Having dispensed diplomatic flattery, generous beyond the norm, the secretary-general expected me to be frank. I recounted the discussion with Bachir, his agreement, and Basri's disbelief. The subsequent 'computer malfunction' had not convinced the Moroccans. 'It was true,' Monsieur Hanneche insisted, 'It was a computer breakdown.' Then there had been Mauritania, that was an important achievement, he said. Of course Basri objected, I said; incidentally, the press release misquoted me. 'They do this all the time,' Hanneche said knowingly.

Neither side wanted progress except on its terms. My strategy, I explained, was to take identification forward, thus compelling both parties to focus on what lay ahead. Conflicting signals from Polisario were unhelpful. Bachir seemed for the process, their minister of defence summoned a return to arms, and Abdel-Aziz brushed both aside with talk of an international conference. 'You must remember,' Hanneche interjected, 'that Polisario is a liberation movement, they put out ideas, seek support wherever they can, and by whatever means. They are not a state with the defined interests of a state.' (That amazed me. Algeria had played a crucial part in having Polisario, as the Sahrawi Arab Democratic Republic, recognised as a state member by the OAU.) 'An international conference,' he shrugged, 'would only work after elaborate preparation. A conference is a forum for publicising what has already been decided.' Did he have any views on a contact group, I asked, to provide a context for the parties to meet and establish dialogue? I emphasised that I had no instructions. He listened attentively, undertook to brief his minister.

Mohammed Dembri, the foreign minister, had a craggy face, strong jaw and aquiline nose, with fierce, piercing eyes mitigated by an engaging smile. He was pleased with the reports he had been receiving, I was to be congratulated on having earned the confidence of both, no easy matter. It was easier for a liberation movement to take up arms than to engage in the uncertainties of political process. In the current impasse Polisario's courageous decision offered hope, Algeria had encouraged them to co-operate with me. The idea of a contact group merited further study, it could permit dialogue in a setting less tense than direct talks and might reveal a solution less radical than integration or independence. Polisario needed an honourable solution to the conflict.

Algiers had been supportive. Good for morale as I mulled over impending problems on the flight to Morocco: premises for identification; guaranteeing security, in particular for sheikhs from the opposing side; accommodating them and observers, with Polisario likely to demand multiple OAU observers; in what order to identify sub-fractions, I had already concluded that the only logical approach was to convoke simultaneously all applicants from a given sub-fraction; how to rule if the two identifying sheikhs judged differently; how to evaluate their testimony? 'Vacancies' due to death of sheikhs elected in 1974 would pose further difficulty. The exchange of prisoners-of-war, confinement of troops, return of refugees were as daunting, but less immediate. Static jolted me out of my thoughts: an announcement from the cockpit. We would be landing in Rabat, not Casablanca. Then a stewardess – with the most stupendous eyes – bent charmingly forward to say that someone awaited me. I was whisked straight to the hotel and given an urgent message from Filali.

Filali had been appointed prime minister that morning in addition to his foreign minister portfolio. He wished to see me as soon as possible. The 'other appointment' had been arranged. Filali, still at the foreign ministry, was relaxed, interested in my Algiers visit. Algeria was in trouble, their east bloc industry declining and they did not have the tomatoes they had condescendingly suggested they would purchase from pre-industrial Morocco, prospects were murky for the military regime. I told him of my meetings. The arguments against an international conference were real: it served but to crown a process. I touched tangentially on the contact group idea, which had interested Dembri – he was nothing more than a '*petit diplomate*', said Filali; Morocco, as expected, found it unattractive. I stressed the need for the parties to discuss – he winced at the word 'parties'. 'What is there to discuss?' he said. 'Either they're independent or they're not.' I broached the idea of regional autonomy. 'Morocco is a country of regions. Why only the Sahara?' he replied. He paused for a word on the phone, apologised. 'The audience with His Majesty will be tomorrow late morning, "*fin de la matinée*". His Majesty had wanted to receive you already this evening, but he has had a tooth out and feels he would not be on form.' Filali suggested I seek the king's ruling on whatever I considered necessary, the audience would be *tête-à-tête*.

Flunkeys in abundance, the royal guard in dress uniform, saluting, a military band in the background, the chamberlain to conduct me: the palace was a theatre of orientalist splendour. Across a great courtyard with fountains dancing, past soldiers on parade, I was escorted to a pavilion and presented to King Hassan and His Royal Highness the Crown Prince. The press horde was corralled in and corralled out. The king seated me at his side; beyond a small table the crown prince sat in silence. The king offered mint tea, let me begin.

When I reached the need for dialogue he interrupted. 'This is a false problem, and a false problem is sometimes harder to deal with.' No, not dialogue at present. Polisario want only to deal with one of my ministers. No. At least for now, maybe later. Should never say never; France refused point blank to speak to the FLN, Algeria refuses to talk to the FIS, he would not do that. But could not say when. As a gift '*cadeau*' to the UN he might be willing to intervene personally at the appropriate stage, but the UN process had first to move forwards. Other countries in the region were in trouble: Algeria and Mauritania. If Algeria had not invested in the Polisario issue they might have been able to introduce democracy, gradually and more successfully, move towards a market economy and find themselves in less of a mess. He was concerned at the situation in the two neighbouring countries, just think where we could be, he said, in five years time entering a new century: Morocco, Algeria, Tunisia opposite Europe on the Mediterranean. He looked to the referendum for the international sanction he wanted. It was, he repeated, he who had called for a referendum. Thousands of armed men roaming the desert, uncontrolled, were a disaster. His hardest task had been to restrain his commanders when they clamoured to pursue the retreating enemy into Algeria. He was himself the most peaceable of men.

More mint tea. Mauritania, when I asked, was not playing fair, he said. He had warned their prime minister about Mauritanians registering as Sahrawis. If not circumspect they would find themselves presenting fifteen thousand of their people to Morocco. Given the overall population, that was equivalent to Morocco transferring a hundred and fifty thousand. And who would not prefer Agadir to Nouadhibou, or Nouakchott for that matter? The king then revealed having written three days ago, to the UN secretary-general promising some 230,000 application forms. We could have swamped you, he said, but we choose to be serious. Smiling graciously he closed the audience: 'We want to work with you,' looking me hard in the eyes. 'A problem needs our attention – timing, priority, for example – you may write, no addressee, no heading, no signature, on plain paper, and pass it through Filali personally. Then we will see you again.' We shook hands. 'A person's face and a handshake play an important role,' said the king encouragingly, and as I moved to bid the prince goodbye: 'Beware of UN New York – the law of the jungle. Our son says it's Amazonian.'

That evening I was invited to Villa America. US Ambassador Ginsberg, in jeans, his former Miss Arkansas wife, more enticingly jeaned, jollied their diplomatic guests into informality. The French ambassador, immaculate in tweed coat, pressed grey flannels, polished brogues, was in earnest conversation with the cravat-wearing British ambassador. They asked me to join them, to hear about the king. They knew of my audience. I was surprised to learn that these two key ambassadors had been received only at the formal presenting of credentials. Mine was a signal honour – it suggested that Morocco was serious about solving the Saharan dispute. How was the king looking, in good health? It was rumoured he was unwell. He seemed fine to me; I ignored the tooth extraction. What were his views on the Sahara? Supportive, I said, but not keen on talks, for the present, though he refused to say 'never'. The Danish ambassador, as happens at a reception, became part of the group. It occurred to him that Denmark, without side in the affair, could provide a neutral venue, like Oslo, which brought Palestinians and Israelis confidentially together. Morocco was unlikely to accept such contact with Polisario without superpower pressure and Washington had other priorities.'Do we really need blood and bodies on television before governments act?'

8

Representation

Polisario refused further action until an OAU presence was assured, in conformity with the settlement plan. Though the Moroccans knew the plan involved the OAU as the UN's sleeping partner they were categorically opposed to OAU participation: the organisation had acted illegally in recognising Polisario as a member state, no way could it be considered impartial. Creative thinking developed a compromise: to have observers personally designated by the OAU president; the current president, Mubarrak, an Egyptian, was well disposed towards Morocco. That should be OAU enough for Polisario. New York was to handle the approach to Mubarrak, by Boutros-Ghali, himself an Egyptian, if necessary. I waited. Polisario was becoming impatient and infuriated when Morocco purportedly ferried another hundred busloads into the territory. Nonsense, said Azmi, there were three buses bringing people back after harvest further north, and even those were at least a quarter filled with 'ordinary' passengers.

From New York came news not about OAU – Salim Salim the organisation's secretary-general was intransigent – but of Yaqub-Khan. King Hassan had written personally to Boutros-Ghali requesting Yaqub-Khan's reassignment for a three-month period, the purpose unclear beyond demonstrating Morocco's refusal to abide by Polisario dictating his dismissal. Boutros was anxious to shore up his own political support: Morocco and Pakistan influential countries. With Boutros-Ghali's assent Yaqub-Khan accepted the king's invitation to Rabat but regretted being unable to resume official functions. Boutros worried that a visit to Morocco alone would reinforce prejudice; Yaqub-Khan should include Algiers, if not Laayoune and Tindouf. The Algerians replied that they were not a party to the dispute but would not object to facilitating contact with Polisario. Yaqub-Khan suggested meeting Abdel-Aziz in Algiers. Abdul-Aziz sent a message that he would come to Algiers only at the behest of the UN secretary-general and invited Yaqub-Khan to Polisario 'headquarters' at Bir Lahlou.

Yaqub-Khan was royally received in Rabat. At an audience, private then broadened to include the crown prince and Filali, they discussed Iraq, the Middle East, the evolving situation in Pakistan and global issues, Mauritania was not mentioned. The king expressed satisfaction at the progress I was making, Yaqub-Khan told me afterwards. With respect to the OAU His Majesty simply reaffirmed Morocco's known objection. I asked Yaqub-Khan if and when he thought the problem might be resolved. 'It will be settled, but take a little time.' How long did he think? 'Six weeks,' but dodged saying why. Anyway the problem was a non-problem, 'What were these OAU gentlemen going to do, cardboard cutouts would serve as well.'

Yaqub-Khan asked how I enjoyed the mission. Good that registration had begun. I started explaining about forms, sub-fractions, the role of sheikhs and how observers would travel and be lodged, the problems I encountered with Polisario – and Morocco. He smiled benignly, in New York many would prefer the settlement plan off the agenda. The official, who concocted the settlement plan for Perez de Cuellar, claimed that Polisario never expected independence but needed the referendum as an honourable solution. Yaqub-Khan then excused himself saying he looked forward – eyebrow arched – to our trip to Algiers.

The Algerian mission in New York had confirmed an appointment with the secretary-general of the foreign ministry, the minister was 'busy'. The meeting lasted a few minutes, Hanneche focused on the OAU as co-responsible for the plan, attempting to divert from secretariat to president was not appropriate. He then confirmed that the Polisario ambassador would call on Yaqub-Khan to receive whatever message he had from the UN secretary-general. The 'ambassador' duly arrived, he stayed frigidly polite, taciturn, while Yaqub-Khan wove very small talk into conversation, skirting the OAU question. No response, no comment, nothing. Awkward silence followed. Without facing Yaqub-Khan, the 'ambassador' recited: 'I am here on instructions of my president to hear what you have to convey from the secretary-general.' There was nothing to convey. More silence, then the ambassador redraped his cloak and departed, with a half-smirk.

Yaqub-Khan's last act, as the old soldier faded away, was to cable that an OAU agreement had been reached. A day later New York called: nothing was agreed. Meanwhile President Mubarrak of Egypt had been succeeded by Tunisia's president as chairman of the OAU. Tunisia had friendly relations with Morocco and had not recognised the Sahrawi Arab Democratic Republic. Morocco mounted an ambitious diplomatic campaign, dispatching emissaries to capitals throughout Africa, to have the OAU summit in Tunis suspend SADR as 'member state' pending the referendum, that would render the organisation credible as an impartial observer. It failed to happen, hardening Morocco's position while reinforcing Polisario and Algeria in theirs.

Blistering heat proclaimed July. It was so hot even the flies grew torpid; when they flew it was at low altitude. I telephoned to wish the American ambassador a happy July fourth; he was at the office – I assumed for air-conditioning. Could the US not use influence in Algiers as well as Rabat? We needed a solution to the non-problem of OAU representation. What were they going to do, get bored? Honour would be saved, surely, and Salim Salim appeased if the Tunisian president proposed two out of four names. The ambassador took note and went off to celebrate. Through an all-obliterating sandstorm I tried passing a message to Polisario that if they wanted to proceed they might try mitigating Algerian opposition to any compromise: sacrifice procedure to achieve substance. New York, when I called, was half on holiday. Salim Salim was stubborn. It did not help that he and Filali had been personal enemies since the time both served as permanent representatives to the UN, and there was little love lost between Salim and Boutros, once rivals for the secretary-generalship.

Prior to Security Council deliberation, with Morocco a member, Snoussi returned to Rabat. We met informally to discuss the OAU problem but he was more interested in the failed Geneva meeting, and my role. I had been instructed to convey a message to Abdel-Aziz, I said, in strictest confidence. Boutros acted behind Yaqub-Khan's back, and made me part of the conspiracy, Snoussi commented; he plays these games, making those round him distrustful of each other. Snoussi was remarkably open, said I could call him any time. Why was it, he asked, Polisario did not want to talk? I said they did. We discussed options, venues, even my 'personal' involvement since Morocco objected categorically to UN sponsored talks. He laughed at the suggestion that I function in a private capacity. What would the UN, the secretary-general say to that? He would be sure to know, I would be discarded. But I could be instrumental in setting up contact. Morocco was ready. That was not the impression I had from Basri, I said. 'Don't speak to Basri on political issues,' Snoussi said, 'just practical things.' Snoussi and Basri vie for royal favour, and dislike each other intensely. Just as Snoussi suggested talking further over lunch, Azmi called for 'urgent' business; he was tense, peeved, mocking the 'grand amour' between me and Snoussi.

Urgency related to choosing sheikhs and the sub-fraction with which to start once the OAU problem had been resolved. I reaffirmed that we take first a sub-fraction indubitably rooted in western Sahara, that only sheikhs from the seventy-four election would be acceptable, and travel in both directions between Laayoune and Tindouf should be simultaneous. He said: 'You always want to chop the whole camel up in small bits to go into your cooking-pot'. Morocco had been vociferous in support of the plan – so long as Polisario objected, with Polisario's agreement came the moment of truth. Polisario, though never fully convinced that the referendum could be free and fair, was confident of Sahrawi votes. A UN managed operation worried Morocco: the fate before the identification commission of many thousand purported Sahrawis who had been bussed down from the north, prospects were not changed by the OAU crisis, only postponed.

Snoussi, returned to New York, intimated to the secretary-general that the latest compromise, which would have the Tunisian president, as OAU chairman, nominate two observers with two to be maintained from among those presented by the organisation's secretary-general, was acceptable. Four days later, after political parties objected vehemently, Rabat signalled 'difficulty' with the formula. The secretary-general responded that he was doing all he could 'If you don't want the peace plan,' he said to the ambassador, 'tell me. We will pull our people out.' He implored the Tunisians to act, and President Ben Ali agreed.

The president's letter endorsing the two plus two formula was forwarded with the request for an urgent affirmative answer, failing which the Security Council would have to pronounce. The Council deferred consultations pending news. Snoussi had no alternative but transmit the letter to both palace and prime minister, fearing Rabat might see it 'as an act of war.' When the Security Council convened Algeria lobbied for a presidential statement to include specific reference to OAU observers. Snoussi took advantage of Moroccan membership to counter that any statement should also reflect the Moroccan view. Acerbic exchanges followed but a presidential statement was agreed: Morocco was requested to issue four entry visas.

I received the cabled text and was flattered to be mentioned in dispatches.[1] I had promised to contact Bachir as soon as the Council acted. At eleven that night came a reply from Tindouf, Bachir was booked to visit Algiers the following day but would postpone his departure. I left on the first available aircraft.

Bachir refused to accept that the OAU compromise had not been as Morocco wished. Everything goes their way, Morocco's views, concerns, emphases prevailed: 'the king's wishes, as if back in the middle ages.' Why should Polisario be pleased? Morocco would create more problems, he said as we reviewed identification procedures: names of party representatives to be communicated to me with me then informing the other side; Polisario sheikhs to be transported by UN flight from Tindouf to Laayoune, while another plane flew sheikhs from the territory; accommodation to be provided by the receiving side, on reciprocal terms. I did not think it helpful to discuss security further, always liable to provoke talk of defection; he made no mention. We agreed that the inaugural ceremony be followed by identifying a token few. My presence was more strategically necessary, he believed, in Laayoune for the opening but I should come to Tindouf afterwards. The initial sub-fractions proposed were acceptable, when it came to sub-fractions sparsely represented he was flexible, very small numbers could be transported, or sheikhs and identification teams moved to improvised premises. I reassured him that those in the '74 census would inevitably receive priority treatment because their cases were straightforward, others from the same sub-fraction were being convoked for practical reasons. 'All Polisario wants,' he said,' is a free and fair referendum. For the Sahrawis to decide.' Then he raised the question of talks.

I thought the Moroccans might be persuaded. They realised, as Polisario must, that either side could easily sabotage the referendum process, without infringing the settlement plan, if only by resorting to endless appeals. A solution was only conceivable if both sides came to terms, that meant talking, dialogue. What Polisario had always wanted, he said. The approach had to be serious, focused, eschewing propaganda. Bachir said that after eighteen years – I corrected him: nineteen – they were not interested in propaganda. For Polisario, he continued, there were two axes: the referendum process, the other what came after. It might be preferable, I suggested, to begin with the second. If a measure of understanding were reached on prospects, it could help agreeing how to proceed, he nodded.

Who would Polisario talk to? The king, he said, the crown prince, possibly Filali. Basri – emphatically no. They dislike Basri, do not trust him. Who might represent Polisario? I asked. At the ministerial level it would be himself, Bachir said, with central committee members, Brahim Ghali, minister of defence, and ministers for external relations, interior and information. At a working level he would still come, but with Emhamed Kheddad and Boukhari, their man in New York. For meeting place anywhere close, outside the immediate region. France was bad: one hundred percent pro Morocco, though it might be a way of engaging France, with its influence and vested interests, to help end the conflict. What Polisario most wanted was to involve America, they had faith in America. Not in Ginsberg, Bachir added hastily, he's sold to the Moroccans. They wanted the UN both as catalyst and guarantor. I said that after the embarrassment of Laayoune, New York and Geneva, Boutros-Ghali might be wary. We discussed a possible agenda: a degree of autonomy? He promised to reveal his 'bottom line' – after I used the phrase – when Morocco, king or crown prince, was ready to reciprocate. Bachir embraced me warmly.

In Casablanca Marc Ginsberg told me he had been received by the king. Snoussi explained later that President Clinton had instructed his ambassador to seek Moroccan participation in Rwanda, there could have been some *quid pro quo*. The king did not object at the mention of dialogue, but foresaw difficulty in dealing with Polisario, their leadership divided, motives suspect. I said that Polisario wanted a third presence: the UN or Security Council member; they reacted positively to the US; Ginsberg thought the US reluctant to entangle itself, relations with Morocco were rather good and America stood well with Algeria, involvement with the Sahara issue would complicate both. Another angle Ginsberg wished to discuss was a possible venue. If Scandinavia, he thought Sweden, which I explained too Polisario sympathetic under the aura of Olof Palme, then Austria. Austria's ex-foreign minister is one of Polisario's staunchest and most public supporters, I reminded him. He said: 'You are rather better informed than I'.

He may be 'smart', in American, and close to the White House, but, according to Snoussi, not core Washington, where he carries little weight. Snoussi was back in Rabat, where the OAU remained an issue. Filali had made so strong a statement in parliament rejecting the OAU that compromise became a threat to his credibility. The suggestion that both OAU officials operate in Tindouf, as Morocco first insisted, gave scope for mischief. One official working with one designated representative might be preferable, and the seniority of Ben Ali's nominees would assure them dominance. I could not but feel the agitation about OAU observers vastly exceeded their significance, observe was all they were mandated to do, they could not intervene or influence proceedings. And without further debate it happened.

The OAU office in New York started booking flights. The UN was asked to authorise travel as for 'experts' and their entering Morocco under UN auspices with the appropriate visa. If they could arrive Sunday or the following morning, as I proposed, they would be able to fly to Laayoune on the Monday by the only scheduled afternoon flight, minimum exposure in Casablanca was less likely to provoke further controversy. Not so simple. I received a note:

Mr Gomes could only come on 9 August; Mr Baricako was available from 7 August with Mr Gomes bringing his ticket (which seemed problematic); Ambassador Cisse would be in Geneva from 2 to 10 August and could be reached by telephone; Mr Chikane had a problem with the dates.

Other aspects were again discussed. Azmi had insisted that Polisario sheikhs and observers arrive before any Moroccans departed for Tindouf. Since both sides were so suspicious of each other the best hope lay in making them equally hostage to one another. For accommodation Polisario had originally suggested a house, then wanted an hotel, which could not be El Massira, because of its name 'The (Green) March'. Azmi offered a house, but a house in the Hotel Parador 'compound'. Reciprocity being the rule I persuaded Polisario, since they had no hotels, to accept this as equivalent to their guesthouse. Neither side was prepared to release names of observers before the other; I worried that at the last minute Morocco would parade Omar Hadrami and Brahim Hakim. Azmi, I suspect, believed Polisario might simply refuse to come.

Basri wanted a last minute meeting, then had me wait before he agreed to see me in the morning at his summer place in Bouznika. At Azmi's prompting I was up early, left hurriedly, only to arrive ahead of the appointed hour and to wait on a flowered verandah, pleasant enough by the sea. The great man, when he did appear, wore faux tartan trews, a clue to where we were headed. He steered me into the front passenger seat of a vast Mercedes and took the wheel. Azmi was parked in the rear to intone responses: 'Yes, Sir, No, Sir, adding force to points made, till we reached the golf course.

Together Basri and I walked all nine holes, serious talk interrupted only by drives, puts, and a single palace call on the cell-phone borne by an acolyte. For an hour and a half we did unbroken business. He was all on my side, he was on better terms with me than with his putter, he said, when putting badly from a good position on the green. I emphasised the need to computerise data provided on the application forms. The mission lacked the Arabic-speaking personnel to cope with the increased volume. Almost casually I mentioned that Polisario were providing cassettes. Every reference to Polisario he brushes aside as if it were of no conceivable value, but he listens. Morocco would provide computerised data. Azmi had told me previously that he did not see how they could: it would require a hundred and fifty skilled operators, where to lodge them in Laayoune, where to find them – the ministry did not dispose of those resources. Basri summoned Azmi from where he trailed behind us. From their quick exchange I surmised that the first batch of applications had actually been computerised. Media coverage was another topic, agreed that press not fly in by Antonov from Tindouf but enter through established routes. I insisted that Morocco admit accredited journalists from serious international media, it was not in their interest to refuse; Basri said they should apply for visas to the ministry of information.

He told me he was a friend, put an arm round my shoulders, said he would work as a 'UN expert', this, when I raised the OAU. Extraordinary how few hackles the OAU issue now raised. After incontrovertible rejection, vehement rhetoric, high-level campaigning, Morocco stomached the organisation's barely diluted presence with little discomfort. Basri was anxious to meet the observers, in my company, before they travelled to Laayoune. I regretted it being impossible for me to return to Rabat in time – without a special flight. Certainly, he said, at moments I relished his crisply arrogant exercise of power.

I was about to go when he asked about Bachir. What did they really want? I restated my conviction that there would be no referendum without some wider understanding. There were innumerable ways of blocking, stalling, sabotaging the process, even within the provisions of the plan. 'There is only one outcome,' Basri declaimed, not for the first time, 'The Sahara is Moroccan.' Then, in a curious shift, he appended a footnote: 'If the outcome of the referendum favours integration, there is nothing to discuss. If independence, then Morocco, an honourable country observing international law, would respect that.' But Bachir should be made to understand: once the population was liberated from the camps and free to return home it would all be over.

OAU observers dominated the ensuing days: one not available till September, another due on 9 August suddenly reassigned due to 'exigencies of the service'; a pompous note verbally presented as replacement an entirely new name, as if, after all the argument, reluctant compromise and screaming about immutability, the OAU could do as it pleased. Meanwhile, Cisse landed and the arrival of Mutsinzi was confirmed. I called Azmi's numbers to advise him and for an appointment with the minister. Azmi said he would phone back, at midnight I tracked him down in Casablanca. Why was I always in such a hurry? The Security Council awaited action. The Security Council! Azmi recognised only one 'patron': his boss, the minister, and His Majesty. It was the minister who had said he wanted us to meet when I recently came to Rabat to see him – you came to see Snoussi, Azmi amended. The minister, I should realise, had much to attend to, Morocco was a sovereign state – don't forget. His tone changed, became conciliatory, and he invited me to spend the weekend in Casablanca.

The weekend, in Laayoune, was nearly over when Azmi rang to say they were trying to locate Mutsinzi. He had landed that morning, now they did not know where he was, which sounded improbable. The minister agreed a meeting for noon next day. Would there be a plane? I asked. It was near midnight when I received confirmation of take-off for nine in the morning. Uniformed pilots stood waiting, saluted and escorted me into a comfortable jet. I worked on my papers, undistracted by aerial sightseeing: light cloud blotted out the view. In Rabat I was driven straight to the hotel where two smartly dressed Africans were instantly identifiable, we introduced ourselves. Muntsinzi, pleasant, with the manners of a senior official, was never without his exquisite crocodile attaché case. Everyone complimented him on his case, he said, his own secretary-general, whom he often accompanied on official travel, commented on the case, the finest crocodile skin, saying he did not have one like that. 'But you don't need it,' had been Muntsinzi's response. Cisse was all ambassador, he was currently ambassador of Senegal in Riyadh, before that in Zaire, and before that the foreign minister's '*Directeur du Cabinet*', as he was quick to inform us. An ample figure, his round face easing plumply into a well-rounded body, he was clothed in a double-breasted suit cut of quality cloth, with a breast pocket handkerchief to echo not match his tie. He carried a burgundy coloured briefcase with a combination lock, which he repeatedly opened and closed, on occasion to retrieve a minute, sophisticated radio; at every gesture he shot an impeccable cuff displaying links, multiple rings, gold Rolex and a heavy gold bracelet, which jangled. The ambassador had many questions about conditions in Laayoune, mentioning casually that he would not be staying beyond 31 August, a week away, about Tindouf his interest quickly faded. Azmi announced that the appointment with the minister had been postponed, Basri having been detained at the council of ministers, later it was confirmed for six o'clock.

Basri smiled his official smile, was unusually relaxed, Morocco had decided to be congenial. Cisse said he thought it preferable to await the arrival of all four African observers before travelling to Laayoune, the minister concurred. Nothing of substance was discussed, even procedure. More handshakes and we returned to the hotel, where Cisse confirmed he would remain in Casablanca until the arrival of Chikane, or his replacement – 'Mandela can have someone here in two or three days, easily.' He and Muntsinzi stayed with their trailer of luggage. I flew back to the Sahara.

Late August, the temperature approaching fifty degrees Celsius, a hundred and twenty-two Fahrenheit. Bachir was in no-man's-land, his 'liberated' strip between berm and border. I had undertaken to brief him as soon as the OAU observers landed and we agreed to meet near a military team-site in this desolate expanse of desert. The endless flat crust, like diseased skin, was blistered with dirty-black mountains, no sign of life. We landed on an improvised strip. The heat pressed with physical weight making every movement an effort, even breathing. Bachir, militarily dressed if not exactly in uniform, guided me to a rudimentary building where we sat in a small room. Before hearing about the OAU he wanted to review – again – the criteria, the census had to be the core, the touchstone, as the plan was before Perez de Cuellar bowed to Moroccan pressure. Why did the UN always bend to Moroccan priorities, always concede what they wanted? He argued that the identification commission should process first those included in the census, only afterwards dealing with applicants under the subsidiary criteria,we would otherwise be swamped by Morocco's population. I explained, as I had before, that it was unrealistic to convoke the same sheikhs, one from each side, several times to identify a small number on each occasion, ours was the only practical approach. I assured Bachir that applicants in the census, already known and computerised, would be handled expeditiously, they had only to be personally identified. Instructions to commissioners were precise, rigorous even, regarding evidence presented by persons who claimed to qualify under the other criteria. He nodded, not entirely convinced, but wanting to believe. The OAU presence was essential, he maintained.

Two observers had arrived, I told him. One each side to launch identification was a possibility. He did not react favourably: should be all four. We were making every effort to have the South African, Chikane, come or for President Mandela to name an alternate. Gomes, from the OAU secretariat, was on schedule. Once four reached Casablanca we needed to move – before any of them began wanting to leave, Bachir thought I was joking. Assemble the group; day two, transfer to Tindouf; day three, opening ceremonies and start identifying. Eighty per cent of those in the first sub-fraction were census listed. All right? Bachir smiled. He was returning to Tindouf, it would take a couple of days overland, but he would be there to welcome the OAU observers.

9

Identification start

Mandela named as replacement for Chikane the man who had represented his movement in India. Mpehle was a distinguished South African with a magnificent deep bass voice, the only drawback that he spoke neither French nor Arabic. Nor did Gomes. But we had four and I authorised immediate arrangements to fly them to Laayoune in our Antonov – fitted with seats. The Antonov, programmed to depart Casablanca old airport at four o'clock, was delayed by an emergency. It was eventually cleared for take-off and several hours late disembarked its passengers in Laayoune. Grating noisily the ramp descended, and OAU observers, one behind the other, stumbled down. Cisse, with his burgundy briefcase, wobbled, recovered his balance and took the lead, Mpehle followed dragging two two-wheeled cases, then the others. While they restored their humour with mint tea I mentioned that Azmi was due any moment. Cisse preferred to wait. Ten minutes became thirty before an executive jet landed and disgorged Azmi together with the Moroccan observers.

Azmi was to provide observer names for transmittal to the other side. I asked him for them. He said sharply: 'We start working tomorrow.' Work starts tomorrow, yes, but I need to provide Polisario your names tonight, as they provide theirs, so that transfers in opposing directions can take place tomorrow, simultaneously. He shrugged his shoulders, the day after would do. No. The details were in writing; he had the letter. I insisted that names were wanted that night for transfers to take place the following day so that identification could begin the day after – which happened to be Sunday. 'We don't begin work on Sunday, at the weekend,' Azmi stated categorically. It was agreed, I said, you remember? That was when he had taunted me: why do you even ask whether we can begin at the weekend when you know that we have been working non-stop, Saturdays, Sundays, public holidays, when he also said the Polisario would never begin, you will see, they will find a reason not to, at the last minute. The other consideration was equally important: Cisse was insisting that he depart on 31 August, which was Tuesday. Two days identification was the very least to launch the process.

The Moroccan observers wanted to know where they would be staying in the camps. Polisario had readied a building for them; I understood it was fairly decent. That was hardly reciprocity, Polisario representatives would enjoy first class accommodation with all they could wish for, a '*salon Marocain*' had even been furnished, while the Moroccans were expected to live in refugee accommodation. Leibek, a former Polisario supporter who had switched allegiance, was particularly scathing, he spoke from experience: the building mentioned lacked sanitation and was impossibly hot. Azmi insisted his were sophisticated people, including governors, accustomed to a high standard of living. I said that Polisario were doing their best, as agreed. No, said Azmi, what had been agreed was strict reciprocity. In fact, what had been agreed was reciprocity in the type of accommodation, it was always glaringly obvious that actual conditions would be dissimilar. Azmi proposed they stay at the base, where our military observers were billeted. I filed this as a fall-back position, if only to have them air-borne next day. Would they permit a suggestion? It was only courteous, and true to every principle of desert hospitality, to visit the accommodation offered by Polisario. If it proved unacceptable we would try to house them at the base although I was uncertain whether the Algerian government, whose base it was, would assent.

Tindouf held as little appeal for the OAU observers. They drew me into a huddle. Cisse, gold accessories flashing, emphasised the important commitments he had on behalf of his government. Mpehle spoke little but when he did commanded attention by his authoritative bearing and extraordinarily deep voice. Since he had no French and Cisse's English was less than modest, I bounced from one language to the other. Muntsinzi remained politely retiring: his input to assert that he would not be staying long, Gomes was the disciplined civil servant. Two would have to operate on the Polisario side. Which two? I reminded them of the political compromise permitting OAU representation, of which they were well aware. Could they give me two names for the manifest? They argued long among themselves, then they offered the brilliant formula of Cisse and Mpehle, both president's nominees, in Laayoune with Mutsinzi and Gomes, from the secretariat, in Tindouf. I could not but wonder whether they were mischievous or refusing to be serious. We rehearsed the niceties of the compromise agreed, how the OAU was to be represented and the balance. Eventually they accepted that Gomes join Cisse in Laayoune and Mpehle accompany Mutsinzi to Tindouf. Settled, when a cable was handed me.

The cable contained names of the Polisario representatives assigned to Laayoune. I immediately told Azmi that I had the Polisario list. He insisted on seeing it, I insisted on his providing the Moroccan names. This he did orally. Persuading him to write them was tortuous, his office was closed, he said, with no secretary available at that hour, he would do it next day. I was adamant, I had to be: delay would undermine Polisario's confidence in everything agreed as well as disrupting the launch. Eventually, irritated, he summoned his assistant and instructed him to produce a letter on official stationery, as I had requested and Polisario demanded, quite legitimately. It arrived, after another wait, awkwardly hand-written, but the paper had an official heading and the letter was signed, by Azmi. The informality would concern Polisario; they might consider it unacceptable. On my way to the office, by now approaching one a.m., I decided to try filling the page with typed names in extra large type to replace the hand-written while scrupulously attentive to spelling and style, and without encroaching on either heading or signature. My brilliant secretary succeeded, in time. The fax went off with instructions that it be delivered immediately to Bachir; at three a.m. he had it, but refused to commit himself to dispatch the Polisario group before consulting. It was five-fifteen, dawn threatening, when I received confirmation that Polisario would be prepared to depart Tindouf at ten o'clock. I had dispatched a trusted member of staff to accompany them when came a crisis message from Bachir, outraged that one Moroccan sheikh was not as agreed, and alleging conscious deception.

I called Azmi instantly – and fortunately found him, he sounded grumpy. Sheikhs for the Arosien and Ulad Tidrarin sub-fractions had been agreed. Yes, but a name on his list did not correspond. He refused to believe me, I was changing the identification sequence. No. It was on the chart I had given him. The chart, he said, was not clear, too '*intellectuel*'. Grudgingly he accepted to check. I wondered whether this was a genuine mix-up. If so, then Azmi had been uncommonly lax in studying the detailed programme, as if he hardly expected implementation. Two sheikh names had indeed been transposed. Polisario accepted the explanation, human error, in good faith, and set off.

Azmi announced that the Moroccans had still to locate a sheikh. At the last moment they did and all boarded – with one man extra as communications officer. The Polisario team arrived in Laayoune and was correctly received, at the hotel Azmi greeted them in passing. The Moroccans having landed in Tindouf were driven with UN civilian police escort to our base. Azmi bearded me: communications were not working and this was unacceptable. I knew that problem, I said; he had the grace to concede some sympathy. He claimed that he was having the greatest difficulty to reach his team and unless I guaranteed effective communication there could be no start in the morning, he would recall his people, he intended communicating with them again later and early in the morning to make sure. His communications officer was instructed to remain at our base, an arrangement in which the Algerian authorities reluctantly concurred, while the Moroccan sheikh and observers were induced into moving to the Polisario camp.

Azmi was equally tense about Laayoune. Protocol for the opening ceremony, speeches, seating, mainly where the Polisario delegation would sit, media access and coverage became contentious. Everything had been discussed and discussed. We had to trawl through every detail again, at the mention of flags Azmi roared that only Moroccan flags flew on Moroccan territory and it was their building. I insisted that, albeit on loaned school premises, the identification centre had to be respected as extra-territorial with a UN flag. That Azmi rejected out of hand, he would cancel the ceremony, he most definitely would, if there were any flag other than Moroccan. A Moroccan flag flew outside the grounds: that was their prerogative; there could be none inside, I told him, except the UN. He threatened to halt proceedings and he meant it. The launch had to happen, if it did not happen then with the OAU finally in place but only briefly, the Polisario sheikh and observers arrived with security assured, the Moroccan group however unwillingly installed in the camps, procedures agreed and applicants convoked, it could all collapse. That might be what they wanted: to scuttle the process. I went myself to the identification centre. In the hall for the opening ceremony the speaker's lectern carried a large UN logo, the UN flag was hung in the room where candidates would present themselves to be identified.

Tension lessened overnight. The morning – it was a perfect day – evoked a garden party. Local dignitaries arrived, government officials, the observers, the Polisario delegation in traditional dress, the media, everyone impeccably turned out, the mood was polite, even friendly. UN personnel were jubilant: we had achieved what years of resolution and talk had not. When Azmi murmured about our confusing applicants it hardly registered, and anyway he was mistaken. Opening day was a resounding success. After a dignified ceremony identification was launched, applicants had their names checked, were finger-printed and photographed before facing the identification commission and a sheikh of their own sub-fraction from each side in the presence of observers representing Morocco, Polisario and the OAU. The procedure, without precedent, convinced both sides and outsiders; no one queried, no one objected.

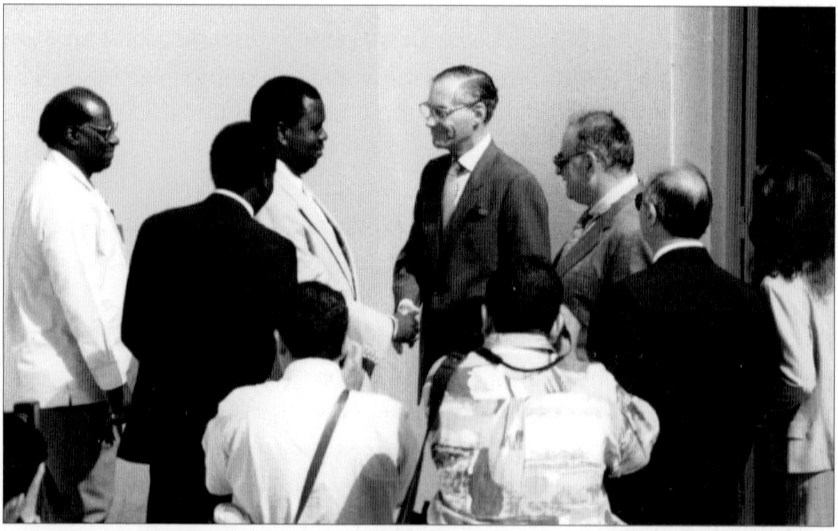

Greeting the OAU Observers for the launch of identification

Bachir, when I met him next day in Rabouni, was guarded. He pointed to 'that Moroccan mix of policemen and traitors'. Why should the OAU observers be in disguise? They ought to be clearly identifiable. They were, I said, everyone knew who they were. 'Because they are black,' said Bachir with more than the hint of a smile. 'They should have a sign and badges. And he criticised failure to highlight the census. Persons in the census merited a distinct approach. Those not in the census should be subject to rigorous questioning following a standard procedure, which I assured him was happening. Most worrying was the lack of transparency, the press in Laayoune was all Moroccan, which had to mean police informers armed with cameras, we should insist on an international media presence. The Spanish news agency, EFE, and the BBC had reported, I told him. With an air of resignation he said: 'If the Security Council decides to give the Sahara to Morocco, we might be forced to accept, but at least we want the world to know how this happened to a small people.' About the opening ceremony in the camps he had no complaints, in his heart of hearts I am sure he was relieved that identification had actually begun. Before leaving I persuaded him that the absence of one OAU observer not be a pretext to stop.

New York had been repeatedly informed that Cisse was departing. The Security Council would never understand why, having finally begun the process, we stopped, I implored action to replace him if he were not instructed to stay. Cisse was observing identification when summoned to take a long-distance call. The secretary described his behaviour as anything but ambassadorial, he erupted, shouted, screamed. Apparently their ambassador at the UN had been mandated to instruct Cisse not to leave. After a violent conversation – in Wolof – he stormed out. It was unclear whether he would go; he did.

Azmi refused to believe that Polisario agreed to work with one less OAU observer, he made it sound implausible. I said it was all right to carry on. 'Don't be in such a rush,' he said. 'I haven't put it to the minister yet. Our position was all four.' But …they were the ones who had rejected any OAU presence. 'Must have it in writing, for the minister.' A letter went. No reaction from Rabat. On Sunday Azmi called to enquire whether a replacement OAU observer had arrived – something he was sure to have known, he had not yet had occasion to discuss with the minister. What about identification? I asked, tomorrow is Monday. 'I'll phone,' he said. No call came. When I tried reaching him, he was out, unavailable, an assistant speculated that he might be on his way back to Laayoune. Around six in the evening he landed accompanied by two senior Moroccan representatives and a pair of OAU observers, who had mysteriously arrived.

No OAU observer wanted to work in Tindouf, those who had completed an assignment in the camps thought it others' turn. When no one volunteered I simply demanded names for the manifest: someone had to go. Much murmuring before they said they would discuss and inform me. Then Morocco delayed presenting their list of representatives and sheikh until assured that I had Polisario's. Polisario named alongside the venerable Sheikh Samba his son. Samba, an indisputably distinguished tribal leader, was old, hard of hearing and nearly blind; he depended on the son. That, said Azmi, constituted an unacceptable increase in Polisario numbers, the laboriously negotiated agreement accorded each side its sheikh, two representatives to observe and one other. That was all Morocco had in the camps – despite impenetrable communications – and all Morocco would countenance in Laayoune. I suggested Azmi add an assistant to their team to handle communication, and thus balance numbers. He wavered; when eventually he agreed I had difficulty in convincing Polisario.

Best I thought to meet the flight from Tindouf. Sheikh Samba was gingerly escorted down the ramp by his son, the observers followed and another. All were admitted without incident, though there was much photography. Samba looks the desert sheikh, magnificently tall, his creviced face deeply tanned, with aristocratic features and bearing, he carries himself nobly, but he can hardly see. Sheikh Samba, Azmi argued, though distinguished was manifestly incapable, it was ridiculous to respect the testimony of a senile man who could neither see nor hear: how could he identify people? The son acted as if he were sheikh, which was unacceptable; the commissioners failed to rein him in, to call him to order. If Sheikh Samba's son appeared at the following session, Morocco's representatives would leave. Sheikh Samba duly came with his son; I did nothing to deter him. The Moroccans walked out, the commission was told to continue working; but general commotion made it impossible.

I insisted that Sheikh Samba's nomination had been generally welcomed, that despite Samba's years and physical infirmity both his mind and memory were in perfect order, he remembered every detail of people in his sub-fraction: as witness there was no doubt as to his credibility. But he could not function, even walk, alone. Azmi said nothing, meaning he found no valid reason to disagree. He had a proposal: that Samba be accompanied also by his eldest son, who was on the Moroccan side (surprised at first, I was discovering that many important families had members divided between Moroccan controlled territory and the Polisario camps). That seemed a constructive suggestion. Could Polisario be convinced? Mansour, the senior observer, agreed: 'You make the road in walking' *Vous faites le chemin en marchant.* Identification resumed, Sheikh Samba accompanied by both sons. The applicants were duly processed.

Then another crisis, Morocco declared our commissioner in the Tindouf camps persona non grata, he would not be permitted to return to Moroccan territory and were he to preside officially at any identification session, the Moroccans would walk out and register formal objection. The commissioner was a former Ethiopian ambassador, Amharic- and English-speaking. In a public statement, Algerian media covering, he had used incautious language on the status and prospects for Polisario. In fairness, the English transcript struck me as almost anodyne, Mpehle, who had been present, could not see what the fuss was about. We blamed interpretation into Arabic. The senior Moroccan representative, Biadillah, took strong exception to the commissioner's failure to respect impartiality and I received an official protest note. Together with a transcript I sent an explanatory letter to Rabat insisting the statement contained nothing reprehensible. Azmi countered that the Arabic version referred to realising dreams, self-determination of the 'Sahrawi people', thus recognising a national identity. Azmi admitted that he had acted on the not normally excitable Biadillah's vehement report. Within a week the charge was dropped.

The sheikhs swore an oath on the Koran but their testimony, their credibility, was not always above suspicion. A sheikh of the Ait Lahcen tribe was challenged because his family had lived for two generations in another tribal zone, of course, he failed to recognise Ait Lahcen postulants. An aspirant wanted to assault him when he denied knowing her: 'You were in my tent for tea.' Morocco accused Mansour of giving little signals: the sheikh, remote controlled, was in breach of his oath. What Polisario wanted, Azmi said, was for Morocco to walk out, for Morocco to be held responsible for the process breaking down, Morocco wished to proceed, he insisted.

The next crisis was not man-made, unprecedented rainfall and flash flooding swept through the Tindouf region. The first I knew was an SOS call that two staff members were marooned in a stalled vehicle, in the midst of rising water, and 'one of us cannot swim'. They were able to radio a position, but a rescue party of three four-wheel drive vehicles became stuck amid swirling water in muddied sand. I authorised the general to deploy a helicopter at first light, ours were not cleared for night flying; should the emergency warrant we might have to break the law. At dawn to everyone's relief the two were safely helicoptered from the roof of the car where they had spent the night. The refugee camps were less fortunate, people were drowned and walls built of rammed earth without straw binding or any reinforcement melted like chocolate into bitter brown pools.

Rain continued falling and hard, a second storm. The water level rose over the impermeable floor of hard-core, rocky desert. Kheddad said that in their twenty years in the camps there had never been rain like it. The lakes that I flew over stretched in every direction: no mirage this, where there had been endless arid dryness: an ocean. The water, only just beginning to recede, stood everywhere. I prepared an emergency humanitarian relief appeal. One could not help feeling that Polisario, with all the deprivation they already suffered, did not deserve this act of God. For us, I expected almost any obstacle at any time and had come to accept the unexpected also, but torrential rainfall and flooding in the camps was beyond imagining; Allah was testing the will to proceed, our Job-like faith in edging onward. El-Aiun camp, closest to the border, had deliberately been sited in the bed of a long dry watercourse, to conceal the camp's existence if threatened in hot pursuit. From the gouged sand there could be no doubting the masses of water that poured through, sweeping much of the camp away. Two women and four children were finally reported killed: one with her baby still strapped to her back and firmly grasping the hand of another infant, was found, dead, several miles away, the other woman, in advanced pregnancy, had apparently stumbled and been unable to escape the rush of water engulfing her.

People were in shock. They might not have lost much of real value but to them it was all they had that was valuable, they had lost blankets, coverings, clothing, simple rations and such household possessions, even floor mats, as could not be dried out. Polisario had encouraged compacted mud buildings to minimise the risk of fire from people cooking in their tents, without binding the mud dissolved. Goats and sheep tethered for the night perished. The enormity of the disaster, the extent of destruction I witnessed from the air, made me wonder whether Polisario might say 'enough is enough': we have survived in these virtually uninhabitable encampments for long enough, even these are now being swept away. Let it end. An Arabic-speaking staff member told me he heard people saying just that, though he reminded me that they were nomads accustomed to the harsh vagaries of their environment. Within days rain-sodden belongings were out drying in the sun and tents, still soggy, were being repitched on higher ground. They would soldier on.

Kheddad quoted a saying among nomads that rain brings twenty times the benefit to what it destroys. Signs of burgeoning vegetation would soon be seen, a surfeit of desert truffles was expected, the region being reputed for them. The more immediate question was whether Morocco would agree to resume identification in Laayoune despite a hiatus on the other side. I tackled Azmi. No way, he maintained, could Polisario send observers in these circumstances, much less the sheikh, who had to be with his people. I guessed otherwise, though Azmi seemed convinced – and he usually knew better. Communications were tortuous, but in two hours I received an answer: Polisario stood ready, observers and sheikh prepared to depart the same day to resume identification in the morning. Azmi, interrupted while resting, turned petulant: reciprocity was essential. 'You are always insisting on reciprocity,' he snapped, as if it were me not Morocco and Polisario who insisted. He could not possibly agree to continue unilaterally, that lay beyond his authority; he would have to refer to Rabat, to the minister, for a ruling. Nor did this comply with the agreed work programme, another Polisario caprice, he implied. No, I said, absolutely not. This was a catastrophe, a natural disaster, not anything that could have been foreseen or planned, he should thank god, *hamdulillah*, that Laayoune was spared.

We need an urgent answer, I said, when Azmi seemed in little hurry to consult his minister, our Antonov was scheduled to depart Tindouf before dusk. Why not wait a day or two, he said, what difference would that make? The Polisario team could fly in that evening and return next day, I suggested, should the minister rule against Morocco participating. 'That's the sort of thing you would want,' said Azmi, 'but we have to defend out interests.' He was categorical, in no circumstance would they admit a Polisario delegation until the minister confirmed that identification could continue in Laayoune without identification on the other side. Hard as I tried I failed to convince him, and rushed off a dejected cable. Unnecessary, as it happened, it reached our commissioner and the Polisario group as they approached Tindouf airfield only to observe the Antonov circle and circle repeatedly before vanishing into the distance. The pilot had been unable to contact the control tower for permission to land. The explanation: electricity failure due to the storm and flooding. Back flew the plane with no one from the other side.

Next morning Azmi accosted me with 'bad news' though his tone suggested otherwise. He had just had communication with the minister, the minister, on instructions from the king, concurred unreservedly in the process continuing. With the same observers and sheikh, he added – this was the sheikh they had accused of refusing to recognise valid postulants. The problem now was to mobilise Polisario in time and arrange travel. I dispatched the most urgent of messages, weather permitted, clearance was given to land. Azmi was astonished when I assured him that identification could recommence without further delay and continue through a one-day public holiday.

Polisario life returned to near normal. Bachir, touring outposts in the southern sector of no-mans-land, suggested we meet at Dougaj. A friendly encounter, much smiling, he and his companions talked of traditional Sahrawi life, the enormous distances traversed in search of pasturage. Flooding had not been the unmitigated disaster first thought, they were accustomed to hardship, and the desert would sprout truffles. They appreciated the aid appeal, but Bachir had another reason for meeting. He wanted more identification centres: in the territory, the camps and elsewhere, not only Mauritania but Europe and Cuba, Polisario lacked the resources to bring people from abroad. I found delightful the idea that we charter a 747, pack it with sheikhs, observers, OAU representatives and the identification commission, and visit Cuba, but I much doubted whether the Security Council would approve. I suggested that Polisario representatives in other countries could distribute forms and return them when completed, now becoming urgent since mid October was the Security Council's closing date for final receipt of applications. Bachir said they needed longer, till the end of the month; the Security Council would not be pleased, I knew, at postponement, but the rains and flooded camps justified deferring the deadline by two weeks, I undertook to make the case. Afterwards I spoke to Bachir alone. He wanted a high-level meeting with the Moroccans, he had concerns about Rabat though the king should be involved, Geneva might be the place to meet – preferable, he said jokingly, to the camps or Dougaj, where we were. In New York, at the General Assembly, Algeria was energetically promoting 'direct talks'; Morocco, less overtly, was warning against dialogue as untimely.

On the day of the revised deadline Polisario promised to submit applications before midnight; I had people in Tindouf to receive them, ready to confirm the moment it was done. Azmi badgered me to know whether Polisario had delivered and how many. I told him of a conversation with Mansour (without mentioning the name): Morocco would expect Polisario to produce its applications first before handing over 'twice' the number. Azmi smiled knowingly. Around eleven he asked for news from Polisario. Nothing yet. He would wait, 'At midnight, I close,' I told him. 'You'll close? You're serious?' He sounded surprised. 'Absolutely,' I said, 'Suits me if no one delivers any more forms. Both sides have received my letter; they know the deadline.' Life would be simpler if we stopped at the ninety thousand we had, an entirely credible figure in relation to the census. Only days before a newly accredited ambassador had enquired about numbers, assuming few likely to be added so close to the deadline; I explained about regional brinkmanship. Azmi began telephoning, he gave instructions for delivery of the Moroccan applications at eleven-thirty, irrespective of information from Tindouf. He had overlooked the time difference, shortly after eleven in Morocco I knew of Polisario's last batch making 42,468 applicants. Morocco presented thousands more, 176,533. The overall total finally reached 233,487, including the 14,486 from Mauritania, where registration was still proceeding – to Azmi's fury, members of Sahrawi tribes perhaps, but Mauritanian nationals.

With these numbers, exceeding every earlier estimate, expanded resources were essential. Basri had no problem, he told me, with increasing the number of party representatives, identification commission staff, even OAU observers, additional centres would be needed. To Azmi, in rear-seat attendance, Basri said: 'First Boujdour,' main thing was to move fast. Then to me: had I seen Bachir recently? What did Polisario really want? I said that Bachir was naturally reluctant to reveal a 'bottom-line'. He knew that only the king could take a final decision, could decide what to offer. For them the ministry of interior had unpalatable connotations but I was confident that, if he came to Rabat and could expect to be received by the king, Bachir might also talk to Basri. Basri, listening attentively, surprised me: 'Of course, he will see His Majesty.' If not, Bachir would opt to meet in some neutral place like Geneva. No, no, Rabat, said Basri, all courtesies would be assured, security, and transport provided. I offered UN aircraft if necessary. Depending on the king's commitments, it could be arranged in the next month or two, I was invited to inform Bachir.

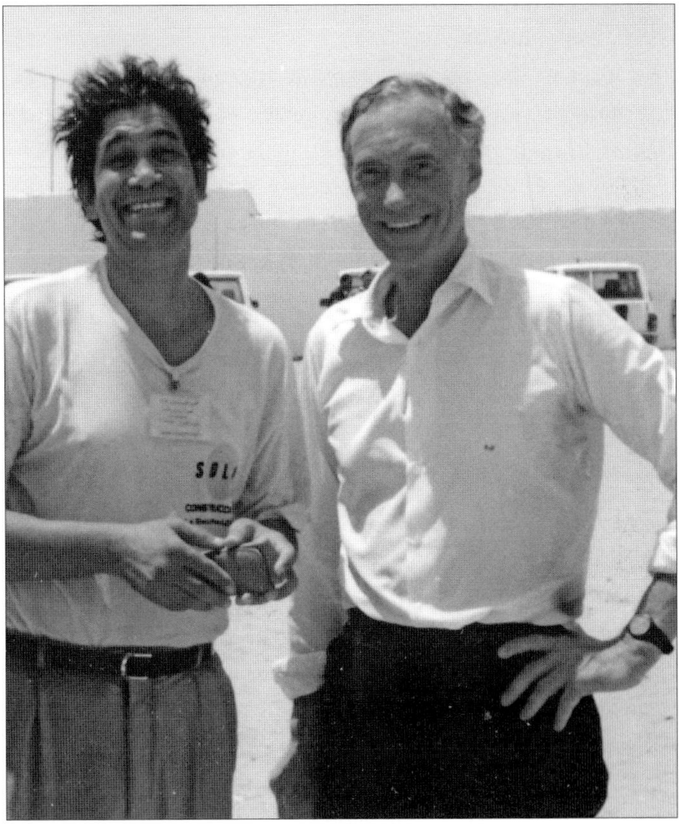

With Bachir at desert team-site

Bachir was still travelling. We arranged to meet at Mijek, like Dougaj an isolated team-site – I chose to ignore Morocco's objection to my encountering Polisario leaders in the buffer zone. The empty desert, broken only by haphazard eruptions of blackish ore between flat-topped mountains in weird isolation, had seen the recent rains bring life to unsuspected vegetation, we landed on sand glazed green with sage grass, thorn-bushes, and the occasional wild flower, even birds sang, flies abounded. The sole sign of human habitation was a mud-walled building, I was led through a narrow passage into a smallish room. As we entered I told Bachir that I had been to Rabat.

Basri agreed to expand the number of centres, beginning with Boujdour. Dakhla would be better, Bachir maintained. Dakhla posed practical problems given the distance and our current resources, though reinforcements were likely to be approved. He said identification was important in advancing the settlement plan but Polisario also wished for dialogue, the draft resolution urging talks, sponsored by Algeria in New York, was Polisario's text. They wanted two irons in the fire, they hoped to use the General Assembly – the parliament, he called it – to counter-balance the 'government' that was the Security Council and where Moroccan influence prevailed. How could anyone object to dialogue? Only, I said, someone familiar with the Western Saharan conflict and its history of talks that failed so conspicuously. But dialogue to the UN is like motherhood, who can be against? he said. I needed no convincing, a constructive exchange rooted in willingness to compromise could permit a way forward. He nodded.

Over lunch, tough camel meat, camel sinew, Bachir mentioned a projected visit by the UN Secretary-General. It derived from an Algerian initiative, I assumed. No, he said, American, the intention to promote dialogue. Boutros-Ghali would be able to say he had made two attempts to intervene personally, and if that failed he could wash his hands of the affair letting the process continue until it broke down. Bachir paused, resigned. Leaning across the table he offered me coca-cola, or did I prefer pepsi-cola? After all my years in America I had never been persuaded to care, or to care much for either, I was happy with water. Water meant life in the Sahara, he said. We talked of the recent rains, which had been predicted, Bachir said, by old-timers, humans always want to predict the future. 'Don't we?' I said. Then, having eaten, I suggested we meet privately and he escorted me to a cell-like cubicle, furnished prison-visiting style with a bare table and two chairs.

First, a matter of visits by Polisario journalists to which Morocco agreed provided their journalists be allowed into Rabouni. Then the core issue: I rehearsed my discussion with Basri, everything about the king, date, discretion and travel arrangements. He congratulated me, was obviously pleased, this was better than expected. If the place were Rabat Bachir would count on seeing the king, there would be no objection to meeting the king and Basri. He mulled it over before reiterating Polisario's wish for dialogue. As to total discretion, I said, my head was on a platter. He nodded.

On the golf course at Bouznika Basri reverted to what Polisario really wanted. I said that Bachir, and perhaps Kheddad, the two leaders with whom I had the most probing conversations, wanted serious talks. Bachir emphasised the importance of dealing with someone who could commit Morocco, hence the king or conceivably crown prince. He was naturally unwilling to reveal any 'bottom line' until the negotiating partner was placed to do the same, and with a mandate to honour whatever compromise might be reached. Before teeing off at the next hole Basri invited me to reassure Bachir.

I went promptly to Tindouf only to learn that Bachir had just left for Strasbourg.

10

Problems

Tension mounted and problems proliferated as identification continued, any pretext served to halt or delay sessions when proceeding served the other party's interest. And the observers were unhappy: Polisario observers in the territory enjoyed limited freedom of movement, Moroccan observers in the camps were nervous for their security and deplored living conditions. The senior Moroccan observer complained they had nothing to eat; in fact, each week the Polisario killed a goat then fed it to their visitors over the days following, Liebek claimed that Moroccans were not used to goat's meat, they did not even eat ram's flesh. For Biadillah it was worse since he lived in constant dread of being poisoned, that his virtually identical brother ran Polisario's secret intelligence service was hardly reassuring. Arab politicking has a long history of poisoning, but I was convinced that for Polisario the treatment of Moroccan observers was a matter of honour. And among the refugees a ration of goat meat counted as luxury.

On the day their return to Tindouf was due the Moroccan observers refused. Not only living conditions but security: unacceptable. Azmi, held me personally responsible, no vague assurance sufficed, transport around Tindouf was dangerous, driving where they might have an accident and be in danger, a senior UN staff member must remain with the Moroccan party. Communication was crucial, access to Inmarsat had to be guaranteed as well as emergency radio contact from wherever they were. The Rabat observers also rejected flying into Laayoune on Saturday, on the only weekend scheduled flight, and spend Sunday waiting in order to depart early Monday. When they did land in the course of Monday morning and were urged to fly on to Tindouf they wanted to eat first.

Azmi, after lunch, called his assistant Abdelkrim to enquire whether the Polisario sheikh had landed. Abdelkrim, visibly nervous, replied that two sheikhs, given the small numbers per sub-fraction, had disembarked and both allowed to stay. 'But I said not', Azmi was angry, he strongly resented being faced with a *fait accompli*. To me he said the Moroccan group would refuse to leave until one of the sheikhs departed. I tried every argument, both arriving on the same flight was logistically rational, simplified air transport arrangements, minimised delays, reduced cost. 'I don't care about your finances,' Azmi interjected. Morocco could add an '*accompagnateur*' to balance numbers, I suggested, but the Moroccans resolutely refused to embark unless one Polisario sheikh departed. Next morning one Polisario sheikh left and the Moroccans flew to Tindouf. Mansour was not pleased. The endless juggling, constant manoeuvring by the parties to limit any perceived advantage to the other, the accusations, the interruptions, unabated tension also took a toll on our staff.

The OAU was little help. The observers insisted on meeting with me personally every Saturday or Sunday evening, at their convenience, to complain: about transport, accommodation, services, lavatory paper – the last a constantly recurring issue. Within our means the best was being done, conditions at Tindouf were hard on everyone. Everything I said had to be repeated in English and French because the African observers spoke either one or the other, not both. They spurned the Chief Administrative Officer and rejected working with the deputy chairman responsible for managing all day-to-day aspects of identification, who was the logical person to brief them. Such was the antipathy between him and the senior African representative that they came to blows, or would have done had they not been forcibly separated.

At an extended meeting on Sunday 20 November, planned to discuss end-of-year arrangements, the OAU rehashed grievances. The African observers would be departing on well-earned leave, their spokesman said, adding aggressively, that in no way must it be said or implied that any delay or interruption in identification could be attributed to the OAU. They had agreed among themselves to remain until 14 December. I asked that they stay at least until the sixteenth, a Friday, we would not be stopping for the Christmas-New Year holiday before 23 December; it would be helpful if just two of the African observers waited till nearer that date. They said they might consider it but gave little hope. When I mentioned resuming work on 3 January, they objected that this would mean those with three day's travel having to leave before New Year's eve.

Polisario needed warning. Bachir, to my relief, accepted a reduced OAU presence if that were necessary so as not to stall the process, commenting obliquely that the OAU battle had no end, but he insisted that identification should not take place without any African observer. We then discussed opening identification centres in Boujdour and Smara in the territory, which should permit equivalent centres in the camps. Over lunch Bachir relaxed describing his early years, he was friendly, complimentary. Afterwards he led me to a small room to talk business: Yes, the king. Basri acceptable but not Basri only. Regarding transport I said that Morocco rejected use of an Algerian aircraft, since a UN plane direct to Rabat might attract attention I suggested a UN flight to Las Palmas with onward connection. With that he had no problem. Discretion: paramount, I reminded him, he gave me every assurance. He would like me to travel with him and to have an '*accompagnateur*'. As for timing he agreed to a date after the secretary-general's visit, unless, conceivably, the king might want to tell Boutros-Ghali that he had already made contact with Polisario.

'Ah, the secretary-general,' Bachir continued with a cryptic smile, when we moved to discussing the visit, he would, unfortunately, be unable to stay long. Where would Polisario prefer to meet him? I thought Rabouni. Bachir replied: 'Smara camp. He will be received by the president of the Sahrawi Arab Democratic Republic', adding cynically, 'On his last visit he came for twenty-two minutes while spending three days in Rabat. It's a brief stop-over. He wants to pretend that he has made a final effort and after "profound" discussion and "long hours" of talk, will conclude that it is necessary to seek a compromise. It could be his way of disengaging.' Bachir was gracious enough to say that, thanks to me, there had been progress, real progress, though it needed to be less 'clandestine', with less Moroccan control. Of the 180,000 applicants introduced by Morocco 150,000 did not qualify, I faced the dilemma of rejecting tens of thousands but only if I did could the process be considered credible. Incidentally, it might help if OAU observers understood a local language, ideally Arabic or Hassaniya. He wanted journalists to visit, suggesting we charter a plane to bring in a hundred and fifty, the Moroccans would obstruct: flights from Las Palmas to Laayoune, he said, were fully booked three months in advance, but arrived empty.

I thanked Bachir for his hospitality and prepared to leave. Every time I visited the camps and saw their bright lively children I resolved to do all in my power to help them to a better future. Bachir was smiling when Boukhari, who had joined us, snapped that the children in the camps, their lives, were none of my business: 'You, your business is the identification process and referendum.' Bachir's appreciative smile over-rode him. Outside a dust storm raised by hot wind off the desert was laying a thick, grey film making it hard to see, visibility barely permitting we just achieved take-off.

The secretary-general's chief of staff telephoned to ask about flying times to and from Laayoune. He refused to believe it took an hour and a half to Tindouf. 'If there is one journey time that I know from painful experience, it's that,' I told him, 'in the Antonov every minute is counted.' 'Ah, but the Secretary-General is not flying by Antonov', he asked me to check jet flying times. Boutros-Ghali wished me to join him at the start of his tour, in Algieria.

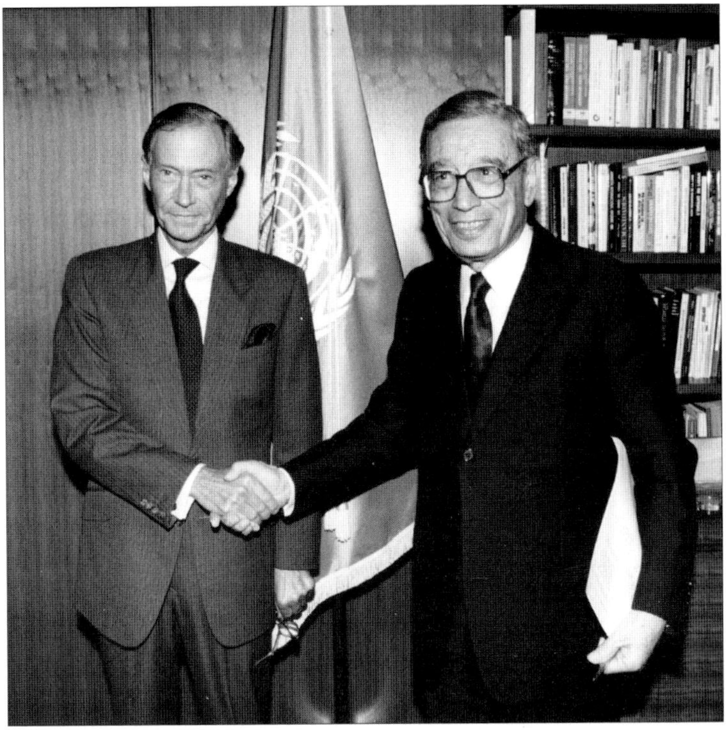

Boutros-Ghali congratulates me on what had been achieved

In Algiers we were hospitably accommodated in the compound for official visitors where I had stayed before. A villa in the grounds was placed at the disposal of Boutros-Ghali and his wife. He took me immediately into the garden to be briefed. This was my first chance to present to him personally my strategy, the strategy which I believed fulfilled the spirit if not precisely the letter of Security Council resolutions, and conformed to his wishes; I needed, though, his seal of approval. I opened with the current joke about Basri. King Hassan received a call from his friend the president of Zaire to say he was planning a democratic election. Apparently Hassan had a man who was excellent at handling such things. Hassan duly dispatched Basri and was shocked when shortly after the election the president called not to thank him but to complain. The king summoned Basri, who sounded very surprised: he thought the Zaire election a great success when ninety-nine percent voted for King Hassan.[1] Boutros laughed, he knew the personalities as well as the issues. He asked how we were progressing. I gave him the facts and then a one side of one page note I had prepared setting out my analysis, the problems and prospects. My core strategy was to take the process forward with no illusion that Morocco and Polisario would cooperate in implementing the settlement plan in its entirety but to engage them long enough for them to realise where identification pointed. Morocco, forced to recognise that it could not be assured of the outcome it intended, and Polisario, convinced that Morocco would never permit a referendum against its interests, might be persuaded to talk. A realistic solution lay through a negotiated autonomy compromise to be endorsed in an act of self-determination.[2] Boutros-Ghali read the note through, twice, said he concurred. He reiterated his support for my approach as we went to lunch.

The Algerians liked his little jokes; one the story of an illiterate man who signed with an X and next to it a small x, the smaller x he explained stood for 'Dr.' After lunch there was no joking, the mood sombre at the session with the Algerian foreign minister and senior officials. Boutros, in professorial style, described the settlement plan: its complexity as well as logistics slowed progress. The Security Council was in no mood to augment financial resources. The UN southwest African operation, it was true, had been larger, but less complicated. In the Sahara work was governed by the parties' willingness to cooperate, if the sheikhs failed to appear or the parties created obstacles, or chose to appeal, the process could take a very, very long time. Attitudes in the Security Council had changed, the Council had previously been reluctant to concede failure and terminate a mission. Now, the US leading, it was prepared to claim that political will lacked and the parties' commitment was insufficient to justify continuing expenditure. The secretary-general said that on his return to New York he would be expected to advise the Council whether or not Minurso should remain.

Boutros urged the Algerians to convince their Sahrawi 'brothers and cousins' that without real progress the mission might have to close. Why did the Cyprus mission continue when there was no progress? Why was the UN still in Yugoslavia? These were of interest, the secretary-general replied, to '*les grands*', the great powers, and they were the ones who paid. He recognised the danger of destabilising the region should Minurso close but was not bluffing.

The Algerian foreign minister thanked him, said they shared his concerns. This was not a civil war in one country but a conflict affecting the region. One side maintained that should the referendum go against them they had to enable their supporters to defend themselves, that he rejected categorically before turning to identification. The enormous number of last minute applications, far in excess of the '74 census, undermined the prospect of an electoral roll respected by both parties, and that was not the only issue. He had spoken to Filali, he said, to urge discussion between the two parties. It ought to be possible to go to the referendum with some basic agreement, an '*accord de base*', he envisaged a 'Lancaster House' (Rhodesia) or 'Evian' (Algeria) conference if Morocco and Algeria could find common ground. Although the settlement plan recognised two parties, two others were concerned; Mauritania, he said, seemed to be slipping from view. Finally, Dembri raised the contact group idea, involving France, Spain and the United States. Boutros-Ghali did not believe that a contact group was the formula, it could even be perceived as a means of postponing the referendum and might encourage those wanting to withdraw the mission. Dembri, before closing the meeting, said it was crucial to break down the wall of mistrust – and paid credit to my efforts.

The subsequent press conference, presidential audience and meeting with the prime minister were interspersed with urgent telephone calls. Boutros spoke to his representative in Yugoslavia about the situation, sliding dangerously out of control, he telephoned the US ambassador Madeleine Albright and just from body language I sensed his aggravation. Further calls delayed our departure next morning and it was in the plane, after we left Algiers, that Boutros ushered me to his private suite. His wife Leah looked in to say I should let her husband sleep, he had been up half the night speaking to the secretary-general of NATO, but he ignored her.

Algeria, he thought, had been quite positive, less insistent on an international conference, perhaps open to an alternative solution. The Algerians might see some advantage in a deal with Morocco to help combat the FIS, and, incidentally, the Moroccans should realise that it was a potential problem there also. Both had an interest in reaching a solution to the conflict in Western Sahara. He acquiesced in the impossibility of direct talks at the moment but asked me to persist in any contacts, and to serve as channel for messages. He paused. It was an awful time to be secretary-general, made responsible for crises over which he had no control and minimal influence, blamed for failure in Somalia and in Yugoslavia, the international situation was bleak, he said.

Tindouf, where we touched down, welcomed the secretary-general. A beautiful Sahrawi girl presented a bouquet to Mrs Boutros-Ghali, who had difficulty in extracting herself from the assembled women wishing to greet her. 'How long is the flight to the camps?' Boutros asked when we boarded a luxurious helicopter. 'Not more than ten minutes,' I told him only to find us circling for twenty minutes or longer giving the Sahrawis time to parade. We landed to salutes, guard of honour, band playing, massed ululating women and a long, long line of dignitaries, sheikhs and other notables. Abdel-Aziz reviewed the guard then led Boutros and party into a tent lined and layered with traditional rugs. Mint tea was served, we had hardly sipped before being rushed to a nondescript room.

Abdel-Aziz addressed us in Arabic, interpreted largely for my benefit. Polisario spared no effort to cooperate, he said. Since I had been made responsible everything was being done to move the process forward, obstruction all derived from the other side, Polisario showed maximum flexibility. The underlying question remained who had the right to participate in the referendum. In spite of reservations about residence qualifications four and five, they respected the secretary-general's criteria, difficult though these were to apply honestly and correctly, it was Morocco that missed no opportunity to hamper and delay. Refusing the OAU, whose role was specified in the settlement plan, had forfeited weeks. Then Morocco delivered a cascade of applications to saturate, drown the identification commission. The plan mentioned the '74 census as basis, some 70,000 persons; Morocco was submitting about 200,000 names – in flagrant violation, with the intention to render the Sahrawis a minority in their land. Either Morocco hoped to falsify the outcome by imposing numbers favourable to their cause or it planned to make the process unworkable. Morocco must not be permitted to convert the referendum into a plebiscite.

Identification had thrown into relief the role of sheikhs. The value of their witness under pressure was questionable. Their immunity was another issue, and why had Polisario sheikhs when in Laayoune been prevented from meeting close relatives? Family members should be allowed to greet and see each other. He turned to the bigger picture: could the UN assure a credible referendum? In the interest of transparency he called for international media coverage, and a more visible UN civilian police presence. Dialogue might provide new impulse, not as an alternative to the settlement plan, rather to speed it up, dialogue should be under UN aegis and at a responsible level. Boutros thanked him.

The secretary-general dealt succinctly with technical issues. The identification commission could be relied upon to accept only those qualified; resources would have to be found to process as many as necessary; the sheikhs, he was sure, had sufficient independence and there was always one from each side. His fear had been for a one-sided referendum. That the UN be obliged to leave was the current danger. The Security Council was losing interest, it regarded regional stability in north-west Africa of lesser importance than ex-Yugoslavia and Somalia. The Council was asking 'how long will this last, how much will it cost? The Council needs a concluding date, otherwise it is liable to declare the mission failed and pull out. Don't complicate things, try to make the process work.' He urged Polisario to support 'my representative', not to bicker, not argue about sheikhs, if they wanted a referendum, they should do everything to make it happen. Recent elections in the US favouring the hard right exacerbated the Council's tendency to a more negative, isolationist attitude. The message of this visit was to have Polisario confront current reality. If they went back to war, so be it, and he stopped. Bachir intervened, in an effort to stimulate an exchange, offering suggestions, but the visit, brief as it was, ended. On leaving I caught Bachir's attention. 'After this,' he said, 'we need to rethink.' I promised to return with news of what transpired in Rabat where I was sure the secretary-general would be conveying the same message. 'Most assuredly,' Boutros confirmed on our flight to Laayoune.

At Laayoune the Moroccans had marshalled a vast crowd of Moroccan flag waving Sahrawis. An honour guard saluted. Having greeted a selection of dignatories the secretary-general drove into town for the lunch that he had had declined in Rabouni, he then visited Minurso headquarters to be briefed by senior staff before leaving for Rabat. Filali, prime minister and foreign minister, was giving a dinner in honour of Nelson Mandela, expanded to honour Boutros-Ghali. The pilot had announced our descent before returning to report that visibility in Rabat made landing impossible; we were rerouted to Casablanca. In Casablanca there was no ground transport to ferry us back to Rabat, a drive of an hour and a quarter, we waited for cars to be mobilised before the convoy set off, reaching Filali's residence more than an hour late. Nelson Mandela awaited us, a commanding presence wearing the dignified, generous expression, which was as characteristic of him as his personalised batik shirts. He showed not the slightest irritation at being kept waiting. Physically more imposing than I had expected and even more charming when we conversed. In his shadow I spotted Mpehle: 'Caught you playing truant,' I said jokingly, 'Shouldn't you be in Laayoune?' 'My president was here and I received a summons,' he replied a touch pompously in his majestic deep voice, before pointedly adding 'My president takes his dinner at 7 o'clock and goes early to bed.'

The secretary-general intercepted me after dining to speak to a politician interrogating him about Sahrawis in the Tindouf area who were unwilling to submit applications through Polisario. Then realising that I was in conversation with Basri, apologised: 'Have to watch out for this man,' he said to Basri pointing at me, 'someone who has the confidence of Polisario and of Morocco, he could be taking my place.' But it was already late and Mandela was leaving, passing us he smiled graciously and said 'It's been a very nice evening.'

Next morning, before departing for New York, Boutros-Ghali went to the palace to be 'tough with the king'. He briefed me on his return to the hotel's 'royal suite' having offered me a guided tour before seating us in an anteroom. 'It's all wired, of course,' he said. He did not explain how the king responded to his lecture. Hassan liked to call Boutros 'the old socialist'; they had known each other for a long time and, whether or not he agreed, the king would have listened.

Laayoune was a shambles, identification at a standstill. The deputy identification commission chairman, a former politically appointed American ambassador and Washington's man with the mission, who had come close to fistycuffs with the OAU, was at constant loggerheads with Azmi. We had to work with Morocco, Polisario and the OAU whether we sympathised with them, liked their style, their conduct or not, I warned him. He disagreed. And threatened to 'destroy' me when I raised non-renewal of his contract. It was not an easy decision and I prepared for the consequences faced with Newt Gingrich's newly elected hard right congress.

Tindouf, Rabouni, seemed strangely relaxing. Kheddad and I reviewed painstakingly all eighty-eight sub-fractions, he confirmed for every sheikh still living the full name – I was beginning to cope, however unpronounceable and triple-barrelled – and suggested alternates for those who had died. Polisario recognised as valid sheikhs those elected in a 1973 election or the eldest son.

Before I left Bachir arrived to say that he was unhappy at the secretary-general's flying visit, and the timing for a meeting with the king seemed less propitious, his attention distracted by the Islamic conference, which was about to take place.

11

Fresh start

TO THE MISSION CAME a new deputy chairman. Seconded from the secretariat, his loyalty was to the UN and he was fluent in French, English and Arabic. Omar Abou-Zahr was introduced to the commissioners and other staff and immediately immersed in identification procedures. Eight centres were now functioning, four each side, with complicated logistics, Morocco had little difficulty in assembling people, Polisario, with refugees dispersed and limited communications, found it challenging.

Given the difficulties, identification resumed surprisingly smoothly, with convincing results. Identification teams were briefed, centre leaders schooled, directives explained and rehearsed. Senior commissioners were instructed to exercise initiative and pre-empt problems, this included a constructive working relationship with local authorities to ensure the two-way flow of information about sub-fractions, their numbers, the arrival and departure of the sheikhs. Our target was to process three thousand applicants per month at each centre,that involved approximately 150 every working day over a five-day week. Hours of work and the daily average were indicative; it might be necessary to work on Saturdays. OAU observers were persuaded to be partners.

Since applicants listed in the census had only to establish their personal identity, they were readily confirmed by the sheikhs. Polisario's initial concern that imposters would present themselves under false names proved baseless. Those not census listed had to demonstrate that they qualified under one of Perez de Cuellar's revised criteria. Case proven when both sheikhs agreed, when a claim was upheld by one sheikh and rejected by the other, the commission sought corroborating admissible evidence, without which an applicant was unlikely to qualify. The final decision depended on a review of all persons from a given sub-fraction to ensure that a relative might benefit from the successful identification of another family member. Only when every applicant from a particular sub-fraction had been before the commission could this be completed; the occasional individual who had been prevented by illness when originally convoked and applicants coming forward not only in the territory and the camps but in Mauritania complicated the review. I concluded it a mistake to publish lists or even numbers until the review had been completed. Polisario criticized me for blocking transparency, which was unfounded since both sides had observers present throughout identification and took copious notes, they heard exactly what the sheikhs said and the conclusion was normally obvious. The Moroccan observers submitted lengthy rebuttals but must have realised that the process carried conviction.

Both sides became increasingly tense as identification advanced, both were reluctant to abdicate control. Polisario wanted the census-listed to be identified as expeditiously as possible, Morocco was concerned that all persons census-listed not be identified ahead of others lest Polisario refuse to continue. If impartial commissioners could not be manipulated the parties deployed alternative means. The settlement planners, who gullibly assumed that sheikhs would simply provide information that a literate civilisation had in writing, knew neither Sahrawi society nor the sheikhs; sheikhs were immensely knowledgeable about the people of their sub-fraction, they were not a reference book. Identification restored to these aristocrats their ancestral importance, a semblance of the power they once wielded.

When identification at one side was interrupted, for whatever reason, it was made to cease on the other by withholding a sheikh, convocation lists then needed revising, logistics were disrupted, and delay inevitable. While practical problems could sometimes be addressed the presence, or absence, of a sheikh was conclusive. Applicants were convoked, in accord with the daily identification target, from a specific sub-fraction. We could never be absolutely certain how many on the convocation list would appear, given weather vagaries and travel difficulty. In the case of small sub-fractions it might not leave enough to complete a day's work, prolonging a session to complete identification of those convoked caused resentment but filling time unexpectedly available was more of an issue. Moving to another sub-fraction implied new sheikhs; despite major effort on my part Morocco refused to countenance the presence in the territory of a second Polisario sheikh on stand-by, and sheikhs from the territory were not disposed to spend additional time waiting under 'house arrest' in the camps.

Twenty years had passed since the sheikhs had been chosen from senior members of their society and most were elderly, many infirm. But both sides were infinitely suspicious when a sheikh was declared unfit, was he being gagged because his views did not coincide with political guidance? When Sheikh Hamuadi Abdelhay Day was reported ill Polisario halted identification. Sheikh Hamuadi had participated in an earlier identification exercise and shown independence of judgment, quite obviously, according to Polisario, the Moroccans preferred him muzzled; his purported incapacity might even be due to maltreatment. I suggested a visit, we could reassure his family; we would also be able to see whether he was genuinely sick. Azmi agreed to a medical visit, then rescinded. Snoussi called from New York: 'You have told the Americans that we are preventing you from visiting a sheikh'; Ginsberg had enquired why identification was stalled. Morocco was being asked to permit a visit or provide medical evidence, our intention to confirm that he was not a victim of physical restraint. 'Ah,' said Snoussi, 'this is the sheikh who has his wife and children on the other side', hence Hamuadi's indisposition, his reluctance to return to the camps. We were allowed to meet him, he had been unwell, he said, but was feeling better. We took his picture in our company for me to give Bachir, Hamuadi had not been eliminated that was obvious. 'Now they'll all want to come and have their photo taken,' Bachir said, adding, with a resigned expression: 'You can't imagine the problems I have with my sheikhs.'

Bachir may have been pleased with the photograph, he was less pleased with the news from the Islamic conference. King Hassan had spoken to the Algerian prime minister who intended focusing on the need to reopen their common border, Hassan launched straight into the Sahara, said he was always willing to receive a 'subject' arriving from 'Morocco' and not by a non-Moroccan carrier. In Bachir's view that closed the door on the meeting we had envisaged, he did not wish to approach through an antechamber, or act precipitately. With a wan smile he looked me in the eye saying 'You can lead us to damnation, but don't rush us, at least let us go to hell at a measured pace'. New difficulty, he believed, stemmed from power struggles at court, Basri was embroiled in forcing the king to abandon his plan, following elections, to form a government of 'opposition' politicians, who made Basri's ousting a condition. Next day, in Laayoune, Azmi called to say that Basri wished to see me immediately in Rabat.

A special plane had been dispatched, my departure programmed for one o'clock. It was noon already and I needed to finish work in the office, I suggested two o'clock. Twenty minutes later Azmi phoned again: the aircraft was about to land; could I please make it 1.15 or 1.30 at the latest?It really was most urgent. I reached the airport by 1.20 only to find lunch had been ordered for the pilots, take-off would be at two. Azmi informed Rabat that we would be there about three, although I knew, as he certainly did, that the flight, even by jet, took a full hour and twenty minutes. On arrival Azmi mobilised transport to the hotel and invited me to relax. I was changing when the phone rang: 'Come at once. The minister is going abroad.' I whipped on jacket and tie before being driven at breakneck speed to Basri's grand residence. I was not kept waiting, Basri waved me in, his mouth half-full, and indicated a chair, he continued lunch while we spoke, eating, not very elegantly, brochettes, salad and cheese. His habit was to repeat the same question, I could never decide if this was a technique to decide whether I gave an identical answer every time, whether he was not really listening – preoccupied by crucial affairs of state, or whether he could not remember, which I doubt. When I expressed appreciation for arranging for me to meet Sheikh Hamuadi he nodded. He was keen that the secretary-general be made aware of Morocco's cooperation with the UN, made the keener by US criticising Basri as part of the problem. 'And Bachir?' he asked.

I had been to Rabouni I told him, where Bachir was pleased with the photograph. The high level meeting needed greater clarity. Basri interrupted: 'What does he really want?' I thought Polisario were nervous, so long as identification had not begun, consequences were too distant to cause concern, after it started repeated disruptions and delays had the process advancing so slowly that Bachir could joke about the end of the century. Now a programme of work was largely agreed and the recent Security Council resolution providing resources made it realistic, the outcome was no longer remote. Our military observers reported Polisario soldiers having no confidence that Morocco would be prevented from manipulating proceedings in its favour; they wanted to take up arms. In the camps people, many people, according to our Arabic-speaking staff, having suffered years' deprivation longed for the referendum: if it produced the desired result, so much the better; if not, it would at least end their refugee existence and offer their children the prospect of normal life. The political leadership was divided, some, like Bachir, sought an honourable compromise, he seemed fairly realistic about circumstances and counted on a measure of autonomy. I had been questioned about the constitutional status of Puerto Rico; the Spanish provinces and German lander were mentioned. I could not reveal any 'bottom line' nor what the king might be willing to concede, but believed this a map for going forward. Basri asked that I accompany him to the airport, he rehearsed what had already been said, to my questions he remained non-committal.

Bachir, having reported to the press his appreciation of an encounter with me at Mijek, which never took place, was back and wanted a meeting. Polisario security both into and out of Rabouni was visibly increased: more checkpoints, more soldiers, more alert, more heavily armed with Kalashnikovs. No military were at the 'farm' where Bachir invited me to lunch, he excused himself from eating because of the fast. I thanked him for his considerate hospitality. He had nothing to recount about his travels; he was concerned about implementation of the settlement plan. Its conduct was clandestine, no international press coverage and no international observers, the process seemed hermetically sealed against independent observation. Census-listed people and a few others were being identified in the camps while on 'the other side' it was mostly a foreign population of settlers from Morocco, the huge number of these, a deluge, was alarming, the commission could be duped. Moroccan sheikhs all took the party line, they functioned like the functionaries they were. What guarantee did Polisario have that all these people would not appear on the electoral roll? He wanted more detail about commission procedures, methods of evaluation. 'We are in the woods,' he said, 'in the dark.' I explained yet again, as I had done so many times already, the procedure, how decisions were reached, that the burden of proof lay with the applicant, the commission could be trusted. He relented somewhat: 'You say we are on the right road. We follow because M. Jensen says so. But let us see with our own eyes.' 'In the desert there are many tracks, what matters is reaching the destination.'

Diplomats too wanted to know where we were. I was asked occasionally to brief the Rabat based ambassadors of Security Council member states. Despite Basri objecting, I thought this valuable – also for the insight it afforded me. At the French embassy Henri Benoit de Coignac, the ambassador, wished to inform me about a meeting in New York. France and the United Kingdom remained supportive of the mission, but the US representative was serious about cutting funds. An under-secretary-general referred to talks as a 'red herring', that I strongly refuted; compromise offered the only realistic solution. Neither side, even Basri, whatever he said publicly, was certain about the outcome of identification, an answer could lie through negotiated agreement, some delegation of powers to the region, a degree of autonomy, a face-saving proposition enabling Polisario leaders to convince their people that this was honourable, worth supporting. I had been entrusted with messages, and Basri did not reject talking out of hand, frankly, without dialogue the conflict would not be resolved. Influential governments, I believed, could bring pressure, France and the US, in particular, might help persuade the king, the timing propitious given the king's American visit. It seemed inconceivable that

Washington would choose such a moment to cease funding Minurso. We had achieved much, much more than appeared remotely feasible a year ago. De Coignac nodded approvingly, he was interested, supportive, anxious to help.

The Moroccan foreign ministry could not confirm that the king would visit New York while in the US, though it was not unlikely. But the secretary-general's executive assistant had telephoned: Boutros-Ghali needed a brief, talking points, for a meeting with the king, tentatively scheduled for the Monday following.

12

Targets

Boukhari revealed that four ambassadors, of the US, UK, France and Spain, had met to discuss the possibility of dialogue, belief in the need to talk was growing. France was increasingly positive, and active, their New York ambassador had taken Boukhari by the arm and allowed himself to be seen speaking to him in the corridor, even gesturing to a Moroccan who passed.

I asked Bachir whether he might be leaving for New York. He had been requested to stay, he said, and asked if I had been summoned. Special representatives were authorised to travel to America only on the secretary-general's specific instruction, for this visit of King Hasssan my presence was not required. In Washington he appealed to US elected representatives to help the UN complete its mission, reminding them that Morocco had been a friend of the United States for two hundred years. In New York he was received by Boutros-Ghali, it was the best meeting, by far, Snoussi called to tell me, that the king had ever had with my 'patron'. I was credited with excellent relations throughout the region; my 'neutrality' was very pleasing '*nous plait beaucoup*', despite recurring difficulties with identification there had been significant progress. Polisario evidently had problems with their sheikhs; reports had also come in alleging a breakdown of discipline in their army, this might suggest some opening to an alternative solution. The secretary-general's discreet, tentative, hint at dialogue was well understood by His Majesty. The secretary-general's personal assistant, Fayza Aboulnaga, added that the king was appreciative of my efforts, pleased with the achievements of the identification commission and especially its 'president', Morocco was firmly committed to moving the process forward. All in all a constructive encounter, supporting my work, it marked a major step forward.

Boukhari had come to learn about the king and Boutros, and to comment, Fayza said. He expressed doubt about the mission's credibility, Sahrawis were routinely harassed and filtered on their way to identification centres. Fayza replied that centre leaders attested to the contrary, none recorded or was able to confirm such allegations. Boukhari persisted, dismissing any suggestion of speedily completing identification, given the obstacles, especially those created by Morocco, direct contact was essential.

Ginsberg returned from Washington with another perspective. Political Washington cared little about the Sahara, wanted it over, even who won was not vital. The situation remained tenuous with a Congress decision on Minurso still lurking, the House of Representatives' intention was to cut tranches of funding from a peace-keeping allocation already approved, including Minurso. The State Department, concerned at slow progress, proposed a figure for identification by end May as a litmus test.

Despite sheikh and other problems prospects for reaching a target figure had improved. Transfers were largely routine and security less of a preoccupation. Personal relations developed cautiously, with constraints, the many who presented themselves at Laayoune centre's large compound found time to mingle with Sahrawis from the other side, I intervened occasionally on behalf of a Polisario sheikh wanting to meet family members at home. One tended to forget these were people at war with each other, bitterness and lack of trust were never far beneath the surface.

With the majority of those belonging to the principal sub-fractions identified there was no evading a difficulty looming. If there had been one unexpected and happy circumstance it was to discover that most sub-fractions had a sheikh both with Polisario and with the Moroccans, which surprised me until I learnt that hedging bets was true to Sahrawi tribal tradition. But my review with Kheddad confirmed what I knew: some sub-fractions lacked a surviving sheikh from the last 'election' in 1973. The Moroccans maintained this was as a non-problem, new sheikhs had been appointed and we were given a list. Polisario refused to recognise any Moroccan appointed sheikh, who would inevitably be beholden to Morocco, but also because he could not be expected to recognise sub-fraction members from the other side. Polisario insisted that only his eldest son could substitute for a deceased sheikh; in the few cases where no son survived any substitute had, of course, to be included in the Spanish census. Azmi said 'no', Azmi knew the sub-fractions and their sheikhs almost as well as Kheddad. The response of both was coloured by intimate knowledge of individuals, though they never admitted political concerns.

'Morocco rejects the relevance of the census to the choice of sheikh', Azmi maintained, 'many distinguished Sahrawis were not in the territory at the time and are not included.' I knew. 'It would be insulting to exclude them. In many cases they are the ones who know the people best.' I allowed him to rehearse the arguments. Valid though some might be, which I conceded, I emphasised the need for sheikh substitutes who could not be contested, Morocco would not wish to be accused of trying to control or subvert the process. Knowing that the encounter between the king and Boutros had been positive, I was quietly hopeful that Azmi's non-acceptance might be kneaded into agreement. We turned to other things: the sea, and the sun setting over the Atlantic.

I allowed time for consultation with Rabat and revised instructions before requesting another meeting. Azmi complied. He kept me guessing by wanting first to discuss the general programme of work and various technical issues, then asked an assistant for the papers. He presented me with sheets, one for each sub-fraction without a surviving sheikh from the '73 election, and waited; on each sheet there were four or three names: eldest son first and where no son survived substitutes were proposed with census numbers beside them. Azmi crossed out a name on one sheet and returned it to me. 'There,' he said, 'they are all in the census. Now you're happy.' I was relieved, though wary of a hidden catch: for example, that they prove functionaries of the interior ministry. Before cabling the names to Polisario we checked our listings and from related information in the census found them all acceptable.

A massive sandstorm next day saw all flights cancelled. The Moroccan observers refused to take their 92 year-old sheikh overland to Dakhla, disrupting identification. We were reorganising when a surprise cable from New York announced a mission of the Security Council in the first week of June, no sooner officially confirmed than the date was brought forward to 27 May; I was to brief the Security Council on Thursday 25th and would have to return instantly, the SG wanted me at headquarters, as of Monday, for meetings beforehand. It was Friday, nearly 11 p.m. in Laayoune, too late to reach the morning departure from Casablanca, Sunday had no flight, making it physically impossible for me to be in New York by Monday. I also had meetings planned with Bachir and Basri; preferable I cancel both, I was advised, though Kofi Annan, under-secretary-general for peace-keeping, felt sure the SG would understand if I were there by Wednesday: 'Incidentally, were we affected by a recent incident?'

The incident concerned a group of youths arrested in Laayoune after demonstrating for Polisario. Azmi, when I had raised it with him, became petulant: 'It's none of your business,' he snapped, 'Minurso is here to monitor the cease-fire and organise identification. What else goes on concerns you not, until the transitional phase that is.' 'That's the official mandate,' I agreed, 'but speaking as a friend I think you should be conscious of increasing international interest and concern about such happenings, especially with a Security Council mission expected.' 'This, *cher ami*, is none of your business.'

My first appointment, with Bachir, was to introduce Professor Roucounas, newly-named as independent jurist to look into issues of political prisoners and 'disappeared' persons. Bachir took advantage to express frustration, he did not believe the UN capable of resisting Morocco. Instead of Sahrawis in the census four additional criteria permitted the import of settlers, 'colons', in their hundred thousands, the proposal to admit oral testimony relied on the sheikhs but the sheikhs 'controlled by the colonial administration the other side of the wall' said exactly what they were told to say, they recognised people before they could sit down, even the very young sheikh knew everybody on his side but refused to recognise others, be it wives and family. Polisario was doubtful, sceptical, in 'free fall,' whether a credible referendum would or could be. 'M. Jensen asks us to have confidence in him. But,' turning to me with his most disarming smile, 'we cannot be certain where we are. The camel calf knows exactly where to go for water having been carried there by his mother before birth.' He laughed: 'Amazing that the she-camel's womb should be more transparent than the identification process.' The cease-fire, he conceded, was effective but the truce offered by Polisario had merely permitted Morocco to consolidate its position, separating the cease-fire from the transitional period had been entirely in Morocco's favour, what had Polisario obtained?

The appointment of an independent jurist showed some concern on the part of the secretary-general, one thousand 'disappeared' persons were unaccounted for in Morocco, including many Sahrawi political prisoners. With Roucounas in his sights Bachir concluded: 'Someone running a flag up an electricity pole or scrawling 'no' on a wall hardly merits the draconian action that Morocco takes.' Roucounas affirmed his intention to apply international instruments: the universal declaration of human rights and the covenant on civil rights. Did Polisario have 'political detainees,' he asked. Bachir said: 'Yes. And we liberated them immediately after adoption of the settlement plan, which called for an amnesty.' He found it hard to imagine that the 'neighbouring country' would submit lists of detained persons and prisoners. While Roucounas studied a document Bachir took me aside. 'With dialogue we could reach a compromise.' He wondered whether the Security Council could persuade Morocco, the Security Council mission would be important.

Roucounas had also to meet Basri, who was in a benign mood and listened amiably to Roucounas between telephone calls and picking at breakfast. The independent jurist was welcomed and assured of Moroccan cooperation. Basri showed greater interest in Bachir's thinking but stopped short when it became evident that there might be more to say than was advisable in the presence of others. Once Roucounas had finished a bland introductory statement, Basri indicated that the meeting was over and Azmi accompanied Roucounas to another room.

Basri instructed, in Arabic that was easy to follow, that there should be no interruption and gave me his undivided attention. I reminded him of King Hassan's '*ni vainquer, ni vaincu*' – neither conqueror nor conquered: was this still valid? 'Yes,' he said nodding emphatically, 'and in calling for the referendum His Majesty sought the seal of international approval.' If that were still the case, I said, Morocco needed to move towards talking, since Polisario might otherwise disengage from a process it believed hopelessly skewed against it, that could leave the Sahara in Moroccan hands but without international approval. Once we surmount the question of form, Basri said, we can talk, we can reach a compromise. Recent efforts to bring both sides together had foundered for specific reasons: the king's competing commitments and Bachir issuing a militant anti-Moroccan statement. When I remonstrated that following a meeting with me Bachir had issued a sharply critical press release, Basri smiled his professional smile, picked at the dry skin on his lip, and asked me to accept this as just propaganda, not for my consumption. 'But how can you negotiate with someone like that?' he added before turning to plans for the Security Council tour and my visit to New York.

Security Council consultations, a context in which the Council does serious business, take place in a conference room abutting the council chamber. It is small and invariably overcrowded, by convention ambassadors are accompanied by at most three counsellors, bar secretariat officials invited to brief the Council no one else is admitted, no formal records are kept. Comparative informality and space imposed proximity encourage more candid views, and, unlike sessions in the chamber, there is neither media gallery nor public opinion to humour. I thanked the president for this opportunity to address members of the Council and began: the 'technical' difficulties faced by the mission were largely political. The process was complicated and increasingly so but it was misleading to emphasise the slow progress, only twelve months ago, following years of warfare and a stymied settlement plan, did Polisario agree to proceed and Morocco confirm its commitment. It was unexpected since Polisario remained convinced that the plan was biased against them; criterion one, they repeated, was for Sahrawis, persons in the census, the other four for Moroccans. Significantly, both Polisario's secretary-general and deputy secretary-general recently presented themselves for identification under criteria four and five, for persons not included in the Spanish census, since like other leaders they were out of the territory at the time. Half of those in the 1974 census had now been identified but figures were not the whole story; statistics failed to reveal burgeoning contact between the two sides, exchange of ideas and information.

Minurso had the capacity and experience to identify a thousand people daily. In practice last minute scheduling changes and stoppages were inevitable, sheikhs, many aged and ailing, were indisposed or held up, sub-fractions were widely dispersed and both sides insistence on reciprocal action caused modification and delay. The greatest achievement had been locking Morocco and Polisario into a process from which they could not easily disengage. The Security Council mission would be invaluable in urging cooperation. The president thanked me, as did others, and Germany took the floor.

The ambassador had some questions: was identification based primarily on the Spanish census? What happened when the sheikhs' testimony was contradictory? Were there problems with access to centres? When an individual was not included in the census, I explained, burden of proof lay with the applicant, cases were common when the sheikhs did not agree and the applicant had then to provide supplementary evidence, which was rarely convincing; the problem was compounded by both sides believing the sheikhs subject to political pressure. Morocco and Polisario provided transport to identification centres; I investigated difficulties when these arose and asked that any obstacle be reported to me. Argentina posed similar questions. The United States expressed regard for my 'hard work' and briefing before querying whether the referendum in Western Sahara would lead to peace in the region and what would happen were Minurso terminated? Were resources being used efficiently? The United Kingdom was appreciative, Botswana had comments, referred to his Namibia experience, Oman, Nigeria and Rwanda also spoke, none showing great insight into the circumstances in Western Sahara, as fully elaborated in reports to the Council. The Russian Federation and China concurred in the four-month extension proposed, the president, Belgium, summing up, was satisfied that the process was moving in the right direction, albeit not as fast as hoped, and urged the parties to show greater commitment.

That afternoon I addressed representatives of the troop contributing countries before meeting with interested ambassadors and the secretary-general. Having done what was possible to generate awareness of the facts,

I returned to Rabat, and prepared to greet the mission. Basri insisted on speaking before Security Council members came, I needed to realise things about Polisario: 'We know them,' he said with his source-of-all-intelligence expression, 'because "*ils sont de nous*" they are one of us – you beat them or buy them.' Polisario was splitting, its top echelon at loggerheads, its leadership tainted, Bachir was complicit in the diversion of relief supplies for sale in Mauritania; an agent had been killed supposedly making off with the profits. Equally significant was the rebellion brewing between political leaders and sheikhs (the sheikhs were becoming uppity, I had told the British ambassador). Polisario did not want a referendum, Basri concluded, they would do anything to prolong the process indefinitely.

13

Visitation

THE SECURITY COUNCIL MISSION arrived on Sunday, 4 June. Guidelines were to impress upon the parties the need to cooperate fully with Minurso in implementing all aspects of the settlement plan and underline that further delay would put the mission's future at risk; to assess progress and identify problems in identification; to identify problems in other areas relevant to the settlement plan. The mission, led by Botswana's ambasssador, comprised the permananent representatives of Argentina, Honduras and Oman with the US and France's deputies. The US had congressional concerns to address, Argentina was of the Spanish-speaking world, France had real interests, others had their own agenda or were along for the ride. Filali received the mission in the new foreign office, in a ceremonial chamber worthy of an ancient dynasty, he welcomed the Council members to Morocco.

A cease-fire had been in place since September 1991, he began, monitored by military observers. Identification had progressed, and reached the point of no return, Morocco was cooperating fully in 'good faith'. Legwaila of Botswana responded: five years had been lost, the UN suffered from a credibility crisis, and faced a financial crisis, time to bring the process to conclusion. The American, Interfurth, emphasised that the current mandate extension was brief pending a critical review, Washington was frustrated at the slow rate of progress, deplored delaying tactics like reciprocity, Congress was prepared to rescind money already appropriated. What would be the impact on the region, the ambassador asked, were Minurso terminated? Given monthly expenses of some six million dollars might Morocco offset more of the cost? The Security Council, with seventeen peace-keeping missions, was looking to reduce costs. Filali responded in his usual mellow manner.

Morocco accepted the plan in 1988 assuming it to be implemented in a year or two, Morocco wanted the problem resolved quickly. 'This is a very important issue for us,' Filali said, and he hoped the Security Council would help. It was the Council approved the peace plan, the peace plan had to be respected, 'On the other side, in Tindouf,' he said, 'they accept only criteria from the census contrived by Spain, they must recognise all the criteria.' Morocco was not concerned with reciprocity. Filali counted on Minurso completing its task, with a free and fair referendum, he hoped in the next six months. It would be highly dangerous to add another destabilising element to those already facing the region, he asked the mission to convey to New York Morocco's determination to end the dispute as soon as possible. Funding was an issue, he realised, with the UN tackling many crises but he rejected diverting resources to other conflicts away from this one; Morocco was already contributing to Minurso though Filali was ready to examine whether more could be done. Argentina commented that helpful though a Moroccan budget contribution could be there was danger of this according them control.

Basri, asked to summarise practical aspects, reaffirmed Morocco's determination to hold the referendum in accordance with the settlement plan, Morocco accepted the secretary-general's adjustments. When identification began Morocco provided lists of sheikhs and representatives; it had never voluntarily interrupted the process. Criterion 4, he argued, was as valid as the others, but was being deployed to reject Sahrawis: forty per cent rejected in Smara and Boujdour against only fifteen in Tindouf. It was humiliating, he said with feeling, for a Sahrawi to be told he did not belong to a sub-fraction or tribe. Polisario it was imposed a ceiling of 150 persons per day. The Security Council and the representative should enforce the plan when the parties disagreed. Basri paused before 'summing up': Morocco would insist that all 181,000 applicants be identified; it stood ready to move 100,000 people to centres in the territory or to transport the identification commission to them, it undertook to increase the number of centres when Minurso was ready and to provide transport, lodging and logistical support, Morocco would abandon reciprocity provided it was not alone in doing so. Any person not found qualified would, of course, have the right to appeal. Morocco willingly accepted the return of refugees guaranteeing their honour, security and freedom. Finally, he concluded, there had been direct talks on fifteen occasions – in vain, independence could be achieved only through the vote; if Polisario wanted to talk integration Morocco would be pleased to respond. 'We are open to any questions' he stopped, then presented, as supporting caste: 'Ambassador Snoussi, whom you all know, emperor of orient and occident, and Brahim Hakim, earlier known as "Davidoff", former chief of Polisario diplomacy, who understands the dossier perfectly from both sides'. But before they could speak

Legwaila had something to say and he was in no mood to be flippant.

The process had lasted too long, he said, and must reach an end, seventeen peace-keeping operations around the world cost three billion dollars, the cease-fire was successful, but insufficient. Ladsous, of France, less aggressive, conceded the Council's impatience, frustration at the slow rate of progress, even scepticism as to whether the plan could arrive at a conclusion, but success was in the interest of all, the people, governments, Morocco and the UN. '*Ni vainquer ni vaincu*', as proposed by His Majesty, might be the way forward. Cardenas from Argentina interjected a comment about fatigue, fatigue on part of actors and financial fatigue, before Brahim Hakim took the floor.

He was among those, he said, students in this very town, who created Polisario. The census had been deployed to block Morocco's recovery of the territory by selecting Sahrawis loyal to Spain. The settlement plan, though good in parts, gave rise to difficulties by reliance on the census, the Spanish census in no way reflected Sahrawi society, for example, none of the Polisario leaders was included in the census. His own father had died the previous year, aged seventy-four; how could he find witnesses to vouch for where he had been born. How could applicants prove that they qualified, having no fixed address and no written records, in their culture '*etat civil c'est le tribu*' – 'civil registry is the tribe', To be rejected at identification was offensive, not to be recognised as belonging to a tribe was profoundly humiliating, to be branded a bastard without blood relations, it was an insult not only to the individual but to his tribe.

Algeria, predictably, was different. Dembri, foreign minister, surrounded by foreign office officials, met the mission in a conference room. Western Sahara, he said, was a case of decolonisation, it was the administering power's responsibility to lead the territory to independence. Algeria's position, moral and political, was based on that principle. Algeria, a concerned country but not party to the dispute, only wanted peace in the Maghreb and development; a solution was essential to regional stability. The settlement plan had been subverted: the additional criteria of 1991 were a disaster. Contrary to what some argued, the census of 1974 had been serious, professional. In the minister's opinion, the '74 census plus a modest percentage could be admissible but the 180,000 submitted by Morocco was beyond reason. The cease-fire remained crucial. He feared a resumption of fighting; Algeria was doing all to ensure that the cease-fire continued to hold. As for costs: the budget was not enormous, he could not imagine Minurso withdrawn until the UN had realised its responsibilities, permitting a durable solution and regional stability.

Legwaila responded that all peace plans depended on compromise, no people got everything they thought they deserved; he gave examples from his Namibian experience. After the Gulf war, he said, the UN may have become over-confident: with success in Namibia, Cambodia, Salvador and Mozambique. A return to war in the Sahara was not a viable alternative; the only game in town was the settlement plan. He would encourage Polisario to cooperate fully, to compromise where necessary, not even to consider dropping out of the process – that, despite their frustration, would be an enormous mistake. Cardenas agreed that the plan offered the best prospect for peace, Ladsous said that Minurso faced an arduous undertaking, but what had been achieved over the last year gave cause for hope. The Algerians emphasised the need to be pragmatic and realistic without losing our vision; they appreciated what I had done and supported my continuing efforts.

Bachir, in unwonted suit and tie, his unruly hair trimmed, greeted the mission on arrival in the camps, announcing that they welcomed this important delegation with esteem, with respect and with hope. Legwaila, responding, said there was no suggestion that the Security Council wanted to run away from problems or paper them over, the Council was aware of the monumental challenge in identifying tens of thousands of people over a vast area, but it was essential to accelerate the pace. Everyone needing to be identified had to be identified for Polisario and Morocco both to say; 'I am satisfied that all my supporters have been identified', we want this to be as fair as is humanly possible. He touched on other issues before reverting to identification: sheikhs must be available on time, they could not be made to excuse slowness, were a sheikh indisposed, a replacement should be found, and let a substitute stand in for the very old. Bachir nodded politely before speaking: 'Allow me to give an assessment of five years of the UN in Western Sahara.'

'I am not satisfied, what has been achieved so far is the cease-fire, which ended one means the Sahrawis had to bring about self-determination and independence, the other side rejects finding a solution through dialogue and direct negotiation. The Sahrawis have a right to self-determination and they look to the fair and correct application of the settlement plan as agreed by the two parties and adopted by the Security Council, specifically, this means compiling a voters' list based on the Spanish census with a modest increase to accommodate population "progression" since 1974.' He emphasised the need for effective UN authority in Western Sahara, to ensure respect for the 'final outcome', if the outcome were not respected then the referendum was 'only a battle for a lost war'.

'What have we, the Polisario Front, had in return for accepting the cease-fire? Accelerated occupation of Western Sahara: after annexation in 1975 of our territory, a settlement programme with over 80,000 Moroccans forcibly encamped beside the occupied Saharan towns, imitating Sahrawi refugee camps. Disheartening, but I like the truth.' He continued, in a long flowing speech, to underscore the need for greater UN assertiveness in face of a repressive foreign power, to assure safety for returning refugees: they must not be forced 'into the mouth of the wolf'. Polisario had not terrorised or used violence, they just wanted independence for their homeland. Bachir referred again to the value of face-to-face talks before finishing: 'The underdog and victims of injustice sometimes speak a lot because they feel people aren't listening enough.' Legwaila responded that never would both parties be completely satisfied, they must not be too absolute.

A visit to Smara refugee camp followed before meeting assembled sheikhs, where every sheikh delivered a homily, in essence similar: 'Seventy-five per cent of the applicants have nothing to do with us.' One refused participating further in this charade: how could he identify 'these dunes of sand borne in from Morocco'. Another argued that sheikhs on the other side were 'yes' men, who admitted to being pressured, even under oath constrained to do as instructed. The eldest sheikh voiced support for 'this UN camel if it is a good one leading to a free and fair referendum; if not, you can save your time and resources, we shall go back to our first camel and fight.' The OAU observers told the mission that Minurso had come a long way in the search for peace, problems were not insurmountable despite difficulties, Minurso withdrawal was unthinkable, that the African continent would not understand, they looked to the Council to encourage dialogue.

The Security Council ambassadors had rooms for the night, Ladsous and I were escorted to two hospitality tents, decked with rugs on walls and floor. A Sahrawi woman addressed me in Hassaniya while pottering about, poured water over my hands, adorned me with a necklace of cloves, sprinkled more rose water, then waited for me to lie down, drew up my blanket and left me to sleep, retired to a far corner only to reappear in the morning with more rose water. By eight o'clock we were assembled for a 'second round of talk'.

Bachir again presided. To his left sat Boukhari, arrived from New York; to his right Majid, as I knew him, now listed as Radi Bachir Sgaiar (most had *noms-de-guerre* as well as their traditional threefold name) and Polisario representative in the Nordic countries, the National Union of Sahrawi Women was represented by Senia Ahmed, a strong personality who filled the part. The others, all thinner, were familiar from identification. Bachir wasted no time, identification commission teams must be told unequivocally that if the two sheikhs disagreed and there was no documentary evidence the applicant was unacceptable. Minurso should be empowered to convoke any sheikh needed and control transfers. If direct dialogue between the parties were helpful, Polisario stood ready, Arabs and Israelis, Bachir said, had talked, Morocco and the Frente Polisario could not be more distrustful, more hateful towards each other than Arabs and Israelis, Polisario was determined to make every effort to achieve a lasting, just solution. The Security Council representatives reacted politely. 'Thank you,' Bachir said with his most ingratiating smile, 'thank you very much.' There had been an accumulation of mistrust and deceit. The sheikhs were people of the desert who loathed lack of clarity, this mission regenerated momentum and hope.

Polisario placed no obstacles, only wished to enhance Minurso's capacity to handle practical aspects, it was not they who imposed a daily limit or introduced holidays and national days; work time was sacred. Bachir was kind enough to say that he had every respect and esteem for me, but the problems were overwhelming and could be resolved only by the Security Council. The mission was then received by 'President' Abdel Aziz, who summarised, in Arabic, Polisario's position. We departed for Laayoune to be greeted by the press.

Legwaila, as leader of the delegation, replied to questions. He asserted that Polisario was committed to the settlement plan, the United Nations would redouble efforts to accelerate proceedings for the referendum to be held by the January 1996 deadline. At the Palais des Congres Sahrawis en masse greeted the mission, the floor was packed and balconies brimmed over with men in blue or white Sahrawi *drah* and dark turbans and women in colourful flimsy *melhafa* with which they fussed constantly, all waved Moroccan flags and as the delegation entered ululated excitedly. The president of the provincial assembly and the governor delivered lengthy formal speeches, they underlined the unswerving commitment of all Sahrawis to their identity as Moroccans and for everything Morocco had done to develop the region. Loud clapping and more ululation. Delays in identification were due to obstacles raised by the other side but thanks to Moroccan good will twenty-seven thousand people had been identified whereas the others had not even achieved fifty per cent of that figure. The member for Laayoune, speaking also on behalf of other parliamentarians from the 'Saharan provinces', reaffirmed the indeflectable attachment of Sahrawis to their '*marocanité*.' Flag waving and clapping, while an interpreter struggled inaudibly to complete the final phrase. A Sahrawi elder denounced the twisted campaign of the 'Polisario mercenaries' to obstruct identification, again stressing the commitment of Sahrawis to their '*marocanité*' and their oath of allegiance. Legwaila replied, thanking King Hassan for the warm welcome received in Laayoune, he assured his listeners that the mission was there to speed the process.

Next day we flew to Mauritania. On the long flight the mission plied me with questions: if both sides argued for greater Minurso control, why was this not happening? The answer, of course, that each wanted Minurso empowered to coerce the other. Legwaila emphasised how both sides invoked the settlement plan; each in their way, and only their way, I said. To speed up identification Interfurth thought mobile teams a constructive proposal. Though theoretically attractive, it was impracticable, the logistics involved in transport, housing, feeding and supplying sheikhs and observers from both sides, the OAU, as well as entire identification teams with their equipment, were as daunting as they would be costly.

President Ould Taya of Mauritania insisted that 'Problems with identification are problems which the parties create'. For Minurso to collapse would be devastating, this was a matter of life and death to the region, he could not believe that the UN might simply withdraw, giving war the green light. A question about numbers identified was referred to me and in answering I slipped in a request to open identification centres in Mauritania. The president agreed at once; this was a major achievement, which I flagged for the ambassadors' attention before they departed to meet counterparts in Nouakchott. Ladsous later confided that Polisario's 'foreign minister' had been received discreetly in Mauritania the night before, from what they were hearing Polisario would certainly consider regional autonomy. Cardenas argued forcefully that the Council should promote dialogue.

No sooner had the mission left than Bachir wanted action. I was to write to both parties, through the Security Council, asserting full immunity for sheikhs and observers, access to communications (at Smara centre, after working hours, power was switched off), freedom to exercise, and some outside contact. Security around centres to be maintained by Minurso civilian police; Moroccan policemen should not be visibly present, they were a '*force de repression*'; Morocco divided people into gaolers and prisoners, and Western Sahara was a prison. Identification should follow a standard procedure, commissioners must, must, he repeated, pose supplementary questions when a sheikh merely nodded assent, it was insufficient for a Moroccan sheikh to say vaguely: 'Yes, I know the face' which was tantamount to admitting he did not know the person. And how did we propose to identify those who were detained or in prison?Then, as I was leaving, Bachir, with his hang-dog look, asked, in a near whisper, that for the time being I not talk about Puerto Rico.

Azmi, equally impatient, called for an evening meeting. Flanked by his acolytes he seated himself across the conference table from me and my immediate team. That he had instructions was obvious: he launched into demands, a long-term programme for identification, to be modified only in exceptional circumstances, the timely availability of sheikhs and their transport as Minurso's responsibility, to cope with interruptions due to 'reciprocity' Minurso should decide to continue working in the absence of one party. I reminded him that we had a complete identification plan but it was necessary to advance in stages. 'No, said Azmi, 'Minurso must impose a comprehensive identification programme to include all the 183,000 applicants presented by Morocco.' Applicants could be identified wherever they were, he said, Morocco would take responsibility to install identification teams, sheikhs and observers, alternatively, Morocco stood ready to move everyone concerned to the territory. Minurso could decide but a decision was urgent. Since the great majority of these applicants claimed membership of northern tribes, grouped in the census into tribal groupings only sparsely represented on the other side, I raised the sheikh problem, Polisario did not have sheikhs who could know individuals drawn from an extensive range of sub-fractions and refused … Azmi interrupted: 'And we reject those people over there.' It was for the identification commission, he said, to prevent Polisario indulging in dismissive pre-identification.

The census listed the Western Saharan Sahrawis in their seven principal tribes; others, like those who followed Spain from elsewhere, were grouped under the heads: 'tribes of the south', 'northern tribes' and 'prophet descendants' as if these were tribes. Most contentious was 'northern tribes', sparsely represented in the census but the category into which the vast majority of persons presented by Morocco fell. Whatever their remote ancestry – it was an accepted fact that certain Sahrawi tribal groups had settled in the north – they could not qualify to vote according to Polisario. The prospect enraged Polisario however many times I assured them that the number of applicants had no bearing on the number likely to qualify. It was also impossible for a sheikh, even if a Polisario sheikh could be found from one of the sub-fractions included, to know and identify the thousands drawn from a multiplicity of sub-fractions, it was farcical. Azmi's answer: 'Take two sheikhs from the party that is willing to cooperate.' 'Fine, 'I said, 'though I wonder how Morocco would react to working with two Polisario sheikhs.'

Azmi changed subject. Flight times were a problem, they were complicated, I explained, by continuing insistence on matched movement from each side – a matter of security, said Azmi sternly, case closed. Restricted hours for aerial traffic in Tindouf did not help; I should put pressure on Algeria; Morocco kept Laayoune airport open day and night to facilitate Minurso's work (as if that were the reason). A related issue concerned the transfer of sheikhs and observers to the Polisario Dakhla camp one hundred and eighty kilometres from Tindouf across stony desert, it was inconceivable that aged sheikhs be subjected to travelling overland. 'I have raised this with Algiers,' I said. 'Yes, maybe,' he replied, 'but there has to be a solution, Polisario would long since have suspended their participation had their sheikhs been subjected to driving 700 kilometres to Dakhla.' I was expecting the Algerians finally to approve helicopter overflights but thought it prudent to await confirmation. Almost as an afterthought, Azmi accused Polisario of running an illegal postal service, returning with suitcases full. I had no objection to 'sheikh-mail', I said, and Azmi came to accept, grudgingly, though only the sheikh, not the representatives – being political agents – might carry correspondence.

The Security Council mission had made nothing easier. Each side looked to the Council, and Minurso, to exert pressure on the other. Morocco wanted commitment to identify 183,000, on its terms, Polisario wanted assurance that this would not happen. Both argued over every detail because they foresaw the consequences, the moment was approaching when most persons included in the census would be identified but only a fraction of the applicant mass presented by Morocco. We were close to finish identifying applicants from the larger sub-fractions, and smaller numbers meant additional sheikh movement, compounding the problem of sheikhs not promptly available, or said to be unwell, or without an acceptable replacement. Then in a day everything changed.

The peaceful demonstrations in Laayoune had led to arrests, that was expected. The Security Council mission had barely returned to New York when the eight demonstrators, young men, were sentenced. Their sentences, fifteen to twenty years in jail, exceeded all expectation. Polisario was outraged. On the same morning, came two 'immediate' encrypted cables: one was a message from Algeria confirming agreement to grant limited overflight rights to Dakhla camp, permitting identification to resume, the other forwarded a letter to the secretary-general from Abdel Aziz announcing suspension of Polisario's participation in identification.

14

End and restart

Sheikhs and party observers were immediately withdrawn. We were asked to help them leave, in opposite directions, simultaneously, no incidents occurred, no hostages were taken. After drafting my report to New York I returned to the hotel around midnight to encounter a cheerful Azmi and his observer team still at table. The mood was positively jovial; rarely had I observed Biadillah so content, they invited me to join them for a glass, which I politely declined. Morocco had achieved the objective of having Polisario withdraw while Morocco continued to respect the Security Council and settlement plan. It came as no surprise when Azmi tracked me down next morning, Saturday, to say the minister wished to see me first thing Monday, he suggested that I be accompanied by my senior staff.

At the ministry of interior, the number two, Ben Hachem, and his advisors spent two and a half hours trawling through a detailed identification programme for over 100,000 applicants from outside the territory. To limit the transfer of more people to Western Sahara – inevitably a bone of contention – what about temporary centres in places where a thousand applicants lived or could be assembled? Azmi said that not all came forward so we settled on fifteen hundred as affording a week's work. Ben Hachem drew circles on maps, which he enjoyed colouring in with a felt tip. The minister wanted specific options, a complete programme of work, to be implemented forthwith. The exercise struck me as surreal since at no point did I believe we could proceed with one-sided identification of all these people, in Morocco to boot. I stressed that Morocco's cooperative attitude was certainly appreciated and Minurso was prepared and technically equipped, but a decision to proceed with one side only depended on the Security Council, it was essentially similar to the first option, option 'A' of the year before – 'Remind me,' said Ben Hachem – which the Security Council did not endorse, to allow identification with only one side participating. Discussion followed with Basri in person, he reiterated what Ben Hachem had said, brushed aside my concerns, seemed amazingly confident that Morocco's position would prevail. When the meeting with advisers finished I spoke to him *tête-à-tête*: might this be a time to pass a message to Polisario? Basri was unreceptive, to whom? They were not serious, he appeared relaxed at proceeding without Polisario. I was at sea, now, deep sea fishing, I reflected on leaving, the challenge to keep the big fish on the hook, giving line as necessary, let it run, but don't let the line snap.

In New York the returning Security Council mission faced the secretary-general with a bleak assessment. Morocco had overdone the emphasis on identifying the 180,000 and heavy-handedness in sentencing the demonstrators cast a deep shadow. The US issued a harsh statement after the Council adopted a resolution mandating a brief extension of Minurso, conditional on convincing progress in the coming two months. The decision signalled America withdrawing, whether others would feel obliged to withdraw was a question. But one thing was clear: the US was determined to convey a message to the parties: 'Get on with the referendum – it's the only game in town – get it over with in the near future, or we get out.'

The eight sentences in Laayoune provoked Polisario to play tough. 'For the international community to take us seriously,' according to a spokesman, 'we would have to go back to war', 'We are cleaning our weapons.' The force commander reported increasing Polisario movement of heavy vehicles, tyres being replaced on armoured cars, issuance of weapons, cancellation of soldiers' leave, and a threatening attitude to Minurso observers on patrol or helicopter reconnaissance. When van Baelen told their fourth sector commander that he expected to be back in a month to six weeks, the commander replied coolly 'Then we will take you hostage.' Fear is that Polisario might resort to hostage taking, other attempts to capture headlines had failed, even to attract sustained international attention, while media coverage when UN hostages were taken made everyone aware of Bosnia, though hostage taking had not been Sahrawi practice since the days when tribesmen recovered shipwrecked infidels on the coast, where shipwreck was common, and held them as slaves or for ransom. I asked for an appointment in Rabouni.

Kheddad was not available, his assistant would receive me if I had something of substance to convey, Bachir needed an official request indicating my agenda but preferred waiting. Azmi meanwhile was pressuring me to move on detailed identification planning. We double-checked records, compiled lists and refined procedural instructions – and held our breath. That Sunday I was walking on the deserted sands bordering the Atlantic – only for serenity to be disrupted by an urgent summons. King Hassan II asked me, the force commander, civil police commissioner and head of administration, to a reception, in forty-eight hours time. I remonstrated with Azmi who had told me that because of drought the king had cancelled traditional events. Our head of administration, on local leave, had to be traced and a special landing organised to collect him. In Rabat, impeccably dressed and uniformed, we were escorted into the king's presence, given precedence ahead of the diplomatic corps and Moroccan dignitaries. I greeted the king, who, dismissing Basri's introduction as unnecessary, shook my hand – no hand-kissing. I acknowledged the princes and moved into the garden. The overcast, muggy day was enlivened by fountains playing and a military band in a corner of the grounds where ornate marquees were lavishly stocked with sophisticated food, pastries and soft drink. Snoussi appeared then de Coignac, who took me aside.

He had been with Filali, he said. Filali was negative about the UN and resentful of unfair reporting, as he saw it, which failed to reflect Morocco's cooperation and wish to proceed, he was annoyed that I ignored him in favour of Basri, though he must have known Basri was adamant that the Sahara dossier had been entrusted to him by the king, was his '*chasse gardée*', his 'game reserve', insisting that I had no business with other ministries. By monopolising my time, Basri did everything to impede my visiting the foreign ministry as well as diplomats. To Snoussi I said that I would welcome seeing Filali, Snoussi invited me home after saying he would convey a message to Filali.

First Basri wanted to meet, to know why Bachir had turned against me. I was not convinced that he had, I said that Bachir had hoped I could facilitate dialogue, organise talks at the highest level, and so long as I was potentially useful they cooperated but they might be giving up. Basri said: 'They can't be trusted. All they do is make propaganda.' Polisario know their weakness, I said, and such clout as they have is bolstered by world public opinion, international sympathy, they play their cards accordingly. Take recent events, they exploited the sentencing of eight youths to fifteen-twenty year jail terms – 'None of your affair,' Basri interjected aggressively – and the one hundred thousand plus for identification to mount a campaign before the OAU summit and in the US. 'Puerile,' said Basri. 'They had barely a headline before being entirely eclipsed at Addis by the attempted assassination of Mubarak, and in Washington their decision to withdraw attracted virtually no attention.' 'In New York there were expressions of sympathy,' I said. He interrupted: 'They faced more criticism than they gained support for their decision to suspend participation in identification.' Their propaganda obsession, he badgered me, undermined prospects for serious negotiation. Basri ended that Polisario would not be returning to the process or at least not in the immediate future. As I rose to leave he said he understood that I had deferred my return to Layoune and would be meeting Filali. Yes, I said, ignoring the query implied.

Filali, refined features and bearing impaired by the accident that left him limping and eye damaged, offered me a chair beside his own, then waited for me to talk. I apologised vaguely for not having seen him more often before summarising my view of Polisario's latest action and the current situation. Morocco wished to proceed, he said, and he resolutely rejected the right of Polisario to veto the process by suspending their participation. Morocco's position had been fully reported to New York, I assured him, but identification could continue on one side alone only with Security Council approval, it would be tantamount to 'option A' of the previous year, which, as he would remember, had not been agreed. Admittedly, matters had evolved since. He made a light-hearted remark and smiled, an engaging smile, though baffling to know which eye was smiling. The mood relaxed, I mentioned talks. Polisario's propaganda obsession made that difficult, he said, 'Besides, who do you talk to? they don't speak with one tongue. Anyway, it's Algeria decides: "His Master's Voice", and unfortunately there is not one master but many, Algeria is divided. Dembri, "*petit diplomate*", no, he doesn't take decisions, the military do, with their entrenched privileges and power.' Filali sounded very pessimistic, Algeria was not genuinely interested in a solution, their country was a mess.

King Hassan, as an act of clemency, following tradition on the occasion of his birthday, commuted the Laayoune demonstrators' sentences.

A press release affirmed Polisario's decision to resume participation in the work of the identification commission. Bachir qualified their willingness to return to the process as conditional on restored credibility: Minurso's lack of control to be remedied, to be boosted in directing identification and other aspects of the plan. And they wanted bilateral negotiations, US assurances – only – carried weight. Azmi came to announce the 'good news' about the return to identification. Basri asked for a meeting, next day.

Only briefly postponed, it began late morning and lasted some two and a half hours. I was confronted by Azmi, Ben Hachem and Snoussi as well as Basri in hard-hitting mood. The process so far in both territory and camps suffered from inadequate staffing, slowness in implementation, interruptions, and other short-term difficulties. Minurso staff lacked impartiality; he accused commissioners of bias in seventy-five per cent of cases. Morocco had been too conciliatory, too accommodating, and would henceforth insist on rigour. Morocco was prepared to pre-identify the 100,000 outside the territory completing this in about six weeks prior to identification '*sur place*', it was necessary to speed up proceedings, it was costing Morocco much; get it over with and get Minurso out – then turning, called me Erik, and said that was not directed at me personally. Grim again, he continued: 'Greater impartiality is essential; commission members should be capable of evaluating the views of the other sheikhs who manifestly act on political instructions'. He planned to invite interested diplomatic representatives and some correspondents for a public statement on Morocco's commitment to the process and intentions with respect to the 100,000, then stopped abruptly to ready for the coming of King Hassan's good friend and new president of France, Jacques Chirac.

Rabat fêted President Chirac while I went to Tindouf. Together with the independent jurist I met Kheddad. Kheddad expressed pleasure at the visit, assured Professor Roucounas that Polisario justice conformed to Sharia law, gave him a copy of Polisario's constitution and suggested he meet their minister of justice. To me he voiced dismay at the 100,000 Moroccan applicants, he counted on the commission: in disputed cases recorded interviews might be valuable. Turning to practicalities, he said that air conditioning was being installed in the premises occupied by Moroccan sheikhs and observers, he would verify personally that it functioned at camp Dakhla. I confirmed that helicopter overflights had been authorised and that Minurso would provide additional four-by-four vehicles if required. Polisario agreed the identification programme proposed – with exceptions: they rejected three census groups: Ait Baamran (H41), Tribes of the North (H61) and Tribes of the South (J51/52). Azmi, after reviewing the programme, had few quibbles except to insist that Tribes of the North and others be included.

On 1 August I flew to Nouakchott primarily to confirm what had been, almost casually, accepted during the Security Council visit. The president, Maaouya Ould Taya, soft-spoken and gentle – shy, Boutros-Ghali described him – welcomed me warmly back to his country and offered dates. Their tradition of hospitality, he said, prescribed offering a visitor dates, dates were first for greeting visitors; secondly, sold for income, only thirdly eaten by family members. The Mauritanian dates I was always given were excellent, I said, thanking him. He asked me to elaborate on progress in identification.

A programme of work had been presented to both sides, I said, but the very large number of applicants from northern tribes posed a radical problem, Morocco insisted on their identification, Polisario refused. In Mauritania some fourteen thousand completed forms had been received and I asked for the president's formal consent to our opening identification centres. Ould Taya seemed visibly surprised, which surprised me since he had apparently agreed during the Security Council mission. Mauritania's involvement, he thought, was limited to authorising offices where Sahrawis could complete an application. The coming and going of various groups, military and police, might jeopardise security and stability and lead to incidents, he had no desire to see the country further implicated. The president paused. The outcome of the referendum depended on whether or not Morocco's 100,000 were included, were they to vote, eighty to ninety per cent might be in favour of Morocco, if not, the result would be too close to call. He considered the 50,000 or so already identified to constitute the bulk of genuine Western Saharans. He congratulated me on all that had been achieved, he remained optimistic, encouraged me to continue; and he supported negotiation between the parties. Reverting to the opening of identification centres he undertook to appoint officials to study the matter; he was confident of finding a solution. Then he nodded to his advisers, who departed the chamber together with my assistant and secretary, leaving the two of us in private.

We needed contact between the two sides, talks, I said. The settlement plan offered a choice between independence and integration, an intermediate option was wanted: some degree of regional autonomy. King Hassan had said: 'Leave me the flag and the stamp; all else is negotiable.' A large disgruntled minority, if the referendum failed to produce an overwhelming majority in favour of one side, would create innumerable problems, also affecting Mauritania. As one who had succeeded his complex balancing act, a man committed to moderation and regional stability, he was an ally I sought to enlist. He reacted with warmth, even complicity in his tone, he said he believed that Algeria, where he had been recently, wanted compromise, as did he, and he was sure Polisario wished to talk. Was Polisario's spokesman still Bachir? I asked. He was, Ould Taya was sure. Who could influence Morocco, I wondered, the US, France? France, yes, he replied, but mainly the US. The ambassadors of the US and France asked to meet me after the audience. The French ambassador promised to be my advocate in convincing the president to allow identification centres, the US ambassador, a refined WASP with beautiful soft eyes, said little in a pronounced accent – we were all speaking French, but she stressed that action was essential in the next month or two otherwise the Congress could be expected to cut funding. A sandstorm was rising when we took off for Laayoune.

Azmi phoned to know why I had seen the president of Mauritania. Mauritania, though recognised as an interested country, was not a party to the dispute and, as the minister had made abundantly clear, beyond the identification zone. Before I could respond Azmi said that Basri was coming and wanted a meeting. The following day Basri arrived in state, flags flying to salute his motorcade; with my senior collaborators I was invited to the governor's seaside residence. Basri placed me in the seat of honour, he was light-hearted, addressed me as Erik, said '*tu*' several times, repeated '*comment ca va*?' and plied us with fine seafood. The working meeting was for later, he said, while making conversation. Then with a torturer's knack of abruptly changing tack announced his decision to proceed to the Laayoune identification centre. Morocco had taken exception to Polisario officials entering centres on the other side, I reminded him; that was different, anyway irrelevant. Certain that he would appear with the customary suite of train-bearers for paparazzi coverage, I dispatched my executive assistant post haste to the centre: to advise Polisario's representatives, stressing that the visitation was in the interest of transparency and wider media awareness, the press would cover the minister witnessing identification, something Polisario said they wanted. I prepared for the worst.

To my relief the response was muted even when Basri with retinue arrived at the centre like a conquering hero come to reclaim his estate. Our civilian police asked permission to open both double gates to admit the vice-regal procession, which I refused; it was best to preserve a semblance of normality. Though there was nothing normal about Basri's media act, he pretended to be an earnest applicant, had his photograph taken and was prepared to be fingerprinted, after which he sat at different desks to be filmed. Departing he reconfirmed our working meeting for five-thirty.

Five minutes ahead of time my senior staff and I arrived at an empty lobby. Three minutes past the scheduled hour came Basri's motorcade, noisily: the minister accompanied by his cheerleaders, obsequious counsellors, and recording media. All were ushered to an expansive conference chamber, its ornate wooden ceiling a testimony to earlier Spanish occupation. Round a massive table thirty to forty personages were packed; behind stood army officers and lesser support staff and a battery of photo-journalists. Basri motioned for me to sit at one of two top seats, with microphones, several microphones, before each. The meeting came to order, reverential silence preceded Basri delivering in his most assertive manner, his take-no-prisoners voice, a prepared statement. Cameras focused, he presented me with two letters. Morocco was organised to open forty new centres; it was committed to identifying 50,000 applicants a month, the Security Council mission had been informed, Morocco wanted to move ahead and rejected obstacles and delays continually imposed by the other side. He trailed off into a sequence of attacks on the other's manoeuvring and prevarication, and stopped. The microphone before me alive: Basri gave me the floor.

I was unprepared for any formal speech and quite unprepared for this particular occasion, we had come for a 'working meeting.' Anxious not to be misinterpreted or misreported, measuring every phrase, I thanked Basri for Morocco's commitment, their offer of assistance and willingness to proceed; the issue of how to continue identification lay with the Security Council, additional personnel might also be required. Basri offered to provide personnel: Morocco had conducted sixteen referenda, had the people and relevant experience. The meeting, a massive publicity exercise, trundled on, Basri reiterated that Morocco would not be subject to Polisario's veto, they were determined to take the process expeditiously forward, they were fully prepared. He called for snap comments from two governors of 'southern provinces', who both, on cue, confirmed readiness, with premises, equipment and all, to open centres the following Monday morning. Basri closed with an instruction to governors and others to resume detailed planning.

Basri counted on my conveying his letters and Morocco's commitment to the secretary-general and the Security Council in New York. I promised, but stressed that only with the Council's endorsement would it be possible to conduct identification in circumstances where one side was unlikely to participate. Action, he insisted, action. Ginsberg phoned next day to check his draft dispatch for Washington that Morocco was opening forty new centres in 'the south' and I, according to Basri, had agreed. That I denied, knowing whatever I said would be meticulously analysed, I had consulted my French-speaking colleagues on leaving Basri. My executive assistant was irate: 'He tried to rape you', but I had reacted correctly, I upheld principles, UN authority untarnished, politely acknowledging Morocco's readiness to contribute but with no commitment to accept 'Moroccan' centres. It was a relief, when the national press arrived, to find, below Basri's voluminous coverage, me succinctly and correctly quoted. As well – since I was about to meet Polisario.

Bachir had agreed and proposed mid-afternoon in Ausserd camp. The temperature at around 50 degrees was blistering, suffocating, just breathing a mammoth effort; at least there was no blowing sand, on a previous visit to Ausserd the camp virtually disappeared in sand dust and the meeting tent blew over. We met this time in a small, almost windowless room in the stifling heat, conditions hardly propitious for compromise. I gave Bachir the gist of Morocco's position, he had already heard; anyway it was nothing new, not worth discussing. Had there been any progress – he thought none – on the appointment of an 'adviser', a deputy to me as head of mission? Bachir was not really interested. My 'additional criterion' preoccupied him; what did he mean? My insistence on 'convincing proof' shocked Polisario, undermining their confidence in me and in the process. I had thought to set their minds at rest, when insisting on 'convincing proof' it was Moroccan anger I feared, not Polisario's. At the outset of identification I had assured Bachir, I reminded him, that burden of proof lay with the applicant; it was not for the commission to prove that someone did not qualify. Rare instances had siblings identified on different occasions and proof of one's paternity could be applied to a doubtful other, though such cases were exceptional. 'Convincing proof' was necessary to qualify. 'Convincing proof' he repeated several times, like a mantra. Had he forgotten it sounded good to the Council mission, including the Argentinian ambassador, a lawyer sympathetic to Polisario? Never before had I experienced Bachir so squashed looking, so remote from the Che Guevara image, captivating smile and bright eyes that enlivened his wild, woolly-haired freedom fighter persona. Perhaps the oppressive heat was to blame. He had nothing more to discuss. Identification, I began, … he interrupted to reject categorically any Polisario role in identifying the 100,000 from the north, even those who might be included in the census, Polisario refused to be involved. 'No,' Bachir said, 'these are not Sahrawis. We have no sheikhs. We will have nothing to do with it.'

Meanwhile, identification of the remaining census-listed sub-fractions was nearing completion. Polisario was entitled, like Morocco, to nominate its own observers, but it was a surprise when Moulud Sayed, their representative in Washington, arrived. Moulud, originally from Laayoune, asked to meet his family, and Azmi said yes, either at the observers' residence or at home, and then, according to Azmi, he did neither; it was pure provocation, to embarrass Morocco, to say that he had been refused permission to see his elderly mother; he devoted every moment outside the identification room to politicking. The Polisario People's Congress was about to open, though Moulud did not mention it. 'Do you think we are going to ask you to our Congress,' my commissioner in Tindouf had been told, 'We are going to talk about you – and criticise you.' Then, after eleven o'clock at night, I received a most urgent message: I was invited with the Minurso high command to be at Rabouni the following morning at 7 a.m. before proceeding to the People's Congress. I replied that I would depart Laayoune at 7 a.m.

Next day, the force commander, new police commissioner, deputy chairman, and I set off, landed at Tindouf before bumping excruciatingly over desert tracks to the October 12 school, where the Congress was assembling. The leadership was awaited, after a while Abdel Aziz entered to take his place on the podium; Bachir, looking uncomfortable, sat to one side. Three or four air-conditioning units in the wall rattled but had virtually no impact on the cavernous space and two thousand people; humanity plus 50 degree temperature created the closest I know to Turkish bath torture. The general and police commissioner were in uniform, I wore a suit and tie like the Algerian ministry and government representatives. I was wringing wet: shirt and trousers soaked as if I had taken a shower fully dressed, the unacclimatized police commissioner grew redder and redder – I feared for his health – as we listened to Abdel Aziz' rambling speech for an hour and a half.

The heat and sweat-generated humidity made it an effort to remain calm, made no easier by Adel Aziz announcing that the conference was running late because of 'the inability of the Minurso delegation, led by Erik Jensen, to arrive earlier.' For that reason speeches by friendly delegations were postponed to an evening session. Relief. We emerged into the heat outside which had the merit of being dry, so dry and so hot that in minutes our clothing had dried. Kheddad greeted me, he confirmed that I was not expected to speak, which I interpreted to mean we were free to leave. Bachir, who had ignored us on entering the hall, appeared, less nervous, friendly, smiling, Abdel Aziz, when I bad good bye, kissed me on both cheeks, the Algerian minister made platitudinously polite remarks. We left.

In Laayoune Azmi was seething. The Moroccan authorities took a dim view of my decision, of this extravagant and ill-judged *acte de presence*, the Polisario Congress was a political event of internal significance, had nothing to do with Minurso. When I hinted that we also accepted the king's invitation to the palace, he exploded: how dare I compare the two! An urgent call came to my rescue, the secretary-general was trying to reach me, Boutros-Ghali would be in Lisbon in two days time and wished me there. Movement control checked scheduled flights and found no connections that weekend to link Laayoune with Lisbon and Minurso aircraft were not authorised to fly beyond the mission area. I had a brainwave, Madeira was bound to have flights to mainland Portugal and our mission area could be interpreted to include Madeira. Late Sunday I reached Lisbon in time for the meeting; Snoussi, unknown to me, had also been invited.

Snoussi was closeted with Boutros. They emerged and I was given, to scan, a letter from Filali. Six pages densely inscribed were hard to skim, but the thrust was clear: Filali focused on the indisputable need to identify the 100,000. He criticised the identification commission as biased, and for hierarchising the criteria – which I refuted energetically – and insisted that there must be no distinction between the 100,000 outside and people in the territory, Minurso had to move ahead resolutely, Polisario could not have a right of veto. The secretary-general asked me to comment. Minurso applied no hierarchy of criteria, I was adamant, criteria 1 to 3 were easy to adjudicate, treatment of candidates under those census-related criteria was therefore straightforward and their cases processed expeditiously, that was all.

With respect to the 100,000 Minurso was technically equipped to handle those living outside the territory as well as those within. If Morocco insisted on identifying the 100,000 I saw a possible solution – but one which I much doubted Morocco would knowingly accept. Polisario did not have the sheikhs, and refused to participate in what they considered a charade. Identification could, theoretically, function with two sheikhs from whichever side – however, for that to have any credibility testimony would have to be underpinned by documentary evidence, and the only documents not challenged by Polisario were those officially issued before 1975. Applicants would be obliged to produce birth certificates showing them children of the man they claimed as born in the territory together with documentary proof of the father's origin and birth. The secretary-general found that convincing, two sheikhs from one side was contentious, of course, but if we insisted on appropriate documentary evidence and eliminated those without, we had a proposal for the Security Council, not an easy sell, but one he would support. Snoussi reflected before, to my utter astonishment, agreeing that the argument was sufficiently compelling, he did not question the documentation to be provided (as if unconcerned that hardly any of the 100,00 possessed Spanish papers), he would urge acceptance in Rabat. Boutros retired and Snoussi asked about my return journey, he invited me to join him on his official jet.

In Laayoune I was summoned to deal with an outrageous, unacceptable provocation. At identification sessions Moroccan observers and Polisario observers sat in the same row, though far apart, both were equally well placed to monitor minutely the conduct of sheikhs, applicants and the commission and to hear every syllable uttered. Both took notes assiduously, Polisario began using a laptop. None of the other observers understood why the opened laptop of Polisario's senior representative excited attention until the Moroccan sheikh, sitting opposite, noticed the lid, emblazoned with Polisario's flag. Everything stopped, the Moroccans reported instantly to Azmi. Azmi demanded immediate action and no one could deal with so serious an incident except me. The Polisario observer, unapologetic, explained disarmingly that the laptop had been a present from his daughter, that it was against Moroccan law to display Polisario insignia did not concern him, he said, and these were UN premises. We talked, eventually he conceded that just as Morocco had no flag or emblem in the identification area there should be none of Polisario, but there was no way he could or would remove the sticker, and he required a computer. I suggested we lend him an unmarked laptop, and finally he agreed. Identification was about to resume when Azmi called, he was not satisfied, if Minurso supplied a laptop to Polisario it must do the same for Morocco; only then would he sanction his people to work. We provided a laptop for the Moroccan observer, Leibek; when I asked him later whether he knew how to use a computer, he said 'no'.

With identification of uncontested tribes and sub-fractions complete in that area work at the Boujdour centre ceased. But when our civilian police began sealing the entrance Azmi demanded an explanation, centres were to remain 'open' until all applicants had been identified and around Boujdour large numbers remained. I was surrendering to Polisario again, granting it a right of veto, precisely as refuted by the minister, the applicants were all Sahrawis. The Security Council would have to decide after seeing the reports, I said, and declined to argue further.

In New York the US asked what was the final figure now Morocco had completed its vetting; Argentina was confused by the number of tribes, the responsible under-secretary-general admitting he was himself perplexed by reference to eighty-eight tribal groups when he had understood there were three or possibly seven. And why had identification in Mauritania not been finished. Botswana accused the parties – 'these guys' – of 'playing with the Council' and had to be reminded that voluntary cooperation was a premise of the settlement plan. I found it depressing that Council members had so shallow a grasp of the facts, with official reports unread or read very superficially. The Council adopted a toothless resolution provoking Morocco to dispatch a high level mission to New York.

It was Friday when I received a telegram from the secretary-general summoning me for Monday morning, ahead of Council members meeting the Moroccan delegation. Basri promised that 'cancelling' the king, who had asked to see me, did not in these circumstances constitute *lèse majesté*. 'I am well-informed' he said, unnecessarily, when we met in Rabat on my way through, 'I know everything, and I know what the chancelleries are saying you have said. What were you proposing to say to the king?' He was angry, he accused me of having manufactured an entirely false distinction between those in the territory and those from outside. Morocco could have presented 750,000, that was the number of those entitled as children of Sahrawi tribesmen, the number of applicants was only 183,000, they belonged to qualified sub-fractions and could be identified in the territory, or New York or Geneva or wherever.

My job, Basri commanded, was to complete identification, to implement the plan, or resign. Talks were what Polisario wanted, even the Algerians were not convinced; they had innumerable opportunities to let Morocco know if that was their wish. I accommodated Polisario, allowed them control while Morocco did everything to comply. He resented bitterly my 'even-handed' reporting to the Council, 'enough, enough of your balanced reports'.We were in his ornate pool-house, and suddenly benign he called me '*tu*', 'Erik' and invited me to join him at table. I complimented him on the surroundings; with a sweep of his arm enveloping the entire swimming-pool, he said 'I give it you. The swimming-pool; it's yours.' And he assured me right of access across his grounds and use of the pool-house. Then, with menace: 'But don't ask me, don't dream of asking me, to give up even the most minuscule thing at the expense of my country.'

Boarding the New York flight I encountered half the Moroccan government. Upgraded, I was ushered by a steward to the front cabin. Basri already seated, with a file open, waved aside the official next to him and called 'Erik, sit here, we are going to work,' and as I sat down, 'There's nothing better than work.' Basri was more honest than I had known him, ingenuous even. Morocco needed to be overinsured in any referendum, couldn't I help get more pro-Moroccans on the electoral roll? By way of answer I simply said this was a UN operation. He was insensitive to international opinion, dismissed as cultural imperialism and American interference, when 'all they care about is their dollar'. I tried steering him to discuss a compromise settlement on the Sahara. He looked thoughtful, as if about to barter in the souk, craftily assessing an opening offer, he asked: 'Well, what might they consider reasonable?' It was not for me to reveal Polisario's bottom line, which in any case I did not know, I replied; 'What would Morocco consider reasonable? But no further confidences followed.

New York was its old self with Fifth Avenue parading in brilliant October sunshine. The UN bustled, the General Assembly in session and preparations in their final stage for the 50th anniversary celebratory gathering of heads of state. Boutros-Ghali enjoyed it. His in-depth knowledge of Western Sahara made him easy to brief, and he remembered our discussion in Lisbon; I saw him after listening to an extraordinary presentation by the Moroccan delegation. The high level Moroccans deployed in a conference room near main committee rooms but attendance was sparse. Driss Slaoui, Counsellor to King Hassan II and former ambassador to the UN, began: Morocco had, did and would cooperate in implementing the settlement plan. 'You have heard of problems', he said. 'Successive postponements of the referendum and delays on the ground suggest that responsibility rests partly with Morocco. As it is, Morocco has behaved in exemplary fashion.' The minister of interior, he concluded, would provide full and detailed information 'to do justice to my country.'

Driss Basri stated that delays were attributable to the other party, Morocco had cooperated loyally with the UN, making repeated compromises to ensure success. Reciprocity was imposed by the others. Morocco respected its obligations, it had no desire to terminate Minurso; never must the implications for regional peace and security be forgotten. Basri tackled the core issue: identification. In overdrive he roared ahead, Morocco rejected any attempt to distinguish between the 182,000 applicants; resident or non-resident had no meaning; pre-verification to reduce the number would be contrary to the plan, to allege that Morocco presented applications from ineligible candidates was unacceptable; Morocco merely transmitted applications, the commission pronounced. Morocco was offering to identify thirty to fifty thousand people monthly and stood ready to open forty additional centres in and outside the territory. Obstruction, systematic obstruction, originated with the other party, they instructed their sheikhs to reject everyone they did not want, even individuals included in the census. Boujdour, Dakhla and Smara centres had all been closed when the others refused to participate. Commitment to a fair and durable solution to the Western Sahara issue was overdue, but Morocco could not accept excluding people, who were genuinely Sahrawi, only to speed it up. Basri referred to a folder, which had been circulated and was available in the room: the folder, overstuffed with documents, described the movement of Sahrawis into Morocco, and more; it demonstrated how all criteria had equal validity, Polisario leaders, including Abdel-Aziz, had applied under criteria 4 and 5. Desultory discussion followed.

To a question about vetting the 100,000, Basri indignantly replied that there were not 100,000, there were 181,787 applications submitted in due time. He repeated arguments about residence, hierarchy of criteria, then dismissed the suggestion of talks, earlier occasions for encountering the others had delivered nothing. 'Should Morocco lose the referendum vote, we will withdraw our army and administration and open a great embassy "*sur place*", if we win we will establish full sovereignty and Morocco will receive its children.' Boutros-Ghali asked me to resume what transpired, it could have been foreseen, he said, and prepared to receive the Moroccan delegation in his thirty-eighth floor office.

His recollection of Lisbon was clear, that way forward was now his decision and he wished me to present it thus when briefing the Security Council the following morning, but, first, he asked that I explain the proposal to the Moroccan delegation. They arrived, Slaoui leading in Basri, General Bensliman, gendarmerie commander, Snoussi and Azmi. Following traditional courtesies, the secretary-general gave me the floor to describe his plan in detail. All listened attentively, nodded, no significant objection or call for clarification; I failed to understand how compliant they appeared. Only Basri intervened to say he accepted with the proviso that should this procedure prove detrimental to Moroccan interests he reserved the right to invoke oral testimony. They departed to talk among themselves, I was left to prepare my address to the Council.

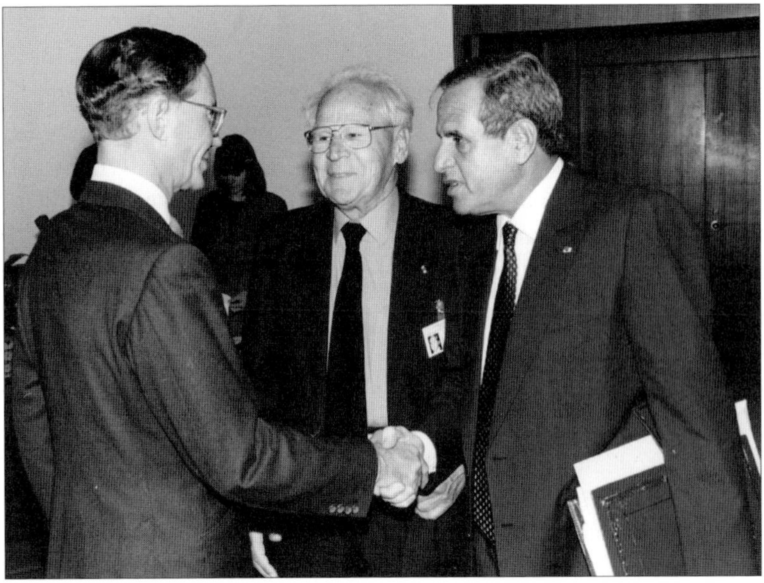

With Basri and Driss Slaoui at the Secretary-General's office in New York

I began by reminding members of the Security Council that the parties were at war. Fear, bitterness, and lack of trust inevitably coloured their conduct; the UN provided a convenient scapegoat. I dealt with specific criticisms: identification could not be said to lack transparency when both sides and the OAU were always present, diplomatic visitors came occasionally, limited media coverage was ascribed principally to minimal interest, though correspondents from America, Britain and continental Europe had visited the mission, television coverage was restricted to prevent its abuse, as feared by Polisario, for intelligence purposes. Firm control, by the parties, could not be denied, excessive though it might appear, it proved no deterrent to individuals coming for identification. Both sides were determined to produce the maximum number of 'their' candidates, and both sides benefited from comprehensive information about the other side; I had specifically requested names of anyone purportedly 'blocked', the very few isolated cases had an innocent explanation. Moroccan agents had been accused of confiscating 'receipts'; true or not, this was immaterial since the so-called 'receipt' was only a chit tokening attendance. More serious was the accusation that the sheikhs acted on instructions, but guidelines for commission members were clear and robust. The transfer and presentation of invalid candidates prolonged the process, it did not affect the outcome. Each case, subject to meticulous review, was checked to insure that all family members enjoyed identical treatment, therefore until all applicants from a given sub-fraction had been identified, in the territory, in the camps or in Mauritania, we could not publish lists.

Despite lack of precedent and both sides' constant wariness identification had endured and achieved more than once thought possible. Some 57,000 persons had been identified, we had virtually finished applicants from all non-disputed sub-fractions and groups, and a surge in tension was not surprising as the moment of truth drew nearer. When I consulted both Rabat and Tindouf and asked bluntly whether they wished to proceed after the stoppage, both said 'yes', with Morocco reasserting its right to present for identification some 181,000 people while Polisario upheld its refusal to identify applicants from the three controversial groups. That Minurso take full control remained purely theoretical so long as implementation of the settlement plan was predicated on the parties' voluntary cooperation. As a way forward the secretary-general proposed a compromise: a comprehensive work programme covering all applications from in and outside the territory, the camps and Mauritania would be transmitted in good time to both parties, they would be invited to observe proceedings as hitherto, alongside the OAU, and to present sheikhs or substitutes; where one side did not wish to take part or had no sheikh or substitute to propose, two sheikhs present could verify the applicant's personal identity while the commission authenticated relevant documents. A birth certificate was essential, issued in the country where the applicant was born, and showing the father's full name, and indispensable was documentation issued before 1975 by the competent authority to prove that the father had been born in the territory. Members of the Council were interested.

All listened attentively. Cardenas of Argentina, who knew the file better than some, emphasised that the *status quo* could not continue indefinitely; his delegation was in general agreement with the secretary-general's proposal. Legwaila of Botswana apologised for the mission having created confusion, he still had doubts, didn't want any of the 100,000 – 'yet we're on board.' Italy, Russia, Indonesia, Germany, UK wanted the SG's proposal fleshed out in writing, for Oman, France and US mandate renewal could not be viewed as routine, but all expressed support, encouraging me to develop my ideas creatively, though always concerned about costs; finally, the president, Nigeria, urged direct talks. My 'useful and comprehensive' statement was appreciated: I was 'most welcome to address the Council again.' But the US looked tired, Russia too, Britain slightly less so, China didn't look. Whether they, or the other member states, grasped the full implications was unclear, or whether they cared profoundly.

Azmi, knowing perfectly well that documents issued by the competent authority before 1975 could only be Spanish, trailed me in New York to say that Snoussi had created confusion. Deliberately or because he did not really understand, Snoussi had reported the documents to be used as Moroccan; that was the impression he gave the king. The king was allergic to any mention of Spanish documents, colonialism's lingering fingerprint. The multitude of Moroccan applicants had no Spanish documentation. Hence, as he prepared to attend the UN's fiftieth anniversary celebrations, King Hassan rejected the secretary-general's proposal: a betrayal 'after what we did in Sinai where we fought to defend what was left of his country, Egypt. Morocco lost men in that war, including a colonel-major.'

Azmi accused me of leading his country to the guillotine. Basri near screamed: 'It's you, Erik Jensen, who are responsible' for an outrageous, unacceptable, untenable move, action close to treachery when Boutros-Ghali's response to the Security Council's request for something in writing was eventually issued. I had prepared a meticulously worded draft, after which I was not consulted. The secretary-general found my draft too 'detailed' and the text elaborated, after my departure, by his New York advisers introduced a radical twist: identification could proceed in the presence of any two sheikhs with oral testimony admissible, as the king wanted, in 'exceptional' cases, but Morocco considered 'exceptional' unacceptably restrictive and Polisario would never agree to any exception to valid documentation. Boutros' attention was diverted by the heads of state and government assembling at the UN for the organisation's fiftieth anniversary.

For the anniversary celebrations King Hassan II took two hundred rooms at the Plaza hotel according to press rumours. He arrived in state, only to fall ill, sympathisers claimed the king's illness a sensitively orchestrated diplomatic reason for annulling a visit to Layoune marking the twentieth anniversary of the Green March. The king's illness was not diplomatic, not only was he ill, he was seriously ill, he was admitted for treatment in a private clinic. When he did emerge for meetings with US Ambassador Albright and Boutros-Ghali both remarked on his poor health. The American ambassador expected a traditional courtesy call and had not been specifically briefed; Hassan, coughing incessantly, launched into a demand for US recognition of Morocco's legitimate rights under the settlement plan, there could be no question of excluding oral testimony, oral testimony in Saharan society enjoyed a degree of primacy, which could not be discarded to accommodate Polisario. Morocco wanted the referendum, in accord with the settlement plan, but not at any price. He counted on American support, he had done much to assist the US achieve its objectives in the Middle East; now he was asking the US to help him in return.[1] Afterwards the king met Boutros-Ghali.

Boutros hoped to receive him *tête-à-tête*; 'It's much easier to talk to him then' he said to me. King Hassan arrived accompanied by the crown prince, Snoussi and 'the old man' – presumably Driss Slaoui. The meeting was neither easy, nor constructive, the king rejected the secretary-general's proposal, which Boutros took personally; he was angry with the under-secretary-general for having released a sensitive text without adequate consultation and for failing to warn of the likely Moroccan reaction. Snoussi blamed me for misleading an innocent SG. 'That's the Moroccans for you,' the under-secretary-general cabled – he was no great fan, 'you're in a tough business.'[2] Azmi warned that New York held me responsible and that the secretary-general was after my head, Morocco was furious and Boutros, anxious to sustain support for his re-election, would sacrifice me. Two weeks later, summoned to Geneva by Boutros-Ghali, I suggested it might be time to appoint another special representative, or did he wish me to remain? 'For another two years,' he said without blinking, 'even if you don't want to.'

15

In Limbo

NEITHER I NOR MINURSO in general was popular with the Moroccan authorities. Returning from New York I was informed that all mission personnel had been summarily asked to vacate rooms in the Parador Hotel by the following evening. The king's planned visit to Laayoune was given as reason for evicting us, the Parador was to receive a complete face-lift to welcome the royal entourage, decorators were already arriving, the Parador would become a jewel, Azmi's assistant said pursing his lips and kissing his finger-tips demonstratively. Minurso staff would be temporarily housed in such hotel rooms as could be found and in apartments. Laayoune, dressed like a bride to receive the royal bridegroom, removed the flags and bunting when the king's visit was postponed. The Parador remained unembellished, but we stayed billeted elsewhere. I flew to Mauritania and Algeria to consult the 'interested' countries.

Dust-covered Nouakchott was never the most welcoming of capitals. When we landed ten minutes after the scheduled arrival time nobody met the plane, the control tower had mistakenly alerted the ministry to a delay of at least forty-five minutes. Then in a dense cloud of sand protocol motored onto the airfield to confirm that the president would receive me in half an hour. Ould Taya was warm and smiling, he listened eagerly to news from New York, regretted having been unable to attend the fiftieth anniversary event. I told him of proceedings in the Council and the proposal for further identification, he approved of insistence on valid documents. I expressed appreciation for his agreeing to open an identification centre; to minimise civil disturbance he wished the centre sited away from where people were concentrated: Choum, the place proposed, was equidistant from Nouadhibou and Zouerate and accessible from Atar, a train service was available at minimal or no cost. Admittedly infrastructure was a problem, he asked for how many we required accommodation. Thirty, I said, or fifty for a centre with two teams. He looked startled, turned to an advisor, and said meekly: 'We were expecting about six.' He promised they would strive to provide what was needed – to Mauritanian standards. On leaving the presidency I was invited to meet the US, French, German and Spanish ambassadors and told them of the president's commitment, they were convinced that with the best will in the world Mauritania lacked means and expertise to deliver in a place like Choum.

In Algiers I was lodged not in the government compound for official visitors but the Hotel El-Djezir, the arrangements, with security noticeably less stringent than on previous visits, contributed to a more relaxed atmosphere. Dembri, the foreign minister, was welcoming, he approved of my approach, had received a full report of my Security Council statement, and not only Algeria thought it good. It was crucial to ensure the UN's probity and credibility. He had spoken warningly, he said, to Boutros-Ghali about the Moroccan flood of names; Boutros simply dismissed the 100,000, only 1,000 would pass, so why worry. He advised me to steer ahead, I had the confidence of both sides – and before I could interject a reservation – or at least their ear, I should not give up. The consequences of failure and UN withdrawal would be grave for the region. Dembri reflected a moment, as if shifting gear: contact, dialogue between the two sides was essential. Algeria, he said, stood ready to provide an aircraft to fly to Spain or the Canaries, or make tickets available for a scheduled flight.

Algeria could be counted as speaking for Polisario. Polisario were satisfied that valid documents from before 1974 proving a father born in the territory had to be Spanish, though they continued to worry that Morocco would bamboozle the commission or apply irresistible pressure. Boutros' admission of oral testimony 'in exceptional cases' was quite insufficient to allay Polisario concern, their UN representative, Ahmed Boukhari, erupted, and naturally held me responsible. Morocco persisted, the king adamant that the settlement plan provided for oral testimony: it could not be excluded any more than some groups could be treated differently. Oral testimony waxed to become, like Basri and Azmi began insisting, of primary importance.

Boutros was pessimistic. He opened, when we met, with Morocco's demand that all applicants be identified, though international opinion, like Polisario, had qualms about the numbers. That everyone be treated the same way seemed logical and the plan provided for oral testimony as well as written documents, but it was difficult to see how one-sided oral testimony could carry conviction. With that I agreed, I told Boutros-Ghali that although it was technically possible to complete identification of all groups, including those disputed, and of all persons, including those in Morocco, without Polisario participation, the exercise would have nil credibility if reliant on one-sided oral testimony. Were that to happen I was convinced Polisario would not hesitate to withdraw from the process entirely. Although their interest, in my view, was to remain engaged, and participating would strengthen their hand, Polisario refused steadfastly to believe the UN capable of resisting Morocco, and quoted this latest development. What if the identification commission, Boutros wondered, were to postpone doubtful cases and with a meticulous record of documents and oral testimony evaluate these later on neutral ground, in Geneva, for example? Two to three thousand cases, at most. Representative sheikhs, party observers and the OAU might be present. We would need to instruct commissioners discreetly. I disabused him of secret instructions, commissioners' sympathies were divided and guidelines, however confidentially conveyed, would become known; implied secrecy would further erode confidence in transparency and impartiality, so dear to Polisario. 'Would there ever be a referendum?' the secretary-general speculated. In my opinion a realistic, equitable, durable solution lay through regional autonomy, Boutros nodded. France did not wish to become implicated, he said reflectively, he had spoken recently to Chirac. 'The Americans?' I asked. 'No, 'he replied, 'they make a mess of everything.'

The Moroccans were furious with me for treating the three tribal groups differently and for requiring Spanish documentation; Polisario were angry because they attributed to me bland acceptance of oral testimony. Attention was diverted briefly by the 'landmark accord' at Dayton, Ohio, with people asking whether bombardment, killing, and war-exhaustion were needed to promote agreement. Though there might be lessons to be learnt, Bosnia and Western Sahara had little in common, I doubted it was Bosnia he wished to discuss when I received an urgent call from Tindouf: Bachir needed to see me.

Since the Polisario congress Bachir had been less visible. Some said that, like Achilles, he had been in his tent sulking, some that he was in Mauritania mobilising a second front against Abdel Aziz, others that he was planning to transfer allegiance. I had no inkling what he wanted, Bodan Kotewski, our commissioner, ex-Yougoslav diplomat and very astute, did not know: 'Perhaps he plans to go back with you.' If he brings a suitcase, we'll take that as a cue, I said. Bachir appeared, punctually, without luggage, but wearing a dark grey suit, classically striped shirt and navy blue Paisley patterned tie, never before had I encountered him so urbanely dressed. He looked well, smiling, relaxed, friendly, we chatted, conversation skirting his visit to Mauritania before he mentioned having been near Choum. For identification it was hopeless;

the Moroccans would welcome somewhere inaccessible to the Sahrawis. The Sahrawis were concentrated round Nouadhibou and Zouerate, yes and Nouakchott, identification near Choum would be a fiction, and eliminate at least three quarters of those who had applied. Bachir implored me to pressure the Mauritanian government, he understood their qualms about Nouakchott, but Minurso was already handling applications in Noaudhibou and Zouerate and there had been no incidents. And he wanted to discuss the 100,000.

He gave an approving nod to Spanish documents before insisting it would be a travesty to honour oral testimony if only Moroccan sheikhs were there to testify, the balance provided by one sheikh from each side was self-correcting, Moroccan sheikhs alone lacked credibility. And did Morocco really have sheikhs for all the sub-fractions that made up these groups? He brightened at my suggesting that Polisario present alternates, as sheikh, to influence proceedings: '*les absents ont toujours tort*' not only in love and war. He still had doubts, but at no point did he intimate that Polisario would withdraw entirely; 'If you want to make Morocco happy, pull out,' a US adviser was telling them.

I sensed Bachir had more to say and proposed a minute's *tête-à-tête*. With the commissioner out of earshot he reminded me of our earlier attempt to organise a meeting with King Hassan, would I repeat the effort? It might not be straightforward, I said, but I could try. The king was dying – he was certain; the meeting had to be with the king or crown prince, as well as Basri. He insisted on flying in a UN aircraft. To rule out any misunderstanding I repeated his request: to be received by either the crown prince or the king or both and willing to meet Basri, with transport organised by me, I promised to do what I could. 'The question of the Sahara will be resolved in the next two or three years,' he predicted as I was leaving.

Azmi, aware that I had landed in Laayoune, wished to be informed. I told him that Bachir and I discussed Polisario providing alternates to identify those groups in the north for which they had no sheikhs. Bachir did not threaten withdrawal, he appeared confident and relaxed, his responsibilities vis-a-vis Minurso not seemingly in doubt. Azmi paused: 'That was all. You rushed to Tindouf for that?' – he always knew my movements. I needed to reflect, I said, on something Bachir had raised. To my surprise Azmi failed to press me further over the next couple of days, I then asked to speak in private and conveyed to him the gist of Bachir's request. Azmi's reaction was instantaneous, he called the minister, he can always reach him when really important. To me he said reproachfully: 'You should have mentioned this earlier,' which made me think I had handled it correctly. He put down the phone, 'The minister wishes to see you without delay.' There would be an aircraft to fly me to Rabat the following morning for a one o'clock meeting with Basri, before he was due at the palace.

A phalanx of impressive cars proclaimed Basri's residence. 'The ministers are here,' said Azmi, and we waited for the ministerial conference to end before I was ushered alone into the presence, punctually by Basri standards. Basri listened with undisguised interest, his attention focussed, questions crisp, to the point. What precisely was the message? he repeated after asking about Bachir's attitude to the latest proposals and sheikhs; he would convey Bachir's request to the king, he was saying, when the summons came from the palace. He promised me a response by the following morning, if not that day, and left, Azmi, on the way out, said: 'Don't call any embassies, will you.' Nothing happened that evening nor for most of the next day. It rained, which everyone bar me found cheering. I was in my room when Azmi announced that a Council of Ministers had ended and Basri would receive me at 4 p.m., the hour was put back to 5.30, then 6 o'clock. At his house Basri emerged looking relaxed in a lozenge-patterned cardigan, he waved others aside so we could talk alone, His Majesty had decided.

Bachir would be welcome, given every assurance of safe conduct, security and appropriate respect, the meeting should be the following Monday. In three days time, I pointed out, and communications with Polisario were never straightforward; Bachir could be hard to locate. Well, if not Monday, then Tuesday or even Wednesday, Bachir would be received by the prince, and possibly His Majesty. When I asked gingerly after the king's health Basri said: 'His Majesty is in excellent health,' correcting himself: 'recuperating fast.' The king had designated the prince and Basri, total discretion was essential, Bachir could be accompanied, should he wish. I said I might come, thinking Bachir would welcome additional security. No problem, said Basri. An aircraft would be available from Laayoune, he continued, transfer from the UN plane had to take place in a remote corner of the tarmac, unobserved. Bachir would not want to fly Moroccan, I knew; since he would be flying from Tindouf with the UN could there be any objection to continuing north? Basri thought that hardly worth discussing, the king was making a gesture, a gesture of welcome, in offering an aircraft of the royal flight, Bachir had asked for the meeting, had he not? Back in Laayoune I called Tindouf immediately and instructed Bodan to convey to Bachir my wish for an urgent appointment.

Bodan ventured forth, after ten at night and again in the early morning. No luck, 'the man' had departed, some reported his leaving for Mijek; they claimed to have no means of contacting him. I left messages with our military observers at Mijek, asked that they enquire locally, and told our commissioner to continue, insistently, his pursuit. Biadillah, returning from identification in the camps, confirmed that Bachir had left for the south. (If Biadillah knew then Azmi and Basri would know.) I stood by throughout the weekend with an aircraft cleared for Mijek, or wherever 'the man' might be, departing from Mijek had the advantage of being easier to camouflage than taking off from Tindouf with everyone, including the Algerian authorities, certain to know. By Monday morning nothing had changed, an assistant still professed not to be aware of Bachir's whereabouts, and that he had no way of communicating. A Monday meeting in Rabat was obviously out, even Tuesday, and Wednesday began looking impossible; speculation as to his movements and the reason for his silence persisted through the week.

It was unthinkable that Polisario were without communication for so long. Either they chose not to convey my message or Bachir chose not to respond, he might have had his knuckles rapped, been ordered to abandon his plan, he had not been secretive at our meeting: when I enquired about the channel for any response, he said, almost casually, the office if he was not available. Then again, he might have decided this was not the moment, the election of Zeroual to the Algerian presidency was heralded as affecting Algeria's position. Zeroual, a general who had commanded the southern region and played an active role in training Polisario forces, was said to have a soft spot for Polisario.

Bachir had indeed been in the south, but I never discovered whether he had changed his mind or been refused permission or whether Zeroual's election had any bearing, Basri, who monitored my efforts to reach Bachir, twice daily, was free to draw his own conclusions. I could not help speculating that Morocco planned to 'turn' Bachir, arriving precipitately on his own initiative; why else had their response been so rapid and arrangements so accommodating. Bachir, when, after more than a week, he resurfaced in the camps glibly told Bodan that there was no urgent reason for him to see me in person. None of this was good for my diplomatic health, I had gone out on a limb for Bachir, and been snubbed, whatever the explanation, I had lost some of Basri's confidence in my ability to deliver, expending more than a sliver of the trust I worked steadfastly to build. It would be a while before I dared reopen the question of talks. UN news was no help.

The Council was near to agreeing a draft resolution when Morocco insisted on modifying a paragraph. The Polisario position hardened from rejecting the secretary-general's procedures for identifying disputed groups in the north to threatening withdrawal, Algeria stepped in with uncompromising arguments,

Zeroual's election was perhaps a factor, or increasingly ominous commentary on the king's illness with the prospect of imminent change in Moroccan politics. Few days passed without Polisario issuing a communiqué on Hassan's health: implying that he had only three or four months left to live, his collapse before the UN fiftieth anniversary celebration led doctors there to diagnosing the advanced state of his emphysema. With the Council far from unanimous, the principal authors of the draft resolution wanted to go to a vote, the time for decision had come: you could not please everyone in this affair. Italy, then Germany, saw cause to seek revised instructions, the US representative stated that if action were delayed to the following week, due to next day's official holiday in Italy, he could not be sure of his position. Voting was postponed. The secretary-general, in Europe for the Bosnia conference, summoned me to meet him.

In the 'salon' at Casablanca airport I discovered Azmi checked for the same flight, I could not resist thinking how expensive to Morocco my constant minding had to be. Azmi disappeared once we emerged from the terminal in Geneva; he may have had work beside monitoring me, I went straight to my hotel, past dreary patches of snow from a recent snowfall, chill permeated even the hotel room. The prospect of the morning's discussion did little to cheer me.

I told the secretary-general that I saw little alternative to the approaches tried: one, with Spanish documents, rejected by Morocco, the other, oral testimony, by Polisario. While identification could trickle to completion in the camps and, I hoped, in Mauritania, there was slight prospect for identifying the 100,000 plus presented by Morocco in the north. Assuming the Council would return the ball to the secretary-general's court we discussed options. He telephoned the Security Council president, the Russian Federation permanent representative, to suggest that the Council defer action until the secretary-general's return to New York when he proposed addressing it and contacted Madeleine Albright, the US ambassador, her voice so strident I heard every piercing word across the desk. He spoke also to others before confirming that the Security Council would ask him to continue consultations for three more months with a view to persuading the parties of an acceptable compromise. But nothing was likely to change, after another three months he would be seen as having failed, the US would close Minurso.

Neither Morocco nor Polisario, I said, nor for that matter Algeria or Mauritania, wanted Minurso withdrawn. Boutros mentioned that only days before Filali made that point. From my information none wanted to abandon the political effort while maintaining cease-fire observers, the conflict, frozen into 'another Cyprus' at considerable cost, held limited appeal for Morocco, while Polisario believed it served only Moroccan interests; it was disliked by Algeria, and dismayed Mauritania. The consequence of total withdrawal was equally unwelcome: serious regional instability, all four agreed.'What does Algeria provide to the mission?' Boutros-Ghali asked. I told him that we had use of Algerian army barracks outside Tindouf, which served as base for our military observers and accommodation for identification commission and civilian personnel. And Morocco? Minurso headquarters occupied a school compound in Laayoune, identification took place in appropriate buildings, and staff, military and civil, were housed in three hotels and in apartments. Boutros was mildly surprised at how much Morocco contributed. 'I have no brief for Algeria,' he commented, 'or, for that matter, the king.' 'Morocco and Algeria,' he mused, 'There is such deep enmity, like France and Germany, like Israel and the Palestinians.' To that extent? I said. 'Yes, yes,' he repeated, Algeria will keep nagging: a thorn in the side of Morocco. He paused for a moment, before saying: 'There will never be a referendum, I think we agree.'

'What we need is to wind up identification of sub-fractions for which there are sheikhs then, knowing the figures, they may negotiate,' I said. He looked me straight in the eye: 'How many are qualified to vote?' We were still identifying and initial findings were subject to review. 'What do you think? Give me an informed guess.' I did, on the basis of identification so far, numbers appeared fairly balanced, with no overwhelming bias, this assumed that a majority, but not all, in the territory would choose Morocco and everyone in the camps would vote Polisario. Identification of contested groups, if it took place, with Polisario participation, was unlikely to affect the voting list much. 'They'll talk, when they know,' Boutros said, 'This is not the time to publish results. When the moment feels right, they must be brought together.' Did he have a special envoy in mind? I asked. (Like Holbrooke in Dayton.) No, he said, and, with a half-smile, sending Garekhan, from his executive office, was not likely to achieve anything. A Security Council mission of the US, France and the UK would be another story, but they would not agree. Did he still want me to stay? 'You're doing a good job, yes,' he said. ' How old are you?' 'I'll be 62 next week.' 'I'm 73'.

Pending action in New York we worked to complete residual identification. Mauritania presented a challenge and was especially sensitive because any Sahrawi opting to be identified forfeited Mauritanian nationality: another example of the complications caused by muddling tribal identity and modern nationality.

The government wanted identification away from the main population centres, after Bachir rejected Choum Atar was suggested. Morocco said nothing negative, it was dismissed by Bachir as a place to exclude the Sahrawis. Of course, neither revealed that the dominant tribe around Atar had allied itself with the French in fighting the Reguibat.

The Polisario were as pleased as Moroccans were displeased by prospects in Mauritania, though even Mauritania paled beside Basri's anger at stalled identification. He resented the implication that Moroccan documentation was suspect, outraged at the very thought that his country could engage in forgery 'We are a state', he asserted, unlike, it was implied, those who were not. It was monstrous to imagine that an ancient, proud country like Morocco might behave improperly, there could be no question about the validity of Moroccan papers. What did the Security Council know, at least some of its members? 'Some are corrupt' he added. 'Corrupt in what sense,' I asked, 'beyond an impertinent assumption of status?' 'Not just that.' No, Argentina was corrupt. He had evidence of contracts in Algeria, so, of course, the Argentinian ambassador played the Algerian card in the Council.

Botswana summarized bleakly when the Council met: 'All the parties seem to do is to find ways of disagreeing with each other. It would be good if the Council could bludgeon them into compromise.'[1] The Council was unhappy, so was Morocco, so was Polisario, so were Minurso personnel with less real work. I went to Rabat but Morocco was in no mood for talking, Basri did concede that he thought Bachir had been honest, that I had not been deceived. Algeria probably got wind of the initiative, Basri thought, and called him off. Why was he not more circumspect? 'That's his style, his brother was the same, they could kill Bachir too', Algeria was suspected of having instigated the 'death in battle' of El-Ouali. Bachir was equally gloomy when I visited the camps.

The drive out of Tindouf set the tone: flat stony desert littered with unsightly black plastic clutching at thorny shrubs and the few scrawny trees. We skirted a vast, endless lake district, where the ground shone like water reflecting the great expanse of cloudless sky, the only 'mirages' surviving. Bachir saw little for us to discuss, he was reluctant to speak of a Polisario delegation to Washington, which had been received, I knew, by the administration but not on the hill, to the US the Saharan issue was peripheral; neither important nor of potential benefit. We drifted, becalmed in doldrums over stony sand.

Like a gust of wind Boutros-Ghali returned to surprise the Council, and me. I think he enjoyed the element of surprise. He ignored talking points he had been given, stating baldly that he had never believed there would be a referendum; it would be good, he thought, to turn identification to account, faced with the facts, the parties should become ripe for direct negotiation. Members were shocked, the other shock was at my expense. He named Garekhan as special envoy to develop a working solution; having agreed with me in Geneva that such an appointment was unlikely to be helpful, I admit to being more than surprised. Garekhan himself told the press that he was no expert on the Sahara, critics warned of his losing the way in shifting sands, the most brutal: 'If we want to make absolutely sure Minurso fails, leaving no stone unturned, why not appoint someone who speaks neither French nor Arabic.'[2] To Garekhan Boutros thoughtfully said: This is my Christmas gift to you. The special envoy was to begin work over the holiday, that meant me too. Christmas in the Muslim world had one advantage: neither Jingle Bells nor Rudolf the Red-Nosed Reindeer constantly blaring, though the landscape again recalled a manger-birth Christmas card on the drive from Casablanca into Rabat and as darkness fell the sky lit up with a panoply of stars. Basri was less Christmas minded.

Relations with Algeria were tense, he explained, when I asked about the abrupt suspension of Moroccan-Algerian cooperation within the Maghreb Union, Western Sahara the divisive issue. Morocco wished to deal with Algeria, Algeria rejected being made a party to the dispute, whatever Morocco claimed and the secretary-general might say. So what new ideas could Garekhan be bringing, he wanted to know, I was in no position to say. 'We shall listen,' he said, 'attentively', high-level meeting was planned and a possible audience with His Majesty.

Azmi, at the hotel, urged me not to unpack, meetings had been set for Marrakech, a special plane awaited. He was sending his cases on ahead, by road; would I like mine to go too? I thanked him but preferred to keep them with me. Garekhan and party landed on schedule and after an hour's rest were escorted out for the flight to Marrakech. We were on the tarmac, luggage loaded, when Azmi was summoned: we should remain in Rabat. Back at the hotel I talked to Garekhan, he had no new ideas, seemed reluctant to venture anything novel although the charged Moroccan-Algerian relationship might offer scope.

Basri, when we met, ran true to form. Morocco was strongly and irreversibly attached to the principle of a referendum, Morocco had been first to propose it at Nairobi and had since made enormous concessions, including agreeing to a UN organized referendum, when all Moroccans considered the Sahara Moroccan. Treating Polisario as Morocco's equal was too great an injustice, the settlement plan attributed to Polisario the same status as Morocco, equal treatment, equal legitimacy, conferring on Polisario the recognition they sought. Knowing they would lose a referendum – Morocco was sure to win – they would never go through with it, if there were only one chance in a hundred for Morocco to win, Polisario would still opt out. Basri's bulldogs followed: Brahim Hakim said that Algeria did not want the issue settled so long as it served to destabilize Morocco. Hasbi, legal adviser, argued that Polisario blocked progress, played games, behaved like children in a school playground, and the UN treated them like a spoiled child, always granting favours. Garekhan replied defensively, he rehearsed the recent Security Council debate and referred to the secretary-general's letter, he had nothing to add. Basri returned to the charge, delays, obstacles were all Polisario's fault. They could not dent Moroccan confidence, 'All will vote for Morocco,' he said sweepingly, 'even Abdel Aziz.' It was time to move forward, on two conditions: all applicants had to be processed; all forms of proof to be considered without distinction.

'Don't despair,' Snoussi said to Garekhan as we left for the meeting with Filali. Filali's style was more diplomatic, his manner more sophisticated, but the substance similar. Garekhan was polite, he repeated the account of developments in the Security Council, emphasized the secretary-general's concern and recognized Morocco's dedication to the plan. The process, stalled, needed help. Minurso was equipped to process all applications, the problem to persuade Polisario. Garekhan appealed to Filali for something fresh to take to Polisario. Filali responded by criticizing the Council's lack of objectivity, lack of balance, everyone could see what Morocco had done since 1988, the king's personal effort, Morocco's numerous concessions. 'We need this referendum as a practical way of dealing with the dispute,' Filali said, 'but not at any price.' Morocco concurred in the SG's October proposition, despite it not reflecting their position, it would have been possible to work with one party, but the Security Council said 'no.' Morocco's message for Polisario was to proceed: they should accept the secretary-general's proposal, everyone knew that the Spanish census was defective, Spain was a colonial power. How could Morocco tell some Sahrawis that 'to move ahead we have to leave you out.'

Garekhan nodded then referred again to action by the secretary-general and in the Council before mentioning talks, the secretary-general was open to holding direct talks, or proximity talks with himself, in New York or elsewhere, whatever format was preferred and with no rigid agenda, he hoped this could be soon. Filali listened, and shook his head, the peace plan had nothing about talks. Before adoption of the plan the king had received Polisario representatives in Marrakech, an experience that proved the impossibility of discussing with them or through them. The real party was Algeria, if Morocco were to negotiate, it had to be with Algeria. Garekhan said that it might sound naïve but the hope was that talks could help keep the process going; he had a letter for His Majesty from the secretary-general. Filali accepted the envelope and explained that the king was resting near Marrakech after being unwell in New York, His Majesty regretted being unable to receive Garekhan.

Garekhan was expectantly received by Polisario. He saluted their twenty years as refugees in a 'war of liberation' before putting their trust in the UN. They had the secretary-general's support, he announced, and the Council was prepared to pay, but only if there was progress. Kheddad said: 'I do not know whether I need to speak Hindi or English to make my self absolutely clear,' then, with dignity, declared in English that self-respect was a sacred right. The Sahrawis ceased their armed struggle without assurance that the peace plan would be implemented in its original form, Morocco was guilty of repeated violations, especially the prohibition against population transfer. The Spanish census remained the only yardstick. The massive Moroccan presence in the territory mocked the prospect of a free and fair referendum. Morocco's talk of a 'confirmatory' referendum was parody. There were two parties: one with a capital 'P', the other with 'p' in lower case. Morocco refused Mr Jensen's proposal in October, so it was altered. Polisario was told to have confidence, but how could they have confidence in the UN's ability to resist Moroccan pressure, given the huge transfer of population, the imposition of more than 100,000 non-Sahrawis for identification, the maintenance of occupation troop levels and security police control. Kheddad's words were endorsed when we left by a phalanx of flag-waving women ululating. Garekhan waved, saying he read their message loud and clear, at that a woman rushed forward screaming: 'Give us independence – or we want no more UN missions.'

Bachir, in his friendliest manner, welcomed us: 'If "*bon volonte*" good will, can deblock, here's plenty of it, we await your message.' Garekhan replied: 'I am a very modest person, and my mission is very modest, I am not attempting to solve the whole problem.' The question was not whether to keep the process going, but how, how to rekindle the necessary faith and trust. Bachir said he understood, he reflected first on the battle in New York – 'it was a battle' – regretting that the US had been partially converted to the French view; if the Security Council thought it could forge ahead without the Sahrawis, let it try. At present there was no confidence at all between the parties, little enough in Minurso, such confidence as had been developing was undermined by the lamentable attempt at talks in Laayoune and the New York fiasco. As to identification Polisario maintained the 1974 census as the sole basis for determining the electoral roll, oral testimony was acceptable only in exceptional cases and only when the two sheikhs concurred. Bachir called for greater transparency: the identification commission should publish lists of those identified to date who qualified, and another list of those remaining to be identified. Polisario would participate in identifying those in the census, those with documents proving their Western Saharan origin, that is Spanish documents, and their close relatives. The 100,000, tribes from the north, and those from the south, had nothing to do with the '74 census – the one and only basis. Finally, he urged dialogue, Polisario sought a just, durable solution – by peaceful means. 'We have fought long enough.'

Garekhan asked that they make an effort to believe him. The UN aimed to be broker, or midwife, it was in no position to impose; dialogue, certainly, he said; the secretary-general, the Security Council, Jensen all favour dialogue. But it takes two to dialogue, confidence was key, between Morocco and Polisario, and that was beyond his capacity to promote. He then undertook, despite my warning him that this posed problems, to publish lists of identification results to date. 'How can we proceed together?' he continued, he had no desire to be a lone horseman 'This is your country (his words); you must assess the risks.' Bachir responded, he had three bad memories: the invasion of Sahara by Morocco; the death of his brother, and losing faith in Minurso, but he reaffirmed their wish to move on given certain conditions, including clarification of the review process, to which I replied. The rest was repetition, Garekhan summarizing: lists to be published; identification and review procedures to be further explained; Polisario to resume identifying persons from sub-fractions belonging to the territory and in the '74 census; pre-1975 documents acceptable or the concurring testimony of two sheikhs, sheikhs being recognized sheikhs of the territory. With that the meeting dissolved, I let Garekhan go ahead then took Bachir aside.

I found it odd, I told him, that after his exhorting me urgently to explore a top-level meeting in Rabat, he vanished. It had been a difficult month, he said, I said 'for me too'. In response his disarming smile: what had the Moroccans agreed to? The crown prince would receive him, and perhaps the king, who was not as sick as they might wish to think – Bachir nodded, a plane to be provided from Laayoune. My communications had not been delivered, or not delivered as such, he wanted me to believe, a misunderstanding, now he was all interest, he suggested our meeting again soon. I tried to convey reluctance at repeating the recent initiative; time was needed. But let us speak in Algiers, or perhaps meet, he said, as we went together into the 'president's' tight security compound and penetrated the bunker.

Abdel Aziz held forth in Arabic, reiterating Polisario's concern about Moroccan 'colon' settlers and Morocco's bid for a 'confirmatory' referendum, wanting to be sure of the outcome beforehand. 135,000 postulants imposed by Morocco had no valid documents, no link with the territory, Polisario had done much but one thing it would not and could not do was to put its seal or signature to a phoney referendum. 'We have nothing left to give, except what is not ours to give.' Abdel Aziz did not doubt the sincerity of the UN, and he paid tribute to my efforts. The decolonization of Western Sahara was a UN responsibility in collaboration with the OAU, best achieved through the settlement plan. Polisario stood ready for a free, fair and impartial referendum with Spain's census as reference. The weaker party was always being pressured; it was time to boomerang, and pressure the other, the alternative to UN action would be war. Finally, the 'president' called for direct dialogue between the parties under UN auspices.

It was for the UN to take the process in hand, said Mauritania's president, when we met him the next day. Ould Taya had been following developments in New York, the UN had to be firm, everyone knew who had the right to vote: those living in the country, who were counted by Spain. Minurso withdrawal was no solution, this was a problem of profound import to the region, for peace and stability, it would set a terrible precedent for world peace should the UN withdraw, leaving the region to war and exploitation, you could not put so small a price on peace. The parties needed to meet and to discuss, which might require pressure. Garekhan said he took note, then briefed the president, who listened politely, on talks in Rabat and with Polisario. I seized the moment to raise Polisario's objection to an identification centre in Atar and suggested Nouadhibou and Zouerate. The president sanctioned Zouerate, I sensed the other would follow. Garekhan was glad to leave for Algeria, to be reminded of the old days when Algeria and India had much in common.

It was a pleasure, he stated on arriving, to be in friendly Algeria. He complimented the Algerians on their energetic and brilliant diplomacy before offering a summary of findings: 'I immediately accepted both his requests,' he said of Bachir's wish to have lists published of applicants accepted and detailed lists of applicants remaining. In return Polisario agreed to participate in identifying all members of sub-fractions included in the census; Garekhan failed to grasp that this excluded any of the contested, though he did ask whether the Algerians might help persuade Polisario to take part in identifying all applicants.

Algeria had a new foreign minister, cast in a similar mould to Dembri, with the same determined jaw. In addition to the peace plan, he said, political momentum on the ground was needed, in Algeria's view best achieved through direct dialogue. The focus had been on identification believing this could be more easily resolved and create momentum, instead it generated problems. The Spanish census, updated, was basic, he could not accept the referential nature of the Spanish census being pushed aside by the volume of Moroccan applications. The October formula, was accepted by Polisario and initially by Morocco, before it made its calculations. Then came the secretary-general's version. He shook his head, paused, before insisting that UN withdrawal would have a devastating effect on the region. This was not a civil war, he continued, nor a conflict between two states, it was a case of decolonization, and for Algeria a matter of principle, the UN had a moral responsibility. It had not exhausted its resources politically, the UN and other countries should work to promote dialogue. Polisario and Algeria favoured the idea of a contact group but whatever the format, direct dialogue was essential to 'bridging' the lack of confidence.

Bachir, when I enquired, had 'gone to Spain.' In Madrid someone answered that he had departed for America, reception gave me another Spanish number to ring where I reached him immediately. He sounded relaxed, friendly, had made enormous efforts to reach me in Algiers, he claimed, and was now on his way to New York; I ought to be there too. He would return after the Secretary-General's report had been considered and any consequent resolution adopted. He remained interested in what the two of us had discussed, I said I counted on his being promptly available, at least for communications. Certainly, certainly. When he returned, we could meet wherever he preferred, Mijek, Dougaj or perhaps Las Palmas, he thought that a capital idea, and promised to call.

Another call awaited me the moment I returned to Laayoune. Azmi wanted to hear how everything had gone, 'our friend' – meaning Basri – was travelling abroad in the morning and anxious to be briefed. I told him that Garekhan had yet to finalise conclusions and planned to report in person. Azmi was determined, insistence seeping through the wires. It was too soon to be specific, I said. Azmi the Rottweiler growled, I threw him a bone, what he undoubtedly knew from their own intelligence: Polisario asked Garekhan for lists to be published, of those already identified who qualified and those still to come before the identification commission, and they agreed to identify persons from census-listed sub-fractions. 'That,' he huffed, 'we know.'

In New York, while Garekhan formulated his unexceptional findings, Bachir worked to convince the Americans of the need for direct talks, he tried persuading them to organize contact similar to Dayton. The US listened, Ginsberg informed me that Ambassador Albright was stopping over in Rabat specifically in that connection. The secretary-general also received Bachir, *tête-à-tête*. Bachir afterwards briefed Fayza Aboulnaga, he mentioned my initiative, told her that he was prepared to go to Rabat, he preferred to arrive by Algerian aircraft; Morocco wanted theirs; he had no problem with a UN plane, as I proposed. To me Bachir said later that the secretary-general's participation was valuable but he considered the foundation I was laying as solid: 'Why add new steps to the staircase?' It bothered him that the report being submitted to the Security Council did not specifically recommend dialogue, nor did the draft resolution. Council members were at loggerheads: most favoured direct dialogue, but Morocco rejected the UN's further involvement and its friends on the Council endorsed the Moroccan view.

Azmi called to make an appointment for me with the minister. Monday, he said. I asked what time approximately to determine whether to leave the evening before. He would tell me on arrival, best to arrive Sunday. It was Ramadan, making the faithful hungrily short-tempered, cigarette starved and sleep-deprived, I should have known better than persist, but I needed to organize my time, I had people to see. 'Not ambassadors,' he raised his voice. I said, 'I want to hear how they assess developments in New York, and I am invited by the British ambassador, as a friend.' 'He's not,' said Azmi at his most petulant. 'We know when you met him, you met him here.' He paused, then: 'If you're going to see ambassadors, there's no point in your meeting the minister. I'll cancel it. I'll tell the minister you're not coming to see him.' It was ridiculous, but Azmi was in no mood for reason, he blurted out nonsense about my accreditation, that I had no business with embassies in Rabat. To me what mattered most was to talk about Bachir's visit, I offered to see only Basri. Never did I rattle more keenly the bars of the gilded cage in which I had to function.

Azmi telephoned next day that he had no news about meeting the minister. Lines in northern Morocco were down, due to flooding; flood damage was extensive, the weather had been wretched. It had rained when we departed Algiers, to general jubilation, drought in Algeria was severe and they were relieved to see rain, Morocco, unusually, experienced a wet year. In the Sahara we had frequent rainfall, strong wind and ennervating sandstorms, herders of sheep and goats and camels rejoiced at the spare coating of green that sprinkled large tracts of sand. I departed Laayoune in pouring rain, the wind lashed at palm-trees outside the hotel in premonition of the climate in Rabat. No sooner was I there than Azmi blew a storm against the latest from New York: lists to be published. 'Morocco will never accept, it does not accord to the settlement plan.' I told him my concern, the need first to review all members of the same sub-fraction, but the plan did not explicitly prohibit publication. That sparked a violent reaction: 'In law a document which says you do something at a certain time implicitly precludes doing it at another time, basic legal drafting.' I reassured him that we could not responsibly publish lists until all members of a given sub-fraction had been identified, to permit cross-referencing and guarantee that related persons received equivalent treatment. All he said was: 'Morocco will not accept it. It's not in the plan, it's a Polisario ploy – to derail the process.' 'The Americans have been urging transparency, you know that,' I said; 'this is supposed to contribute.' 'Gharekhan's brilliant diplomatic compromise,' Azmi said with heavy sarcasm, 'under pressure from Bachir.' Transparency was a long-standing Polisario fixation, I said, and fuelled their criticism of Minurso and me, transparency was championed by the west, most especially America; Gharekhan came intending to promote it, and he virtually offered this to Bachir. 'We know Gharekhan,' Azmi said, 'his non-aligned background, his sympathies and his shallow diplomatic achievement, and what does he know about the process?' His master's voice: like a dress rehearsal for Basri.

16

Basri and Bachir

THE MINISTER KEPT US WAITING. In his office antechamber I was offered a choice of tea or coffee before being told that the kitchen was closed for Ramadan. When ushered into the presence we found Basri in conversation with the justice minister. He introduced us, followed by rapid fire greeting, and, immediately, the lists, it was not in the plan, Morocco would not accept publication of lists, they had conveyed that to New York, to Snoussi. 'You understand? Is it clear?' The habitual peremptory commands, and the interview was over. I was half way out of the door when Basri turned to say we would meet again in half an hour, no time for lunch, but it was Ramadan, and twenty-five minutes later Azmi arrived to conduct me. We set off in pouring rain, away from town. 'Where's the meeting?' 'At the golf,' he said with a wry smile while I stared at the windscreen wipers in overdrive, 'I assumed we were going to the office, I see no reason to walk around in puddles and mud.' 'It's not muddy,' he said, and he was right: greens and fairways were impeccably trimmed, the grass like an English lawn, the rain had eased when someone handed me a raincoat. For five holes I walked with Basri, interrupted only by his drives, his puts, and the automatic round of applause, which hailed most shots, from the fan club, including three ministers, grouped behind at a respectful distance. Basri launched into the draft resolution being considered by Security Council members.

The precise wording of paragraph six, which was, of course, intended as a call for dialogue, what did it really say? I told him: ways of building confidence. He summoned Azmi, and Azmi confirmed the exact wording in French, quoted correctly, but said the implication was talks. Yes, I agreed, it was code for dialogue, but its face value was genuine, about building confidence, Basri mumbled. Another drive took his ball far down the fairway, assured of his undivided attention I told him I had spoken to Bachir and planned a meeting on his return from New York, I needed to be sure of the Moroccan position.

Basri confirmed, and reconfirmed with only minor linguistic variation two holes later, that Bachir was welcome home '*chez lui*', he would be received by the crown prince or His Majesty or possibly both depending on how talks with Basri evolved. Regarding flights, I said it might make sense to fly to Anfa, the old Casablanca airport devoted mainly to non-commercial traffic and where UN aircraft sometimes landed without attracting attention. He liked the idea, and to ensure there was no misunderstanding I repeated everything. Basri added that as '*demandeur*', it was not for Bachir to impose conditions. Fearing that threatened the certainty of his seeing the crown prince or king, I checked again. His reply amounted to a guarantee, and Bachir could be accompanied, by two, three, even four, if he wanted, but no Algerians, no Algerians, his security would be assured and status respected, he would receive every courtesy and full hospitality. With regard to dates – Morocco was not prepared to wait for ever – it should be the 5th, 10th or 15th of the coming month, in short, in the next couple of weeks. Bachir, when I reached him in New York, was pleased I had a proposal that sounded reasonable. No details over the phone, so when could we meet?

The Security Council had still to adopt the resolution, Bachir said, and the secretary-general was labouring on an initiative. From hints I deduced that Boutros-Ghali was trying to organize contact, in his presence, between Bachir and Snoussi, but was prepared to 'eclipse' himself leaving Bachir and Snoussi alone together. Bachir did not expect this to generate anything valuable, however, he had promised to be available and now awaited a telephone call 'inviting us two old gentlemen to tea.' He looked forward to seeing me as soon as he returned. Azmi, of course, was impatient to know how Bachir reacted to Basri's invitation, 'you must inform Basri,' he said, passing me the cell-phone while he dialed Basri's secret number. I explained that Bachir was standing by for a possible encounter. Basri snapped '*Il te mente*', he's lying to you, trying to impress with his importance, end of conversation. Azmi wondered what on earth had been said, refusing to believe that anything could take place in New York without their knowing, but that evening, at the appointed Islamic hour, Bachir broke the fast with Snoussi.

It was presumably *tête-à-tête*, I said. Ye-es, Bachir replied, though Snoussi certainly had his policemen somewhere around. And you? 'We don't have the budget,' Bachir said. 'Snoussi started by saying he had come to listen. I came to listen too, I told him.' It had been pleasant enough, a social occasion. No commitments, although Bachir expressed his wish for serious dialogue, when propitious. Snoussi promised to report. Apart from that, he just told jokes, a 'joke tank' said Bachir. We agreed to meet in the Canaries the following Sunday – in secret, he insisted.

For forty minutes I sat on the tarmac waiting for clearance to the terminal building before being marched through a crew entrance across large empty spaces until I saw Bachir, by himself, on a bench, reading a newspaper, very discreetly. We made our way out and drove towards Las Palmas while he described happenings in New York. In all crises with which the Security Council was concerned the call was for dialogue; only in the case of Western Sahara was dialogue to be excluded, Morocco had campaigned aggressively against a relevant paragraph in the draft resolution. Everyone on the Council wanted dialogue, except perhaps the French, and even they were not genuinely opposed, just supremely cautious about alienating Morocco. 'Where does Chirac go for the new year?' Bachir asked rhetorically, answer: Taroudant. 'As though there aren't enough prostitutes in France. But it makes little accommodations easier to arrange.' We agreed on the need for dialogue, identification would not resolve differences over the four-month Minurso mandate extension, but dialogue when and how?

We talked in a café over orange juice. Bachir is not over-scrupulous about Ramadan but he doesn't drink – except once, he confessed, in North Korea, and 'it tasted horrible.' He seemed to be back-tracking, he could meet Basri, but outside Morocco, he was nervous that despite assurances a meeting with the crown prince or king might not take place, the prince or king might be 'indisposed' and he would have come to Rabat just to see Basri. France, or Geneva, England, anywhere else was acceptable, the Nordic countries, which I suggested, would be excellent. I faced a quandary, I pointed out that it was he who first requested being received by either the crown prince or the king, were he now to refuse their 'invitation', the Moroccans would say that he did not know what he wanted, or that he was a person who changes his mind. A visit to Rabat might also offer insight into the king's health and the overall situation, including the succession, initial contact could lay the basis for substantive talks. He listened attentively, reflected for a moment or two, drained the last of his orange juice, and gave me his disarming, boyish smile. He had not been entirely open, he confessed, when breaking fast with Snoussi, he had passed a message and had now to await a response, before that came he was unwilling to move. The reply might be delivered through me or whatever channel the Moroccans chose, he could not say.

How to defang Basri? A message conveyed through Snoussi was credible enough, and a valid reason for Bachir postponing his answer to Basri's offer.

I wondered though about that message. Azmi greeted me on my return from the Canaries with a copy of the planned identification programme fingering the identification bar chart, which he claimed was designed to camouflage unacceptable elements. I began explaining; he stopped me. 'To serious business. How did it go, your meeting with the Spanish authorities?' inverted commas audible. The Moroccans always knew my cover. I gave him the gist. 'I told you you couldn't trust him,' Azmi said, insisting I inform Basri. Tomorrow, I said. 'No. He's waiting.' It was after ten thirty. 'Doesn't matter. He's waiting.' I called. After several attempts it emerged that Basri was at dinner in the palace with the Spanish prime minister, he was expected around midnight. I told Azmi that I had no wish to wait up only to be shouted at. 'He. Never. He's always polite.' At one in the morning Basri came on the line. Bachir much appreciated, I said, the offer to be received in Rabat by the king or crown prince as well as meeting Basri, but at the encounter organized by the secretary-general in New York he had passed a message through Snoussi, he had still to hear back. After prolonged absence he would have to return to Rabouni for consultation before travelling again. Basri said nothing.

Whatever urgency the Security Council sought to inject into proceedings, both sides stayed the course, unhurried. They welcomed extension of the mandate; they were not disposed to compromise on the way forward. Polisario had no intention of identifying in the north, or even contested groups in the territory, and stipulated that lists of those found eligible be published prior to any identification. Morocco refused to modify its demand that all groups be identified, reacting virulently even to contested groups being deferred from the initial weeks of identification, nor could Morocco accept publication of lists. It's only what Polisario demanded, Azmi repudiated reference to Garekhan's 'compromise', 'What compromise? We never agreed to any compromise.'

The South African foreign minister, on an official visit in Rabat, was no help. On presenting myself at the minister's suite I was greeted by two familiar faces: one Coen van Wyk, from the OAU observers, the other the stubbled and pockmarked South African I recognized from his years with the UN Centre against Apartheid when he habitually brandished the same knobbly stick. The minister, physically unprepossessing, was the antithesis of Nelson Mandela, we shook hands and he requested me to summarize the initiatives taken recently and the last ditch effort of the secretary-general's special envoy. Prospects for resuming identification were bleak since both sides insisted on measures that they knew unacceptable to the other. The four-month extension bought time for dialogue, the minister told me he had seen Filali and mentioned dialogue.

There was no real response; an aide added 'he didn't bite.' The minister also had an audience of the king, nothing in the king's demeanour suggested terminal illness, he said, when I mentioned that Polisario seemed convinced that Hassan was unlikely to live long and counted on a new political dynamic. Talk with the king focused on recognition of SADR, South Africa being urged most strongly to defer. 'In three months the problem will be solved,' Hassan had said, I asked the minister if he knew what that was supposed to mean. 'No,' he emphasized the strength of public opinion in South Africa in favour of recognizing Polisario, 'We are committed to the OAU and this is an OAU decision.' Not all African member states had recognized Polisario, I pointed out. 'But the majority has,' he said, 'and it's an OAU decision.' We discussed the OAU role in Minurso, I paid tribute to Mpehle and to Coen van Wyk before summarizing the OAU dilemma. The organization was seen as having taken sides by admitting SADR to state membership, the UN secretary-general believed that recognition by South Africa of Polisario at this stage in the settlement process appeared to prejudge the referendum. The minister listened without comment. As I was leaving he impressed upon me how unsettling Minurso withdrawal would be for the region, very unsettling, he repeated.

Basri asked to speak immediately, he was about to review the enormous extension to what was already Africa's largest port. In good spirits, he dispatched the driver to another vehicle and took the wheel of his copious Mercedes, me beside him, the minister of finance and Azmi behind. We shot off at high speed – the speedometer touching 100 mph. Containers, Basri said, pointing as we passed, were for shipping me out, that was the only joke, nothing about South Africa. He launched into heated criticism of plans for identification: 'I knew when Garekhan came it was to tread on your toes, to cut off your head. It is outrageous, illogical, unacceptable to relegate certain groups to the Greek calens, which never comes, before the end Polisario will call a halt, and these people will never be identified.' He brushed aside that our programme covered all applicants. He had a proposal, somewhat against Azmi's advice, Basri suggested that two contested groups be identified in the middle. I found that constructive, it accommodated their justified concern that Polisario call a halt while permitting time to explore how to identify them, but we had to recognize that Polisario did not have sheikhs or alternates for all groups. That was summarily dismissed. Minutes passed in a barren exchange about Minurso taking control and proceeding with or without Polisario sheikhs, Basri hoped to see me again that evening.

He appeared, dark suited, ready for the palace. He was unusually formal, addressed me as '*vous*', used only my surname. He enquired about the message Bachir passed through Snoussi, I had no knowledge, he looked disbelieving. What were those regional autonomy models? 'What exactly does he want?' 'I don't think he can say precisely, or that there is total agreement among Polisario.' Basri reverted to the encounter between Bachir and Snoussi: they ate together, he said, amazed, at the Waldorf Astoria. 'What did Snoussi say?' I told him I did not know, beyond some jokes, Basri closed his eyes, shrugged his shoulders. With an abrupt change of tone he asked why identification commissioners were biased in favour of Polisario, a judgment I disputed. 'We know, we know,' he said, 'we have files of information on them, and how could it be that numbers were to Polisario's advantage?' I did not have precise figures, let alone know how those qualified would vote. 'Don't give me that, 'he said. 'Don't pretend you don't know, of course, you know.' If he deduced that identification numbers favoured Polisario it might be because most of their candidates were straightforward census cases while on the Moroccan side many relied on oral testimony from sheikhs, who often failed to agree. With only his expression to refute me, Basri rose to leave. He turned, and, raising his voice, said: 'If those lists are published, or their contents become known' – he insinuated that Minurso staff were giving information to Polisario – 'I shall hold you personally responsible and the UN will be out in forty-eight hours.' He left for the palace, I returned to Laayoune.

In Morocco they spied the new moon. After swirling sandstorms and rain, heavy cloud, further downpour and a thunderstorm, Ramadan culminated in Eid-el-Fitr. The Eid had been proclaimed a day before in Algeria; I chose the moment to deliver my official letter of greeting to Abdel-Aziz with a wish for God's guidance. In Tindouf the weather was perfect: the sky brilliant clear blue, a gentle mirage spread lakes to our left as we drove towards Rabouni. Bodan had advised Bachir of my coming, leaving him to choose whether or not to meet. He was there and I gave him the letter for Abdel-Aziz, he seemed ill at ease, talking non-stop, restating, repeating their insistence on 'transparency', time had come for Minurso to emerge from opacity, the secretiveness of its work, the obscurity surrounding identification, and publish the lists. Garekhan had promised and the secretary-general reported the decision, no approval or endorsement by the Security Council was required, whether or not in accord with the settlement plan was immaterial, other deviations had been effected by the secretary-general. The lists had to be provided, published openly; making them available confidentially could only mean we had something to hide, up to me, Bachir said. I explained, again, the provisions of the plan, Morocco's inflexible stand and that we depended on the parties' voluntary cooperation.

Was I the king's representative, he asked sarcastically, adding that he was perhaps alone among Polisario leaders still to have confidence in me, and that was ebbing fast, continued confidence depended on my providing the lists. If the lists were published, I asked, would Polisario participate in identifying all who remained?

Bachir and an assistant, who was present, reacted in unison and forcefully, there could be no quid pro quo. I reminded them of Garekhan saying 'now give me something in exchange'. Bachir smiled his disarming smile, Polisario would take part in identifying members of sub-fractions included in the census, as confirmed to Garekhan. I pointed out, tactfully, that the statement sounded cooperative, giving the impression of Polisario's willingness to complete identification, but he knew, and I knew, unlike Garekhan and most in New York, that this effectively excluded the contested groups and many more. That, he said, was the plan – both sides insist on punctilious observance when it suits.

I waited until we were alone before asking about a response to his message; he had not heard. The two of us should speak, he said, after the Fête du Trone, when the king might announce something eventful, he promised to be available and embraced me warmly as I left. It perturbed me that Bachir, indeed Polisario, having prayed so fervently for direct contact, for a meeting at the highest level, now wavered, I was tempted to ask whether he did know his own mind, or whether he had the authority for independent action, or whether he was genuinely troubled by the prospect of a visit to Rabat being twisted into defection. His chameleon qualities were undeniable. Azmi, whose wife was a Sahrawi, maintained that mind changing was characteristic of Sahrawis, notably men, they sat watching their camels munch and occupied their time in inter-tribal plotting and counter plotting, devising razzias, raids and revenge forays, the uncertainties of life, the unpredictable environment, good seasons interspersed with bad when there was no grazing, inhibited longer-term planning, and consistency.

Bodan, on our return journey, did his utmost to convince me that the lists be published. Even if we set aside the need to crosscheck all family members, which could be accomplished only when every applicant from a sub-fraction had been identified, I did not believe that publication would permit identification to continue. Fine for me: everyone would realise that, against the odds, our motley identification commission had worked assiduously and with integrity. But I feared that the moment Polisario had figures officially confirmed they would halt further participation, bar perhaps some tailends;

they already intimated being prepared to sacrifice potential support in Mauritania. Morocco would express outrage and denounce Minurso for bias and failing to identify the overwhelming majority of their candidates. We needed the plan, sinking but still afloat, and sufficient uncertainty on both sides as incentive for talks.

An American initiative injected another dimension. Assistant secretary of state Pelletreau had detailed a counsellor to encourage Polisario, who saw the US as natural champion of their independence struggle and believed that only the US had power to coerce Morocco, in developing a negotiating position for possible direct, discreet talks. In New York the US was arguing for phased withdrawal of Minurso, though other Security Council members considered that premature, believing it too soon to abandon the plan and identification. Basri telephoned me, twice, to ask what the Council intended, as if he did not know better from his own sources; no blame must attach to Morocco for the hold-up in identification. Simultaneously I was informed by Ginsberg that he was engaged in a two-pronged attack: to persuade Morocco to abandon or defer contested groups and, in exchange, have Polisario shut up about lists, although he felt that publishing the lists would 'give the king something to think about'. He expected to be received by the king and would pressure Morocco while the US also leant on Polisario, 'We are working in tandem,' he said, 'you and I are locked in a velcro bear-hug for the weeks ahead. You have a problem with that?' 'Not at all,' I said, 'except for the difference in weight, in both senses.' The European Union ambassadors requested a meeting. Nothing new emerged bar the Italian ambassador divulging afterwards confidential information from the early seventies: Polisario-SADR was an invention of Brezhnev who sold it to Boumedienne, Morocco was the only north African country linked to the west and the Soviet Union, through Algeria, sought access to the Atlantic. The seeds of discord were scattered, ready to sprout.

As I informed the European Union ambassadors we still juggled residual identification cases. Problems never ceased: a sheikh defected, in Polisario words, or came over, according to Morocco, causing disruption; another, in advanced old age, could not travel and his eldest son was untraceable; a sheikh on the Moroccan side claimed to belong to a different tribal group. The only course of action, I decided, was to hold fast to our comprehensive plan of work as the final compromise, not subject to adjustment, it proposed three weeks to identify all remaining uncontested tribes (A to G) followed by the tribal groupings (H, I and J) from week four, with the most contentious (H41 and 61) as of the seventh week.

Identification was upstaged by Pelletreau's presence in the region and speculation where the American initiative might lead. His transit in Algiers without visiting Rabouni proved mistaken, Bachir was to explain afterwards that he had been summoned at absurdly short notice, and he was told that the meeting was conditional on Polisario foregoing insistence on publication of lists. That had been discussed by them and was a concession they might make but were not prepared to accept as a precondition. Bachir still hoped that the US initiative could produce results though he said so without conviction, 'American diplomacy is far from subtle.' What of the French? I asked. They knew the issues, they knew the region, and it mattered to them, he said, and they were clever diplomats. But the Americans might be more sincere. Polisario leaders confided in Bodan their losing confidence, unsure what to hope: 'We have suffered twenty years. We are at a crossroads. A meeting could give all a chance for peace. We can negotiate with Hassan. Not that he is in position to give anything; he just thought he could co-opt the UN to rubber stamp a false vote.' They had offered the Americans a paper – which I was not shown – but heard nothing further. In the Security Council the US threatened closure. My next report had to spell out the conflicting positions and prospects, to be sure I reviewed Polisario's stand with Bachir.

For three hours we talked, in the presence of Boukhari, over from New York, and others. I reaffirmed the identification programme they had been sent, in reporting to the Council I wished to reflect exactly Polisario's position on identifying the contested groupings (H, I and J), I also sought their views in general: should the process continue in whatever way possible, should the mission close, or should a small political office remain and a reduced military presence? Bachir welcomed my desire to clarify their standpoint, they wanted the process to continue on the basis of Garekhan's report, which, he insisted, had been approved by the secretary-general. What induced me to determine that the other's concurrence was necessary? Polisario was in favour of cooperating with the UN, in favour of the referendum. 'Ours is a liberation movement. Our people are weak'; they could not be compared to Morocco, but they had the right to self-determination, and they wanted peace, hence the UN's importance and responsibility. 'Withdrawing the UN will do nothing for our people, whatever happens the Sahrawi struggle will continue.'

Boukhari interrupted to ask why I refused to implement the decision about lists. When I repeated the arguments and lack of agreed guidance from New York Boukhari shook his head. I suggested giving them numbers orally; together with their own observers' records that would provide a fair assessment. Bachir recalled visiting a chocolate factory in Austria where he was offered an army of chocolate soldiers, I offered them a nameless army, these were individuals with names and surnames, that was what they wanted. The work of identification was scrupulous, I reassured Bachir, burden of proof lay with the applicant – tough to sustain without documentation and if the sheikhs did not agree, applicants included in the census had the advantage of documentary evidence. The Moroccans were the more dissatisfied, they accused me of rejecting 'all these people'.Boukhari burst in: 'Then they have the results, the lists.' 'No,' I said, 'no lists have been released, lists can be finalized only when members of a given sub-fraction have all been identified, in the territory, in the camps, in Mauritania. The Moroccans have their observers, as you do, and they deduce the probable figures.' Bodan, who had been listening, explained that the identification review was to ensure that all family members benefit from comparable treatment. Bachir kept nodding, he was satisfied with the procedure as explained, but then 'why no transparency, why not publish the lists?' Boukhari conceded that the work might have been correctly performed, as I maintained, but my refusal to provide lists made them suspicious. 'If you did have the lists,' I asked, 'would you participate in identifying all tribal groups?' Bachir replied categorically: 'We accept to identify sub-fractions included in the census.'

'I need to be absolutely clear on this point,' I said, 'Polisario agrees to identify persons from census-listed sub-fractions only. The tribal groupings (H,I and J) are not sub-fractions…' 'They are tribes or groups of tribes,' Bachir broke in. 'H are from the north, meaning Morocco, J from the south, mainly Mauritania, and I claim descent from the prophet giving them special links with the king.' What of the famous Ma-el-Ainin in the 'I' category, surely they were Sahrawi. Sheikh Ma-el-Ainin was indeed a Sahrawi, Bachir admitted, who pledged allegiance to the Moroccan sultan, but accepting them would mean including all other prophet descended tribal groups. 'We want compliance with the settlement plan and insist on transparency.'

I attempted once more: eighty-five of the eighty-eight sub-fractions on which working agreement was originally reached included H, I and Js apart from the most contentious: H 41 H 61 and J 51/52. What prevented Polisario taking part in identifying the eighty-five? Their sheikhs were under no obligation to recognize applicants they deemed unqualified. 'What is the point,' Bachir replied, 'since we have already deemed that they do not qualify.' I said that Minurso had received applications in due time; they required processing. 'How many were submitted individually and how many by the Moroccans?'

Bachir asked. He and I both knew that most forms were completed with the parties' help, Polisario as much as Morocco; only in Mauritania was registration handled entirely by Minurso. Every applicant was entitled to come before the identification commission, with the commission deciding on eligibility. 'Give us the lists, by sub-fraction included in the census, showing the criteria claimed for eligibility,' Bachir said, 'if it's a father born in the territory, we want to check.' Boukhari asked permission to make three points.

One, the principle of transparency was not negotiable, it was a 'must' for the UN to respect. Two, Polisario remained committed to implementing the compromise proposal: to identify Sahrawi sub-fractions included in the census, implanted in the territory and for which there were sheikhs. Three, were the UN to abandon the plan, Minurso should withdraw completely, withdrawal of Minurso would not end UN responsibility however: to ensure decolonisation and the right to self-determination. The next report of the secretary-general, with a Security Council decision, was due by the end of May, were the UN then to admit failure in accomplishing its mandate, Polisario would discuss options, Bachir said.

When I asked how I should report to New York their unwillingness to identify certain applicants, Boukhari erupted: 'You maintain that Polisario rejects identification of H, I and Js. You intend reporting that to the Council. It's not true. Polisario does not reject anything. We are ready to proceed in accord with the secretary-general's compromise: transparency. It's up to the UN to make the other party, Morocco, respect that compromise.' As to the future, Bachir said cryptically, no-one wanted to see their father die but the father still died. UN involvement had to be within the parameters of its traditional responsibility for decolonization and self-determination.

Under the current mandate the UN had no means to force the parties, I said: to impose a solution. I sought a way out of the impasse that both might accept. Boukhari interrupted: 'For you it's an impasse, for us it's our destiny, either the UN is weak and makes a present of Western Sahara to Morocco, or it is still credible, that credibility becomes questionable if the UN is unable to implement transparency measures because Morocco opposes.' If the peace plan failed UN military observers would only serve to control Polisario and protect Morocco's army of occupation, Bachir concurred. Boukhari switched on an adversary's diplomatic smile, expressed admiration for my personal persistence and courage in a task aggravated by lack of support in New York – which he knew only too well – and said: 'So, are you considering packing your bags?'

17

Proposals

THE SECRETARY-GENERAL summoned me to Geneva, mine was his last meeting of the day, to make it open-ended. He was visibly unwell, I overheard him asking for a doctor's appointment in the morning. He wished a full account of the situation in Western Sahara.

Morocco, I told him, was poised to move ahead with identifying all applicants and rejected any distinction between them. Polisario insisted on publication of the lists before resuming identification and continued to deploy the phrase 'sub-fractions included in the census'- the precise wording that I respected in drafting my official report only for it to be edited out in New York as too technical. It sounded accommodating and correct to anyone not conversant with the ethnology of the Spanish census, but I knew, and Polisario knew that I knew, this excluded not only the most contentious H 41, H 61 and J 51/52 tribal groups but all the H, I and Js as groupings divided into tribes and fractions but not categorized in recognizable Sahrawi sub-fractions. Polisario held to this language, fully aware that it would be otherwise understood. They latched onto publication of the lists during Garekhan's visit, as restated in the secretary-general's report, for their own purposes and confident that would embarrass Morocco, the Moroccans, to whom it had not been mentioned by Garekhan, held their cards close when the report appeared and a resolution was first under consideration, when forced to declare their hand they could argue that the proposal had not been discussed with them, had not been specifically endorsed by the Security Council, and did not accord with the settlement plan, open and shut. The secretary-general looked annoyed: 'But I said my intention was not to issue the lists. I mentioned it to you last year.'

It was in the report, I told Boutros. He had missed it, 'I cannot be expected to read every word they put in front of me,' he said irritably. I was appalled, not that the secretary-general overlooked a detail in rapid reading of a draft, but that Garekhan had not drawn it to his attention before signing, that was what advisors were for. I had not forgotten Boutros' words of the year before – nor had I forgotten that on the same occasion he saw no value in dispatching Garekhan as special envoy, I assumed that under pressure for transparency he had also shifted position on publishing lists: transparency a fashionably American catchword, as irreproachable as motherhood and apple-pie. In consequence the process was now deadlocked, we might achieve three further weeks of identification to complete the A to Gs, but then? I was convinced that both sides were well aware of the facts, that they had approximate figures, if I could guess without checking records, then the parties, equipped with computers, supplied with detailed applicant rolls and constantly present, could easily make reliable deductions. The lack of transparency was a fiction, the process was altogether transparent. I told the secretary-general that I offered Bachir to give figures orally, and confirm what they surely knew already. He rejected the offer, insisting on names, full names, Polisario wanted irrefutable facts now that we had completed identifying nearly all those applying under the census-derived criteria and belonging to uncontested Sahrawi sub-fractions. My concern was that they would halt the process and lure international opinion into sanctioning a referendum on the basis of those identified, precisely what Morocco dreaded. Boutros-Ghali had been listening attentively, reflecting, without saying a word, he became decisive.

'We have a solid body of work to show. But have reached a critical deadlock. Whether we publish the lists, or not, whether the three tribal groupings are accepted or not, the outcome will not change. Let us cease identification and move all documentary material and computerised analysis of completed identification to Geneva. The UN presence in Western Sahara will be reduced to my special representative and fifty military observers.' (Fifty, I think, was picked out of thin air; peacekeeping experts queried the precise function of thirty milobs, reduced from fifty in garbled onward transmission.) A solution could be found, the secretary-general continued, through direct contact between the parties, a new initiative was required.

The US did not agree. At a meeting with Pelletreau, Boutros-Ghali outlined his proposal to reduce the mission, drawing down both military and political components. The Americans were not prepared to scuttle the settlement plan, they rejected complete dismantling of the process, wanted it kept alive. Military observers were needed for peace and stability in the region, though a smaller military presence might suffice. Boutros mentioned the idea of appointing an arbitrator, but that was ruled out since Morocco refused to accept any decision as binding. Pelletreau was pessimistic about his own effort, Polisario had provided a paper, with some positive elements, but he was skeptical about their commitment, and he had not been encouraged by a meeting with King Hassan. The secretary-general raised the idea of regional autonomy, which the Americans could bolster. Next day Boutros received a call from the king expressing concern at his intention to downsize the mission, Polisario was equally unhappy.

In Rabouni the force commander was harangued. Monitoring the cease-fire served Moroccan interests, Polisario units were controlled but there was no control at the northern border, overflight violations were common, the UN military observers helped the occupation by giving Morocco security and removing pressure to negotiate. The cease-fire had been accepted to allow a free and fair referendum, without a referendum, the cease-fire lost relevance. To me Bachir said that the identification commission was the locomotive with the whole peace process in train, if identification ceased, the process stopped: the locomotive was at standstill in a tunnel, no light, no transparency. He did not mention reverting to war, though it was implied; Kheddad was saying that there had to be an alternative to the resumption of hostilities but he could not see what. Polisario leaders faced a problem with their supporters, of credibility, they had campaigned for people to accept the settlement plan, the compromise proposal, additional criteria, and to trust the UN to deliver a free, fair and transparent referendum. That having failed, a return to fighting gained increasing support. Kheddad said they wanted direct talks; he hoped Morocco could be forced into talking.

The US State Department assigned a young diplomat to monitor the fading American initiative. Polisario were not responding as hoped, their non-paper had little of substance, they agreed to eschewing publicity, looked to dialogue and wanted support in overcoming mistrust. The Americans saw an achievement in the omission of specific reference to independence. Boukhari protested that Polisario had expected more, much more of America and interpreted US efforts as petering out. At a meeting of the Sahrawi National Council the chairman made a statement to the effect that since their population was very small it would not be to their advantage to start another war, however, all diplomatic efforts to advance the peace process appearing fruitless, they were forced to reconsider a military option, he still hoped that the peace plan, or direct talks with Morocco could help resolve the issue and avoid a bloody war.

At Security Council consultations the secretary-general reported on nine conflicts. Of the seven in Africa he singled out Western Sahara to remind the

Council that Minurso's current mandate was due to expire in under a month. Identification was deadlocked, both sides claimed commitment to proceed but on incompatible terms. He proposed presenting plans for a phased withdrawal: the identification commission would be suspended and military observers reduced in number without affecting adversely on operational capacity. Comments were scatter-shot, Korea had calculated costs and found the price excessive for each person identified, France insisted that avoiding war made it worth every penny; they were not petty accountants. Boutros-Ghali retorted that Minurso had assured the cease-fire, war would have cost ten times as much, look at Rwanda, the price of genocide there. Chile wondered about a cease-fire without political process? Another asked, if the process was deadlocked, where was the exit strategy? The secretary-general wanted to explore alternatives, we needed to find a way to compromise. US Ambassador Albright said she shared the general frustration, she would welcome any idea how to resolve the problem, adding that she had heard Korea, the same message coming from Congress. Botswana said he was almost crying. 'It's pathetic. Why can't we talk sense into these guys.' 'Put everyone in an aeroplane,' said the chairman, 'like the Americans did for Bosnia.'[1]

I was due to visit Algiers and Nouakchott. Nouakchott, when I landed into the sun-blinding murk of whirling sand, was blistering hot. Exceptional headwinds had delayed our arrival by nearly an hour and I was hustled into a waiting vehicle to be escorted direct to the presidency, dripping perspiration evaporated in the Sahara's all-blotting aridity to render me presentable for audience. The president, open and friendly, had us pose for television crews and cameramen before inviting me to talk *tête-à-tête*. I briefed him on recent developments and expectations for the secretary-general's report. Quite a relief it was to explain the controversy about 'sub-fractions represented in the census' to someone who understood the implication. He was amazed at Polisario rejecting Ma-el-Ainin, the great sheikh had raised Sahrawi troops, also in Mauritania. The controversy about lists I also explained, transparency was not really at issue. The president was hardly surprised that the American initiative faded; it had been insensitively handled. A reduction in military observers, I assured him, would not be detrimental to their mandate and current deployment, with that he was much concerned, it was also, he said, the Algerian position. The military had to remain as cease-fire monitors, their withdrawal would entail serious consequences for stability in the region with renewed hostilities likely. It was essential to maintain the political momentum, he continued, suspending identification risked lessening pressure for a political solution. What did Polisario hope for? I asked. And were there differences among them?

The president thought not. From what he knew of the Polisario leadership their policy objectives were not much at variance, differences related to personal rivalry: Abdel-Aziz and Bachir were rivals, not wide apart in position. Regional autonomy, was that realistic? Ould Taya said that when the idea was first floated it might have been premature; current circumstances were different. The two sides had to talk, he repeated as I was leaving. Before my departure I met informally with the ambassadors of France, Germany, Spain and the US and representatives of the European Union and UNDP. The American ambassador confirmed that, to the best of her knowledge, attempts to nudge Polisario further were being abandoned, the Spanish ambassador stated that he had been aware of the idea to appoint a mediator but it failed when none 'saw light at the end of the tunnel.'

In Algeria I met the foreign minister, Ahmed Attaf, the foreign office secretary-general, Amar Bendjama, Lamamra, their permanent representative at the UN, and directors of relevant departments. As always in Algiers discussion was serious, focused and well-informed. I was asked to elaborate on developments subsequent to Garekhan's visit, these covered arguments for and against the publication of lists and the prospects for continuing identification, Morocco insisting that all applicants, whose forms were submitted in due time, had a right to be identified while Polisario refused to identify persons other than those belonging to 'sub-fractions included in the census'. In a comprehensive programme covering all remaining applicants, we proposed three weeks to identify those remaining from non-contested groups, Morocco agreed provided there was explicit commitment to treat H, I and Js from week four. Even if lists were published Polisario would work only with the A to G categories. In the circumstances Boutros-Ghali had told me of his intention to suspend identification; military observers would be reduced in number: the force commander believed a reduction achievable through a leaner medical unit and headquarters staff without affecting team-site deployment and monitoring patrols. The secretary-general was determined to retain a political presence, which, I said, led naturally to the question of talks.

Following discussion with Bachir I had obtained Rabat's agreement to a top-level meeting, but when it transpired that the US was exploring an alternative way forward, Bachir thought it sensible to await the outcome of the American effort. Logical, I admitted. Pelletreau's visit to Algiers followed, but his projected meeting with Polisario did not take place, nor did a subsequent

American mission to Tindouf make headway. Now, I said, we had King Hassan II's official visit to France, I could not know whether something helpful might emerge from his talks with Chirac. Attaf, who had been following with rapt attention, smiled in disbelief at the last, he wanted, first, to address specific points.

Algeria, with other countries, had invested substantially in launching the settlement plan, they believed it the path to a just and durable solution, there was no alternative to the plan; it alone had been accepted by both parties. The secretary-general's intention to withdraw the identification commission left those concerned without real alternative. The minister rejected financial consideration as principal argument, UN systematic disengagement from African conflicts – he cited Somalia, Burundi, Rwanda, Sierra Leone, even Liberia – delivered a political message, did it mean that financial concerns applied more stringently in Africa? Thirdly, he insisted that Minurso was and continued to be a political mission, that was its primordial function, the military dimension was subsidiary, supportive and valued for ensuring a peaceful environment for a referendum. He strongly opposed withdrawal of the identification commission, the decision was precipitate, taken hastily. In his oral report to the Council the secretary-general offered hope by promising a political alternative, Algeria had counted on a substantive proposal but news from New York implied this amounting merely to an appeal for the international community's good offices in bringing the parties together. Algeria had always urged direct contact in overcoming obstacles to the settlement plan, it was necessary to breach the wall of mistrust, for the two warring parties to meet face to face. Minurso's presence had cemented the cease-fire, but it needed political action, ending that would legitimize a return to arms. The minister concluded by reasserting his government's full cooperation. I thanked him, I looked to Algeria for support in the coming political phase. In the corridor Lamamra told me he was returning urgently to New York for the Council meeting, he thought it possible that members might decide to deliver more than the secretary-general requested.

New York, focused on reduction, had dispatched an administrative team to visit Laayoune, Tindouf and military team-sites. Option one would involve twenty percent reduction in the number of military personnel, the others forty and eighty percent respectively. The last provided for a static, purely symbolic presence; the first two meant cutting current activity. The new force commander, Major-General Leandro, though uncomfortable at presiding over a diminished force, was politically sensitive – he had earlier been Portugal's governor of Macao. He argued persuasively for a slimmed military, with twenty percent cuts overall but leaving units equipped to perform similar tasks to the past, with deeper cuts the military observers would be unable to meet such obligations. General Leandro had my full support, I reported accordingly to New York, but I was unsure of priorities in the secretary-general's office and the Council.

In Laayoune I received a draft secretary-general's report for the Council indicating a forty percent cut in the military. General Leandro was outraged. Given how Boutros had briefed Council members and what he said to me personally I saw two possible explanations: the first, more subtle, was Boutros being manipulative by proposing less than necessary, as a cost-cutting measure, to have the Council responsible for increasing expenditure in line with cease-fire essentials, the second, that my recommendation had been sabotaged in New York. I telephoned at the earliest realistic hour. While Garekhan, and, from hints, the department for political affairs upheld this reduction, Kofi Annan, head of peace-keeping operations, objected; he confronted the secretary-general:'If cuts were inevitable, it would be better to choose a purely symbolic presence.' Boutros-Ghali compromised: 'Then let's split it. Let's go for thirty per cent.'

The force commander was diverted by an urgent summons to meet Polisario's 'minister of defence'. I authorized his immediate departure – it happened to be Saturday – and pondered the reason. It was 1 June. Polisario had declared they would respect the cease-fire until 31 May when the existing mandate expired. General Leandro returned late, confused by the lack of urgency in what Brahim Ghali had to convey: failure to monitor Western Sahara's northern border, ineffective action on overflight violations and the untenable situation for Sahrawis living in Moroccan dominated territory. The cease-fire would continue to be scrupulously respected, it was all that remained of the settlement plan and, as such, vital. Ghali explained that he had called for a meeting since he would be absent travelling round their military regions. An aide moaned that the exodus of identification commission staff deprived the Sahrawis of hope, the military staying on enabled Moroccans to sleep peacefully. Polisario, while ready for armed action, looked to the new political office for diplomatic momentum, though contemptuous of our ability to deliver.

Polisario agreed to seeing me as an 'act of courtesy'. At the chicken farm I was greeted, with minimal politeness, by a man who identified himself as director-general at the presidency, everyone, he said, was exceptionally busy but the 'prime minister' would receive me later. Meanwhile, critical issues needed addressing, transparency was paramount so why did I refuse to implement the secretary-general's 'decision' and bow to Moroccan pressure? And could I please clarify what 'burden of proof' meant. I stated, yet again, that it was for the applicant to prove that he or she qualified, which depended on written evidence or concurring testimony from both sheikhs. The director-general looked skeptical, he cited one group of three thousand applicants, 'all Moroccans'. 'Our sheikh Breika tired waving his hand in refusal, so he waggled his forefinger from side to side, we called him the windscreen-wiper. A complete waste of time.' 'Just give us the lists', why conceal the outcome if what I said was true? If lists were published would Polisario agree to further identification? I asked. That he rejected categorically; it should be unconditional. And have identification end? 'Tomorrow there will be another special representative,' he summarised. There was bitterness in the air, a sense of somewhat irrational disappointment, while expecting a '*deus ex machina*' to impose their view on Morocco. I felt wheels spinning in the sand.

Mahfoud Ali Beiba, 'prime minister', arrived to 'receive' me in the absence of Abdel-Aziz 'out of town', Bachir 'in the south' and Kheddad in New York. He had no comment on the report to the Council or the resolution, he had no new ideas, preferred to hear anything I had to say. I mentioned political prisoners: I had asked the independent jurist to return before the end of the month with Rabat under pressure to cooperate fully. I was also working to interest governments in enabling the release and return of prisoners-of-war. Thirdly, Polisario had long insisted on direct talks, which Morocco refused, would they, I wondered, welcome exploratory contacts? Ali Beiba said he would transmit my thoughts and provide an answer when possible.

The mood in Morocco was equally dispiriting. When I asked Azmi for an appointment with Basri I was told it would be arranged in Rabat. That evening Azmi telephoned to say I should postpone coming, Basri was preoccupied with the Argentinian president's state visit before travelling abroad. I had meanwhile made appointments, which Azmi urged me to cancel, the timing was most inopportune. When next day I landed, half an hour behind schedule because of headwinds, actual as well as allegorical, I faced a disgruntled Azmi, he complained: having to wait, having missed work at the office. Gruffly, how had my visit to Tindouf gone? Had I seen Abdel-Aziz? – as if he did not know. Abdel-Aziz was away, I said, I met Ali Beiba. Abdel-Aziz was there, he said, or at least returned that day. Had Polisario agreed to identification? When were they going to? Fortunately, Azmi had a commitment and we parted. Before talking to the Moroccans I was anxious to hear what the American ambassador might have achieved.

Ginsberg congratulated himself on his influence in maintaining Minurso and he had other irons in the peace plan fire. In Washington many lawmakers argued for US withdrawal from Minurso, ending financial support, it was because of confidential initiatives in recent months, Ginsberg claimed, that Congress had not pulled the plug. He was disappointed that Morocco chose not to engage more positively. What were my ideas? I told of my meeting in Tindouf and described the general dismay, how it affected the morale of people in the camps and military personnel, previously buoyed by the prospect of a referendum. Minurso and the identification commission being drawn down led the refugees increasingly to despair of escape from the camps. I mentioned the ideas presented to Ali Beiba, an exchange of prisoners-of-war would happen only if governments intervened, Ginsberg said that agreement to an earlier exchange was the king's 'gift' to the US. On political prisoners a visit by the independent jurist might be helpful. He had nothing on talks.

Bodan, instructed to follow up on the meeting with Ali Beiba, was twice rebuffed. The 'president' would not be available to meet me; the Polisario leadership would name a representative in due course, Kheddad might be designated but he was travelling, his return date unknown. Then came an invitation to meet Kheddad and Boukhari in Madrid. The Spanish authorities confirmed that a conference of Sahrawi supporters was planned, with Abdel-Aziz attending, in a strictly private, non-official, capacity as far as Spain was concerned. The Spanish government was reluctant to see me involved with this Polisario propaganda event, where a media ambush should be expected, a trap: Polisario would announce my presence and corner me with aggressive NGOs plus manipulative press, I could not expect a fair hearing, much less a constructive exchange. I thanked Polisario for the invitation, I would welcome a meeting with Kheddad and Boukhari, both well-known to me. Since Madrid lay outside the mission area I needed the secretary-general's authorization and he was travelling which might make it difficult to obtain approval in the forty-eight hours remaining, should it prove impossible to meet in Madrid, I hoped to see Mr Kheddad after his return to Rabouni. From New York I heard that Kheddad had stayed in America before flying directly home without visiting Madrid.

After speaking to Kheddad back in Rabouni, I received a message: ' I can confirm our being available in Las Palmas on Tuesday 2 July 1996. We are also available to meet the independent jurist.' Las Palmas was welcoming to Polisario, their slogan sculpted in bleached rocks widely visible on a hillside above the airport.

18

Towards dialogue

SPAIN GENEROUSLY MADE AVAILABLE a conference room in an overpowering, somewhat gloomy official building from another era. At the entrance Boukhari and Kheddad introduced themselves. Once inside Boukhari assaulted Roucounas, for genuine, worthwhile work he should obtain names of political prisoners from NGOs, vague statements were all hot air. 'It's a year since your appointment, what satisfaction do you think our parents, children, families derive from your blandly accepting Morocco's statement that there are no political prisoners?' Kheddad said that the Americans, not the UN, pressured Morocco into releasing eight some months earlier. Barbarism had increased since the UN came, 'What is Moroccan law: that anyone who disputes, insinuates, hints that the Sahara is not Moroccan is guilty of a crime.' He paused. 'We were written off twenty years ago. We are still here, we will still be here in thirty years.' The identification process was derailed when thousands, from tribal groupings not included as sub-fractions in Spanish records, were imported from Casablanca and beyond. Polisario agreed, pragmatically, to start but had been 'made to swallow vipers'. They did not want tears or sympathy, Kheddad said, they wanted action, without pressure on Morocco progress was impossible. Transparency was an obligation, lists should be published, only those qualified who belonged to a sub-fraction included in the Spanish census, Polisario stood ready to identify anyone belonging to a census listed sub-fraction, and who submitted a request himself or herself. Boukhari had something to add about recent arrests in Boujdour, which Morocco maintained were not political in character, all such events had a political aspect; they were in reaction to Moroccan occupation of the territory. Roucounas insisted he had transmitted his concern to the authorities; Boukhari snapped: 'You are not just a courier. You have a mandate.'

They had an inalienable right, Kheddad said addressing me, to self-determination. Whatever any eventual concession, compromise or deal to end conflict, theirs remained the inalienable right to independence through self-determination. How could their people sustain morale, faced with a cadaver? Where was the secretary-general's political office, what its mandate? Kheddad saw nothing happening to implement the settlement plan. Without transparency the process made no sense, we worked in total obscurity. The question of sub-fraction membership was crystal clear. And the cease-fire, which only served Moroccan interests, with UN military observers complacent in tolerating Moroccan troop movements, reinforcements and overflights, could not be an end in itself. Polisario found itself checked, blocked, stopped in its rightful aspirations. Before I could speak Boukhari said that he had had enough of me talking and achieving nothing – except what Morocco wanted, he was shocked by the latest report of the Secretary-General, I had promised and failed to reflect correctly the Polisario position. There was no referendum because Morocco did not want it, except to confirm its occupation, only the cease-fire remained, which insured the colonization of Western Sahara. In real politics, he went on, they were just a small people, Morocco was stronger. How did I think that I could use whatever remained of my authority to overcome current problems? Transparency was not negotiable, the lists had to be published; that was a decision of the secretary-general not an idea of Polisario's. Only sub-fractions included in the census qualified for identification. They demanded their right to a free and fair referendum.

I waited an instant before cautiously raising the possibility of dialogue. I suggested informal and preliminary talks as a first step, Kheddad argued that only dialogue that was structured and at a responsible level served any purpose. When Morocco was ready for that – then Polisario was quite ready. The meeting ended with discursive talk of a new secretary-general, Boukhari adding something about another special representative, and we parted. After hours' bombardment, Roucounas, exhausted by unwonted abuse, retired to his hotel. Next morning we flew to Laayoune where the Moroccans lay in ambush.

Azmi attacked me for having gone to Las Palmas, I bent over backwards to humour the Polisario when all they wanted was my scalp, they were doing all they could, he said, to discredit me, in their eyes I was '*brulé*'. He told our chief of administration that I was '*brule*' – burnt out, finished – also as far as Morocco was concerned. So what was it they demanded? he asked petulantly. Transparency, the publication of lists, I said. 'It's against the plan, you have no mandate to publish lists at this stage, you know that perfectly well. And their rejection of H, I and J is ridiculous, they're made up of sub-fractions like the rest.' When I mentioned the great number he reacted furiously, it was not uncommon during anti-colonial struggles for people to seek refuge abroad. To be frank, he said, I was useless, the UN was useless; we were incapable of imposing compliance on a refractory Polisario.

Roucounas' discussion of political prisoners was equally uncomfortable. The two senior legal advisers in the ministry of interior took advantage of his diffidence and their superior French. It was almost a joke, Roucounas commented afterwards, a bitter joke: Morocco did not concede anything, stating only that some prisoners had died, some had been released, and the eight remaining, the eight sentenced in Laayoune the year before, after having their sentences commuted were due to be freed in an act of clemency on the king's birthday. A propos the king's birthday Azmi told me not to expect the usual invitation, he saw no need to remind me of their outrage when I compared attendance at Polisario's Congress with the royal birthday, but at the eleventh hour a courier delivered the royal summons.

Arafat was guest of honour, he hovered beside the receiving line, where the king welcomed other special guests. My fall from grace was not reflected at court, I was accorded precedence and King Hassan greeted me graciously. Like a feudal scene from Shakespeare select guests and members of the diplomatic corps forgathered in a central court, where part obscured by columns, Basri slipped conspiratorially from one distinguished personality to another, as if plotting. That suspicion returned when, after the garden party, he drove me to Bouznika, past the palace at Skhirat, where on an earlier birthday Hassan was almost assassinated. Basri was fully informed about my talk with Ali Beiba and the encounter in Las Palmas, their intelligence was impeccable. He upbraided me fiercely for addressing Ali Beiba as 'prime minister' – the UN did not recognize Polisario as a state. He said he had a copy of something I had written. (True, 'prime minister' would be improper in official correspondence, but this was a very informal note; I could not help wondering how the Moroccans obtained a copy.) I said to Basri that since he knew all, there was little for me to add, what was his analysis of the current situation and what did he think could be done?

Basri, who liked to ask questions, to repeat questions, to interrogate, was less prone to answering, except to dictate. His usual response was: take a firm line with Polisario. 'Listen carefully,' he said. He began by summarising the state of identification, his numbers largely accurate from what I knew, though I was not asked to comment. 'If we have the figures Polisario have them too', with which I agreed. He counted on me to convey the 'real reason' for blockage to the people in the camps, to promote defection, their secession from the

Polisario side without offering a clue as to how this be done or why I should wish to do it. Bachir was erratic, he continued, but a meeting was still possible provided it took place at Bachir's request. He wanted my evaluation of the Polisario leadership, and an assessment of those remaining to be identified and expected to qualify. It was quite extraordinary: for Basri to make unrealistic, unreal requests that he knew I neither could nor would implement, unless the intention was to confirm my uselessness in Moroccan eyes, only the reference to Bachir made sense, and that almost incidental. I speculated that the king had ordered Basri to persevere, and he did not know how.

Polisario had no clearer vision. Boukhari in New York sounded bleak, the American initiative had failed: they simply told us not to mention independence, and Pelletreau, when in the region, did not even meet with Abdel-Aziz. He piled criticism on Boutros-Ghali, who, happily, would be going at the end of the year- though a departing secretary-general could be dangerous viz. Perez de Cuellar's last minute input. Boukhari favoured dialogue, but without pressure Morocco would never agree; nobody seemed willing to bring pressure on the king, certainly not the UN. Curiously, he said nothing unpleasant about me; and if I could create a framework for direct dialogue they were prepared to consider it, I should speak to Bachir, who was back in Tindouf, Boukhari adding wryly: 'At one stage you might have thought he and Jensen were engaged'.[1]

Neither Morocco nor Polisario wanted the political process to stop. Both sides, I was sure, were able to assess the outcome of identification to date, and thus well placed to guess at the end result should all be identified. Polisario, albeit confident in convincing support for their cause, seemed certain that Morocco would never submit to a referendum it was destined not to win, and that the international community would not compel it to do so. Basri was as determined as ever to manipulate the settlement plan but at a loss how this be engineered to achieve the global seal of approval that the king desired. Plans for regionalization gave scope to devolving regional autonomy, but Morocco would still need nudging into dialogue by sharpened awareness of where identification was headed. The combination of certainty and uncertainty could provide an incentive. Polisario had regularly expressed interest, they had conditions, but these did not appear insuperable, their commitment, however, depended on Algerian concurrence.

Arrival in Algiers was once again marked by maximum security. From a slalom course outside the airport circling inverted saw-blades and concrete blocks we were driven at high speed on the wrong side of the highway, against approaching traffic waved away by motorcycle outriders. The familiar tranquility of the government guest compound provided welcome respite before we proceeded to the ministry. The foreign minister, Ahmed Attaf, relaxed and friendly, was accompanied by Bendjama, secretary-general of the ministry, the director-general for African affairs and the director for multilateral relations; I had Bodan Kotewski with me. The minister began: their President Zeroual had seen Boutros-Ghali at the OAU summit and been assured that the Saharan peace process was not at an end. He invited me to elaborate on developments since our last meeting. I gave an account of my visit to Polisario, the ideas floated, and subsequent discussion in Las Palmas. On the Moroccan side I mentioned Basri's complex reaction. My concern was that Polisario opt to await King Hassan's disappearance and a change of UN secretary-general, not that either development would necessarily facilitate a solution. If, by the end of November, no progress was reported the Security Council would be tempted to make draconian reductions if not close the mission entirely. Well though I understood Polisario's quandary, danger lay in doing nothing.

Attaf responded at length. He favoured a 'package deal' covering all aspects of the plan, and to that end advised direct negotiations. He said his was the longer-term perspective: at first Morocco refused even to hear of self-determination, later the king agreed, albeit as a '*referendum confirmatif*', Algeria urged direct negotiations and the OAU in 1984 called for the exercise of good offices, again Morocco said 'no' before relenting in 1988. Morocco never made a move except under compelling domestic or international pressure, but circumstances might be ripening for negotiation. Of course, one should understand Polisario, they were unwilling to make further concessions with nothing in return. Transparency, Attaf continued, was for them face-saving. I enquired what he felt about influential countries coming together with Algeria and Mauritania as a first step. He paused before replying: Mandela suggested just that.

The minister had a prior commitment that evening and dinner was hosted by Amar Bendjama. I liked Bendjama, a sophisticated, travelled man, and decided this was the moment to declare my hand. It happened almost of itself when their top official for African affairs asked rather pointedly how I envisaged 'neither winner nor loser', the phrase, as they knew, attributed to King Hassan. Bendjama said: 'It would be very interesting to have your opinion, frankly, and off the record.' I told them what I thought: 'Do nothing, waiting for a miracle, and the Sahrawis will remain in camps indefinitely, under the harshest desert conditions. Second option is to resurrect identification and the settlement plan, though, in all honesty, I don't think the chances are bright. But let us assume that a referendum does take place and the vote goes in favour of independence. Do you really believe the Moroccans will meekly withdraw from the territory? And if they don't, do you see the US or France, or NATO or the UN, mobilized to force them out? Again, no. Would Algeria go to war with Morocco to liberate Western Sahara? Regional autonomy constitutes my third option. The world knows many models, some as extensive as Germany and Spain, others less so. Morocco is in process of constitutional regionalization; the king is ill, although we don't know how seriously, and anxious to settle the issue during his reign; this could be the moment to negotiate.' Bendjama had been listening attentively. He reflected a moment. Then he asked whether I had discussed this with the Moroccans, and what was their reaction. I had, I said, probed, but only tangentially. I faced a challenge in working principally through Basri. King Hassan, of course, would decide.

The Director for African affairs butted in that regional autonomy was no new idea. The Americans had recently floated an informal paper going beyond Moroccan regionalization, but it went nowhere near far enough. He warned against piecemeal implementation of the plan, UN sausage slicing was the wrong approach. The failure of identification . . ., he was saying, when Bendjama intervened: the situation had evolved and might be conducive to negotiating a political solution. Morocco never voluntarily moved ahead, every advance had been achieved under pressure, including contact with Polisario, and that often to buy time. Serious negotiation was indispensable, Morocco had to be made to understand. Polisario remained suspicious, knew themselves the weaker party, yet, Bendjama said, they had nothing to lose. They would not make further concessions without guarantees in return, they would not wish to negotiate 'without a parachute'. The lack of confidence between the parties . . .'Huge mistrust,' I agreed. Bendjama finished: 'Since we are talking frankly, let me point out that your mandate is limited – to the plan. One must not forget that. One has to be very cautious if pursuing what goes beyond.' 'Understood,' I said. 'But you are not against my exploring?' 'Certainly not.' Only given the green light from Algeria could Polisario commit. The caution, though, was well taken, in nudging the two sides towards dialogue I would be venturing onto waters for which I had neither chart nor travel authorisation.

Algeria's President Zeroual had just visited Mauritania, it was important to know if anything transpired in relation to the Sahara. For Zeroual's state reception the Mauritanian presidency had been stylishly equipped. A new, female, protocol officer, dressed in traditional Sahrawi '*melhafa*' adorned with silver stars, ushered me into the refurbished audience chamber. The single, throne-like chair had been replaced by a resplendent yellow leather sofa, regally imposing in a roomful of fine carpets. Ould Taya was friendly and welcoming while the cameras worked their photo opportunity. That done, he was keen to hear about recent developments, my encountering Ali Beiba and meetings in Rabat and Algiers. I concluded with what was said about regional autonomy. When he asked I made it clear that the Algerians had not explicitly agreed, but nor had they disagreed. Morocco responded only to pressure, the president confirmed, and this could be the moment. Did he think regional autonomy worth discussing? It might not be ideal for Polisario, he said, but it was what Morocco could offer. This was not something, he added, that had been discussed with Zeroual.

Polisario was in a quandary. UN military reported a Polisario field commander divulging a plan to take Minurso hostages, strike into Moroccan held territory, and deploy the hostages as a human shield against counter-attack, people were nervous. Convinced that inaction would only aggravate the situation, I asked Bodan, back in Tindouf, to arrange an appointment with Bachir. Bodan, who had earlier been brusquely warned that I would not be meeting high Polisario officials, except at their specific request, was told: 'Mr Bachir was ready to meet Mr Jensen any time anywhere.' Next day, Sunday, I went to Rabouni. 'Need to wear a tie?' Bodan asked, 'Only if Bachir does,' I said, which seemed improbable. The heat was extreme: 50 to 52 degrees centigrade. Bachir arrived, immaculate in a white shirt, silk tie and well-pressed trousers. I said how pleased I was to see him, it had been a long time since our last meeting. He nodded, yes, he had been travelling and enquired where I had been. I asked whether he wanted a detailed account of my discussion in Algiers, as well as Nouakchott, or was that redundant since he was presumably informed. Again he nodded, his distinctive nod; I interpreted it to mean that further briefing was unnecessary. We dealt succinctly with outstanding issues: Polisario's reluctance to release another batch of prisoners-of-war except in context; a date for a visit of the independent jurist; the debatable merit in three further weeks of identification if leading to stoppage. Then the crux: the idea of dialogue, with others in the room I was cautious about proceeding, but he insisted.

The settlement plan had gone far but was blocked. Figures did not look as giving Morocco a decisive majority and even identifying all the disputed was unlikely to change that. I conveyed to Bachir the gist of our projections

– we should publish the lists, he interrupted. With Morocco in process of revising its constitution the timing might be propitious for talks, a meeting could perhaps take place in Morocco, or, I mentioned the Nordic countries, Norway or Denmark. What was the capital of Denmark? he enquired vaguely. Copenhagen. Ah, yes, he remembered having been there on his way to meet Khomeini (a curious route, I thought) and lying awake waiting for twilight to become night before falling asleep as dawn broke. We debated questions of level, size of delegation and were about to discuss an agenda when Bachir, smiling cryptically, said that we were largely 'back to square one'. Lunch was announced.

Lunch over, I suggested seeing Bachir alone. We needed to be absolutely clear on several points. He reconfirmed that Polisario was committed to dialogue, he agreed with my proposal for a small group from each side: I suggested himself plus two and offered to try convincing Basri of the same. The meeting should take place outside Morocco, he said – Denmark fine except in high summer – unless talk was with the king, not merely, he added, 'an audience', in which case Bachir would come to Rabat, the agenda to be unstructured '*à batons rompus*'- without a fixed agenda. I suggested the first encounter, in secret – absolutely no propaganda, no publicity – begin by setting an agenda; he proposed a lasting political solution, '*solution politique durable*'. Perfect, I thought, assuming we both spoke similar coded language. I enquired about the American initiative, he said they had a paper that was to have been a basis for discussion. Could that paper be used? He was doubtful, there were reservations, amendments on both sides and needed the US for enforcement. (I had been promised America's backing but the burgeoning feud with Boutros-Ghali had me doubt whether the US would intervene on the UN's behalf.) Closed session over we were interviewed by 'National Sahrawi' radio, Bachir kissed me on parting and promised to stay reachable.

I had barely returned from Tindouf when Azmi called: Basri wished to see me urgently. I prepared for a 9 a.m. appointment at the minister's seaside residence by memorising complete identification figures and projections assembled with my computer expert's calculations and insight: for ammunition, there would be no piece of paper I could be cajoled into surrendering. The first of August was warm even in the morning, Azmi collected me promptly then railed at the driver for an inappropriate turning till we reached Bouznika, in good time. Ushered into the presence we witnessed the minister for fisheries given short shrift, told to make another appointment, he had a speech for urgent clearance, he muttered to me and left. Basri, spruce and energetic, ignored the splendid outlook over his exclusive bay, and breakfasted. He devoured honey dipped pancakes and a fried egg before announcing that we would talk in the car.

Basri, driving, asked me in Arabic to begin. Azmi, awkwardly perched in the middle of the back seat lent forward to interpret, but I understood. You raised with me certain issues. 'Points', Basri interjected. To tell the people in the camps why identification stalled I used an interview with Polisario radio (this would have been monitored). Other direct contact was impossible, which I knew he understood perfectly, and fomenting secession could hardly be my task. As far as assessing the leadership: frankly, Morocco had known and knew the personalities much better than I. Lastly: meeting with Bachir.

I gave an account of my discussion. I had proposed Bachir plus two and in counterpart would urge Basri plus two. Talks, in secrecy, should begin without a rigid agenda, the focus on a durable political solution. What did that mean, precisely? Basri turned to ask. A negotiated compromise, I said, in the spirit of '*ni vainqueur, ni vaincu*'. From my perspective two considerations predominated: whatever the outcome of a referendum Morocco would not voluntarily relinquish the Sahara, nor was it likely to be expelled by force, on the other hand King Hassan wanted Morocco's presence in the Sahara validated internationally. A measure of regional autonomy offered a possible solution. Where to meet? If for discussion with the king in Morocco, if not, I suggested preliminary talks abroad, to be followed by a meeting with the king in Rabat. Basri listened throughout, paying meticulous attention; Azmi told me that he had been driving at up to 150 kph – with me in the suicide seat. He agreed that the moment might be ripening, the situation had evolved. That was when I chose to lob my grenade: identification results were not overwhelmingly in Morocco's favour, I said, far from it, and rattled off figures, 'Yes, yes,' he said, 'that they knew, and Polisario know.' But, I warned him, projections for identifying all H, I and J applicants promised limited change, which he disputed by shrugging a shoulder; he shook his head. I shot off more figures, estimated from what we knew, and they had to know better, I wanted Basri, and through him the king, to realize that a referendum, free and fairly conducted by the UN, would never deliver the only result they were prepared to accept. They had to talk, they had to compromise.

Bachir, having been temporarily sidelined, could be looking to reassert a political role, a good moment to exploit. Basri did not disagree. On where to meet, he had other views, he said he had met Bachir once in Lisbon, and elsewhere, why not Morocco? Could be Rabat, which was best, or Agadir, or Laayoune, or another place, in Morocco he could discuss with the crown prince – and be received by His Majesty. A strong preference for Morocco was evident but I wanted to be clear whether this was a condition. Summarizing his argument, I confirmed my understanding that he was prepared to meet Bachir, but not abroad. No, he responded sharply, meeting elsewhere was not out of the question, but a meeting in Morocco, anywhere in Morocco, was preferable. He became extremely insistent, aggressively so, reverting to '*tu*' and Erik: 'Talk to no one about this. Not to the ambassadors, not to people at the UN, not to Snoussi.' I said I had no desire to jeopardize what I had been working long to achieve. He repeated, word for word, what he had just said. 'We'll meet again tonight.'

Basri was in the pool-house at his principal residence. An expansive television set showed a French detective film. He looked round, tired but satisfied, a 'social dialogue' had been agreed with union leaders and signed after months hard bargaining that culminated in a twenty-four hour lap. A marathon, I said, he liked that, the accolade of having completed a marathon, and switched off the television. In Algiers: who did I see? He wanted me to confirm what he certainly knew. I met Attaf, the minister, and over dinner the ministry's secretary-general Bendjama, together with senior officials; speaking frankly and off the record, I had sketched three scenarios: one, a referendum won by Polisario – Basri shook his head in theatrical disbelief – but no competent power poised to drive Morocco from the Sahara, two, continuing inaction imposing a heavy humanitarian cost on people in the camps and nurturing instability throughout the region, Algeria and Mauritania included, three, a 'peace of the brave', in the king's words '*ni vainquer, ni vaincu*', based on a measure of regional autonomy. That was the gist, if not my precise words, I said. What did he say? Basri asked. He did not disagree.

The first encounter should have no fixed agenda. Both would speak '*a batons rompus*', discuss whatever was on the table, I said, glancing down at the coffee table before me. Straight independence is off one end – and I chopped beside the table; integration pure and simple is off the other end – and I chopped it away. Talk could be about anything on the table, excluding those extremities,[2] Basri broke in: 'And we'll move towards each other.' We can talk to Bachir, he continued, the only one with any openness of mind, flexibility of approach. Abdel-Aziz was rigid, the puppet of Algeria, Bachir was intelligent and had the authority and status among his people to make discussion meaningful, he was an Reguibi of standing. Bachir was the man they wished to meet, the rest, Basri argued, were technicians, advisers, civil servants, like Ali Beiba, ironically titling him 'prime minister'. Assurances and conditions would apply as discussed before these were sidelined by the American initiative. The Americans had been heavy-handed, Basri said, not diplomatic, they threw their weight around, it culminated in mutual frustration, a feeling that the other could have done more and done better. He saw no point in working with Ginsberg, who seemed to imagine he was some kind of Kissinger, and he dismissed involving Carter or any other eminent American. Finally, he said, for 'your ears only' that when identification resumed Morocco would exclusively present qualified candidates expected to pass muster. We had finished, I thought, when he accused me of evading one question.

The figures, he pronounced, after a pause. He sought greater precision: what was the basis for my projections? I said that in light of experience we estimated around eighty percent turn-out for identification. Those in the census qualified and others census related, claimants under criteria four and five were acceptable if they produced documents, but those who indicated only vaguely their fathers' place of birth rarely obtained both sheikhs' recognition. Admittedly mine were guesstimates but I believed they were fairly reliable, he looked unconvinced. What are your projections? I asked. Without a second's hesitation and with a degree of certainty I found astonishing, he rattled off figures: Polisario had at most a further two thousand, 'They're finished. In Mauritania another two thousand at the outside. We have eighty to eighty-five thousand more, they're definite, no doubt about them,' he ended triumphantly. My turn to look dubious.

Azmi cornered me as we left. He said he understood how I reached the rough division of thirty-eight thousand for Polisario with just possibly forty-eight for Morocco. Minurso favoured Polisario. I insisted that the identification commission was rigorous and impartial, a candidate seldom qualified when one sheikh said 'no'. Azmi retorted that while that principle was unremittingly applied against Moroccan applicants, the identification commission had accepted the testimony of Polisario sheikhs when the Moroccan sheikh dissented, which I found hard to believe. According to Azmi, Polisario could count on about twenty-four thousand, he doubted more, and Morocco between eighty and ninety thousand. It was a brave show, he knew I was not convinced.

My projections served a purpose. Precise figures were less important, the message was to convince the Moroccans that an honest, UN brokered referendum should not be counted on to deliver the decisive outcome they planned and in the circumstances a political compromise became attractive. Similarly for Polisario, they would be unwise to barter on conclusive implementation of the settlement plan in their favour, but their showing in identification conferred negotiating power.

As the Antonov approached Tindouf I surveyed the vast expanse of desert, grooved like an ancient face with fern-like wrinkles, before my head began to clear. Our new Russian colonel, Malekov, greeted me at the base. Fifteen minutes later Bachir arrived, in jacket and tie. He was relaxed and friendly, had a word in Arabic with Malekov. Admin first: a date for Roucounas, which Boukhari was designated to handle; I had been trying to reach Boukhari but he was 'out of town'. 'The FBI tell you?' Bachir asked. 'The UN works closely with the FBI, doesn't it?' Bachir pursued his little joke. 'Given current relations between Boutros-Ghali and the US, we daren't rely on the FBI,' I said. Boukhari would be back shortly to make arrangements. Bachir was interested in Roucounas' visit to Rabat, the Moroccans, I told him, agreed to provide information regarding all individuals whose names were supplied by Polisario as suspected detainees. 'Polisario will do that,' Bachir said, 'Then Morocco will state this one is unknown, this one has been released, this one is dead. We have no great expectations.'

Bachir, once we were alone, gave me his expectant look. I had met Basri, I told him, and Basri accepted the proposal for a small confidential meeting with a flexible agenda, Bachir to be accompanied by two others. As to place, Basri preferred Rabat. I knew Bachir's position on Rabat, indeed anywhere in Morocco, but he had earlier expressed interest in talking to the prince, admittedly when he believed the king terminally ill. Bachir pondered, said nothing for a moment, before responding, it was useful that Basri agreed to a meeting, small, and without a precise agenda but Basri had been unforthcoming on the important issue of where. If it were to discuss with the king, then as a matter of courtesy, 'I am neither king nor president', he would go to Morocco, not otherwise; perhaps at a later stage, the initial meeting should be on neutral ground. Though Basri argued for Rabat or somewhere in Morocco, he had not dismissed going abroad. I asked Bachir to name places he would be unwilling to go, and whether he had a preference. Denmark, I recognized, was far away, whatever the hours of daylight. Denmark would be fine, he said, or Switzerland, Spain. France? I enquired tentatively. Slightly to my surprise he said France would be all right – it might even offer advantages. Like Evian, I suggested (where the Franco-Algerian accords were concluded, no need to remind him). The French could easily provide a setting, he said.

Bachir wanted to hear more about Basri. For Morocco stamp and flag, emblems of sovereignty, and recognition of the sovereign were not negotiable,

Polisario would be starting from a position short of independence. As with Basri, I demonstrated, using exactly the same chopping gesture off the ends of a small rectangular table to delineate the area for discussion, excluding integration off the table at one end, independence at the other. What remained on the table was the subject for talks, then, in Basri's words, 'we will move towards each other.' He said that! Bachir was genuinely surprised. 'If our extreme position, off the table, is independence, what is theirs?' Integration, straightforward integration, also off the table, I repeated. He ruminated. 'If we discuss, we will reach a solution,' he said using similar language to Basri, and seemed to mean it. If Morocco's willingness was based, as often in the past, on assuming Polisario would not accept the terms, its bluff was called. I said I had no wish to co-ordinate a meeting unless both sides came with constructive intent, confrontation, propaganda would be entirely counter-productive. Did he think this the right moment to begin talking, or might it be preferable to wait? This was the moment, he said, definitely, for many reasons, without explaining what they were. Was he prepared? He was ready 'to begin tomorrow'. To fix a date I needed Basri's concurrence. Might he be going on holiday? Bachir asked, it was August. 'I doubt it,' I said, 'the man is a worker without equal.'

Azmi, equally passionate about work, was, unexpectedly, preoccupied with leave arrangements, his wife and daughter were in Marbella and he planned to join them. I apologised for being inconvenient but I needed an urgent appointment with Basri. Basri was in Paris, Azmi replied, with no return details fixed; it could be in the morning, he promised to keep me informed, and before noon next day I was told Basri had returned and a meeting was possible. Literally five minutes later Azmi was again on the line, proposing we meet 'at once'. Basri at the seaside was already at ease, he had his shoes off and feet up on a neighbouring chair, he threw aside a stack of newspaper and invited me to sit. Bachir, had I seen him?

I gave an account of my talk with Bachir, including the graphic illustration of limits to negotiation when I chopped off independence at one end of the table, straightforward integration at the other. Whatever remained was subject to discussion in the hope of moving from extreme positions, inevitable at the outset, towards a common ground of acceptable compromise. Basri asked me to repeat the demonstration. Bachir, I continued, had used language similar to his own in the belief that serious talk would eventually lead to a solution. A small group, meeting in strictest confidence, without a fixed agenda was agreeable. I thought the first encounter should serve to establish contact, lay a foundation on which to build confidence, discuss a framework for a meeting to follow, and to fix a date and place for it. On the venue question Bachir had reiterated his willingness to come to Rabat for discussion with the king, but otherwise expected the first meeting, at least, to be outside Morocco. He had no strong preferences and excluded no country. Switzerland was a possibility – or France. I said I had queried the suggestion of France thinking they would object. 'Why?' Basri commented. 'They have good relations with France.' Basri repeated arguments favouring Morocco, Rabat as the place that would give Bachir opportunity to be received by the king. The crown prince was not mentioned. Then, seamlessly, he moved to meeting abroad. France was a good choice, he thought, very good, he mentioned localities in and around Paris and beyond. He rambled, as others might perusing a travel brochure, though rambling was unfair to Basri, his grasp of pertinent facts, names, dates and other detail was stupendous – seeing anyone else's point of view was what he conspicuously lacked. For a moment summer, sunshine and the sea beyond his verandah inspired holiday anecdotes as he mulled over geographical options.

The Marrakech formula: flag and stamp, sovereignty, was inviolable, Morocco would control defence and be responsible for foreign affairs. After every item he said: '*tu me comprends*?'- you understand me? As if he could be misunderstood. Other constitutional pillars had also to be respected, such as finance and taxation, though these could be subject to negotiation. The range was broad, he hesitated at full autonomy internationally guaranteed, as opening the door to secession, short of that – anything. Morocco had no problem with talking. 'Recognition' was irrelevant, the plan already recognized two parties: Morocco and the Frente Polisario, Morocco had accepted the plan, alas, which was tantamount to recognition. He was astonishingly relaxed about issues argued elsewhere with fiery commitment and without flexibility. Did Algeria have a role? I asked. Basri volunteered that Algeria's position was known, and with its internal problems it was content just to create difficulty for Morocco. Whatever Algeria's minister artfully said to me, or when they received me hospitably, they would revert to rigid insistence on electors listed in the Spanish census and be equally unbending on other aspects, the Soviet Union was no more but Algeria remained Soviet in mentality. Personalities counted, he went on, and he liked Bachir notwithstanding appalling things said about the king. Bachir had qualities – not least his apparent dislike of the Algerians, Abel-Aziz was a different affair altogether. He paused. I took the chance to raise a sensitive issue: my presence.

From discussion with Bachir it was clear he insisted on me accompanying them. If Bachir wanted it, would that pose a problem for Morocco? As soon as the delegations had been safely introduced I could disappear. Much better that I did not come, Basri stated without hesitation, no reason for it, he understood why I might be asked to escort Polisario to Morocco, but abroad, he saw no reason for it. Inevitably that would implicate the UN, the secretary-general, if I was only spotted arriving, the security people, who always accompanied Bachir, would be sure to photograph me and they could produce whatever montage they desired. Basri offered to provide a transcript or recording of Morocco's position as enunciated at the meeting, he was adamant that there be no presence other than Morocco and Polisario. Then, in a more accommodating tone, said he saw no objection to delegations staying in the same hotel, on the same floor even. In France security would be no problem. His team had visas; Polisario could have theirs issued on arrival. Back to hotels, he named the Ritz, in Paris, or Meurice at Celle St Cloud and the Pavillon Henri IV, which he favoured because of its powerful sentimental association as the place Mohammed V stayed before returning to Morocco and where many had come to show allegiance – including Sahrawis. Otherwise Grenoble was possible, or Bordeaux, or Biarritz, the French authorities might suggest somewhere. Should I advise them once a meeting in France was agreed? I asked. 'Morocco will,' he said categorically.

Bachir needed to provide the names of those accompanying him, two to three, who should be like-minded. Basri started demanding that Bachir bring credentials signed by Abdel-Aziz but thought better of it: Bachir's hands ought not to be tied. And the date? I asked. Basri awaited the king's 'green light'. He had consulted His Majesty after our last meeting and was confident of the king's blessing, 'tomorrow' we should have the royal assent. Basri counted on me transmitting this immediately to Bachir before returning to Rabat to settle final details. I could tell Bachir to expect an interlocutor who was 'courteous, well-informed, open'.

19

To Geneva and beyond

Next day I waited. When the telephone did ring the line went dead, finally, in the early evening, Azmi called. Had the 'patron' spoken to me? 'No,' I said. Geneva was now the place, Azmi continued, without explaining, could I please inform Bachir and return at once to Rabat, in two days' time. That I refused, communications, he knew perfectly well, were complicated but I would do my best. Miracle of miracles, Bachir responded promptly when I called from Laayoune offering to fly over as soon as it suited him. 'Why not tomorrow?'

The August heat lay heavy. Our Antonov felt claustrophobically hot and uncomfortable, hardly the climate for gathering thoughts or reflection. It amazed me how keen Basri had become, his sense of urgency. They wanted Bachir to come, perhaps they planned to separate him from the other Polisario, when accompanied by only two or three like-minded, even buy him. In the souk there was no morality, only a deal. As Polisario once admitted, any sheikh could be bought, including one of theirs, and Morocco had more money, though Azmi, in a moment of indiscretion, said that with all it cost to bring Brahim Hakim over and set him up in appropriate style, that was an exercise not easily repeated. You could never be sure. The temperature when we landed and drove to Minurso's base touched fifty in the shade; Bachir arrived punctually, wearing a dark suit and tie, with hair bushy and sand blown as his freedom fighter's insignia. Once alone together we came quickly to the point.

I confirmed having met Basri promptly after his return from Paris. He showed genuine interest: no fixed agenda, and I repeated, as in Rabat, the illustration of chopping off one end of a table then the other to exclude the two extremes: independence and straightforward integration. Concerning the place, France initially found favour but the Moroccans came to prefer Geneva. I had expected them to choose France – 'No, they would probably rather not,' Bachir interjected – but Geneva seemed a good choice. We discussed where to stay. Bachir said the Canton of Geneva disposed of houses but he had no objection to any hotel that was central and busy. Would he require a visa? I asked. He thought not, Switzerland was easier to enter than the European Union, after Schengen, he would check. I mentioned his brother, from what I had heard Polisario representative in Geneva. Bachir said his brother was in the camps pending reassignment to Canada, they had no one currently posted in Switzerland. I asked who would be coming with him. Sadafa, he thought, their 'ambassador' in Brussels, and perhaps Baba, his brother, or it might be Majid the 'ambassador' now in Bonn.

He had no problem with an early date, on the contrary. The following Thursday, which Basri had mentioned, was that too soon? He had no objection: could be Thursday or Friday. Finally, the issue of me, Basri stressed that I and the UN had no mandate, and thought it better I not be there; he wished me to serve as channel for communication in setting up the encounter but not be further implicated. Bachir demurred, he accepted that I might have no mediating role or be present during the actual meeting but I was needed to facilitate the encounter. With Snoussi in New York, he said, it took days merely to fix a breakfast appointment, who should call whom? Who call first? Who decide where to eat? Who pay the bill? My presence in Geneva was indispensable if only to oversee logistics and to alert the two delegations where and when to assemble, once they had been introduced, I could withdraw. I agreed, and undertook to tell Basri. Other Geneva business made it simple to justify my being in Switzerland. It followed that I would not be at the airport to greet either the Moroccans or Polisario. Basri had offered to provide me an account of proceedings after the meeting. Bachir, saying he would likely do the same, rose to check, through their 'ambassador' in Algiers, flights and visa requirements. He returned immediately, visas were no problem, flights from Algiers to Geneva departed Mondays and Saturdays. He suggested Monday the following week; I preferred Saturday, then they could take the Monday flight back, and he was happy to agree.

I urged Bachir to feint at Polisario's negotiating range in Geneva, but warned against being too ambitious. The first encounter was to establish contact, lay a foundation for serious exchange, seek to build sufficient good will for both sides to detect readiness in the other to move the process forward. One decision was necessary: to agree where, when and in what format to meet again. Circumstances could be opportune: Algeria had major political and economic difficulties and Morocco faced problems, not least massive unemployment, both stood to benefit from an end to conflict in the Sahara. The present situation, I imagined, was difficult also for Polisario. Bachir nodded,

'Very much so,' he said. Powerful countries beyond the region might be helpful: the US, of course, but not only the US; France and Germany, possibly other Security Council members; my idea was to invoke pressure, once dialogue was established, once it became clear that Morocco and Polisario had begun to discuss seriously. Bachir said he thought the timing right. (We may have underestimated the full implications of a US presidential election coming to a head and the secretary-general, unpopular with the Americans, campaigning hard for another term.) Bachir made a point of assuring me, for me to reassure Basri, of their total discretion: no press coverage, no photography, and no declaration to follow or statement. Basri had asked me to convey to Bachir that he could expect an interlocutor who was courteous, well-informed and open; those were his words, I said. Bachir requested that I pass a similar message in return.

At Tindouf airport I sat boxed in, suffocating inside that airless metal container, broiling at fifty plus degrees. Once again a crewman had to be ordered out with a small fire-extinguisher to squirt and squirt till finally the engine ignited and we were airborne. Heat exhausted, rattled by noise and vibration, a headache forcing into my eyes, I returned to an immediate message, Azmi wishing to speak.

Straight to the point: 'Have you got agreement?' Yes and no, I said. He became tense: 'What does that mean? Is it all right for Thursday the fifteenth?' No, I said. We checked flights between Algiers and Geneva and Thursday was not feasible. He could come on the Saturday. Azmi's sense of relief was palpable: 'Oh, well, that's only two days difference.' Extraordinary, I thought, that after all these years' repeated postponements, twistings of every tentative engagement, tricks to have months pass, a day sooner or later was becoming an obsession. Basri expected me without delay, Azmi continued; I told him that the Sunday Boeing had been cancelled, I could fly on Monday. 'No,' he said, 'you must come tomorrow.' 'If the minister needs me that urgently,' I said, 'I suggest he arrange a special plane.' That was going to be very difficult, Azmi said, aircraft had all been assigned, but I suspected the necessary effort would be made.

The following day I departed Laayoune by a Learjet of the king's flight. Pilot and co-pilot, smartly uniformed, saluted, and an elegant stewardess waited in the cabin. It made a pleasant change of travelling routine. An hour and a half after take-off we landed at Rabat's military airfield where Azmi greeted me. Basri, meanwhile, had left to spend Sunday with his family on the Mediterranean coast where the privileged summered in luxury, but would be back. Next morning, ready and dressed, I called Azmi, who sounded half asleep. At 11.30 I phoned again, still nothing, then minutes later he was at the door: we should leave instantly. To Bouznika? I asked as we sped out of town. The minister wanted us to meet on the autoroute. At the first major turn-off Azmi ordered the driver to the roadside, instructed 'no flashing light'. I waited for a vehicle to crash violently into our rear; Azmi waited for Basri, and became increasingly nervous. Suddenly, a car emerged driven the wrong way down the turn-off, frantic hand signals indicating we should follow, we did. The guide car accelerated, asserting automatic priority against oncoming vehicles, lights and policemen, crazier than Algiers. We halted, abruptly, beside a large Mercedes with Basri at the wheel. A minister, secretary-general of the government, was unceremoniously ushered out of the seat next to Basri and I invited in. We shot off, Azmi bruising his leg as he clambered into the back with the car already moving: direction Skhirat, the summer palace.

By the time we arrived I had briefed Basri. He rushed to the king, asking that we meet afterwards at Bouznika. I could not resist telling Azmi that I regarded last minute alert, postponement, delay, bizarre roadside rendez-vous and mad car chases as taking discretion, or secrecy, too far, and frankly putting a strain on my self-respect. If, as he repeatedly said, I was more than an ordinary ambassador in Moroccan eyes, how did they treat ordinary ambassadors? Azmi tried convincing me that it should be taken as a compliment, he had been amazed at how freely Basri spoke to me, saying things only a trusted high level Moroccan would be privileged to know. Basri arrived, changed rapidly, and minutes later descended onto a chair opposite me. He glanced towards a stack of signature files beside his favourite rocker, twice asking, '*comment ca va?*' without expecting an answer. He looked preoccupied, I was beginning to wonder from his manner, apparent reticence, what to expect. After a longish pause, he announced that His Majesty had approved Geneva as the place for a meeting on the coming Saturday without a rigid agenda.

Geneva was fine with Bachir, I confirmed. Polisario had no current representative there, Baba being reassigned to Canada, but visas were not a problem, nor was security an issue in Switzerland. Bachir nevertheless preferred that the Geneva authorities be alerted. 'Why?' said Basri. In my day the authorities appreciated being aware of political visitors, I said, and could see no harm in this if Bachir insisted. Basri raised no objection, though he reiterated there being no need, Morocco would not be advising anyone, all could enter as tourists, like a private visit. Who would be coming was what mattered. Bachir, I said, expected to be accompanied by two counsellors:

Sadafa, Baba or Majid. Majid, because he belonged to a Fokra sub-fraction, struck the Moroccans as 'virtually Algerian', but it was left at that. I asked Basri who would accompany him. Two, possibly three, of his senior officials, he answered, Azmi for sure, other names were mentioned. I requested, and received, absolute assurance that no '*rallié*' turncoat/returnee, such as Omar Hadrami or Brahim Hakim, would be involved; to Polisario these were traitors, and the stumbling-block at earlier encounters, and that included Biadillah. The date was governed by scheduled flights between Algiers and Geneva. Basri nodded: His Majesty had given his approval. Discussion of hotels ensued.

The most prestigious, Les Bergues, the Richemond, the Beau Rivage were all central, and expensive, as were the Noga Hilton and President. 'A UN hotel?' asked Basri. Waldheim always stayed at the Intercontinental close to the Palais des Nations, Boutros-Ghali preferred La Reserve outside town. Basri reflected, picked Les Bergues, instructed Azmi to book a suite and two rooms as well as a suite for Bachir plus two rooms. I wondered whether Bachir, even if content to stay in the same hotel, might be uncomfortable with somewhere so expensive. 'Tell him we'll cover the cost,' Basri said. That was appreciated, but I remained almost certain that Bachir would feel unable to accept Moroccan largesse. 'For him to decide,' Basri concluded. 'We meet at the hotel. We will be available as of 6 p.m. on Saturday evening', I was to stage manage the initial encounter. One further meeting on Sunday should suffice, I assumed, the main purpose being to decide date and place for the high level contact envisaged, provided this preliminary contact went well, Basri nodded. Despite earlier reluctance, he now took my presence in the area for granted, best that I be there in advance, 'discreetly'. That prompted me to convey Bachir's assurances regarding discretion: no press, no photography, no declaration – and my belief in his good faith. I had one question.

When to brief the secretary-general? Basri, sharply: 'When His Majesty says so,' in the peremptory tone of a royal command. This was and had to remain secret, absolutely secret, he repeated, only on that basis had Morocco seen fit to proceed. I knew that neither the UN nor I had an official mandate other than the settlement plan, however I had instructions from Boutros-Ghali to bring the parties together, and even acting in a 'personal capacity' was still identified as the special representative. 'You tell him and the secret is out; he will immediately talk about it,' Basri said. 'He will imply that he, not you, brokered a meeting between Morocco and Polisario and use it in his campaign against the Americans.' I guessed this to be the king speaking; it reflected Hassan's view of Boutros. It left me in a delicate situation, but fortunately, the secretary-general was on holiday and had issued orders only to be disturbed on matters of the greatest urgency. I arranged travel to Geneva for a meeting on the Friday and with HCR the following Monday; by chance I overheard our ticketing clerk mutter to his neighbour about the 'crafty so-and-so' giving himself a holiday weekend in Switzerland.

This was the weekend when Basri met Bachir and reached agreement for the high-level encounter on which so much depended.

20

Rabat

THAT SUNDAY EVENING, toward the end of one of the most pressured, most tense and most important weekends in my working life, I walked to a hauntingly empty Palais des Nations. I had a handwritten draft of the coded cable I proposed sending the secretary-general 'for his eyes only'. It was ultra-discreet, not too specific, and emphasized that Morocco demanded absolute discretion: no one, but no one, should be informed. We had surmounted the first forbidding ridge but, I think it was Wilfred Thesiger, the Arabian desert explorer, who said, you cross one mammoth ridge of dunes only to face another, and then another.

Bodan telephoned on my return to Laayoune to pass me Bachir, who came on the line sounding reasonably cheerful, repeating '*bien, bien*', before announcing that 'the friend had called', and he had lost the number to call back. I told him the special number, which Basri himself had once given me for exceptional circumstances. Bachir promised to call again after they had spoken. He did. The two sides would foregather in Rabat on 2 September for talks lasting two to three days, arrival details to be decided. I offered to make available a UN aircraft; he thanked me but they expected Algeria to provide transport. He was most insistent I should be in Rabat. Shortly afterwards Azmi was on the phone, Basri intended visiting Laayoune. Three days passed, then Driss Basri before eight in the morning: 'How are you? Did I wake you? What is the weather in Laayoune?' Windy, I told him, with blowing sand. 'I'll see you this evening.' What time? 'Have to arrive first, then we'll fix the hour. *Inshallah*.'

Police on duty at every corner throughout Laayoune confirmed the impending presence. At seven-thirty I heard that a special plane had landed. After two hours in the office, I asked my driver to take me to provincial headquarters. Approach roads were cordoned off but we managed to penetrate by resolute insistence on my right of access and bluff. Outside the palatial building motorcycles with lights flashing, engines revving decreed imminent activity. A guard recognized me and saluted, a plain clothesman tried blocking entry but by invoking an appointment with Basri I had reached the base of the great baronial staircase when the minister emerged higher up. He greeted me saying we would talk at the governor's residence on the coast.

Within a circle of caidic tents the grounds smelt sweetly of new-mown grass. Indoors, ministers discussed earnestly, dignitaries and regional governors conversed, while waiters, in white mess-coats and snappy black ties, dispensed drink, Black Label flowed. Basri, seeing me enter, rose and invited me to an adjoining salon, he confirmed his conversation with Bachir and the date agreed before saying he had tried to reach Bachir again, without success, Polisario leaders were reputedly in conference. That corroborated news I had from Bodan; I said I was aware of a high-level gathering. Yes, Basri said, there was discord among them, 'What matters is that Bachir comes.' Like a throwaway line, adding: 'Well, if he doesn't want to, that's just too bad.'

Bachir was obliged to take into account views other than his own, differences could well be reflected in the group coming with him. Basri wanted to know who would accompany Bachir to Rabat, and other details needed settling. He preferred that Polisario arrive by UN aircraft. When I said Bachir mentioned an Algerian plane Basri repeated preference for the UN. He was noncommittal how long the meeting might last. The delegation would be received by the king, working sessions were planned with the crown prince and himself: 'We are going to work.' I promised to meet Bachir at the earliest and obtain delegation names and flight details. Basri volunteered how positively he had been impressed at Geneva and I told him that Bachir appreciated his attitude.

Early next day in the throes of organizing travel to Tindouf I received a call: Bachir wishing to speak urgently. '*Bien, bien*,' he said when I asked how he was. To my relief he did not sound tense, he had just spoken to Basri, and apologized for not speaking first to me. Monday was confirmed, with Polisario arriving at 10 am, modified, after discussing flight times and time difference, to 11 o'clock. He counted on my being there to receive them, unless I liked to accompany them on their plane, they would fly by an Algerian aircraft. Six in all, himself plus five, as well as the crew. Bachir enquired about lodging arrangements, they did not want to be sequestered 'for security reasons' somewhere remote, accommodation should be as normal as possible and transport. He wanted, again, to be assured of my presence 'in the wings'. Fifteen minutes later it was Azmi on the phone. He spoke in code – who spies on whom here? – without specifics or names, did not believe another meeting with Basri necessary, then asked me to come immediately.

The governor's town residence overflowed with dignitaries, in their best suits. I was invited to eat though the others had finished. Basri completed licking his fingers, he confirmed having spoken to Bachir and finding him on good form, they would talk again to settle arrival details: whether Sunday evening or Monday morning. There would be six of them. When I raised accommodation and transport he pretended not to grasp the point. 'They will be treated impeccably, housed palatially, given government cars – Mercedes,' he thought. He was uncomfortable about my being in any way involved. (I chose not to mention airport reception.) I could be in Rabat, where I often came, but should keep a low profile. In hectoring mode: 'No ambassadors, not the English, not the French, not the Americans!' If anybody guessed, it would be impossible for matters to remain confidential, and discretion was of the utmost importance. '*Tu me comprends*' 'You understand?' he said, twice. 'They want direct talks, they will have direct talks, no one else is involved, not the UN, not the Security Council permanents; had they wished they could have settled the Sahara issue long ago.' Getting up to go, he promised to keep me informed, me personally.

Morocco made confidentiality the over-riding condition, one they claimed Polisario failed previously to honour, any breach would scuttle the proceedings. Bachir I trusted and he had given his word; but others were bound to have an inkling. Bodan reported meeting Majid in Rabouni and being asked what was moving. The wind, he replied, jokingly. Majid turned serious: 'Monsieur Jensen is trying to fly a helicopter by himself. And there is nothing secret going on either. Nothing is secret.'[1] I prayed that whatever was rumoured in the camps would not begin to percolate. Bachir and I spoke again, he planned to be in Algiers with the delegation Sunday evening and suggested we talk then. Saturday he telephoned to say that he had heard from Basri and the meeting was postponed to the following Wednesday. Why? He gave as reason the launch in Morocco of a referendum on the revised constitution.

That he would have known all along. It was hard to understand, could there be a 'real' reason: tit-for-tat for the delay in Geneva, or provocation? Either way it was dangerous, liable to undermine confidence building and trust. Two days later Bachir called for my assistance: 'Once more UN mediation is indispensable.' Basri had telephoned the Polisario representation in Algiers before the appointed hour and missed Bachir, who was now unable to establish communication with Rabat. Could I help? I dialed Basri's private hot line. He was unavailable; I said it was most urgent, concerned Bachir and Basri came on at once. The most tantalizing, exasperating exercise in telecommunication followed. Our communications unit made every effort to create a link via Minurso lines between Basri and Bachir, they were cut off, and cut off, time and again till eventually contact was achieved just long enough for Basri to say that Polisario's flight should land at Tangier airport. Was this a military or civil airfield? Bachir asked me. Civilian, I thought, but might be both. And was it far from Rabat? – as if he did not know. It was some way, I said. Why there? he said I seemed surprised, and I was. This latest Moroccan manoeuvre perturbed me, first, the changed date, next an airfield in the north without explanation. Bachir did not sound too disturbed, and he surely knew where Tangier was; he had made no attempt to remonstrate with Basri. I planned to reach Rabat on the eve of Polisario's arrival.

The lovely Antonov engine refused to start. Not failing to ignite, but battery failure. With a replacement battery installed we were finally airborne. At Rabat Sale I was told that rooms at the Hyatt had been booked for Polisario – they would be perfectly accommodated – while I was dispatched elsewhere. Bachir was not in when I tried Algiers but someone insisted his flight had been slightly delayed and 'he's coming, he's on his way'. An hour later he answered, his immediate question: had I spoken to 'our friend'? Briefly, I said, and he let me understand that he had provided answers. Not really, Bachir said, it was still unclear why Tangier, and was it a civilian airport? It was a civil airport, I understood, and chosen for confidentiality. The meeting would not be there; accommodation had been reserved in Rabat, very satisfactory. He counted on my presence when they arrived. I said the Moroccans were ill at ease with my visible involvement. He much preferred that I be there on arrival but, if that proved impossible, he would telephone me at once. He wished to be quite certain that Morocco posed no obstacle to my being on the fringe and always available. They accepted that, I thought. Loud banging on the door. I gave Bachir my hotel number and room. More banging.

It was Azmi. Why had it taken me so long to open? Who could I have been speaking to? Bachir, as a matter of fact, who had arrived in Algiers and had some questions. He seemed excessively suspicious, said Azmi – though both sides attributed dubious motives to any query, change or delay, as well he knew. Azmi reconfirmed that Tangier was the only exclusively civil airport, apart from Agadir, and chosen for that reason. Bachir and company would continue to Rabat by road. Then the surprise, the minister concurred in my being there to greet Polisario's arrival; it would be helpful, I said. A car had been designated to take me; I would have to be on the road before seven in the morning, it was a long way. Azmi was barely out of the door when the phone rang: Basri to confirm cryptically what I had just been told. I informed him of my conversation with Bachir, and the queries, they ought to speak. When I tried to reach Bachir minutes later, the line was busy. Afterwards Bachir called me to say he had talked to 'our friend' who had explained about the airport before asking for views on my presence, Bachir said he had insisted and it was agreed. We wished each other good night.

By seven I was embarked on the three hour drive to Tangier. To my astonishment, beside the motorway pay booths stood Azmi's senior colleague, Ben Hachem, like a hitchhiker. He declined a lift, said he was waiting for someone. Azmi lay in wait at the next toll-booth to ambush the driver of the palace minibus, who was not permitted to know in advance where he was headed, and dispatch him to Tangier, before driving back the wrong way past mystified policemen to collect his colleague. At Tangier airport I was deposited in the VIP lounge and asked not to step outside: someone was bound to recognize me; nobody came near. The incoming aircraft from Algiers was labelled a domestic flight: therefore no immigration formalities, no passport control, an air of mystery combined with interior ministry top-level representation evoked a narcotics haul. Only briefly delayed, the plane was announced, then said to be circling. It landed. Bachir appeared with an impressive delegation, Basri phoned to greet him; much good-natured laughter and '*barakalaufik*'. Ali Beiba was friendly, even Brahim Ghali, Sadafa especially so, thanking me for 'my inestimable help' with great sincerity. Kheddad though less warm, smiled when I reminded him that our last encounter had been war; 'There's no armistice yet,' he said, 'but no shooting.'

The Polisario delegation was escorted into the palace minibus, not the most elegant form of transport. I was seated with Azmi and Ben Hachem in their car. The Polisario leaders were being accommodated at the Hyatt, Rabat's premier hotel, I would be at the Tour Hassan. Basri remained categorical, adamant that the meeting not be construed as UN sponsored, or organized, or with a UN presence, if I were seen as involved, he would end proceedings instantly, even if someone noticed me in the vicinity, and, Azmi said, 'everyone knows who you are'.

The Tour Hassan may have been a fine hotel; it was no more. In that jaded cage I spent the day waiting, both Basri and Bachir had promised to keep me abreast of developments. Basri was to greet the delegation on arrival at the hotel and a meeting was planned for the evening. I could only be patient. Sadafa called to give me Bachir's room number: 600 – a very fine suite I knew. Bachir had left, someone said, when I telephoned. For a meeting? Yes. I waited, confined to the room because the operator maintained that technical problems made impossible transferring an outside call to either terrace, bar or equally gloomy dining-room. Room service delivered greasy Bolognese over soggy pasta. By half past eleven, not having heard, I tried Bachir's number, I recognized his voice, half asleep, saying he had tried to call multiple times but there was no response. I told him I had been there all day, waiting. He reassured me that everything was all right so far and suggested we speak in the morning.

It was just nine-thirty when I heard from the Algerian ambassador. 'Our friends at the Hyatt', he said, had tried to reach me many, many times, without success. Would I please phone them, they were being told that lines to my hotel were out of order. Bachir needed to see me as soon as possible in suite 600. No time had yet been set for a meeting. That had me worried, what game was Basri playing: making it impossible for the Polisario to contact me and failing to respect the timetable. I was not meant to appear near the Hyatt, I knew, but I thought if I went straight to a back door, I could take the dedicated lift direct to the sixth floor virtually unobserved. At the entrance a uniformed guard stood sentry and the moment I stepped from the car another rushed forward to guide 'Monsieur Erik' to the special elevator. Sadafa greeted me. He said they had raised the phone problem with Azmi: lines being blocked. As he was speaking Azmi came into the corridor, he looked grim, decidedly not pleased to see me. I was there because Polisario had been unable to reach me by phone; he professed disbelief. And, anyway, I had entered unobtrusively by the back entrance. 'You,' he blustered, 'you – all Rabat knows you, you are as instantly recognizable as the *loup blanc*' – a white wolf. Basri would be livid if he knew. 'With this Polisario can to blow the whole thing. They still want to make publicity and they'll use you. Whatever you do, don't go into the suite. Call Bachir on an internal phone.' Tempting as it was to ignore Azmi, the last thing I wished was to provide Basri any pretext not to proceed. I phoned.'Where are you?' Bachir asked. 'Are you here in the hotel?' 'Well come to room 600.' I said it might be preferable to avoid any possible publicity. 'I can see who I want,' he said, 'I think you should come up.' 'Why don't we meet down by the pool, where we aren't monitored', I suggested. 'it's in the open air.'

Bachir strolled over beaming, Ali Beiba with him, both in crisp white shirtsleeves. 'You are the UN, why care what Morocco thinks,' Bachir began. I said that I did not want to give any excuse, any reason, for Basri to say 'I told you so.' And here in the open no walls with ears surrounded us, I added smilingly as we settled at a small table. Bachir and Ali Beiba ordered tea, which

Ali Beiba insisted be minted and strong, Sahrawi style. Bachir dispersed my gloomier assumptions with his account of the previous evening. They had been received at a 'palais' by the crown prince, Morocco was represented by the prince and Basri; no other Moroccan was involved. 'Good,' I said, at least that commitment was being honoured. Did the prince know the dossier? Not that well, not the detail, Bachir replied, but well enough; that could be an advantage in permitting new attitudes. The prince led the discussion, he made it clear at the outset that he was not prepared to discuss independence (as agreed), he described plans for regionalization and Morocco's willingness to accommodate Polisario: proposals were malleable and could be adapted. They also talked about identification.

Bachir explained that for them the defining entity remained a sub-fraction represented in the '74 census. It was for people included in the census to pronounce on the territory's future. Then the prince had left for some minutes; Bachir thought he had an electronic wink. Basri resumed discussion, emphasising commitment to the five criteria. Bachir did not dissent but raised the tribal groupings: the northern tribes, southern tribes and Chorfa: these were not single tribes composed of sub-fractions. He thought he detected a glimmer that Basri admitted some validity to the argument, what Basri did was to insist that all who deemed themselves entitled should be able to come forward and it was for Minurso to decide who qualified. Bachir had then made a statement.

History could not simply be forgotten: the departure of Spain, the Green March and Morocco moving in, Polisario's response and the founding of SADR. Twenty years had passed creating a fact, nationally, regionally and internationally. However, if there were willingness to go forward from this point, to seek accommodation with honour, an accord that was '*honorable, equitable et durable*' – honourable, fair and enduring, Polisario was prepared. The atmosphere was good, he assured me. He did sense some openness to moving ahead. That was crucial. There was to have been follow-up after they saw the king seven years previously, said Ali Beiba, before confirming Bachir's account. 'Then it was autonomy, now it's regionalization.' That could be semantics, I said; autonomy is flexible as is regionalization. 'We'll be seeing the king, which might clarify matters, Bachir thought, the audience was tentatively planned for later in the day; Bachir said he might come to my hotel afterwards.

With Miss Marple for grainy company I waited, then telephoned the Hyatt: Bachir was expected back 'soonish.' Two hours later I called again. Bachir answered sleepily, he went straight to bed on returning to the hotel.

An evening meeting had gone 'all right', though less well than the earlier one. They had not yet been received by the king, now proposed for the following afternoon. Azmi, when I tracked him down, would only say that the meeting had passed reasonably, there would be more next day.

In the morning Sadafa put Bachir on the line, to brief me. The session had lasted a good one and a half hours and been somewhat 'bitter'. 'Our friend', bristling with nervousness, resorted to a degree of brinkmanship, always pushing to extremes. Extreme positions had to be expected at this stage, I said. But the crown prince was impressive, Bachir continued, was 'great', very self-controlled, Bachir admired and appreciated him. At the first encounter Prince Mohammed had shown amiability; on this occasion he displayed further qualities: discipline and the ability to face issues constructively. 'Our friend' was due around midday. Bachir assumed that after some minutes' discussion they would proceed to the palace to be received by King Hassan, Bachir saw a meeting with the king, after their positive contact with the crown prince, as opening the door to serious negotiation. This could be the beginning, to begin was what mattered. He invited me to Rabouni the following week to discuss the next stage. For their return flight he thanked me for proposing UN transport but they had decided to accept the offer of an aircraft of the king's flight. Departure was likely soon after the audience.

The audience was postponed to the evening. The Polisario had still not been received by the king when I reached Bachir at 11 o'clock, they had spent another hour and a quarter in session with the crown prince and Basri. Since there were no new elements, according to the Moroccans, the king decided to await further development. Bachir reflected that in the seven years since Marrakech Polisario had conceded the cease-fire 'against the wishes of many,' and much more. The king, on that occasion, deployed agriculture as analogy, after seven years the crop could be ready to harvest. The evening had ended with discussion of time and place for further negotiation: 'in two weeks', 'not more than a month' each side was to prepare a position paper. There was no agreement where to meet, Polisario wanted a neutral country, Basri insisted on Morocco if the crown prince were to stay involved. It was a dismaying end to yesterday's expectant mood. But the door had been opened, a sliver, to serious talk. Basri offered to come by in the morning before we leave, Bachir said; 'If he doesn't, that's rupture.' Azmi, when we spoke, sounded more positive. Basri would brief me the following day after seeing off the Polisario.

Basri arrived at the Hyatt before nine-thirty next morning and since neither he nor Bachir had eaten they breakfasted together. Basri also spoke to the other Polisario representatives before, with much embracing and prolific expressions of friendliness, they departed for the airport. By noon they were airborne. Basri drove straight to the palace to report to His Majesty. He hoped to see me later, Azmi called to say. I decamped from the Tour Hassan with Azmi seeking to mollify me: talking mattered and the meetings had gone surprisingly well, they made progress in overcoming mutual distrust. It was a worthwhile beginning, although, of course, only a beginning. Incidentally, he said, I should be aware that the Algerian ambassador had been in and out of the hotel.

The Basri appointment was postponed until the following day. I had to be back in Laayoune by evening, I said. It was essential to encode my confidential report to the secretary-general, the sensitive account that I was drafting. Shortly after eight next morning Azmi called: Basri awaited me at Bouznika. I was ushered into the presence past a minister who impatiently expected his turn. Basri, informally dressed for summer by the sea, was in good humour. He thanked me at the outset, with apparent sincerity, and thanked me again before I left. Before lecturing me on the proceedings, he declared that 'His Majesty has authorized your reporting to New York,' then reviewed the process, beginning with Geneva, punctuating every few words with '*Tu me comprends?*' – you understand me? Geneva was fine and the first meeting in Rabat excellent: Bachir's talk of autonomy had been music to Basri's ears. At the second meeting Bachir mentioned independence, that meant no audience, he had failed to respect the gentleman's agreement reached through me that independence was not on the agenda – he had agreed, had he not? – and honoured in Geneva and at the first session in Rabat. Yet again the suspicion that you cannot trust these people. I had to insist that an introductory speech incorporating the phrase 'independence with interdependence', invariably a module in Bachir's political pronouncements, hardly infringed what had been agreed, and should not rule out an audience. Independence was not on the agenda, Basri reiterated.

He had spent another two hours in *tête-à-tête* conversation with Bachir before the Polisario departed. Their talk was free ranging but one thing had to be clear: any suggestion of independence, the word even, must be excluded. Acceptance of Moroccan sovereignty was the point of departure; from there on all options could be discussed. When Bachir suggested that they focus on alternative scenarios, Basri refused 'and spring independence on us later. No. Moroccan sovereignty has to be evident.' He quoted the World Court recognizing Moroccan claims. 'Were you ever a state?' he had asked Bachir rhetorically. Nobody was going to drive Morocco out of the Sahara; Morocco would bolster its claim with force but the basis was legal, a legitimate right. To 'independence with interdependence', whatever that might mean, the answer was 'No', Basri told Bachir bluntly, while insisting he remained his 'best friend'. There could be no windscreen-wiper politics, now swinging one way, now the other. Basri was a negotiator and assumed the same of his interlocutor. 'I expect a response and I react. I am used to tough negotiations and don't presume ready compliance.' That could also be said of Bachir.

When Bachir had spoken of twenty years struggle Basri shifted to history measured in centuries. In exasperation, Bachir had asked 'Do you expect us to run up the white flag – to capitulate?' No, Basri had said. 'We are not a pair of greengrocers haggling over the price of tomatoes and potatoes. These are matters of real importance.' Finally, as if he had overlooked something key, Basri told Bachir that if pushed to a referendum Morocco was sure to win, they had meticulously calculated votes; the alternative, therefore, offered the most honourable solution for Polisario.

Basri was desperate to regain control. The encounter had gone too well, too fast for his calculations, opening the door to pressure from the US and others. Polisario had behaved impeccably, respected the conditions. It was inevitable that Bachir utter 'independence' in an opening statement that would proceed to exploring alternatives 'on the table'. Basri had to make this his bone of contention, and that the Algerians intervened.

He reverted to the report. The talks had been that, not 'negotiations', which would imply a degree of recognition between equal parties; they had taken place at Polisario's request, were without any UN mandate, and my role was entirely personal. The king knew the UN in New York, where confidentiality was non-existent, and he did not trust Boutros-Ghali, it was imperative that I respect these sensitivities. Basri was adamant that no UN context, no reference to Security Council or secretary-general be included, I needed to minimize my formative role. Recognition of Moroccan sovereignty had to be underscored, he added, and that independence could not even be mentioned. Presumably it was thus Basri had interpreted the project to King Hassan, or, at least, claimed how it was managed. His nightmare was international pressure, that the Security Council or great powers use the clout that I lacked to induce Hassan into conceding genuine regional autonomy. A tense, disagreeable exchange followed when Basri tried dictating elements for the report. I strongly resented this unwarranted interference and told him so.

However emphatically labelled confidential and encoded, it would have been naive to imagine that I could dispatch a cable to the secretary-general and not expect the Moroccans to become aware of its content. I knew as well as the king that confidentiality at UN headquarters was in short supply. I counted on briefing Boutros-Ghali personally, I had delivered precisely what he strove for and had asked me to do, and whatever the Moroccans maintained, it was one hundred percent true to the spirit of Security Council thinking if not in the letter of a resolution. The two sides had met, under excellent conditions. Polisario presented an unimpeachable array of its leadership and made no move to exploit the event for propaganda. Morocco fielded not the turncoats considered traitors by Polisario but its crown prince and Basri. For the first time the two sides talked showing mutual respect. Thus the seemingly insuperable obstacles to opening negotiation had been overcome. This was a major break-through. No recriminations followed Polisario's departure and both sides looked to a further meeting in the near future. They only disagreed as to where. All this and the arguments I used in persuading them to meet was what I planned to tell the secretary-general.

No representative of the secretary-general was permitted to depart from his region of responsibility without authority; he could come to New York only if summoned. I fully expected a call the moment Boutros heard the news. Given the prospect of providing the secretary-general a complete account, including my confidential projections, I acquiesced in heeding sensitivities in the provisional report. Retaining the trust of both Morocco and Polisario remained critical to further progress.

Next morning Azmi arrived: the minister wished to talk further. I 'thanked' him in quotes: this corresponded to a Muslim being made to stuff himself all day during Ramadhan. Azmi stifled an uncertain smile. I rarely tried jokes on Basri. Too fanatical for a sense of humour. It is hard to imagine someone with a sense of humour, or sense of the absurd, becoming a fanatic. In the event Basri was less fanatical than the day before – having received royal clearance. His Majesty was satisfied, and he thanked me with his sinister smile while picking at the dried skin on his lip. He looked forward to seeing me again soon. I returned post haste to Laayoune to complete, encode and dispatch my report to the secretary-general. The following afternoon came an urgent call: Basri.

The foreign minister of Spain emerging from a meeting with the Algerian foreign minister had made a statement referring to direct contact between the parties. You see, Basri said, the Algerians talked. I had suspected something when fielding a probing enquiry from EFE the Spanish press agency. 'I know you didn't say anything', Basri conceded. 'It was the Algerians, probably also in New York. You see Morocco is the only serious country. And I am the most serious man in Morocco.' I said a sense of humour was sometimes helpful. 'Yes. I know I'm hard when defending my country' – 'You certainly are' – 'but I maintain good spirits.' He wanted to know whether I had sent my report. 'Let me know after you've seen Bachir. I shall show you the complete *compte rendu* of the meetings in Geneva and Rabat. (He never did.) We must proceed "*doucement*"- gently; it won't be resolved in two or three encounters.'

The process remained on track by the sound of it. Basri not excessively concerned about the inevitable leak. As predicted 'all' New York already seemed to know: of all sieves it was the greatest. The desk officer, on her first day back from leave, was asked why she was not at 'the talks'. From the camps meanwhile Bodan reported that Polisario awaited my visit. Bachir received me warmly. We talked of Boutros-Ghali's re-election prospects and American objections. Of more immediate concern, however, was keeping our objective in view, not too distant, while always allowing enough time. He invited me to join him in private for an assessment. The meeting with Basri in Geneva had been good, much better than expected, they agreed three things: to meet shortly in Rabat; to hold a working session with the crown prince and Basri, and that Bachir would be received by the king. The Moroccans had not kept their word. He resented being obliged to land at Tangier, a considerable distance from Rabat. The hotel was fine though access to communications had been deliberately hampered, it was only the unexpected need for an additional room that enabled them to telephone freely, to me and the Algerian ambassador.

Basri, and I went to some length in mentioning the positive comments he also made, blamed Bachir for failing to honour a commitment not to speak of independence. That was why the audience with the king had been cancelled. Bachir paused before replying. How could he not mention independence? If he opened with autonomy he would, in effect, accept the Moroccan position before beginning to negotiate. He repeated several times that he understood the eventual solution to lie in the autonomy range but he had to begin by staking out Polisario's officially preferred option. They could not be instructed simply to recognize Moroccan sovereignty then talk; recognition would come as talks advanced. You had to be sensitive to twenty years struggle, the Polisario Front, SADR, and historical memory, which could not just be made to evaporate. The long-term solution, he explained, speaking as a realist, lay in an appropriate measure of autonomy with respect for Sahrawi identity (*specificité Sahraoui*), not merely a region like any other. We agreed that as realistic. I looked to King Hassan to show the largeness of spirit he had displayed on some issues. What should I tell Rabat? I asked Bachir.

He wanted a further meeting, to continue dialogue. Not too much time should elapse, ideally within a month. I suggested they might agree to discuss options alongside those spelled out in the settlement plan; the plan spoke of independence or integration, therefore mention of the plan tacitly retained these basic positions. Excellent, he said, it could be a way to proceed. Any solution would have to be honourable, fair and enduring, he reiterated, hinting that he held no illusion about independence – though others of the leadership did. But he was not prepared to open negotiation by surrendering his best card. The place for the next meeting mattered, Rabat was acceptable only, and only, if an audience with the king was assured, otherwise it should be on neutral ground. He looked me in the eyes; he was genuinely ready to move forward, he said. He wondered whether Morocco was merely going through motions while waiting to deal with Algeria, or trying to destabilize Polisario by fostering polemic among them – or was it serious?

The next day, after I had left, the secretary-general of the Algerian foreign office, Bendjama, and his director for African affairs paid a surprise visit to Tindouf. They spoke to Bodan, who had been with me in Algiers and knew them both. Bendjama was supportive of my efforts to have the parties talk. He regretted not seeing more sign that the Moroccans were prepared to negotiate seriously, the king failing to receive the Polisario delegation showed Morocco at its old game, buying time. Polisario, had observed absolute discretion. Bodan mentioned that the Spanish foreign minister when visiting Algiers was first to reveal publicly that there had been dialogue. No, Bendjama reacted fiercely, it was the secretary-general in New York: 'He mentioned contacts at a "closed meeting" of the African group – and you know how "closed" these meetings are at the UN.'[2]

Snoussi, at the same meeting, while protesting Boutros-Ghali's use of 'Sahrawis', appeared not well briefed, as if awaiting instructions. Boukhari was reported as lobbying actively though it was unclear for what.[3] I looked forward to being summoned: the centre of gravity had shifted to New York. Meanwhile Azmi was to convey to Basri the gist of my discussion with Bachir and unusually for him took written notes. He wondered out loud about Bachir, speculating that the Algerians, instead of leaving him dangerously free range, might be reining him in. Days passed without reaction from Basri, he had been briefed, Azmi assured me before explaining that Basri was preoccupied by the referendum on a revised constitution, but with that now successfully organised hoped to see me. Bachir also requested another meeting; he was leaving for New York. We agreed that I fly to Tindouf the following day after seeing Basri. '*Bien, bien*' he said.

Basri looked haggard, huddled over a telephone in his private office. 'You never know what to expect,' Azmi said. Eventually Basri raised his head to greet me amiably. The discussion with Bachir; yes, he had heard from Azmi, but he would prefer my account. Bachir, he said after I finished, should understand that reference to independence was out of the question, 'independence' was excluded from speech, writing – and dreams. I ought not to encourage him to refer to the settlement plan if 'independence' was subversively lodged at the back of his mind, he had to abandon his 'independence through interdependence' or any similar phraseology. That must be absolutely clear, 'Then, but only then, can we discuss.' He awaited a working document with proposals for autonomy and regional delegation of powers. Such proposals, and any discussion, must remain strictly confidential, Basri resented, as a breach of trust, Polisario making a statement after Geneva and Rabat – I shook my head in disbelief. He continued by suggesting a date for a meeting after the opening of parliament, in two or three weeks time; since His Majesty had mandated the crown prince to head the discussion the place could only be Rabat, while Basri himself might go elsewhere to accommodate Bachir, the prince could not be asked to travel abroad, and there was no merit in someone being nominated in his place. Morocco would provide an aircraft and fly Polisario to the most convenient airfield; an Algerian plane could only be authorized to land at an entirely non-military airport. It was for me to convince Bachir not to go to New York – and open the door to external pressures, if he went to New York and began discussing Rabat or Geneva, it would be 'rupture', which Azmi echoed. 'Bachir starts talking negotiation at the UN, then it's off,' Basri ended with an air of finality, this was something outside the UN. When I asked about the audience with the king, he pronounced: 'The king concludes, he does not engage in discussion, he will receive Bachir and company when ideas are specific.'

Basri had become inflexible, less comprehending than ever, determined to reassert control. Morocco was preparing again to state that it had made an effort and 'look – Polisario are not serious, not trustworthy'. I asked Azmi whether there was real will to reach a solution. Definitely, he said. No way, I told him, could I persuade Bachir not to go to New York, nor would I try; in his shoes that is precisely what I would be doing, an international context might loosen the straitjacket imposed by Basri and permit realistic negotiation. Arab sales technique, I reminded Azmi, differs from the European. In the west if you are buying or selling a house, the seller inflates and the prospective buyer reduces the price both by an intelligible margin. In the souk the Arab begins bartering with an asking price that is ridiculously high and the buyer by offering absurdly little. Neither takes offence. It is perfectly understood that the price asked and the initial offer do not reflect a true valuation. Bachir's 'independence' honours that tradition.

In Tindouf Bachir insisted on the UN being closely, as closely as possible, involved, in furthering constructive dialogue, concerned and influential states might help. Both sides should eschew extreme positions, recognizing the imperative to move forward, they needed to consider an intermediate position, between the settlement plan options of independence or integration. This involved the UN since an endorsing referendum would be essential for both parties' honour and integrity, a UN presence would also inspire confidence and provide a witness. While the palace had done well to select the prince and Basri, Morocco's persistence in treating this as an internal matter was unacceptable. Bachir said that if Basri persevered in rejecting any use whatsoever of the word 'independence', as a preliminary condition for talking, it could mean rupture. Were that the objective, Polisario would be forced to acknowledge it. We had made a good start, he continued, could not have expected more at this stage, Polisario looked to settle the problem, but they would not be stampeded into recognizing Moroccan sovereignty. A formula could be found, but foundations and roof were not built simultaneously. A paper was in preparation for the next round, which he hoped would take place soon after his New York visit.

21

In New York

At that 'closed' African group meeting Boutros-Ghali had indeed spoken about African issues, in alphabetical order, adding, after his report on Zaire, that there was something he had forgotten to mention: 'We have arranged "direct negotiations" between the Moroccan government and the "Sahrawi party".' When Tanzania accused him aggressively of abandoning Western Sahara, he reacted: 'Didn't you hear what I said? We have arranged "direct contact" between the Moroccan government and the "Sahrawi party".'[1] Most surprising had been the impression that Snoussi was not in the picture. He telephoned Rabat and spoke to the king. At the UN Snoussi then insisted that these were mere preliminary contacts and had to be seen in the settlement plan context, Filali, arriving in New York to address the general assembly, said the same. In the Polisario camps Bodan had several encounters with key people. They wanted direct talks, they were prepared to consider options but mention of independence could not be eliminated beforehand. From hints Bodan surmised that if Morocco moved to serious negotiation Polisario might drop insisting on reference to independence given appropriate international guarantees though they had reservations about the UN, Boutros-Ghali in particular. As for me: 'Jensen has built the helicopter but must stop trying to fly it by himself.'[2]

Exactly. I had brought the parties together to discuss a realistic compromise; they had met respectfully and talked and agreed to meet again. This was the breakthrough that took us over the seemingly insurmountable hurdle that had stymied Yaqub-Khan, Boutros-Ghali himself as UN secretary-general, the US and others. In that achievement I took pride but I was keenly aware that further progress depended on the pressure Morocco dreaded. The sooner Basri faced reality, that the UN could not be excluded from further developments, the better. We had opened the door, it was only ajar, but it had been opened. Autonomy in greater or lesser degree was on the agenda and both sides had agreed to discuss it. Pressure was needed, pressure such as the Security Council and especially the US could bring to bear, or the secretary-general with US support.

My State Department contact assured me of Security Council, or at least US support: 'You have our admiration,' he said,[3] but I needed the secretary-general to be aware of my assessment and prognosis, which could only be conveyed in person. The summons to New York had not come. The Algerian foreign minister, Attaf, had seen the Secretary-General and spoken approvingly of the contact I established which he hoped would continue. As a suitable place he mentioned UN headquarters, which Boutros dismissed: confidentiality, discretion would be impossible in New York, even Jensen, he informed the minister, had been asked to stay away from New York for that very reason. He urged Attaf to persuade Polisario not to squander this opportunity for direct talks, they should be encouraged to moderate their position, and not think of independence; the Americans were telling them to be sensible. At the same time Morocco needed to be less arrogant.

Bachir was received by the secretary-general and listened attentively to Boutros-Ghali. Polisario had campaigned for dialogue ever since earlier efforts failed. It was important not to compromise the recent breakthrough, another blockage and suspension of contact would make it most improbable that Morocco could be brought back to the negotiating table in the foreseeable future. An understanding that independence not be mentioned had made possible the latest meetings, by insisting that independence not be excluded Polisario risked provoking Morocco to suspend contact. Bachir should be aware of the danger of publicly involving intermediaries, discretion and secrecy allowed the parties and the special representative latitude and flexibility in developing creative solutions. Bachir nodded, he wanted the process to continue. As he left, forty-five minutes later, he turned to Boutros' personal assistant saying 'We are pleased things are moving – thanks to UN efforts', and smiled his inscrutable smile. Then he went to lunch with the American ambassador Interfurth.

To the Americans Bachir implied that the secretary-general considered the settlement plan dead. Polisario needed it 'as cover', Bachir explained, though what was happening of value was outside the plan. He thought a solution possible, if Basri had offered autonomy, Bachir believed he could have worked with hard-liners and carried his people. Instead Basri provided copies of the Moroccan constitution and insisted on talking about regionalization. Bachir looked to the US and other Security Council members to facilitate talks.

Interfurth urged Polisario to be realistic; they should 'make the Moroccans an offer they could not refuse' by proposing autonomy.[4] For their part the Americans would advise the Moroccans, through the ambassador in Washington, to be receptive, counselling them to be magnanimous because they had the upper hand.

That my telephone was bugged was taken for granted and that cable traffic, especially confidential and encoded, was under surveillance. In normal circumstances this did not trouble me unduly; it even served to disseminate ideas. Real secrets I transmitted face to face and it was now imperative that I make Boutros-Ghali, and certain Council members, aware, in confidence, of all that had occurred and, equally important, of the estimates used in convincing Morocco and to an extent Polisario. Having studied in detail the outcome of identification to date and given insight into Sahrawi conduct and tribal allegiances, we had assessed the final voting pattern after every applicant had been identified. (Even though Basri had rejected the estimates as vociferously as he did, years, effort and treasure later, those projections proved remarkably accurate.)Morocco was not assured of a comfortable majority, which with an element of uncertainty served as spur to negotiate.

The Rabat coming together achieved exactly what Boutros-Ghali and Yaqub-Khan had striven for, it was what the US at various levels had worked towards, it was what Security Council members urged. I had taken the process as far as my powers permitted, in fact, way beyond. Only the secretary-general and powerful states could exert pressure, carrying on the relay to give the process its own momentum, precisely what alarmed Basri. But instead of confidential briefings in New York I was instructed to draft a report for the Security Council that did not focus on Rabat or call for talks: the one item of supreme importance to be mentioned only in passing, if at all. King Hassan had addressed a personal letter to Boutros-Ghali, arguably drafted by Basri, the precise contents of which were not divulged, to me or from what I heard to others in New York, but the thrust was clear. The forthcoming report to the Security Council should not describe the Rabat talks or suggest any follow-up action by the Council. Following the king's letter, Morocco reinforced its campaign. Snoussi treated New York to his gloss. Morocco would oppose intervention by the Council in favour of negotiation, and resist any initiative from powerful states.[5] He explained that the king had never refused to see Polisario as he had 'a duty to all his children'.[6] Polisario had requested a meeting with the crown prince; they were asked to be discreet but had not respected secrecy, Snoussi queried their current behaviour before describing Morocco's constitutional changes and regionalisation plan. 'We view regionalization as you view autonomy,' he replied to a question. When someone asked whether the talks were under the settlement plan he said they were outside the plan. Morocco did not want the Council to urge talks, he insisted; were that to happen Morocco would have to refuse.

Snoussi intervened again in the fourth (decolonisation) committee of the General Assembly. 'His Majesty the King or his representatives receive and will always receive those we consider our brothers who have been separated from us, to bring them back to reason and the motherland.'[7] He emphasized that it was not in Morocco's tradition to proceed with contacts on instructions from any outsider. The settlement plan remained the only rule. Bachir dismissed this as childish. He wanted reassurance regarding Morocco's commitment, its engagement to proceed; Polisario had a proposal, he hoped Morocco did too. He stood ready to continue dialogue once the place had been agreed, he had no problem with dates: could be that month or early November.

The secretary-general and the US, the two with obvious potential for influence, had other priorities. Boutros was campaigning with ever growing anxiety for re-election. He had been voted secretary-general – the British ambassador quipping that he had already been sixty-nine for too long[8] – for a single five-year term. He was the first secretary-general from Africa, Egypt being in the African group at the UN, and recent secretaries-general had all been awarded a second term in office. Boutros dismissed the single term condition, arguing, with OAU backing, that Africa should not be denied what other regions had enjoyed. Washington had been comfortable with his original election but the Somali debacle and crisis in ex-Yugoslavia as well as his style, he was nicknamed 'Pharoah', created tension with the US administration, exacerbated by mutual antipathy between him and the permanent representative at the UN, Madeleine Albright. Boutros was made scapegoat for failings, including many manifestly not his. The US presidential election threw everything into high relief, the Republican candidate in campaigning speeches repeatedly mocked the secretary-general, calling him Boootros Boootros-Ghali, and made the UN an electioneering whipping boy. Madeleine Albright, ambitious to become secretary of state in a second Clinton administration, had no qualms about offering Boutros-Ghali's head.

Western Sahara was left to flounder, beneath the radar, the spark of achievement barely flickering. With the official report to the Council being edited to skirt gingerly round any allusion to direct talks the wind was taken from my sails. I drifted.

Summoned from the doldrums by the secretary-general it was to Paris, not New York. Boutros-Ghali had come to lobby France on his behalf. He was being received by the French president at 11.30 with my appointment at noon. Blandished by the luxuries on display at the Hotel Meurice, I was startled by the secretary-general's prompt return. In evident good spirits he ushered me to his suite, his wife Leah said how long it was since she had last seen me but the Sahara obviously suited, then left. Boutros seated me on the sofa beside himself and came to the point. He had seen the Polisario number two and had emphasized in no uncertain terms that Polisario now had its long sought opportunity and should be sure not to waste it. Abdel-Aziz had refused to meet Khadiri when Boutros-Ghali brought them both to Geneva, Polisario ought not repeat that error, they should make every effort to engage in discussion of reasonable terms. If the present attempt failed, or failed to continue, then it would be another eight or more years before it could be repeated, when it might be too late for Polisario. Boutros said he had asked the French whether they could be helpful, with the Algerians; Chirac replied that France's relations with Algeria were not of the best and France preferred keeping the issue at arm's length. The Americans, I told him, had been to the region, Abdel-Aziz might be wanting to re-engage them. 'Doesn't he realize,' Boutros cut in, 'that the Sahara is not important to the Americans?' And the mediator proposal, which had been floated, he dismissed. It barely merited serious comment; he had no one in mind, least of all an American. Abdel-Aziz, he continued, had no imagination, was not very intelligent. Bachir was the better prospect.

The secretary-general was intrigued to know how it could be that I had succeeded where all others failed in bringing the two sides together on terms both would accept. He listened attentively, made rapid notes in the special book he carried in an inner pocket. I explained how I gradually overcame the pervasive lack of trust, the arguments then deployed, more specifically the projected outcome of a vote, which I spelled out in detail. He nodded, approvingly. Basri, with his French lawyer's training, should be able to develop a formula, Boutros said: 'Regionalisation can be made to mean whatever you want. Give the king his flag and his stamp and recognize his sovereignty over the Sahara, the rest is negotiable. The trouble with Basri', he mused, 'is that he will never settle for anything less than everything, he lacks all sense of compromise.' With that he turned to the Security Council report.

How the talks should be reflected vexed him. Snoussi had mentioned them publicly, I said. Snoussi was Khadiri's man and closer to Filali, who was not fully in the picture. This was Basri's show and he wanted any credit. 'Have

Basri produce five lines,' Boutros concluded, 'to reflect whatever Morocco is prepared to have said about talks.'

Boutros-Ghali brightened visibly when I enquired about his audience with President Chirac. It went well, French support for his candidacy was assured. The 'lady' had gone overboard, become too excited – that was Madeleine Albright for you – it would be disastrous for her to prevail. The US campaign to impose its view unilaterally had been rejected by virtually all member states. A successor secretary-general appointed under US insistence would be lame duck from the outset, perceived as an American stooge. The likeliest compromise lay through an abbreviated mandate, he admitted. Africa was behind him; others who supported him, he presumably meant France, would need to make their position forcefully known. At which juncture he offered to extend my contract: how long did I want? I thought a year. Was that really as long as I wanted? Yaqub-Khan, he went on to explain, had to remain on the letterhead, only *pro forma,* of course; Pakistan was highly sensitive to being snubbed by Algeria. Boutros-Ghali was back on his own electioneering track. He had nothing further to invest in Western Sahara from what remained of his authority and diminished influence with the Americans.

That re-election campaign and international focus on the US presidential election submerged other concerns. With a UN secretary-general fixated on nudging, cajoling, mustering support, and America obsessed with domestic politicking, our process was in limbo, for me with Basri to confront. We met the day after I returned from Paris. He seemed ominously relaxed, an impression enhanced by the absence of telephone interruptions; he remained as stubborn as ever, any mention of independence constituted an insurmountable obstacle to progress and that applied equally to 'independence with interdependence' or other fanciful phraseology. On a venue for talks he was as inflexible, I contended that Bachir preferring somewhere neutral was not unreasonable but Basri refused to budge. It was inconceivable that His Majesty be asked to dispatch the crown prince abroad. A meeting without the prince would serve neither's interest. Why, he wondered, could they not meet in Morocco? Did they feel themselves under pressure? Living in the best hotel with complete freedom seemed a most congenial form of pressure, one which Basri would personally welcome. Perhaps with the telephones working, I said, before changing the subject.

I described my conversation with Boutros-Ghali and his suggestion that I agree with Basri a few lines for the Security Council report noting the talks. 'What for?' said Basri sharply, 'They are not in the UN mandate. They took place outside.' Azmi, who had been silently watching, echoed this before they both brushed aside my reference to the confidence building measures called for. Only after protracted argument did Basri concede that since everyone knew talks occurred, ignoring them in the report would simply provoke more questions, Snoussi had made mention in a fourth committee statement; I assumed they would have no problem with similar wording. Basri slowly, reluctantly, nodded, but he would insist on vetting the text. Might he prefer to contribute a few lines and be quoted? I asked, although straightforward reference in the report seemed better, with which he agreed. Basri ruminated that Polisario were nearing the end of the road, they could stew in their own juice. He showed no generosity of spirit, no willingness to help Bachir lead his people to a settlement, not a glimpse of the French legal training that would enable him to devise a formula. I left, depressed.

Basri was not mollified by the wording, however camouflaged and distilled, proposed as an 'observation' towards the end of the secretary-general's report to the Security Council. The draft read 'I have been informed that there has been contact recently between the Government of Morocco and the Frente POLISARIO and that further contact is expected. I am hopeful that this development will contribute to creating the climate of confidence essential to full implementation of the Settlement Plan.' No, said Basri.

In Laayoune, United Nations Day, I addressed the assembled staff, military and civilian, and had just presented service medals when summoned for an urgent call from New York. The Western Sahara desk officer panicked that Council members' expectations would be massively disappointed with a text in which the talks were seemingly ignored or mentioned only in passing. How could they know what was happening and vote to continue the mission? How would they realize what the UN had accomplished? (Nothing to what I felt.) It was the secretary-general's decision, I explained, after receiving a letter from King Hassan, which I never saw. Then I flew to Tindouf to meet Bachir.

'I'll be over again to say goodbye', I said. No, no, he laughed, you are still needed. Polisario wished to resume identifying. They continued to respect the cease-fire, were committed to the settlement plan, the only framework remaining. Tone and subject changed the instant we were alone. Bachir reverted to talks, Morocco had to concede some measure of reciprocity, the next meeting should be on neutral ground, anywhere other than Morocco. He rejected Tangier and, even more firmly, Laayoune: nowhere under Morocccan administration. Accepting that would be Morocco's token of serious commitment. Of course, if they were looking for a pretext to break off contact ... With a conspiratorial air he revealed that not many in the Polisario leadership believed Morocco serious about engagement; he was one of the few. Not uttering 'independence' failed to help Bachir in persuading others who were less enthusiastic. The prince presented a problem, I explained, for the crown prince to travel abroad might involve too visible a public gesture. Bachir wanted the prince to continue; his presence had worked well in Rabat but if the meeting had to take place without him, so be it, regrettable though it was, a neutral setting was essential. Their paper was ready, he said, at the next meeting the two sides could merely exchange position papers though it was greatly preferable that some discussion take place to maintain momentum. Bachir guessed that Basri had planted a rumour about a 'second' Rabat encounter, as disseminated by the official Moroccan press agency, to sound public opinion. Bachir believed that Moroccans in general were positive about talks.

Azmi met me on arrival at Casablanca. He was in attack mode, there must be no mention whatsoever of talks, they were still working on public opinion. He rejected my suggestion that refusal to permit reference in the report could jeopardize the undertaking. No, he insisted somewhat aggressively, it was our fault, the UN, by shifting the process from the secret, the discreet, into the open. I had no mandate, he repeated twice, nor had the UN, talks were entirely outside the framework of the settlement plan. He warned me of exceeding both my mandate and official position: I needed to take more care. There could be no meeting except in Morocco; it was inconceivable that the crown prince be asked to leave the country, Basri was unwilling even to suggest it. What if the prince went skiing in Switzerland, for example, and the meeting happened to coincide, I offered gently. No, Azmi replied, no, it would be presented otherwise. And to make it crystal clear, any mention of independence was ruled out, Bachir needed to understand. Anyway, Bachir seemed increasingly marginalized or incapable of leading, unable to engage and make a commitment. Azmi accused me of trusting Bachir too much. I found him sincere, I said. 'He's a great actor,' whose power and influence were on the wane. Polisario had missed an opportunity, Morocco's regionalization plan was now complete. It was only a matter of time before Algeria decided to expel the Polisario remnant from their territory and the hard core rump could decamp to Mauritania where they might take over. Azmi was more amenable next day.

He let slip that a meeting without the crown prince was conceivable. He suggested I look at the Polisario paper to ascertain whether it had elements to make progress possible. I asked Azmi to assure Basri that Bachir had confirmed readiness to resume talks any time, in a week, two weeks, a month, anywhere except Morocco, though volunteering to return to Rabat for a subsequent meeting. The hard reality is Basri: determined to downplay what has already taken place and to evade any UN involvement or great power pressure. Only apparently changing the subject Azmi asked why I was going to Mauritania, as I had mentioned in passing; he saw no reason. What would I be telling them? Mauritania, like Algeria, I reminded him, was officially identified as an interested neighbouring country; I needed to confirm Mauritania's view for reporting to New York. He grumbled disagreement.

Incidentally, Basri was on his way out. With the opposition controlling parliament under the new constitution Basri would cease to be minister of interior. 'And no more Azmi,' he added gloomily. He grew increasingly morbid, launching into a tirade against the white man as source of slavery, imperialism, economic exploitation and, not least, selective imposition of human rights – on others. I seemed personally exempt. I could not help liking Azmi, despite our conflicting purpose and many confrontational disagreements. He was a patriot in every tissue of his being, proud of his country and unquestioningly committed to serving the king who embodied Morocco's history, tradition and future. That loyalty encompassed Basri. I did not say that it seemed improbable for King Hassan at his age and this stage in his reign to replace the minister of interior whose fidelity was assured, though I thought it over on the long, tedious, uncomfortable flight to Nouakchott.

Buildings, the scant vegetation, and spaces between were as ever brushed with a pallid whiteness deposited by ever blustering sand. Sand confronted me on descending the Antonov ramp. I was escorted to a presidential guest-house lavishly marbled, its technical installations were less impressive: elaborate spouts embellishing a large bathtub emitted only the feeblest trickle, from an ornate shower attachment – nothing. Instead of a bath-mat lay a doormat. When a cockroach scuttled from behind the bath I stamped on it and wiped my foot on the doormat. A pulsating air conditioner was no match for the heavy heat, which engulfed the room, I washed as best I could and lay down. An audience with the president was confirmed for 11 in the morning and before that locally accredited ambassadors hoped to see me.

The ambassadors of Spain, Germany and the US arrived together with the European Community and UNDP representatives. All seemed informed about the talks in Rabat and discussion in New York. The Spanish ambassador mentioned the need for an accord respecting Saharan identity. The German ambassador, with a visiting deputy foreign minister in tow, spoke positively of what I had achieved, his government in cooperation with the US was now working with the ICRC to repatriate the prisoners-of-war Morocco had agreed to release. The American ambassador nodded before turning to me sweetly: 'You have lit a candle, a small candle, but you have lit a candle.' 'Don't speak loudly,' I said, 'or you may blow it out.'

The president was friendly and forthcoming as in the past. I congratulated him on the conduct of recent elections. Law and order prevailed, he said, and they followed correct procedures, European and American friends might find it difficult to grasp why the opposition was poorly represented but that was the people's verdict, Mauritanian voters chose personalities who commanded respect, theirs was a society where individual qualities were known. He paused, then congratulated me on my achievement. I thanked him for his valued advice, which I had followed in ensuring Algerian concurrence. Algeria's role was critical, he said. He approved the composition of the Polisario delegation to Rabat and the arrangements; he was obviously well informed, even about arrival in Tangier. The president attached great importance to the role of the crown prince, the perfect choice, the prince implicates the king, the king cannot himself negotiate, the prince is ideal. It would be regrettable to meet elsewhere if that cost the presence of the prince. Above all the process must continue, he insisted. He denied energetically that Mauritania would prefer the status quo, a solution, honourable, fair and enduring, was foremost in the interest of Morocco and Algeria and, of course, Polisario, but would benefit all countries of the region. It would enlarge markets and investment opportunities, release funds for development and bolster the Maghreb as a whole.

Before departing Nouakchott I received a message from New York confirming the transfer of Polisario POWs from Morocco to Tindouf. This was Morocco wanting to divert attention from talks, to counter criticism in New York, to 'look good'. Germany provided an aircraft to fly the men under Red Cross auspices from Agadir to Tindouf. The 31st October was 'a black day in the history of our people', Sahrawi National Radio announced, marking the 'occupation of our land by the authoritarian Moroccan regime', but on this twenty-first anniversary it became an historic event of great significance[9] Ambassadors of the United States and Germany joined Polisario leaders to witness the prisoners return. Kheddad exclaimed as they landed: 'There you already have the referendum: all sixty-six have voted for us by opting to return to the camps' despite inducements: housing, cars, employment, to woo them into settling in Morocco. The German ambassador spoke, calling on both Morocco and Polisario to respond to every initiative likely to help resolve the conflict. In conversation Kheddad and Abdel-Aziz lobbied him and the US ambassador for the appointment of a mediator, preferably an American. They recognised Morocco's modest concessions in Rabat but Polisario had only one concession to make. In making that they would depend on a great power to bear witness and underwrite compliance with what was agreed. They wanted to talk – insisted on being able to mention independence at least at first – but they relied on a mediator with the weight to lean on Morocco. It was profoundly disturbing that Morocco could block the secretary-general from informing the Council honestly on the recent talks.[9]

Basri was now demanding, and invoking the king's authority, that the report to the Security Council make no reference at all to what had taken place outside the settlement plan. He rejected even the fleeting reference proposed or wording similar to that he himself had used earlier: 'In keeping with its traditions Morocco has had contact with representatives of the Frente Polisario in August and September and expects this process to continue.' Boutros-Ghali instructed me to present a further compromise to read: 'I had a meeting with my special representative in Paris on 16 October. He informed me of his efforts to establish contact between the parties' or 'help create a climate of mutual confidence between the two parties' and 'the result of these efforts is encouraging at this time.' The secretary-general found it impossible to be entirely mute on the subject of talks. He had himself mentioned the contacts in briefing the African group and they were widely known in New York, even Snoussi in addressing the Fourth Committee acknowledged the fact. The Security Council would consider it bizarre were the report to contain no reference to this most significant development. I asked Azmi for an appointment with Basri; he could not promise. I said I would catch the flight that evening, it was Sunday, and go directly from Casablanca to Rabat. It will be very late, he said. 'Too bad, but that way I will be available first thing Monday morning. I have to report to the secretary-general urgently.' No appointment had been confirmed when I arrived.

Azmi called around ten fifteen the next morning to say he had been unable to speak to Basri. I waited. At one thirty Azmi admitted to having seen Basri – in the lift, by chance, for less than a minute. Was I in Rabat? Basri had asked. When Azmi told him I was and what I wished to discuss Basri said he had no time that day – a leading politician had died – but perhaps the day following, or better on my return from visiting Tindouf. In any event Morocco's position was clear, as stated by His Majesty: no reference to contact in any form in the report. Azmi elaborated, as I am certain he was ordered to do: there was no

UN mandate, hortatory references in a resolution were not within the plan as agreed and not binding, and the UN had not been involved, I had acted unofficially as a 'friend'. The UN and the secretary-general could not claim any credit, which was what they sought to do, and if some achievement were attributed to me, Morocco would have to deny it, calling it a lie. The Moroccan position was increasingly surreal.

Countering an Algerian *démarche* for talks to be reported as the highly significant development they were Morocco resolved to make quite certain that the report contain nothing whatsoever on which the Council could hang an operative paragraph aimed at endorsing direct talks and have Council members exert influence.Any mention of talks, even oblique, and Morocco threatened to close shop, end all contact with Polisario, eject Minurso and see me out on the next plane, or so Azmi said.

I left Rabat early to disembark, deafened and shaken, after long Antonov hours, at Tindouf where I was requested to join Bachir at an unfamiliar place, another one and a half hours of spine-rattling cross-desert drive away. From unrelieved rocky hard sand emerged a compound, buzzing with life and with two small trees and a real bird. The 12 October school had been transformed into a reception centre to fete returned prisoners-of-war. Men and women milled about. I was greeting Brahim Ghali, 'minister of defence', when Bachir appeared together with ex-prisoners. They recognized me, they said, from Moroccan television and pictures in newspapers. When I asked about their detention, one said he suffered from heart disease and had been transferred to a hospital for treatment, but refused surgery on discovering that he was classed as 'Moroccan'. This was later corrected, he admitted, before lecturing me on UN failure to distinguish between victim and aggressor. Bachir directed me next door to eat.

The ex-POWs had already feasted and I was not hungry. We sat in a corner, pleasant and airy. Bachir was friendly, albeit detached and melancholic, he had not been much involved with the American and German ambassadors, nothing very new, he thought, except perhaps the mediator. On talks it seemed to him outrageous that the secretary-general might not report fully to the Council. Boutros-Ghali had never inspired their trust and under Moroccan pressure he was now refusing even to inform the Council of the direct talks he himself had so long endeavoured to organize, it was precisely what Boutros had been trying to achieve, and about which he encouraged Bachir at their latest meeting. That he also failed to provide me whole-hearted support seemed dishonest as well as undermining my authority. Desultory discussion of another round followed, he was vague about the Polisario position paper, implying first he had not seen a final version, then that it was ready and he was familiar with the content. Did it move beyond independence? I asked. He could not say, everything relevant was in it. He added that he also knew the substance of the Moroccan paper: as expected. A further meeting had to be somewhere neutral, if the crown prince did not attend that would alter the level of the Moroccan delegation, in which case he, Bachir, would not be going. So much depended on the secretary-general's report. Why should Morocco's position always prevail? Reference to the talks was essential, otherwise they would be converted into a non-happening, with a conspiracy of silence to pretend there was nothing. And, with his engaging rueful smile, Bachir concluded: 'there will be nothing – except another disappointment, more bitterness.'

Memories of the Green March were stirred the following evening when King Hassan addressed his people. Rumour of talks had sparked speculation. The king chose to preempt gossip by making public his interpretation, he described 'mislead sons' for whom the palace doors remained always open, as to the prodigal, provided any notion of independence was first set aside. Astonishing though it was to hear the king mention openly an encounter that had been enveloped in such secrecy, his tone, his terms, emphatically enunciated, made it harder to envisage Polisario returning to the table. Azmi insisted that it was better to have it out, in the open. 'The Polisario aren't serious,' he repeated like a mantra. 'They had their chance. The dog barks but the caravan passes.' I suspect that Basri had intended keeping contact secret but when that failed was determined for Morocco, in the king's person, to retake the initiative and be first to announce what, in their ingenious translation, had occurred. Whatever Boutros-Ghali had said in briefing the African group, or was rumoured in New York, or might eventually appear in a report, Morocco had regally imposed its version on the record. Bachir, when we spoke on the phone was, to my surprise, sanguine about the king's speech: 'He has to say these things to his subjects in order to galvanise his own people, especially the Sahrawis on their side.' At least the king referred to 'mislead sons' and not 'traitors' and 'mercenaries' as in the past. That he never said 'negotiations' was a quibble, it was good that Hassan acknowledged contact and also mentioned the returning prisoners-of-war.

Azmi was wary. Basri, who had of course not been replaced, had been damaged, according to Azmi. He was unwilling to risk further calamity, 'after being bitten by a snake a piece of rope is alarming' in the Arabic saying. Despite the king's speech he was still arguing against any reference to talks in the Security Council report; if anything were said it had to be pared to the ultimate minimum. The secretary-general submitted a final draft: 'I have been informed that there has been contact recently between the Government of Morocco and the Frente POLISARIO and that further contact is expected. I am hopeful that this development will contribute to creating the climate of confidence essential to full implementation of the Settlement Plan.' We were to be damned with the faintest of praise. But it was enough, in the Council, for the British on behalf of the 'group of friends' to present a draft resolution with a second operative paragraph reading: 'Supports the activities of the acting Special Representative in continuing the dialogue with the parties and the two neighbouring countries and in facilitating, in the context of the Settlement Plan, other efforts to set the parties on a course towards an agreed formula for the resolution of their differences, and requests that those activities be accelerated.'[10] Morocco reacted vehemently, were such wording adopted Snoussi would issue a statement disassociating Morocco, and refusing to comply with the resolution except in respect of paragraphs concerning the extension of Minurso. Council members persevered. Repeated consultations failed to reconcile Morocco's refusal with US and others' wanting unambiguous reference to talks. The much modified resolution eventually adopted gave Polisario just enough satisfaction for 'Sahrawi National Radio' to report that 'Our people's just cause scored a political and diplomatic victory of great significance.'[11] Snoussi, looking grim, circulated a statement in New York distancing Morocco from the Council's decision, which 'Sahrawi National Radio' gleefully noted. Others shrugged their shoulders, member states were losing patience with a marginal conflict, their focus on the US presidential election and Boutros-Ghali's likely replacement.

Bachir responded to my call later in the day: 'What, still in the office'; it was eight-thirty. I said they could reproach me many things but not for failing to stay late at my desk, he chuckled, but his voice had none of its habitual warmth. The situation was alarming, the battle at the UN proved beyond all reasonable doubt that Morocco was not in earnest, their heavy-handed determination to obliterate reference to direct contact could only have one consequence: no more Minurso, no cease-fire. Current circumstances were worse than ever, they offered no hope, apocalyptic was the word he used. That inadequate, merely glancing reference in the report had to be my responsibility and even the resolution he considered partly my fault. The final version helped but it was all too obvious that Morocco withheld cooperation. He saw no point in our meeting at this stage, everything was blocked, confused and profoundly discouraging. He still wanted to say farewell to General Leandro, the departing force commander.

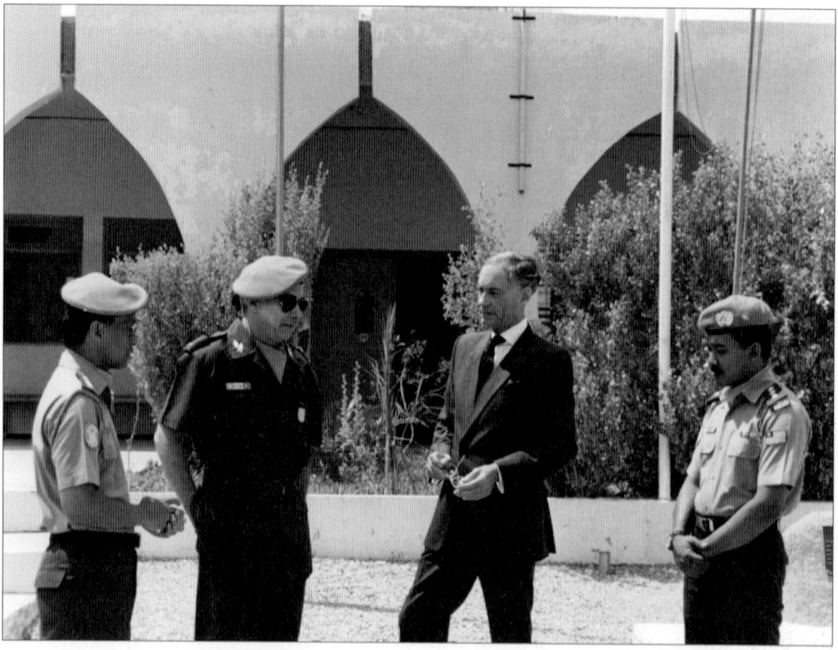

With General Leandro after presenting him his service medal

Bachir accused me of being instrumental in Leandro's leaving under pressure from Morocco. The general might be less popular with the Moroccans, but he was an excellent force commander and politically astute – honed by service as Portugal's military governor in Macao, and I had no wish whatsoever to see him replaced. But after one extension, which I had strongly recommended, he was being recalled to his country. Leandro, on his return from saying goodbye, reported finding Bachir a saddened man. He had been extremely disappointed by the 'doughnut report', characterized by what it omitted, not what it contained, for which he continued to hold me partly responsible, and disillusioned by the Council's failure to act decisively. All was back to before summer or before that. He looked to a new secretary-general – and a new special representative. Back in the camps Bachir retired to his tent where he was left to brood.

Polisario were thoroughly disillusioned, the secretary-general, the UN, the Security Council chose to ignore the real import of direct talks: under Moroccan pressure they downplayed what occurred giving events the twist

Rabat demanded, and without sequel. Polisario awaited the appointment of a secretary-general less biased in favour of Morocco. Morocco too looked to a less biased secretary-general: Boutros-Ghali had failed to eliminate 'talks' from the report and to prevent any mention in the resolution.

Azmi, reached after multiple attempts, said the minister was exceptionally busy: no idea when a meeting might be possible. Did I have anything specific to propose? When eventually I flew to Rabat it was at Snoussi's instigation. He was in the capital to report to His Majesty and offered to brief me on developments in New York. Azmi met me on landing in Casablanca and during the drive to Rabat I mentioned a dinner engagement. Yes, he knew Snoussi was in town. He retrieved a mobile phone and ostensibly out of my hearing mumbled in Arabic. From '*si, Sidi*', repeated as he rang off, it had to be Basri. Azmi said the minister was now aware of my being in Rabat. Nothing about an appointment, instead I was lectured on the need not to speak of the talks – they were no business of Snoussi's – or about confidential exchanges with Bachir – Snoussi was famously indiscreet – anyway the whole affair was not his concern.

Azmi was there when I approached the car sent to collect me. As I was saying politely 'good evening', he opened the door before following me into the back. Snoussi, on our arrival, feigned mock pleasure at seeing Azmi. We were offered the customary generous hospitality and excellent wine; Snoussi prides himself on connoisseurship. The conversation rambled without infringing sensitive areas. With Snoussi this is easy, he likes retelling stories and that evening he included some that I had not heard before. As to New York, Snoussi turned to the secretary-generalship, Boutros-Ghali's departure was no great loss. The year before when given ideas for implementing the plan, he failed; after my drafting his Security Council statement, he produced something else, and after accepting my judgment that dispatching Garekhan was pointless, he did just that. Morocco had objected strongly to nominating Garekhan as someone too close to the Algerians. Most of my problems arose from that decision, Snoussi concluded. Azmi remained silent. Talk moved to the settlement plan and continuing obstacles to its implementation. It was weird experiencing two key players ignore the one significant development of recent weeks, the reason for Snoussi's presence in Rabat. Pervasive mistrust extended beyond the parties in conflict into their own society, enfolding me with straitjacket and minder.

Basri wished to see me: late morning; as soon as he returned from the palace; then later in the afternoon; till around 6.30 came confirmation of an appointment for 8 o'clock. A brief downpour and potentially ferocious dogs welcomed me. I was kept waiting long enough to marvel yet again at the gilded lily of gold-leafed plaster ceiling. Basri was in a side salon, seated in an armchair, golf-dressed and wearing a cap, which he removed as I entered. Azmi, who followed me in, was instructed to switch on the television, then raise the volume, then produce a Davidoff cheroot and light it, then place an ash-tray strategically on the arm of a sofa next the great man. His authority firmly established Basri returned to picking at his lips, the vitilego disease looked worse, the skin at his mouth was dry and blotched, white patches and pink covered his hands,. The customary Moroccan salutation: how are you? How is your health? How is the family? anticipated no more response than the English 'how do you do?' Basri watched the crown prince on television, being hand-kissed by an array of dignitaries prior to an official visit to the US, next, the younger prince presiding elsewhere. The programme following had Basri holding forth on the electoral process, he told Azmi to switch off and turned to me. 'How is the Sahara?' 'Still there,' I said. 'We don't need Minurso for that.' He paused. 'I respect you,' which I took as the cue to be serious.

One thing was evident, he began, independence could not be mouthed or in any way imagined; a document in which it appeared was unacceptable. Surely a position paper, I said, could move to devolution of power and regional autonomy after recognising there was no prospect of independence. 'No,' he stated categorically, 'there must be no mention of independence whatsoever, even the king could not permit that. Independence in interdependence has no meaning and is not legally known. But let them dream what they want, provided the Sahara is indubitably part of Morocco.' Basri said he wanted a solution, he was ready for a face-saving solution. 'But independence – only one road to that: grab it, seize it, take it by force. Let them try,' he said. He drew on his cheroot, picked at his lip before continuing. Morocco had awarded the Sahara three regions. 'Yes,' I said, 'and included Smara with Goulemine and Tan-Tan[12] to make things tidy.' Azmi half-smiled, Basri ignored the pointed irony. He then urged me to renew contact with Bachir. He, Basri, was the only one willing to talk to Polisario, he said, in Rabat they asked why they were not received by Filali. 'Because Filali refuses', though they were given a more diplomatic excuse. 'No one will speak to them, just Basri.' Last time they were treated like kings, Basri said he chauffeured them himself, next time it would be even better. He meandered on without ever wobbling on the two immutable conditions for further contact: no thought of 'independence', and it was inconceivable that the prince be obliged to travel abroad or have someone take his place. Azmi next day asked when I planned going to Tindouf. He became dismissive of Bachir, he was ham-strung by his brother's legacy: what El-Ouali stood for and had fought and died for, making it near impossible for Bachir to renege on his brother's ideals in the eyes of the following he had inherited.

Bachir, in Vienna, responded to my call without enthusiasm. Was there anything new? What had I been able to wheedle out of the Moroccans? Basri wanted to resume contact. I could hear the question mark in Bachir's mumbled 'Hm?' That was it. No to 'independence', and Morocco insisted that the crown prince be present and could not be expected to travel outside the country for a meeting. Bachir said: 'No ladies in Morocco these days go abroad more than the prince.' 'Polisario is ready and prepared to meet in any neutral place, for Morocco to respond.' There seemed little point in my coming to Tindouf; Bachir had no idea when he would be back. He said 'Better wait for a new secretary-general to be appointed and see whether there will be a new "dynamic".' The new year might bring new faces, new ideas and renewed hope.

22

New Secretary-General

MADELEINE ALBRIGHT'S SELECTION was announced as secretary of state in the next administration, assuring the American veto that put paid to Boutros-Ghali's last ditch campaign. With insufficient time for the Africans to rally behind one of their political own, a UN insider emerged as candidate, the Ghanaian under-secretary-general for peace-keeping. Washington liked his soft-spoken, accommodating manner and part-American education, the French accepted that his command of their language was adequate. Kofi Annan was generally liked, he had risen through the ranks of international civil service and being a UN man endeared him to many. That Annan was

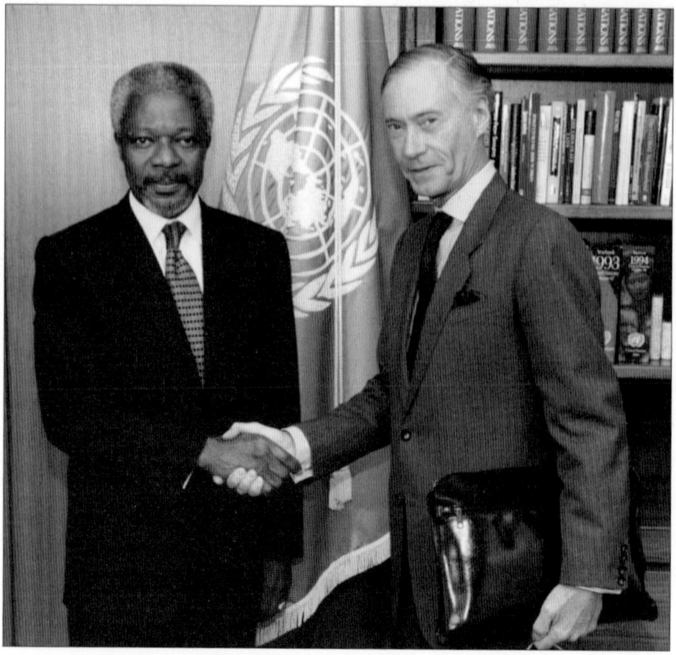

Congratulating Kofi Annan on his appointment

perceived as the American candidate had one advantage in restoring US sympathy for the organisation after confrontation with Boutros-Ghali and the damaging presidential electoral campaign. I welcomed the appointment of Kofi Annan, had known him for years, though not closely, and thought well of him. His endorsement by the US encouraged me to believe that the Americans might relax their carping about mission costs and, more important, could become involved in bringing pressure on both parties to reach a negotiated agreement.

A peacefully negotiated solution was at the heart of the action I proposed to Kofi Annan. For talks to resume Morocco would need persuading and the Polisario reassuring. Only a mediator, with political weight, from a powerful interested country would be capable of exerting influence, the power that I lacked. Of the two most obvious countries France, with long involvement in the region, was perhaps too close to Morocco and had a complicated relationship with Algeria, from Boutros-Ghali I already knew that Paris was unlikely to undertake a mediating role. That left the US. I suspect others gave similar advice: to involve the Americans directly. An emissary was dispatched to Houston to approach James A. Baker III. Baker had a distinguished career as Ronald Reagan's chief of staff and secretary of the treasury before becoming secretary of state under President George H.W. Bush, he had played a key diplomatic role at the cold war's ending and in liberating Kuwait from Iraq – noted with glee by Polisario. Baker, who had intimated interest in a high profile international appointment, agreed to possible nomination as the secretary-general's personal envoy.

How this affected my position was not immediately obvious. Ginsberg was urging the appointment of a new representative, being reluctant to pardon me for having succeeded in bringing the two sides together without him. Snoussi argued that with a new secretary-general he saw no advantage in a new special representative. A replacement would take months to agree: if acceptable to Algeria then not to Morocco and vice versa. He would be unfamiliar with an extremely complex problem at a peak of political sensitivity, it would be at least a year before he understood what it was all about. It was preferable that I be given maximum authority: 'We are not in love with Jensen' (he used '*amoureux*'), 'but he is the only representative to have achieved a degree of confidence on both sides, and the only one to produce results.' When Snoussi reported the exchange to me, I admit to being pleasantly surprised. The message from Tindouf was different. Boukhari, back from New York, told Bodan that I had been around long enough and he did not believe I could do more than I had already done.

My State Department contact reported an 'awful' encounter in New York, at which he was present, between the Moroccan crown prince and the American ambassador Interfurth. It lasted some two hours and had been very, very difficult.[1] The Moroccans dismissed the talks as unrelated to the UN, an internal Moroccan affair and of no concern to the US or the Security Council. Despite the Americans' best efforts, and, I was assured, they tried extremely hard, the Moroccans rejected every argument, and accused the US of not 'helping'.

The secretary-general had summoned me and departure was imminent when Azmi called that Basri insisted on meeting. 'But I'm leaving, early tomorrow.' 'Yes, it'll be all right. The appointment with Basri is at 8 a.m.' It was not. When we met at the golf club, Basri stated, without any embarrassment as to how he knew, 'Your appointment with the secretary-general isn't till the day after'. He switched to being friendly, it was a long time since he had seen me, had Polisario thinking evolved? I said that I detected no change, Bachir would surely stand by his commitment to resume talks but in a neutral place. As regards identification Polisario insisted on lists being published for those already identified and stood ready to identify applicants from all sub-fractions included in the census. Polisario now awaited whatever initiative the new secretary-general decided on.

Basri listened. No comment. Then abruptly changed tone: 'Talks, they're an internal affair, not the UN's concern,' end of subject. 'We want to deblock identification. Lists – no, anyway Polisario already has them.' No group of applicants to be excluded, the suggestion that only some census categories qualified was unacceptable. Whoever coined 'disputed groups' did not know what he was talking about. Basri then convoked his top legal advisers to eliminate any lingering doubt. Waiting for the lawyers I strolled for a few minutes soothed by the delicious morning air.

The legal advisers appeared, dressed for jogging. Both had just been named to university appointments, as rector, respectively of the universities of Casablanca and Kenitra, I guessed to quell student unrest. Hasbi, the senior, who was frequently interrupted by important telephone calls, began by demanding how the UN intended to proceed, how I, as special representative, would impose the plan to which there was firm commitment. He elaborated loftily with legal-sounding exposition – not the first time he had lectured on the subject. His colleague nodded affirmation. Principle had to be respected, every applicant had the right to be identified, he categorically rejected distinguishing between census groups. It was politically untenable to postpone 'disputed groups', disputed by whom? he asked rhetorically. That was a Polisario plot to identify those they wanted, then declare the process complete, leaving many, who had submitted applications correctly, unidentified. He dismissed my efforts to clarify, even the problem in finding sheikhs to identify individuals drawn from many different sub-fractions, there was nothing to discuss. They were as dismissive of the Security Council and of Snoussi – as substantial as air – as they were of my arguments, the lawyers summarized, delivered judgement. Basri, it seemed, continued to believe in his capacity to manipulate the process, to reject compromise, and to buy time.

Whatever Morocco's wishful thinking, nothing convinced me that Polisario would capitulate and their supporters return to '*la patrie*' – the homeland. That was not going to be. The leadership had invested too much in their independence campaign simply to surrender, they had faith in their cause, and they had international support. Polisario genuinely believed that they would win in a free and fair referendum but doubted such a referendum ever taking place. The excitement generated by Geneva and Rabat was making Morocco wary, it dreaded mounting pressure for concessions leading to internationally guaranteed regional autonomy. Despite all he said to me at the time, years later, forced into retirement, an exile in Paris, Basri revealed his visceral opposition to serious autonomy: it predestined disintegration of the kingdom.[2]

Identification, if resumed, would never end in resolving the conflict, of that I was sure, at best, it would prolong the process inconclusively, at worst, it would entrench positions and make concessions more elusive. Identification so far had achieved the objective of facing Morocco with the likelihood of an unacceptable electoral roll, this was the juncture when an alternative solution could be made appealing. Morocco, of course, knew that an American mediator had the potential to exercise pressure for meaningful negotiation and to offer guarantees. Baker's rumoured nomination delighted Polisario, who saw it as a step in their favour; Morocco took comfort in his staunch Republican credentials, refusing to believe that the US would work to undermine Moroccan stability. Though it worried His Majesty, Snoussi confided indiscreetly: 'We''ll let Baker walk about, putting big, flat feet on the table, with big size shoes, but make sure he understands just how far he may go.'

On 17 March the appointment of James Baker was officially announced. The secretary-general's spokesman referred to Baker as a most distinguished statesman, who enjoyed a high international reputation and commanded universal respect. 'His appointment has been warmly welcomed by the parties.' The formal terms of reference were: 'to review the situation ... and assess the implementability of the plan in its present form; to examine whether there are adjustments ...which will significantly improve prospects of implementing it ...; if there are not, to advise on other possible ways of resolving the conflict.'[3]

In New York Boukhari was taken to lunch by an American and a British diplomat. After some amiable banter they suggested that Polisario be open, not reject a proposal, even if it was not exactly what was hoped for. 'The tide is against you. Don't turn down an opportunity.'[4] The word autonomy was used more than once. Boukhari became increasingly heated: 'If it's autonomy we could have had it without Baker.' 'If Baker cannot make the plan work, God himself cannot do it.' Polisario intended making their case when the envoy came to Tindouf, they counted on his staying at least twenty-four hours – not like the secretary-generals who flew in and out. America should be expected to sympathise with freedom fighters. Kheddad was being especially emphatic: 'I fight for a cause; they (the Moroccans) defend a regime,' I was told on arriving in New York for Baker's briefing.

It was April Fool's day, but no jokes. The responsible heads of department lacked precise ideas. All found the arcane detail confusing. In leaving me to brief Baker they warned me not to delve excessively into 'all that business about sub-fractions and disputed groups'. I said that if Baker failed to grasp 'that business' he would fail to understand the problem. Next morning James Baker arrived.

With him came John Bolton, infamous for his hardline neo-conservatism, who was already known for his antipathy to multilateralism and the UN while assistant secretary of state for international organizations affairs. On this occasion he merely glowered. I was given the floor and explained succinctly about the region, recent history and the settlement plan, the agreed cease-fire, crucial and continuing to hold. Uncoupling the cease-fire from other aspects of the plan had reduced leverage, but voter identification, core of the referendum process and its biggest challenge, eventually began. The two sides had incompatible views as to who should qualify to vote and, of course, saw that as crucial to the end result. A census conducted by Spain, in a late colonial move, recorded the nomadic population in tribes, subdivided into sub-fractions, the key unit of Sahrawi society, though it emerged that three of the census groups were not actual tribes but tribal groupings comprising individuals from a multiplicity of fractions. Baker broke in. 'I have a question, 'he said, adding: 'Do you mind if I interrupt you as we go along. If you prefer, I can wait till you've finished but then I'm liable to forget what it was I wanted to ask.' No problem, I told him. He needed more detail about these tribal unities, and about sub-fractions, he followed one probing question with another, Baker was tenacious. He also enquired about the talks, the background, and their outcome. Instead of a twenty-minute mission statement with the odd question afterwards we embarked on an in-depth dialogue lasting nearly an hour and a half. At the end I felt that Baker began to understand what had been achieved, why the process had stalled, and in what way it might be possible to advance.

The chairman asked how Baker wished to operate and what staff he required. He could choose to maintain distance and work independently of the UN or, if he preferred, select whatever support he thought useful. Baker replied that he hoped to bring one or more of his earlier collaborators in Washington – he mentioned Chester Crocker, sometime assistant secretary of state for Africa, and John Bolton – and, nodding at me, 'I would like to have him'. He would travel with his own secretary and interpreter but would appreciate UN logistical assistance. I departed New York looking forward to work alongside a statesman of Baker's caliber, here was someone, who seemed to latch onto issues, with authority and power to influence events. Basri, naturally, insisted on meeting the moment I returned to Morocco.

As predictably, he changed one appointment after the other. The habitual deferment, rescheduling, postponement had me waste a day. Basri, when finished with the French prime minister, union leaders and the king's business, did have the courtesy to apologise. He was desperate to hear about Baker and the Americans, 'They're sovereign, now super-sovereign,' he said. Having listened to what he certainly already knew, he became conspiratorial. Morocco would never dismiss H, I and J applicants, and Basri undertook to pre-vet and submit just 50,000. I returned to Laayoune to prepare Baker's visit to the region.

A violent storm broke as we landed. Wind whipped sand into a frenzy of thick cloud, which bursts of lashing rain failed to settle. In few days the desert would sprout and flamingos return to a newly formed lake. Only a soothsayer would know to interpret the tempest as harbinger of Baker bringing unsettled weather or the moisture to nourish the land and nurture growth. From New York came news that Polisario reacted furiously on hearing that Baker might not stay overnight in the camps, they demanded equal treatment with Morocco, and that he see the parties to the conflict before meeting others. Question of security, they were told. They remonstrated with the secretary-general's chief of staff, blamed the UN for bad experience in the past, were expecting better from James Baker. As with every new face they discredited predecessors and appealed for fresh sympathy. Baker might be proving less malleable than they wished; his security concerns imposed severe restriction on movement, privately to me, he threatened simply to meet Polisario leaders at Tindouf airport. An audience with the president in Algiers being scheduled for the morning we were to fly south was certain to dismay Polisario by further reducing time available. The programme for Rabat, which came first, was less contentious: an audience with the king, meetings with Filali and Basri; accommodation at a royal guest house.

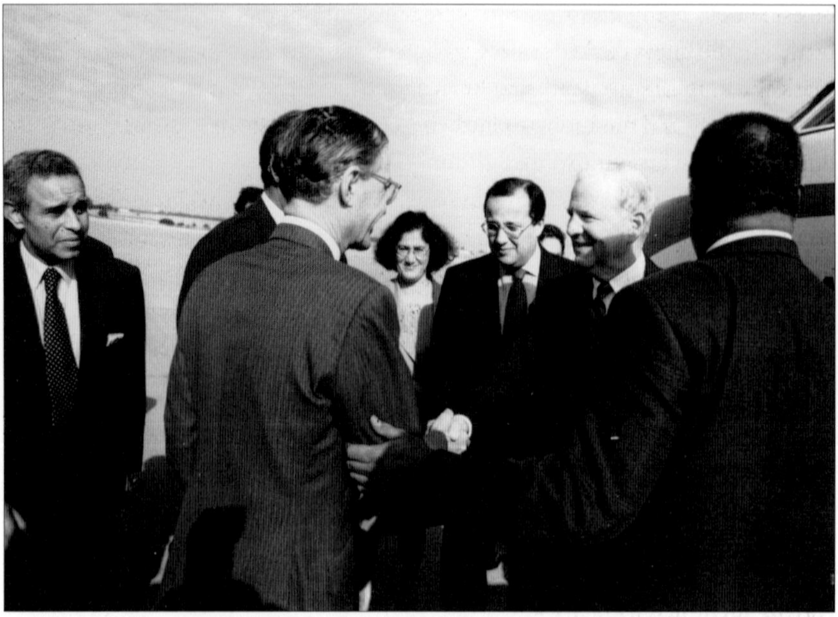

Greeting James Baker on his arrival in Rabat

King Hassan greeted Baker as an old friend with whom he had much to talk about.

Once we were seated round an opulent conference table at the palace, the king took his place at the head, nodding to where both princes, his chief ministers and we sat. He would always remember, he said, Baker's handling of the lead-up to the Gulf War, how he presided over the Security Council at its culminating session – and the taut expression on his face pending China's vote lapsing into glad relief when the Chinese abstained. Legality, Hassan continued, was the main attribute of a nation, countries were not all nations. He summarized his own nation's quest for international legality,

Morocco submitted its case to the International Court of Justice, as king, he accepted holding a referendum, Morocco agreed to the settlement plan and relevant resolutions of the Council. Morocco remained respectful of the plan, 'Ambassador Jensen,' he said looking in my direction, 'can confirm that we have always cooperated.' The prime minister, Filali, would meet Baker in the morning to discuss detail. Baker thanked His Majesty and presented him with a one dollar bill bearing serial number 0000017, signed by Baker as treasury secretary and personally countersigned. Even if the dollar was worth less these days, this was something, Baker explained, that he liked giving to a person he esteemed highly. He usually selected a serial number reflecting the year of birth, and he knew the king's – a year before his own – but in this case chose to mark the king as seventeenth in line of the Alaouite dynasty. Hassan thanked him profusely and the audience ended. At the royal guest house Baker took me outside: 'Come for a walk,'

He recalled briefings in Washington and at the UN, from Council members and others. All the best informed agreed that continued identification would not channel into a referendum and urged talks. 'Give me those identification facts again.' I did. I told him that we had identified nearly as many persons as were in the Spanish census and convoked more. Polisario would be delighted to proceed to a referendum on this basis – precisely what Morocco dreaded. Well over one hundred thousand further applicants, not identified, were drawn almost exclusively from groups that Polisario rejected as not authentically Western Saharan. Polisario doubted the identification commission's capacity to resist Moroccan pressure to have these accepted, and without them being admitted as voters Morocco would never voluntarily submit to a referendum. Having identified as many as we had, and after analyzing the implications, it was possible to project the result were identification massaged to the bitter end. Morocco might command majority support, though even that was uncertain, but it would be far from the decisive vote in favour the king needed. I had given – orally – to Basri round figures and my prognosis, whether he transmitted them to the king I could not know, and had come to doubt that he dared. The figures and analysis were to persuade Morocco to engage in direct talks. Morocco needed to compromise but was strongly placed for negotiating so long as Polisario remained convinced that they would never have the referendum they wanted. A compromise on regional autonomy, while not ideal from either perspective, took and gave in almost equal measure, it offered an equitable prospect.

Until now Polisario had been doing all to engage the UN and Security

Council in furthering talks, while Morocco stretched every muscle to evade potential pressure. With Baker's appointment the chemistry changed; American high-level engagement had implications. Polisario now wished to resume identification because they believed in US influence ensuring their 'free and fair' referendum, Morocco chose to revive the settlement plan as bulwark against being pressured into conceding regional autonomy. Identification would inevitably entail more time and money, hardly pleasing the Security Council, but worse, I was convinced it could only lead to a hardening of positions making compromise still more elusive. Ultimately, Morocco would be sure to challenge the result, presumably invoke the appeals process as authorised by the plan, thus threatening to repeat the entire operation. Polisario, like the dog with its bone at last, would have no incentive to relax a grip on the electoral roll they favoured. Baker listened attentively, nodding now and then. 'Give me those figures of yours again,' he said. I began. 'No, it's too complicated, I need a bit of paper.' I promised, reluctant though I was to commit this to writing. 'I want you in the loop,' he said, 'There will be no secrets from you – on one condition. Nothing goes to New York, no written reports, nothing.'

Next morning Filali received us in the foreign ministry's sumptuous new office. As always gently spoken but resolute. The conflict had lasted far too long, neither Morocco nor Algeria had interest in permitting it to continue and fester. He urged full implementation of the settlement plan. Baker said that a reason for his accepting the assignment was the great friendship and respect he had for Morocco, this was a problem Morocco did not need, and needed to put behind it. That morning he had played golf with Basri, who promised that 'if I can show a way for Morocco to get out of this problem, he'll show me a way to get out of sand traps and bunkers – at which he is very good.' It was the second or third longest running problem for the UN and some Security Council members talked of ending Minurso. The secretary-general looked for a new initiative with a new face, someone with experience in conflict resolution. Baker asked, first, whether political will existed on both sides to implement the plan in a reasonable span of time; second, if there was little chance of bringing the settlement plan to closure, might other initiatives lead to a solution. Failing that, the Security Council was likely to conclude that the mission in Western Sahara was over. He recognized the danger of resumed hostilities, that was another reason why the problem should be resolved – in the interests also of Algeria and the Maghreb Union. Could the plan be implemented?

Baker had seen a Moroccan letter to the secretary-general. It signalled good faith and wish to move the process forward but gave rise to questions. The publishing of names was an issue. Did Morocco object to the UN publishing aggregate numbers of those deemed eligible to vote? For Baker to hold meaningful discussions with Algeria and Polisario he needed to know exactly what Morocco had in mind. Basri elaborated over a three-hour meeting, which began when we left Filali. Morocco had done everything to comply with the settlement plan, they were diligent, impartial in defending legality, and scrupulous in observing the right to apply, he rejected any charge of stuffing the ballot box. Their applications were presented on time, whereas Polisario submitted one list on time and others later. Their main concern was to implement the plan, with respect for the five criteria. Their sheikhs, like their applicants, were always present; on the other side sheikhs were constantly ill or otherwise unavailable, causing delay. Casually, he said: 'The territory is now and for ever under Moroccan sovereignty', explaining 'I am not a diplomat.' He turned to the publication of lists. This would contravene the plan, which provided for publication only shortly before the referendum campaign. But Morocco was a democratic, open society and he was prepared to discuss with Baker in due course when names could be divulged. He then chose to address 'fundamental' issues.

182,000 persons had legitimately applied to be identified. That Morocco, a nation state rooted in legality, could have falsified applications was inconceivable, however, to accelerate proceedings he agreed to pre-vet and submit some 50,000 of those most certain to qualify while a solution for the rest remained pending. Baker interrupted: 'We don't want an interim solution – the UN or the king.' 'No one can ask Morocco to violate the plan,' Basri replied. 'No,' said Baker, 'but I can suggest to Morocco, and Polisario and Algeria, to adjust the plan and permit it to continue, otherwise, it's the end.' Basri changed tone, saying they looked to Baker as their physician, capable of prescribing pragmatic treatment. More compliments followed. To me Baker whispered: 'When they start talking nice to you, that's when you have to watch out.' To Basri he expressed the feeling in many quarters that the plan was inherently unworkable because the parties seemed unwilling to take political decisions to make it work. Basri refuted criticism of Morocco, which endeavoured to implement the plan while Polisario blocked. As we left Baker admitted to me that he was more and more convinced that it was not workable.

Political party leaders, at a gathering afterwards, took an equally rigid line. Asking a Sahrawi whether he was Moroccan was comparable to asking a citizen of Detroit or Chicago whether he was American, said the first speaker. Morocco would not be split by the Algerian nutcracker. The Madrid agreement of 1975 recognised the Sahara reverting to Morocco, Moroccans had accepted the referendum only under pressure from friendly countries. 'They are determined to have you jump through the hoops,' I said to Baker as we left, he understood perfectly, everything he had heard was predictable. Hope remained that King Hassan would use his unassailable authority to steer the conflict out of gridlock. A final audience was planned for the seaside palace at Bouznika.

Inside the security wall paddocks with white-painted fences lined a long drive with an impeccable stable block in the background. The palace, an elegant single story building, fronted the sea across a nine-hole golf course, the grass immaculate. Both princes waited in the entrance to greet us together with Filali and Basri. The king appeared, recognized us graciously, and drew Baker aside. They left to walk outside, backwards and forwards as we watched. The crown prince made conversation but small talk was desultory. Basri, surprisingly, whispered to me 'We all know what Baker is aiming for: autonomy with international guarantees.' Half an hour later King Hassan and Baker returned. We said our farewells and departed. 'Erik, sit here beside me,' Baker said as the driver opened the door. 'Know what. They want the settlement plan, identification.' He heard me sigh, I could have screamed. They had discussed various issues, Baker continued. On 'transparency' the king would not object if Baker deemed it necessary to publish lists of those so far found eligible to vote in order to relaunch the process. The king gave a gentleman's agreement to deferring, perhaps indefinitely, the most contested H41, 61 and J 51/52. Regional autonomy had not, it seemed, been considered. I could not but wonder whether the projected outcome of identification was mentioned – with figures. I said: 'You know identification will never deliver a solution to the conflict. It may only make a negotiated compromise harder to achieve.' 'When they peer into the abyss,' Baker said, 'they'll talk.'

With Baker for our next appointment was Chester Crocker, urbane academic from Georgetown. Crocker had made a distinguished contribution as assistant secretary of state for Africa. His expertise was sub-Saharan but he was knowledgeable, cultured and pleasant company. Once airborne, en route from Rabat to Algiers, Baker, relaxed, reminisced, chatted about holidays, he told jokes, was delightfully indiscreet. He had had a call from Jimmy Carter before leaving America, dismissive of Ginsberg. The former deputy chairman, who had tried to lobby, claiming to know more about the issue than any other

American, was written off as 'such a nutcake' and a 'disaffected bully'. We were into anecdotes about Reagan when I was invited for security briefing: security in Algiers demanded extreme measures. After exhibiting Baker's bulletproof coat – incredibly heavy and torture to wear – the security chief, an experienced Australian, detailed procedures in the event of ambush: if the driver has been killed, push him out – 'there's nothing you can do for him', if he is wounded you squeeze in, take the wheel and drive like hell, when necessary use the vehicle like a bumper car to create a gap. But we drove into town incident free to the government guest hotel where I had stayed previously and on to our first meeting with Attaf, foreign minister.

Was the plan implementable, Baker asked; what would it take?Attaf thought direct negotiations unavoidable. He felt that Morocco was readier than before for negotiation, Polisario certainly was – on two conditions: that talks take place in a neutral place and with the presence of a third party. Discussion of a political solution needed to be based on specific proposals, reference to 'large autonomy', 'links with the kingdom', 'internal guarantees' remained to be fleshed out. As to the plan, he said, there were complexities beyond identification. Baker responded: 'The train has stalled. Can we get it back on track and moving? Should we put aside the plan and focus on a political solution? The prime minister insisted that Algeria had long desired an outcome permitting Morocco, Polisario and Algeria to live together in peace and stability. Algeria had no territorial claim, no national interest, it sought a solution acceptable to Morocco and Polisario, but wished it to be legal, ensuring security and stability, and lasting. 'A problem with the referendum,' said Baker, 'is that it delivers one big winner and one big loser, which may be why the settlement plan won't work. So how can we move towards a political solution?'

The prime minister replied that if the settlement plan was not enough, and he believed it not enough, then perhaps Baker could help foster political will on the Moroccan side, Algeria was ready to nudge Polisario towards a peaceful solution. Baker thought, and the prime minister concurred, that direct talks might be focused, not on the plan, but on a political compromise, which could then be confirmed by referendum. Over dinner with Attaf and Bendjama, secretary-general of the ministry, Baker heard a detailed account of both Geneva and Rabat meetings from their perspective. The opening day in Rabat began auspiciously, the second day saw the prince introduce the new Moroccan constitution and regionalization proposals and Bachir's insistence on mentioning independence, but the final day went well enough with agreement to meet again. I was pleased at confirmation from the Algerians, their implicit endorsement of what had been achieved and the way forward. The president received Baker next morning.

President Zeroual assured Baker of Algeria's continuing commitment to a definitive solution. Algeria had long called for dialogue, for the parties to sit at the same table. He also stressed the importance of maintaining Minurso, its withdrawal would create a dangerous vacuum. Baker reassured the president: the Security Council would not terminate Minurso unless it became obvious that the plan was not workable and political will lacked to pursue any other initiative. True, many in Washington preferred to end the mission but Baker also encountered support in both the administration and Congress. He was an optimist, though only the night before, when the secretary of state asked how things were going, he replied: 'This problem makes the middle east look easy.' Mauritania beckoned with a sandstorm.

The foreign minister welcomed Baker. With his experience and the new secretary-general's will they were confident a solution could be found. Baker took a pen from his pocket and held it up. 'The magic wand,' he said, 'Let there be peace.' The prime minister, in a larger office, added that the withdrawal of Minurso would be a disaster, a catastrophe for the region, leading inevitably to hostilities. The president insisted on reviewing events since August, he was concerned why the initiative, begun with Geneva and continued at September talks in Rabat, had not proceeded further. He looked to the US to foster dialogue, to Baker he said: 'You have played a great role, as a mediator', Mauritania would support any proposal of Baker's, while emphasizing that they were 'neutral, totally neutral.'

Arrival in the Polisario camps next day felt anything but neutral, Sahrawis waving Polisario flags were marshalled on either side of an extenuated approach route, at least half a mile long. The women screamed, cried out and ululated piercingly – 'don't wiggle your tongue at me', entreated the security officer – the men shouted, made 'V' signs, exhibited placards marked independence invoking the liberation of Kuwait. So close they were that many could and did bang the car-sides as our cavalcade passed slowly through. Eye contact was inevitable, a few smiled, more bellowed slogans, I recognized '*istiqlal*' – 'independence'. Baker in his bulletproof raincoat looked imperial and hot, and was visibly relieved at being able to remove the coat after entering the complex where we were to meet.

Bachir, as Polisario's principal spokesman, welcomed Baker effusively, regretted the brevity of his time in the camps, and moved to substance.

Identification was the core, criteria four and five were impossible to implement reliably. If only Morocco would cease imposing a foreign population identification could proceed. All Polisario wanted was to exercise their god-given right to self-determination. Kheddad said that for them the referendum was a democratic process leading to a decision, the others planned the referendum to impose a solution. The Spanish census counted some 74,000 inhabitants; how could that translate into 181,000 or more? He instanced 46,000 applications presented on the basis of 503 persons listed in the census under 'Various Tribes', it was no solution simply to defer their identification. Baker asked what they needed to restart the process, how to find a way out of the bunker. 'We just want the settlement plan,' said Bachir, they were sure to reach a peaceful, lasting solution if only Sahrawis came for identification. 'Morocco is absolutely convinced they will win, I am sure you are convinced you will win', Baker said thoughtfully, 'Heck of a big roll of the dice. Helluva gamble. Might it not be better than risking all to consider an alternative, offering much, if not everything, you would like.' Bachir said their top priority was to resume identification and implement the plan. 'That's no use if you hit another hump in six months time,' Baker replied. Bachir said he hoped Baker would come again, many times. 'No, I'm not going to do what Erik has done, this is your last best chance.' Bachir smiled wanly then rose to introduce the sheikhs present before escorting Baker to meet Abdel-Aziz *tête-à-tête*. Abdel-Aziz was predictable.

Baker said as much when, to Polisario's consternation, we departed immediately afterwards. At the airport the Algerian authorities insisted on serving tea. Baker chatted briefly to the governor, the Wali of Tindouf, confirmed with me some practical arrangements, concluded last minute courtesies with Kheddad who was seeing him off, and prepared to board. He was flying direct to London, I was returning by Antonov to Laayoune with a heavy heart. An American friend wrote when Baker was first appointed that for him this was a win-win situation: achieve a solution and it's the Nobel prize and enhanced international standing, declare political will lacking, mission impossible, end Minurso, and he is a hero to his own republican right – never should we forget that he remained an American politician. All I sought was neither political credit nor great honour, but an honourable end to the conflict and a future for the refugees and the region. From the meeting with Abdel-Aziz I had no expectations but I had had hopes for King Hassan. I wanted to believe that Baker was biding his time but the prospect as Baker's plane took off felt gloomy. Kheddad beside me looked visibly pleased, I should be happy, he turned to say, to have great power backing. He embraced me, something he rarely did, and Boukhari embraced me and then Moulud. At which moment I was summoned to take an urgent message from Laayoune, where the governor wished to speak personally.

We met on my return. Baker's tour, he began, generated dissatisfaction among Sahrawi notables and intellectuals – 'there are at least twice as many on this side'- they failed to comprehend why Baker had not visited Laayoune. He would, I felt sure, when next in the region. But the governor had more urgent business and he opened a folder containing an official-looking document. For five years, he read, Morocco had generously supported Minurso – he quoted figures – but could not continue doing so, for financial reasons his government had decided no longer to contribute board and lodging in Laayoune with effect from 1st March. After only a slight pause I expressed appreciation for Morocco's generosity and the significant contribution to the mission. They had the right to cease voluntary payments, however, I feared New York would have reservations about this being made retroactive: had I heard correctly '1st March'? We were in mid May. Discussion of the mandate, budgetary procedures, the impossibility of backdating, followed, but this was a decision that the governor had no authority to debate, only instructions to transmit. A matter with significant financial implications, I explained, would have to be communicated officially to the secretary-general.

It was a bewildering message to submit to New York, Morocco had but recently offered to contribute more should cost be an obstacle to maintaining Minurso. Azmi, when I sought clarification, said Morocco was within its rights: 'Anyway, there was nothing in writing to say we'd pay.' I asked to see Basri, urgently. That posed a problem with new governors to install and electoral business, and the official visit of President Mubarak, Basri was fully committed. And, as it happened, all Rabat hotels were booked solid. I had not yet received New York's reaction to my report on the governor's communication but knew this would trigger a *demarché* in Rabat. The new British ambassador had invited me to stay, I phoned to ask whether it might be possible to spend a night or two. He was most gracious, I was welcome, and even if he were called away the house remained available. I confirmed to Azmi that I would come to Rabat and stay with friends. Who? He demanded. The British ambassador. What will all the other ambassadors think? Azmi asked dramatically – as if they cared. 'It's private,' I said. 'You can't be private, you have an official position. Everyone knows you.' Minutes later he called back to say that a small suite had suddenly become available at the Hotel Tour Hassan.

He would meet me on arrival.

Azmi reiterated how inopportune my visit was. The timing was dictated by Morocco, I said, the governor had conveyed a message with major financial implications that was not merely urgent but retroactive. Morocco had already contributed so much, Azmi said, and they had their own budgetary problems. With the visit of President Mubarak and joint Moroccan-Egyptian commission meetings Basri was fully occupied. All of which Azmi repeated when next morning I conveyed my instructions cabled from New York to make an immediate *demarché* to the minister. I persisted until given a possible time, which was first postponed, then cancelled. Next day the same. I decided to phone Snoussi in New York knowing my call would be monitored. Snoussi offered to check with the palace. Within the hour he cabled advising me of his enquiries and to confirm – with relish at putting the minister of interior in his place – that it was not the intention of his government to modify their political or material support for Minurso, he had informed those concerned at the UN. Azmi came on the line soon afterwards to invite me to meet Basri who was making a very special gesture to accommodate me.

The appointment was for eight in the morning at his country house. This was my first visit to Basri's place at Ben Slimane. We approached through a formal garden, past fancily caged songbirds in full throttle and a display of flowers smelling sweetly. The house was rustic French reconfigured with a Moroccan interior courtyard and ubiquitous rugs. Beneath the beamed ceiling two massive boars' heads aggressed the room. The panelled walls were decorated with photograph upon photograph of King Hassan, princes and princesses, with and without Basri, enjoying informal pursuits. Basri, dressed for golf, entered exuding friendliness. '*Comment va Erik?*' 'How's Erik?' and to a servant 'Give him some coffee,' as if two old friends were joining up for a round of golf on a fine summer's morning, not a word, nothing at all, about the threat to modify Morocco's contribution to Minurso. Basri talked about Baker, what he had achieved so far, which was marginal, and his aspirations.

That evening Baker called, asked how I was, 'still building castles in the sand?' He dismissed the Moroccan move on payments, which I interpreted as an awkward way of having the Security Council recognize what Morocco contributed and was capable of withholding, with 'Too damn much emphasis on symbols, not enough on substance,' it was time to cut through the chaff. Baker had concluded that regional tours were unproductive and intended inviting the parties to a neutral venue – he preferred London. He needed my views on Algeria and Mauritania, should they be invited? Algeria definitely, its influence and interests both at stake, Mauritania for 'ego' reasons. Baker expected representation at foreign minister level. For Morocco he preferred Filali, but Filali was also prime minister, otherwise Basri and perhaps Snoussi with his line to both Filali and the king, for Polisario he wanted Bachir and Kheddad. The dates he had in mind were 11 and 12 June.

It was a couple of days before Azmi called to gouge me for information. Had I spoken to Baker? I had. What exactly was he planning and when? I was unable to say for sure. Azmi accused me of lying – 'and when you lie you become ill.' I told him that Baker was contemplating the second week in June. That was impossible, Azmi retorted, elections on 13 June meant that everyone, above all the minister, was one hundred percent busy, it could suit Algeria, their elections over on 5 June, but be quite unfair to Morocco. Baker might not be planning another tour of the region, I thought. What did that mean? That he was less keen on returning to Tindouf, perhaps. 'Would the meeting be in Rabat then?' Azmi asked. 'With Polisario – hardly.' He reflected: 'But Baker was coming to Rabat?' I refused to be drawn. Azmi reverted to the date, it was for me to ensure that Baker's mission not take place till after 13 June. I professed limited influence, Baker was someone who took his own decisions. That decision was already being communicated in New York, where it was Snoussi's turn to remonstrate, he resented the choice of date 'just as we have our elections', and naming specific individuals 'to represent the king' lacked all sensibility to etiquette. 'You would never have done that,' Snoussi commented sweetly to me. True, I could not have selected King Hassan's representatives, nor would I have ventured to impose a date and place to meet. That was the difference between the UN cajoling parties to cooperate and the American big stick.

Baker called for briefing on unresolved aspects of the settlement plan: identification, refugee repatriation, confinement of troops, the referendum process, he needed to understand how the parties viewed these provisions. 'The plan isn't working, is it?' he concluded, 'The only way forward is through direct or proximity talks.' He also wanted to hear about Moroccan regionalization. Polisario, he deduced from a non-paper rejecting autonomy or similar compromise, was hardening its position; it could be posturing. 'See you in London.'

The London flight departed from Casablanca. I was checking into the usual hotel the night before when Azmi phoned. He would be with me within the hour. When he did arrive he insisted on Black Label before announcing that Basri had to see me before I left for London: eight a.m. at Ben Slimane – again.

I found this inconsiderate, outrageous even, I told Azmi. 'He treats you as he would a friend,' was the reply: I should decide which side I was on, I could not always play this impartial, neutral role. How absurd, I reminded him of my contacts with the Algerian foreign ministry and with Bachir, unless I remained even-handed I was useless, as useless to Morocco as to the UN. The identification commission, Azmi continued irritably, was biased, unprincipled, incompetent, most members just desperate for employment, they followed whatever Polisario sheikhs said but never respected the Moroccans. Simply untrue – I stressed that the commission had accepted under criteria four and five over six thousand applicants on the Moroccan side and some six hundred in the camps. It was past midnight before I escaped to bed, slept badly and by seven in the morning was geared to confront Basri.

At Basri's country house the battery of twittering birds greeted us. No other sign of life. A shutter opened to one side of the front door as we approached. Out peered Basri, rumpled, unshaven, in his pyjamas. Inside he shook my hand before disappearing to emerge minutes later dressed for golf, still unshaven. He set to gobbling breakfast before attacking Baker: 'What does Baker want? What does Baker intend doing?' The timing of the London meeting was ill-judged, and certainly not with Moroccan interests in mind. I reassured him on two aspects: Baker had expressed interest in Moroccan regionalization plans and he unquestionably recognized the relevance of Algeria to any solution. Basri wanted detail. I told him, honestly, that I was far from privy to all Baker's thinking. Basri persisted, counted on a call from London when I knew Baker's 'game plan,' which could be decisive in determining whether he came in person. It was time to leave, outside Basri surveyed the clouds, said I was a bringer of bad weather. I replied that in the Sahara clouds were an excellent portent, and left him to play golf – and feeling miffed, indignant, no, furious, that Filali had been chosen to speak for Morocco in London.

23

London, Lisbon, Houston

In London Baker began by asking Filali bluntly whether Morocco was sure it wanted to proceed with the referendum, it could be close, he hinted at a marginal majority. Filali, defiant, replied that they had more than three for every two for Polisario. How had Filali reached that conclusion, Baker wondered – but it left no doubt what Morocco decided to believe. Baker shrugged; he detected no incentive to reach a compromise on autonomy, even discuss it. To deblock the settlement plan the only avenue lay through talking, 'If we can't get to that I don't believe we can implement the plan. Got to cut through the diplomatic needlepoint.' He told Filali that otherwise he would have to advise the secretary-general that the plan was irredeemably stalled; the Security Council would likely end Minurso.

Polisario, of course, favoured discussing under UN auspices. Baker asked the Polisario delegation whether they had anything else to say? Bachir, who was accompanied by Kheddad, Boukhari and Majid, apologized for not wearing a tie. Things were not easy, Polisario wanted Baker to succeed, the alternative would be disaster. With a smile slipping into a grin Bachir assured Baker of the great esteem in which they held him, they heard him clearly, and promised sincerity, readiness to deal, for give and take. Baker replied firmly: 'No one else can deliver talking with the UN at the table, even I may not be able to do it. Think about it.' Bachir, in English, was quick to insist they were turning nothing down, but it could be costly for them to buy this with all they had left. To understand someone's problem you had to be in his ... Baker interjected 'moccasins.' He wanted confirmation by eight-thirty next morning, rejecting Bachir's request for more time. When Majid said piously: 'We will abide by the plan,' Baker snapped: 'Don't give me that, that kind of crap, give me that and I'm out of here.' The moment Polisario left the room Baker asked 'Who the hell is that guy? I don't want to see him again.'

Baker has a certain style. He wears a well-cut blue suit with a white shirt and tie, which always has red in it. Polite, normally gently spoken, he spices his conversation intermittently, pepper-mill fashion, with specks of profanity.

He reverted to Filali, always addressed as Mr Prime Minister. Morocco believed there was no other solution than to apply the plan. As a way out of the impasse they renewed the offer to present 50,000 persons, from the 'sub-fractions' challenged by Polisario, for the identification commission, not Morocco or Polisario, to decide who was qualified to vote. After interminable debates at the OAU and the UN, decades of military confrontation and armed conflict, a solution was imperative, Morocco could not leave this hanging over its head forever. To ease Mr Baker's task, Filali affirmed His Majesty's authority to discuss meeting with Polisario. Baker thanked him, he proposed nothing like an international conference, to which he knew Morocco objected, but Morocco together with Polisario, Algeria and Mauritania present as observers, under the auspices of himself as the SG's personal envoy. He would not impose but might offer 'bridging proposals'; nothing would be decided until everything was decided – no slicing off of concessions. The sole purpose would be to discuss implementation of the settlement plan and such adjustments as the parties might agree to. He proposed holding talks where easily accessible from the region, enabling Morocco to check with the king and Polisario with their secretary-general, Lisbon might be appropriate.

Lisbon, Filali responded, was convenient, only forty minutes flying time. He queried observers and asked about seating. Baker thought observers potentially helpful, it could be important to have Algeria close if discussing confinement of troops in the Tindouf area, he was not 'hung up' where they sat. 'Algeria created this problem,' Filali said, 'Polisario are on their territory, militarily supported by them, financed, provided with Algerian passports to travel the world, but for Algeria this fiction of an independence movement would not exist. And it intervenes on behalf of Polisario in New York.' That prodded Snoussi into arguing that Polisario was always on the lookout for publicity and propaganda and would exploit being in Lisbon with Morocco, Algeria and Mauritania under UN auspices: there should be no press. Baker said that press coverage was occasionally helpful in providing leverage. He believed Algeria's presence mattered. Snoussi said it was Algeria spoiled the Rabat encounter; he did not elaborate. Filali suggested that Baker, not the UN secretary-general, invite Algeria, Mauritania really had no role, but he accepted Algeria being involved, Polisario might otherwise be tempted to wriggle on and on.

Polisario returned punctually, suited and tied. Baker came straight to the point, to break the logjam, he said: 'You and Morocco both want to implement the settlement plan, there is no point discussing anything else.' He proposed their meeting under his auspices. Morocco, though not enthusiastic, did not reject this out of hand, but talks were not yet assured and he warned Polisario that if they told the press that there were going to be talks, there would be no talks. Morocco had still to consult the king, if he agreed, they would begin in Lisbon on 23 June – the date tentatively accepted by Filali. Bachir paid fulsome tribute to Baker, his key role as facilitator. Morocco must not imagine that Polisario wanted talks as an end in itself, as token of recognition, they saw it as the way forward. Bachir listed the salient issues: identification, repatriation of refugees, confinement of troops. They had confidence in Baker: 'We are ready to embark in your boat, take us on the high seas as you wish, advise us how to steer'. On identification their position was known, repatriation was complex, it had to be based on the sacred principle that the individual was free to choose, security being crucial, the confinement of troops needed to be seen in context: 'should national troops withdraw from the country while alien forces remain?' Polisario was unwilling merely to comply with Moroccan whims but would address real security concerns; their own military would obey. 'We are small,' Bachir concluded, 'we are no threat, but we have our dignity and honour. Morocco constantly picks at our wound to make it hurt.'

Baker commented succinctly: talks would operate with the rule that 'nothing is decided until everything is decided, we won't slice you up like a piece of salami, neither you nor the Moroccans' – not a very Islam-sensitive analogy. Regarding identification he was unclear whether Polisario was prepared to resume or only under specific conditions. Kheddad and Bachir both reacted, Boukhari summarised: 'The peace plan is the denominator, differences of implementation can be settled with goodwill in the presence of Mr Baker.' Subfractions included in the census remained the marker, no masses from H, I and J, and they wanted names of those found eligible to vote and explicit confirmation of identification commission criteria. Bachir said they were opening their heart, because it was Baker and they trusted him.

Baker briefed the Algerian foreign minister. Attaf, in ornate French, praised Baker's statesmanship, his patience and perseverance, before assuring him of Algeria's every wish to see the mission a success and offering to cooperate fully. Without any preamble Baker, smiling politely, said: 'I'm going to pick up that chip,' meanwhile congratulations should wait until something was achieved. The Moroccans were not yet on board, though he hoped they would agree. The Mauritanian delegation was also informed, they reiterated support for the UN peace plan, for a free and fair referendum, and expected Baker's nomination to lead to rapid deblocking of the situation, and were confident that their president – to whom Baker conveyed his respects – would approve their coming to Lisbon, if invited.

Filali next morning agreed in principle to Lisbon, though he quibbled about Algeria's presence, Snoussi said the Algerians had an interest in only two of the four main issues. Baker argued the importance of implicating them: 'You can't have it both ways, saying that Algeria is the real party and at the same time refuse to talk to them.' Filali opposed any press conference. That this was not an international conference was self-evident, Snoussi saw no need to spell it out, better to say it, said Baker, 'we don't want the OAU there, nor do you – or any other international organization.' 23 June was decided, Polisario beamed at the news and Attaf smiled. Basri's first words when I returned from London: 'So what are you complotting with Baker?'

Basri was, of course, fully informed. As if thinking aloud he wondered whether I had any inside knowledge or insight to help evaluate Baker: 'Is the sixth fleet steaming towards the coast? Can he call in the F16s or summon the marines?' What Basri really wished to know was whether Baker commanded American power, whether Washington was solidly behind him, whether he wielded the big, big stick, and if so, what was the US planning to achieve in the Sahara. His intelligence was certainly far better than mine, I said. They did not entirely trust American motives, I felt, America's cold war bond with Morocco was weakening, Algerian energy resources increasingly significant. Basri conceded his doubts about resuscitating the plan. Polisario would never go through the referendum process, complete identification of all applicants, allow refugees to be repatriated, they would pose impossible conditions: withdrawal of Moroccan administration, closure of borders, with UN control and command. And the Algerians? They were the wiliest, the most cunning. Reverting to Baker he said: 'With the sixth fleet and sqaudrons of F16s and the marines, he could impose a settlement; the US is the superpower, but short of that.' He paused. Then interrupted his stream of consciousness to dismiss Polisario: 'They will never go to a vote. What do they want? A miracle', before ferreting about Algeria: what have the Americans to offer? What is in it for the two of them?

Privately I wondered whether Baker's strategy might be to declare the situation hopeless: to report to the secretary-general and the Security Council that the plan would not work, that he had tried insistently, but political will was lacking. Or he might wait and exploit failure of the plan – when both sides faced the abyss – as springboard for a negotiated solution. A third scenario could be to relaunch the process, claim credit before letting it collapse under UN incompetence, at which point the US steps in and imposes a settlement. Whatever his vision Baker keeps that shrouded, unlike his crisp, transparent negotiating style, he horse-trades: you want this, they want that, and cuts to the quick. For Lisbon Baker asked that I focus on a detailed identification brief, identification was the immediate obstacle to be overcome. There was no merit in discussing other contentious issues, the return of refugees, release of political prisoners, confinement of troops, conduct of the referendum, until the parties compromised on how and who to identify as qualified to vote.

Polisario welcomed talks and five days after London Morocco agreed: date and place were not open to discussion; delegations to be small. The Portuguese government generously made available the splendid 16th century fort S. Juliao da Barra, which commanded the estuary leading to Lisbon. Vaulted rooms and passages, with unexpected winding staircases illuminated by narrow shafts of light, had been sympathetically configured to provide all delegations separate areas, equipped with telephone lines, fax machines and photocopiers. The conference chamber was a magnificent knights' hall, strewn with fine carpets, as a film set for Hamlet's Elsinore. Not surprisingly, the Portuguese foreign minister proposed an opening ceremony. Baker declined, he wished minimum diversion from substance.

Morocco and Polisario were to sit facing each other, only direct exchanges in good faith would enable Baker to determine whether the plan could be implemented or implemented with adjustments. That was the agenda: to test whether political will existed, we were not to lose our way in symbols. Baker reminded everyone that nothing was decided before everything was decided – we were, again, not slicing salami, Snoussi, in a stage whisper, suggested substituting mechoui, before Filali was given the floor. Filali paid tribute to Baker as guarantor to reaching an honourable compromise, after much time lost, secondary differences and procrastination must not continue sidetracking the plan. Morocco, in London, had reaffirmed agreement to full implementation of the settlement plan, and to resume identification, it was necessary to establish why it stopped and have it restart as soon as possible. The second essential was for UNHCR to fulfill its mandate.

Filali, in addition to being foreign minister, was prime minister. Polisario, consequently, felt constrained to be led by their 'prime minister', Ali Beiba, who replaced Bachir. Ali Beiba, interpreted from Hassaniya, thanked the Moroccan delegation for its presence and expressed appreciation to the prime minister of Morocco, after congratulating the personal envoy. Polisario and Morocco shared two things: both wished to adhere to the plan, both regarded highly and trusted Mr. Baker, they should start from that solid base, as solid as the fort where they found themselves. He was open to discussing obstacles to identification from whichever angle was preferred.

Baker, pleased with the tone of both statements, called for discussion that would avoid becoming bogged down in 'legal minutiae and diplomatic needlepoint'. Since Polisario had more problems with identification than Morocco, he suggested Polisario begin by indicating specific points before Morocco explained its difficulties, then see if there was a way 'to compromise these differences', he hoped to arrive at trade-offs. Baker implored both to speak in all frankness, not looking backwards, not revisiting the past, but focused on how to proceed.

Ali Beiba delivered a measured speech. He rehearsed provisions of the plan and their shock at Perez de Cuellar's revised criteria which they accepted because they believed there had to be progress. The electoral roll could never be divorced from persons counted in the Spanish census, persons belonging to a Sahrawi sub-fraction, with evidence to prove that they were in the territory during the Spanish time, and relying on oral testimony only when affirmed by tribal leaders. Concluding, Ali Beiba asked whether Morocco accepted the compromise put forward by Boutros-Ghali, that an applicant had to be a member of a sub-fraction included in the census and that oral testimony be admitted only in exceptional cases. A muddled exchange followed after Kheddad described the complication of 'tribal groups', which were not composed of sub-fractions. Baker summarized, as too much oral testimony and the tribal groupings not qualifying, before giving the floor to Filali.

Filali did not wish to meander in the labyrinth of the past, revisiting the past would only waste time. Morocco accepted the Spanish census as a basis but it did not have unlimited confidence in the colonial power. Were the contested applicants, he asked rhetorically, from sub-fractions, members of a Sahrawi tribe, or did they come from the moon? The identification commission existed to determine eligibility; it was for the commission to accept or reject, the commission should be enabled to resume its work, and submit lists for publication when complete; it would be contrary to the plan to publish provisional lists, as Polisario was demanding. Ali Beiba intervened with a Sahrawi saying: 'When you have to run, you have to look.' Identification had stopped, Filali said, because it failed to respect the basis agreed. Ali Beiba said:' Let's let bygones be bygones, let us define the basis for a fresh start,' which made the Moroccans laugh. Following repetition of known positions Baker suggested a break. To me he said he had to remain optimistic, he was a 'balcony person' unlike those 'basement persons' at the UN, always listing problems and stressing poor prospects of success.

Baker told the parties that he wanted to believe we had agreement in principle to resume identification, sufficient to advise the Security Council and ensure financing, but if we failed to agree on terms for identification that would collapse. Polisario had a problem with applicants from the groupings H, I and J, most especially H41, H61and J51/52 with 50-60,000 applicants who did not 'represent a sub-fraction', Polisario was also troubled by lack of transparency, and objected to oral testimony other than in 'exceptional circumstances'.

Kheddad thanked Morocco for accepting the Spanish census as basis before elaborating. The difficulty was to see how some 70,000 listed could justify 182,000 applications. He cited figures, for engorged sub-fractions, traditionally a smallish entity of which the sheikh knew family details, how could one sheikh possibly have relevant knowledge for over fifteen thousand people, even if a sheikh could be found? At best the sheikhs' role was difficult, and skepticism about political influence, control exercised by the parties, undermined confidence in oral testimony. Filali reverted to those not census-covered, they should be allowed to present their case to the identification commission. Subfractions, he commented opaquely, made up a tribe, had not appeared by spontaneous generation. Were the role of sheikhs challenged the entire identification edifice would collapse. He proposed setting aside the sub-fraction issue – to be pragmatic.

Baker said he understood the objection to H41, H61 and J51/52 but did not appreciate why other H, I and J applicants were rejected. Kheddad replied that Polisario accepted those applying under the criteria that were census-based, for the other criteria the applicant had to belong to a sub-fraction included in the census. To Baker's query about tribes and tribal groupings Kheddad insisted that every tribe 'at least in this desert' comprised fraction and sub-fraction. Boukhari said a 'dramatic nuance' derived from the Spanish census where a category might have just two or three individuals from a particular sub-fraction out of a tribe numbering many hundreds, the implication was like admitting every Latin American if two Mexicans had the right to vote, were all H, I and J accepted then the whole Maghreb would be able to participate in the referendum. Kheddad emphasised the problem of finding sheikhs for the contested groups. To and fro discussion followed about the Spanish census, how people were grouped. When Snoussi enquired whether Baker had ideas to propose, he asked for time to think about it: 'We have tackled but we haven't wrestled to the ground. Maybe we'll have better luck tomorrow.'

That evening he asked me to develop 'trade-offs'. By condensing the argument into four disputed areas – H41, H61 and J51/52; other H, I and Js; transparency, and oral testimony – Baker created a paradigm for compromise, he hoped to make this a pattern for ongoing use. We debated an identification quid pro quo: if Morocco were to drop H41, H61 and J51/52 bar persons in the census, Polisario could be asked to accept the other H, I and Js; if Polisario were to accept oral testimony, Morocco could be asked to agree to the release of the number, if not names, of those identified. Baker wondered what I thought the Moroccan reaction would be to dropping H41and H61 almost entirely. I was certain they would object.

The following morning Baker showed his hand-written version individually to Filali and to Ali Beiba. Filali rejected it. Morocco offered amendments that modified slightly provisions relating to 'other' H, I and Js, release of numbers identified, and admission of oral testimony, but changed radically what was proposed for H41, H61 and J51/52, the commission had to respond to every individual request for identification from persons in these census groups. That Morocco would not accept complete exclusion of these groups was to be expected, it was equally obvious that Polisario was not about to capitulate. New wording, based Baker thought on the king's attitude, would have 'The parties agree that they will not directly or indirectly sponsor or present for identification anyone from tribal gropings H41, H61 and J51/52 other than persons included in the Spanish census of 1974 and their immediate family members, but the parties shall not be obligated to actively prevent individuals from such tribal groupings from presenting themselves.' The Moroccans reacted badly; to me Baker said that if they would not honour what their king agreed then 'it's all off'. Polisario, predictably, was also unhappy. The afternoon passed inconclusively. Events would have to take their course, Baker decided, after demanding, with media present, that both parties respond no later than the Friday following – in two days' time – after which he would be 'out of pocket', on holiday. Polisario began to quibble, would need till Saturday, which Baker refused, urging that they contact Abdel-Aziz without delay.

The Polisario delegation left dejected. The revised paragraph was unhelpful: 'You close the door than leave the window wide open.' Their official response, received in time, affirmed acceptance, Polisario would be resigned to work on the basis of the revised draft, with minor changes, but always provided that applicants belonged to a sub-fraction included in the census, that documents accepted as proof be those issued by Spain as administering power, and that oral testimony be admitted only in exceptional cases. Morocco, without enthusiasm, confirmed agreement, but for individuals who presented themselves to be identified as soon as possible. Baker interpreted both replies as a qualified 'yes' but was unsure how to assess the qualifications, he asked me the meaning of Morocco's additional phrase. I took it as Morocco anxious to ensure that H41 and H61 were not left for identification after all others, when Polisario might simply disengage. Polisario's response struck Baker as reiterating old arguments.

That I returned to Laayoune by way of Madeira irritated Azmi. He said that it was to avoid discussion in Rabat – being 'interrogated' I would call it – when he telephoned to ask whether I had the 'texts'. No, I assumed he meant the replies, and I did not. He was decidedly cool, frosty even, when I suggested meeting the minister, if I wanted to see Basri I would have to explain why. I spoke to Bodan to arrange an appointment with Kheddad. I had barely finished speaking when Azmi called to say that Basri hoped to meet me the following day, he was travelling to Spain, it had to be prompt. I reached Kheddad before Bodan had traced him and we agreed a provisional appointment for the following week.

Basri was less unfriendly than Azmi. Though Basri considered the Baker proposal outrageous, extracting outsize concession from Morocco in return for lame paragraphs restating what Polisario was already obliged to do. Why had Bachir not been in Lisbon? Did this signify a harder line? Basri talked away, interjecting frequently *'tu m'a compris?'*- you have understood? I was not always sure that I had. About Baker he knew what there was to know, except to be certain, looking over his shoulder, whether the sixth fleet was steaming into view. Morocco would honour its commitments; Polisario would not, would never go through with the process. Morocco would attend the next encounter, Basri continued, without enquiring when and where. He was dismissive of Filali who did not really grasp the fine points, and Snoussi's presence amounted to, he paused looking round, a television set in the room. Finally, did Baker have something up his sleeve, a card to be played when his concerted effort to resurrect the settlement plan failed?

Baker announced the next meeting for 19 and 20 June in London – 'to nail them to the mast'. Kheddad suggested that we meet beforehand at the airport in Las Palmas. After a cursory rehearsal of Lisbon he focused on how the identification commission could deal with H41, H61 and J51/52. The thousands imported by Morocco bore no relation to numbers in the territory at the census, this was inflation of absurd proportions, true, every country had its minorities, as did the Sahara, but that is what they were: minorities, and with the thousands of other H, I and J applicants Morocco did not even need the H41 and 61. Kheddad quoted figures before reverting to the real problem: no sheikh, could one even be found, was able to recognize and identify on that scale, the human brain had its limits, might in rare cases cope with up to a thousand, just conceivably, but certainly not more, no Sahrawi sub-fraction ever approached such a size. How could the identification commission function?

The sheikhs were essential to confirm the individual's identity, and to qualify as a voter both sheikhs had to agree. I explained, for the umpteenth time, that when they disagreed the applicant did not qualify. Exceptions were extremely rare when corroborating evidence became available from another family member or one sheikh's evidence proved significantly more compelling, for example, the sheikh who knew every family detail, how many camels they had, the great-grandfather's name. Kheddad rebutted: 'Precisely the sort of theatre in which some excel and not necessarily more reliable than the sheikh who just says 'yes' or 'no' or merely nods in assent or shakes his head.' I assured him that it was quite exceptional for the commission not to abide by a sheikh's rejection – the 'veto' deployed to Morocco's consternation. He quarried for detail. I confirmed that in the camps most people qualified, he smiled: they knew, they also knew, I was sure from my conversation with Bachir, the situation in the territory: did acceptance reach ninety percent? No, most of those accepted were in the census. Not all, he commented somewhat bitterly. (Bodan was to tell me that Kheddad had analysed the Polisario observers' reports and deduced the rejection rate as around 5 percent in the camps and 35 percent in the territory.) I reassured him that identification commission members, most of whom they knew personally, were decent, capable and conscientious people; decisions were double-checked with other members and extensive computer cross-referencing provided further safeguards. He nodded.

I had the sense that Polisario would make the compromise necessary for identification to resume. Would Morocco, Kheddad asked? And what was Baker's objective? It seemed inconceivable for a man of Baker's stature, wealth and interests, to undertake the mission merely for the plan to be abandoned, he believed Baker wanted success, focusing first on the plan because both Polisario and Morocco opted for it and were not tempted by the regional autonomy solutions floated, if forced to conclude that political will was lacking Baker would then pass to other options; he did not elaborate. They liked Baker, his transparency, his honesty, the way he involved the press, he did not play tricks, we agreed. Kheddad reverted to identification, all aspects had to be settled. Polisario sheikhs must not be subject to Moroccan security checks; security to be handled only by the UN, indeed all arrangements relating to sheikhs to be administered by the UN. Kheddad turned on Morocco, cataloguing 'why we hate them'. The king ruled, and only he; most countries had another layer, not Morocco. The king was old; he wanted to die saying 'The Sahara is Moroccan.' Kheddad's animosity towards Morocco startled me, Bachir never spoke thus. It was easy to forget that the Polisario leaders had different backgrounds: Kheddad, unlike Bachir, brother El-Ouali and others, had no Moroccan ties or inherited veneration for the sultan.

Hassan celebrated his birthday more modestly than usual. Shepherded as always by Azmi, who was telling me how disillusioned they were at my conceding everything that Polisario sought, I was directed by the palace chief of protocol to an inner sanctum. A handful of ambassadors stood about with distinguished guests in Gulf and Saudi dress. Basri engaged me conspiratorially behind the pillars of a keyhole arch, he enquired, *sotto voce*, whether I had met Kheddad. I said I had and that I believed Polisario would accept to resume identification, on certain terms. They were? And Baker? At that moment His Majesty entered from a side door, looked about him, before marching into the larger court adjoining where he walked the circuit briskly, smiling and nodding but without greeting anyone individually. The king returned to the inner sanctum and as he passed he took my hand addressing me by name, he recognized one or two other guests and departed. The diplomatic corps concluded that he was ill; three ambassadors, on reassignment, were sorely disappointed having been advised to expect a decoration and after choosing ties not to clash. The only certainty here is uncertainty, one said, resignedly.

Back in London Polisario stated that clearance was still pending; Abdel-Aziz had been impossible to reach. Baker expressed surprise, he counted on having Polisario's firm reply to the identification compromises by day's end, at the latest before he left on the morrow for New York where he was to brief the Security Council. Filali, a little smugly, said that his government had responded positively two days after Lisbon and wished to move on. Baker proposed addressing the refugee issue and the role of UNHCR.

Repatriation was one aspect of HCR's traditional mandate. The plan had the referendum take place 'in the territory' without specifying where, the refugees, according to UNHCR enquiries, opted overwhelmingly for repatriation to the 'liberated' desert west of the berm, which lacked towns or settlements, returning to their place of origin only after a 'satisfactory' outcome to the referendum. That made a mockery of an electoral campaign as well as posing an unthinkable logistical challenge. Baker thought that best addressed under the referendum code of conduct, he moved to an equally contentious issue: the confinement of troops.

Ali Beiba referred to the plan, which permitted Morocco to maintain 65,000 military personnel in the territory, and that not including paramilitaries. Polisario had difficulty in swallowing a presence that conferred undue pressure on voters, but that had been, reluctantly, accepted, he could not see how a few thousand Polisario troops, confined in the territory, could possibly pose a threat. Filali intervened: there was only one army in all, all, the territory, the FAR. Morocco was militarily responsible, on the ground, in the air and at sea, for the entirety. Polisario's 'minister of defence' Brahim Ghali asserted that UN military observers came to supervise two forces, separated after seventeen years of protracted fighting, throughout which Polisario had fought within the territory. The UN was not there to present to Morocco what it had failed to acquire through force of arms. Baker said the plan was specific about Moroccan forces, but vague about confinement of Polisario troops, some, being eligible to vote, would rejoin their families at voting stations, but he asked where others should be confined. Ali Beiba insisted that the overwhelming majority of military personnel would be voting, the troops remaining constituted no threat. Was it a question of confining about 2000 men in the territory? Baker asked. Maybe a little more. Less than 4000? Yes.

Filali said the plan was explicit about troop confinement, Polisario forces could not be assigned to an area that the FAR might re-occupy overnight. Kheddad refuted any implied disparagement of Polisario forces and rejected the claim that the entire territory was Morocco's responsibility, twenty years of war had bequeathed one area to Moroccan occupation and another to 'no-man's-land', which 'we proudly call the liberated zone.' Baker said that it was for the referendum to establish what was 'no-man's-land', liberated zone, independent territory or part of Morocco. At that moment Polisario, having heard from Abdel-Aziz, confirmed agreement to the compromise identification proposals.

Baker was welcoming this achievement when Filali asked to speak. Morocco had accepted the compromise, as emended, for paragraph one, but had not agreed to the wording of other paragraphs. Baker was as astonished as I was, that was never raised in Lisbon. 'We did not get beyond the first paragraph,' Filali maintained, 'because it raised problems, we had to return to Rabat for the king's instructions.' Baker asked what difficulties they had. Consultations followed, perusal of texts in French and English (with some Arabic translation). For the fourth paragraph Morocco insisted that the identification commission 'must' take oral testimony into account. If 'may' were changed to 'will' would that do, Baker asked, and including 'as provided for in the settlement plan?' Filali conceded that would be all right. Polisario accepted, with Boukhari looking daggers. Filali reverted to the publication of lists; that departed from the plan. Baker clarified this as about numbers not names. Morocco could not agree to names, Filali stated, but would not object to numbers. Polisario seemed satisfied, Attaf, on behalf of the Algerian government, congratulated Baker. Mauritania added a tribute and good wishes for progress. The parties initialed papers agreeing to the identification compromise and lists on the principle that nothing was agreed till everything was agreed. Morocco declined signing on the same piece of paper as Polisario.

The numbers emerging from identification were already known, broadly, to both sides, although Polisario preferred them officially confirmed. Oral testimony was already considered. Persons from disputed tribal groups who were themselves census-listed had been accepted by Polisario. Opening the door to individuals from H41, H61 and J51/52 to 'present themselves' was, to anyone familiar with Moroccan practice, tantamount to admitting a surge of applicants, without qualified Polisario sheikhs to identify them.

Did he really believe they would go all the way to a vote? I asked Baker. 'They say so, but when they stare into the abyss, they might think differently.' 'It's their affair,' John Bolton intervened, continuing emphatically that, from the American angle, 'success' lay in closing a UN mission. Baker's tone in briefing the Security Council was more conciliatory but he found both sides relatively comfortable with the current, stagnant, situation. Though they told him that they wanted to proceed with the settlement plan it remained subject to divergent interpretations and led to a winner-take-all ballot. He reported on the preliminary contacts and meetings in London and Lisbon before recommending that the UN mission be extended, with the minimum financial provision required. Baker hoped after two or three further rounds of talks to be able to conclude that the referendum could be held according to the plan or that it could not.

Arrangements were in hand for a second meeting in Lisbon to finalise matters relating to confinement of forces, political detainees and prisoners-of-war, and begin discussing the referendum code of conduct. The first item,

Baker announced, was confinement of troops: Moroccan armed forces would be reduced and confined in accordance with the settlement plan, Polisario forces, it was proposed, would be confined with not more than 2,000 on the territory east of the berm, no more than 300 in Mauritania, the others in Algeria. Baker had squeezed this concession from Attaf, invoking the chip to be picked up after repeated offers of Algerian cooperation. Filali asked for a French translation and time to study it; an hour passed.

Ali Beiba, lauding Baker's efforts, saw no need to repeat what had been stated. Baker interpreted this to mean Polisario recommending that their secretary-general approve. Ali Beiba said: 'The Sahrawi side would not be an obstacle in respect of the compromise proposal'; he hoped to confirm 'during this session'. Baker accepted that as affirmative. Filali objected, insisting on clearer articulation of Polisario's position. Ali Beiba thought the conclusion drawn by Mr Baker clear enough. Filali: 'If I understood the other party right, they have sought instructions from Tindouf, yet Mr Baker says they have agreed.' That's my interpretation, Baker said. Filali insisted that Polisario provide a 'definitive' answer and on that basis the Moroccans would make their views known, then relented: Morocco could, in principle, accept the text as proposed. (The king had evidently authorized what his senior general earlier dismissed out of hand. Snoussi said to me 'None of us would have accepted; it's His Majesty's decision.') Baker ruled that acceptance, subject to the usual qualification. Algeria requested a minor precision while congratulating Baker, Mauritania reiterated support for his lofty and delicate mission. Baker believed that with such 'very good rhetoric' they wanted the mission to succeed and that the statements amounted to agreement. He passed to the next item: political detainees.

Filali affirmed having no difficulty in conforming to the provisions of the settlement plan. He had one query: Morocco had received informally a list of 140 to 143 political detainees but needed particulars since a great number of these individuals were unknown. Ali Beiba replied that they did not have full details concerning political detainees largely because Polisario was denied contact with families; available information had been conveyed to the independent jurist. Filali wished the text emended after reference to political detainees to read 'if they exist', Baker said you could speak of them only if they existed, and proposed 'any and all', 'That protects the Moroccan position,' and, turning to Polisario, 'doesn't harm yours.' After some quibbling about the French version, both agreed. Baker turned to the code of conduct.

Filali stated that comprehensive discussion required police, gendarmerie, even military expertise as well as further study, he suggested meeting again in two weeks time. Ali Beiba asserted that Polisario was ready. Baker said that this was the fifth time he had flown over, he had travelled far for very little business; there really had to be material progress. After a pause Filali suggested starting with general observations, Ali Beiba concurred. 'Who first?' Baker asked. When neither answered he tossed a coin, Polisario was given the floor. Ali Beiba spoke followed by Kheddad and Boukhari before Filali and Snoussi intervened for Morocco. Animated exchanges revolved around administration and security, responsibility for law and order, it was for the UN to organize and supervise, according to Polisario, Morocco with 'its long history and attachment to law' refused to abrogate its duty for security throughout the territory; the code spoke of no military or administrative pressure, it never said eliminate entirely a military and administrative presence; the UN had limited means. Filali called for a few days to review the situation with security experts. Baker offered to stay over the weekend if Morocco could fly home and return in two days' time prepared to discuss.

No, would have to adjourn. Meet in two weeks in the US, Baker proposed, at the Baker Institute in Houston, the meeting to continue as long as it took to reach closure, 'You'll be right at home,' he said, ' it'll be oppressively hot.' Back in Rabat, to the Moroccan media, Filali described progress made at the talks before declaring this an affirmative referendum on the Moroccan nature of the Sahara, which was Moroccan even before Spanish colonialism, was Moroccan today and would remain forever so.[1] Polisario's Sahrawi national radio news announced the achievement of direct negotiations and recognition that the conflict was between 'the Sahrawi people, led by the Frente Polisario, and Morocco.' The commentary continued: 'let Hassan the Second...be certain that the victory for the Sahrawi people is coming no doubt, because of the justice of their cause, the strength of their argument, the solidity of the stand of its friends ...the Sahrawi people will continue to ... make sacrifices until they force the final departure of the invading intruders and return to their home, triumphant and victorious, with their heads held high.'[2]

Baker opened proceedings at the Baker Institute for Public Policy by pointing out that the secretary-general's reference to 'breakthrough' did not emanate from him, we were not there yet. He suggested taking the draft code of conduct for the referendum line by line, though 'this text will only be as strong as the commitment of the parties to implementing it'. He wanted to 'avoid cosmetics' and bracketed the first disagreement for later consideration; how to ensure that conditions were met for a genuinely free and fair referendum, provoked argument, who should be allowed to campaign was contentious: Polisario wanted only those eligible to vote, which Morocco forcefully rejected, and even Baker considered rather 'unusual'. Under gatherings, before a reference to 'groups of persons', Basri wanted to insert 'legally constituted'; Boukhari asked what that was supposed to mean. In what body of law? Baker wanted to know, and suggested 'approved by the SG's special representative'. More brackets. Differences too about independent observers and non-governmental organisations, to have only the UN and OAU observing would be laughed out, Baker commented, Snoussi said it would not just be New York laughing if the referendum were to be observed only by the OAU with its mixed record. For public meetings Basri said the customary threshold requiring authorisation was seven persons, to be coordinated with Moroccan security forces, Kheddad found fifty standard and reasonable, with UN civil police supervising. How could the UN, Snoussi wondered, with limited resources ensure security except in coordination with local police? Kheddad asked how one might aspire to a free, fair and transparent referendum, the UN's business, when there was one party, with settlers, military and police, determined to exert control. Basri thought it realistic to speak of 'Moroccan police' not 'existing police forces', which provoked Boukhari into a speech about the Sahrawi state, recognized by the OAU, with its police and army and administration. Filali said it was the first time we were hearing about a state that might or might not exist, if already a state what were we discussing? Baker, irritated, said we were there because both sides maintained that they wanted to implement the settlement plan, failing agreement at Houston he would not recommend the Security Council extending Minurso's mandate beyond its expiry date at the end of the month.

Discussion quietened to the need for educating those who were to vote, many illiterate and unfamiliar with such a process. Habitually done by the UN when organizing elections, Baker said, citing Namibia and Cambodia. For the parties to do, said Snoussi, Morocco had extensive experience of local and other elections, Basri insisted, and 'we never engage in polemics'. Kheddad, reminded of the character in French literature who spoke 'prose' without realising it, thought words could be polemical without the speaker knowing. The referendum had not to be confused with elections in Namibia, Cambodia and Nicaragua about who was to govern, this was an act of self-determination on the future of the territory. Filali thought it sad that Polisario had not educated people over twenty-two years, he agreed entirely that they needed education, on television all he saw was flag-waving. Baker took a decision: voter education would be UN responsibility, strictly non-partisan, he counted on the parties' cooperation. It was for the SG's special representative to call the referendum once convinced that conditions for a free and fair referendum were met. 'We will take up flags after lunch,' Baker ended.

The Moroccan position was crystal clear, Filali said, restriction on flying flags applied only to referendum related sites; elsewhere the Moroccan flag would, of course, fly on public buildings. Boukhari argued that the Moroccan flag should be flown only after a vote for integration. Kheddad said that in such a campaign it was essential for both sides to be able to display their colours, symbols, flags. Filali smiled: the flag was the symbol of a nation's sovereignty. 'Those across the table from us are trying to create a sovereign state, at present there is no state, therefore no flag.' Following Boukhari's heated reaction Baker calmly decreed that, flags being divisive, each side should have a symbol under which to campaign and that symbols be permitted, both appeared to accept.

I discussed with Baker the many points bracketed, which had still to be resolved. The next day he took them one by one, with crisp redrafting suggestions. The speed of accommodation confirmed my conclusion that neither Morocco nor, I think, Polisario genuinely expected all this to be implemented. When Basri, with an obliging smile, repeatedly expressed no objection, Baker retorted: 'If you do that so easily the other side is certain to object; they think it's a trap.' Prohibition of bribery reignited disagreement, but mainly semantic, to Basri 'bribery' sounded pejorative, we should choose something 'nobler, more consistent with the region', Baker proposed 'corruption'. Discussion moved to media access and control; this could be settled only in conjunction with Algeria, Mauritania and the Canaries. The remaining brackets were almost disposed of when a portable phone rang loudly – Snoussi's.'The ambassador has a call from his bookie,' Baker said.

Baker concluded the session by repeating that nothing was agreed till everything was and 'is everything now agreed?' Both sides nodded, and Filali departed presumably to submit 'agreement' for the king's seal of approval. Revised wording and textual amendments in fair copy with translation, as well as a half page on 'practical measures for the resumption of identification', were distributed. Some political analysts praised 'constructive ambiguity'. I was asked to release figures, not names, for those found eligible to vote – Kheddad gave me a mildly surprised look of approval- and prepare immediately to resume identification. First, Baker wanted a word.

A photographer had been summoned for a 'celebratory' picture. What we celebrated was less in focus. Baker began by paying me generous tribute and presented his doubly signed dollar bill. I was still needed, he said, only I knew which were the minefields and where the bodies were, they counted on me to restart identification. But, of course, after four to five years in action I had some scars, as he had in Washington; it was inevitable, the consequence, which I had foreseen, a new special representative to be named, and, it was understood, this ought to be an American to ensure continuing support in Congress. I had so much wanted to see the process to an honourable conclusion; had I believed that the Houston Accord, as it became known, would lead to resolution I should have been extremely disappointed to hand over responsibility, I was not. The obstacles to full implementation of the plan remained squarely in place, it was to be seen how many of the H41, H61 and J51/52 thousands would present themselves without Moroccan sponsorship, but Morocco was not enjoined from preventing anyone, and I knew Basri. When a journalist asked Baker how many had still to be identified he guessed eighty thousand. Morocco reacted angrily, insinuating that the figure came from me; it was pure conjecture on Baker's part and way short of my guesstimate.

Numbers were to an extent irrelevant. Even if Polisario could be induced to participate and the commission were to identify everyone who had applied, including all applicants from the disputed groups, the outcome was predictable. At that stage Morocco could resort to appeals, as provided for in the plan, involving a re-run of the whole process – unthinkable. Polisario would be salivating, eager for their referendum. I was profoundly depressed, less by the prospect of leaving Western Sahara in these circumstances, than by the opportunity missed to arm-twist the parties into negotiating an alternative solution to the conflict. Possibly, just possibly, I thought that if the resurrected process were to crash almost at once, the moment could be seized and that might be Baker's plan. If it were he gave no hint when I promised to set identification in motion as expeditiously as possible, recruiting qualified personnel – most ex-commissioners were by now in other situations – and interpreters, setting up centres, retrieving files from storage in Geneva, preparing convocation lists and more; we would act immediately following Security Council endorsement.

24

New beginnings

Basri asked for a meeting on my return to Morocco, to hear what Baker had actually done. Assorted ministers, advisers and dignitaries were being steered in and out of the presence while I waited, an outbreak of cholera, I gathered, was being kept secret until brought under control. Basri greeted me with a friendly: '*Ah, le serpent!* Should put your head on a spike in a public place,' and invited me to be seated while he had his hair cut. I had witnessed Basri tousled and unshaven but this was more revealing of his self-image – assuming airs of a royal levee. Azmi and Ouchen, the Laayoune governor, were ushered in as Basri demanded what, in reality, Baker had brought to the process, what was to digest. When he was appointed everyone expected him to arrive with new elements or to introduce new elements, but what was new in the 'agreements' reached in London, Lisbon and Houston? And why Houston of all places? Baker had brandished the American big stick to impose compromise proposals little different from those I had already put forward. The one new element, I offered, was American involvement, to which Basri responded: for Morocco it was hard saying 'no' to Washington, for Polisario, of course, Baker was god.

With Polisario primed for action I flew to Tindouf to discuss arrangements. At a working session with Ali Beiba, Majid and others the mood was positive, though guarded 'We must be prudent,' Ali Beiba repeated. They assumed that identification could restart within a month till I explained that not only did we have to recruit, and in some instances train, personnel, recover files from storage, reopen centres and update sheikh records but I was committed to providing convocation lists thirty days in advance, for which we first needed the files and staff. Bodan had explored the availability of centres, at Smara camp the old facilities were ready, elsewhere buildings required work and there was an issue with accommodation for Moroccan sheikhs and observers. Before I left Bodan reported conversations with Polisario leaders, who were convinced that they would win in a truly free, fair and transparent referendum, should they lose it could only mean that the referendum was not truly free and fair.

Polisario and Morocco both wanted to begin with the three most contested groups – for quite different reasons. Kheddad believed this would test, from the outset, willingness to implement the Houston agreement honourably, Basri wished to ensure these groups were not eclipsed, or postponed sine die. Both agreed that we issue convocation lists for four weeks of identification, convoking those named in the census. Basri maintained that Morocco would present only eligible candidates before asking how many I expected, quoting dismissively the 80,000 figure that Baker, according to Basri, claimed he had from me. Basri volunteered to provide practical help and logistical support to accelerate the process, the UN was doing everything, I assured him, to have the relevant staff deployed urgently. John Bolton, out of the blue, telephoned to say that Baker was worried about losing political momentum and wanted action. This was a chance, Bolton said, for the UN to prove itself capable of doing anything, and may have added under his sneering breath that he expected it to fail. I fought to convince New York of the need to speed recruitment when Iraq was being given priority.

Recruitment was hampered by both sides' sniping, Polisario accused Morocco of 'buying' new identification commission members, Morocco, critical of bias and political sympathies, rejected certain candidates by name. The search for commission chairman was hard: he had to be of acceptable nationality, be competent in French and English, with the managerial skills to handle a large multinational staff plus sheikhs, observers and the OAU, as well as having the diplomatic and political astuteness needed to work with all parties. Azmi grumbled that a new chairman knowing nothing of identification procedures and a new special representative unfamiliar with the mission would set the process back not six months but a year.

Bodan cabled that a sandstorm had prevented the dedicated aircraft bearing records from Geneva from landing, it was being rescheduled. A first of December start date looked increasingly challenging. We worked intensively with the personnel available, who included, to my relief, the brilliant French computer expert, whose employment Morocco had endeavoured to obstruct on the grounds that his mother was communist. By mid November we had advanced sufficiently to believe that with super-bureaucratic effort identification could be relaunched on both sides as targeted, and as both sides desired. The catch: this would rule out thirty days notice for those convoked and we could not begin with the populous and complex contested groups.

Kheddad was concerned, how could Polisario be expected in so short a time to gather 'from all corners' those convoked; Morocco wanted to know why we deferred the contested. Both were mollified by my guarantee that within the month persons from the contested groups, who were census-listed, would be covoked with due notice.

Identification restarted. All went smoothly, the sheikhs cooperated, chatting with each other, mission staff, newly arrived, proved dedicated, keen to proceed. The unwonted calm was barely ruffled by a letter criticizing living conditions for Moroccan observers and sheikhs in the camps, Bodan saying that the one complaint he actually received was from Biadillah about a reading lamp, which was provided.

Tension mounted with impending identification of the census-listed from contested groups, H41 the vanguard. We announced that those not listed but wishing to present themselves in accordance with Houston provisions should do so while their group was being identified, should more persons present themselves than could, for administrative reasons, be registered during the session they would be requested to come forward subsequently. The first batch convoked comprised 830 individuals. Applicants additional to those convoked began arriving throughout the morning, some came by minibus and assorted transport, disembarking behind a container area, others, in threes and fours, appeared on foot from different points, more and more they came. 3,927 had arrived by the end of the first day and in the succeeding days another 8,613. How many more would there be? I asked Azmi's assistant. 'We don't control this,' he said blandly. I laughed.

The newly appointed chairman of the commission was overwhelmed: how could orderly identification be planned for non-convoked walk-ins on this scale. The walk-ins vented their frustration, shouting 'Why can't we be identified – today?' 'We are Sahrawis, we are supporting our king.' One woman screamed: 'They made me come here', others ululated, a few applauded. The crowd turned aggressive, looked ready to storm the identification centre, until dispersed by a sudden, heavy downpour, our *deus ex machina*. Kheddad was outraged, this was back to Moroccan manipulation, Morocco was not honouring the spirit of Houston, even the letter. Polisario reacted, not by withdrawing, but by augmenting their presence, they dispatched as an observer their 'minister of defence', Brahim Ghali, but his name appearing on the manifest as Brahim Glub provoked another incident reminiscent of the past – accusations of masquerading under false names – until it emerged as genuine error. Redesignated 'minister in charge of the occupied territories',

Morocco still rejected Brahim Ghali as observer – too much blood on his hands, according to Azmi. There were problems also with those designated to accompany sheikhs, emphasis on reciprocity, accusations of provocation – the rocks, snags and rapids briefly submerged by the Bakerene tide.[1]

Snoussi accused the UN of applying arbitrary limits, Morocco had made a concession at Houston 'purely of form', applicants had every right to come forward. If the commission was understaffed it was for failing to plan for these people, the Moroccan government could not handle the political ramifications should individuals be excluded. Each side was waiting for the other to blink, Baker thought, neither wanting to be blamed for failure. He decided that we identify those who had come forward on convocation days, seeing ninety percent or more not qualify Polisario might realise that sheer numbers constituted no threat and Morocco recognize that allowing unqualified persons to appear en masse served no purpose.

Practical planning continued apace to accommodate increased numbers and encompassed identification centres in the north, in Morocco, where large numbers of applicants resided some of whom were census-listed. Kheddad became exercised but (with Algerian encouragement, I heard) accepted the logistical argument. A programme for February was agreed to include sessions in Morocco and Mauritania. Despite nervousness, exchange of insults, the occasional slight and accusations, and a demonstration in Laayoune, identification stumbled on. When I handed over responsibility to my successor the total figure for those identified came to 94,161. Some 65,000 non-census-listed from groups H41, H61 and J51/52 remained in limbo.

The new representative of the secretary-general was named, as expected an American. Charlie Dunbar had been a US ambassador in the Gulf, spoke good French and some Arabic, the mysteries of identification were another matter and it was decided that we overlap to permit apprenticing him in the craft. Following sessions with Basri and the interior ministry team the king received us. Centred in a salon with panelled walls and brocade-covered gilt furniture, on a chair embellished with the Moroccan coat of arms sat His Majesty Hassan II. Looking small and older, not well, he pinched a tablet intermittently out of the exquisite pillbox he retrieved from a fob-pocket, he smiled his tooth-perfect diplomatic smile, but was less warm than I had known him. The crown prince, invariably dapper, Filali, Driss Slaoui and Snoussi were the silent supporting cast.

The king began by drawing attention to lack of impartiality on the part of some Minurso personnel, not all, but some. He did not ask they should be 'for us' but nor should they be 'against us', he recognized a worldwide tendency to sympathise with the underdog, but insisted Dunbar be alert to bias. Lists came next: 'Ambassador Jensen will remember,' Hassan said, 'at Bouznika when we were all standing together with Mr Baker, he asked why we opposed publication of the lists. I decided to agree.' At Houston numbers were released though nothing was decided about further lists, could I confirm that they might be processed monthly? The king moved to the wider political arena, Algeria was not honouring its commitment to the plan, Algerian ambassadors in Spain and Senegal had stated publicly that the Sahara question remained a means to create difficulties for Morocco. 'That's all they have left', Hassan said, 'and they are using it against us.' Algeria controlled Polisario, it had only to cut off fuel supplies or food shipments, could impose its will at any time. Incidentally, the king found it of concern that Polisario had changed ministers: those at London and Lisbon, the doves, had been replaced by hawks. He himself thought in geopolitical terms, he continued, and picking up a book from the desk behind him and opening at a map of the Maghreb explained how influences, movements, notably Islamist, travelled from east to west. Egyptians brought Islamic fundamentalism to Algeria; its recent, dangerous, expansion was spreading from central areas to the western frontier, which abutted Morocco.

Hassan II concluded the audience by criticizing Boutros-Ghali for not taking sufficient interest, not making a real effort to resolve the Sahara issue – like leaving a car parked. We should not imagine that you could now put a key in the ignition and have it run, the car would need fresh oil, a tyre change perhaps, and fuel. He enjoyed the analogy, Boutros, the mechanic, had failed to maintain the vehicle in his charge. The challenge was to get it on the road – and the need to do so. With that injunction His Majesty said he would not keep us from relaxing any longer, rose and left.

That Hassan was unwell seemed obvious. He decided to grant an audience, and he was parsimonious with such, presumably because he wished to appraise the new man on the spot: Morocco was unsure about Baker, nervous at the prospect of American pressure, and the king needed to evaluate the executors. Dunbar took pride in being able to assess people; I said that what mattered equally was how people assessed him.

At audience with the president of Algeria, Zeroual's intense glare peered sideways at Dunbar while expressing fulsome tribute for my contribution. Afterwards, the minister, Attaf, rehearsed the Algerian view of the Western Sahara conflict, they looked to someone with knowledge of the region –

Dunbar had earlier been posted to Algiers – to complete identification and the mission.

For my farewell visit to Polisario I was escorted from Tindouf to the '*Presidence*' to be received in style with military honours, a full company on parade presented arms, the smartest, best turned out Polisario military unit I had seen, our Russian colonel agreed. Kheddad, beside me, interpreted the official welcome before guiding me to a reception. Nearly a hundred sheikhs and notables were assembled, one after the other they shook hands with me, most with a supplementary thumb hook, their weather-etched Saharan faces warranted Durer, eyes blurred with age strained piercingly from deep sockets, beards, greying, were neatly trimmed. All carried themselves like the desert sheikhs they were, all wore the flowing blue '*drah*' and a black turban. Abdel-Aziz waited, in army fatigues and matching khaki turban, which he removed on taking the floor to deliver a eulogy in my honour.

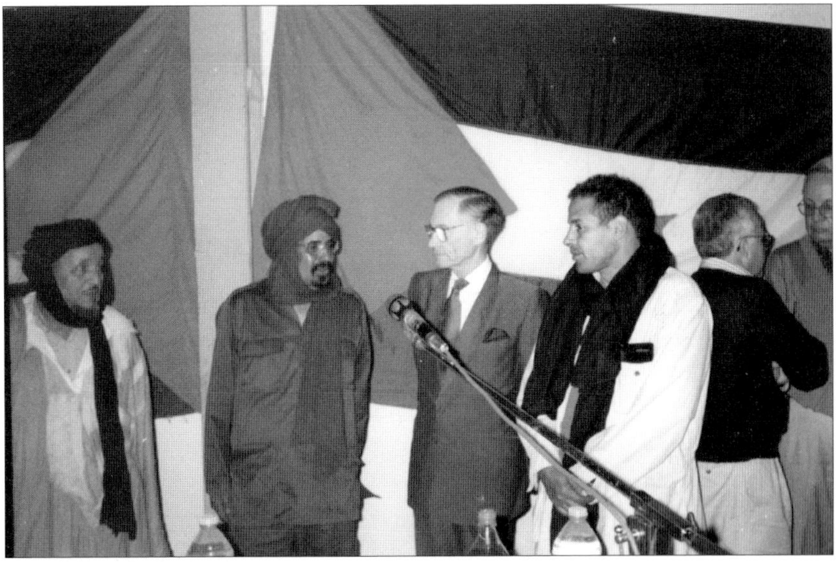

POLISARIO paying tribute prior to my departure

He credited me with laying foundations and building walls. It was now for Baker to roof the building. As president of the Sahrawi Arab Democratic Republic Abdel-Aziz awarded me Polisario's order of 20 May. The citation read 'For his integrity and ability as Chairman of the UN Identification Commission and for his patience' as the secretary-general's representative, the citation recognised my handling of identification and that I delivered a result they respected; knowing they had had, or many of them had, doubts and knowing that they lobbied for an American to replace me, I appreciated this recognition. Kheddad translated into Hassaniya my thanks, sincere and simple. The assembled crowd was offered nuts, soft drinks and camel brochettes, after which Abdel-Aziz embraced me, kissed me and took his leave, or rather indicated I should leave. I was to dine with Kheddad in his tent. No sign of Bachir, his name not mentioned.

Kheddad entertained me with impressive generosity: salads, grilled meat, chicken, couscous, fried potatoes, noodles, vegetable stew, bread and fruit, on which we made slight impression despite the help of my security escort: two bulky west African UN civil police. It was Sahrawi tradition to provide lavish hospitality when occasion warranted, I was touched by the tribute. The people in the camps were seriously undernourished and I liked to believe that our uneaten food would be benefiting others while Kheddad and I talked late. They were determined to go through with the referendum, confident that a genuinely free and fair referendum would be in their favour, American pressure was vital and they counted on Baker. Kheddad agreed that their commitment to implementing the plan was new, he sensed Morocco showing some will to move ahead prompted perhaps by the king's sickness, the spectre of his mortality, reluctance to bequeath unfinished business to his heir – the time-bomb Hassan did not wish to leave to his son. Alternative solutions lost relevance, Kheddad said as we parted, with Sahrawis becoming a minority in the territory. The stars were spectacular, circling over us on the drive away from the encampment. With the engine off silence became audible. There was no sound – even the breathing of air.

I paid one final visit and said goodbye to Ali Beiba, who saw a crisis looming but was unsure in what form. To my real regret I had no opportunity to take leave of Bachir.

In Morocco Basri was confident of asserting control, always the gambler, he never threw in his hand, he doubled the stakes. The great numbers 'presenting themselves for identification' might not be true to the spirit of Houston but a pedant could argue they did not contravene the letter, that they would arduously prolong the process without affecting the outcome was what he refused to admit – perhaps still counting on Polisario to call foul and abandon the plan. I was about to quit Laayoune when a letter came from Basri rendering 'homage' to my contribution as head of the UN mission, I was to be privileged with a diplomatic reception in Rabat. Thrice the date was changed and on the actual day the hour confirmed before being twice postponed; Moroccan ministers and officials kowtowed to Basri's whims, the senior ambassadors, who had all been invited, were less amused. Basri arrived late to deliver a generous speech and present me with an ornate casket. I thanked him, with light humour touching on our various encounters. Houston had permitted identification to resume; the icebergs, still there, demanded navigational skill, much depended on M. Basri's seamanship. In conclusion I expressed appreciation to the minister's collaborators, notably Azmi, wishing them success in achieving a just, fair, durable peace leading to prosperity in this important region. *Le Matin* newspaper next morning carried my picture on its front page and paraphrased what I had said into fulsome tribute to the understanding, aid and cooperation I always received from Morocco. I read it on my way to the palace.

King Hassan was to accord me a farewell audience. Protocol escorted me through reception chambers to a salon, like a boudoir, which was furnished in pink: pink silk stretched on the walls, furniture covered in pink and on a small table a bouquet of pink roses. A discreet television set showed cartoons with the sound reduced to being inaudible, eclipsed in any case by a guard of honour outside the French window stamping at every shouted command. The commanding officer bellowed a louder order, the guards roared in unison, saluted, presented arms, the grand chamberlain thrust the door aside, proclaiming 'His Majesty', and in walked the king. He greeted me 'ambassador', before saying he had learnt from Basri that I was ready to depart. Being away from the mission, Hassan believed, offered me greater freedom to assess the situation and he urged me to review critically even the Moroccan position, I would be returning, he hoped, 'to visit us from time to time'.

With centres functioning in Mauritania and at places in Morocco where applicants were living the number of those identified continued to rise. Included were those from contested tribal groups who had presented themselves on the days census-listed persons were convoked, but H41, H61 and J51/52 remained contentious. The nearly sixty-five thousand applications from these groups represented more than 25% of the total received; in the census individuals belonging to the same groups accounted for 3.4%; H61, in particular, with only 536 persons census-listed had 46,875 applicants, the great majority, over thirty-five thousand, from the Ait Ousa, the Ait Ousa was a Sahrawi tribe, but long integrated in southern Morocco, even enlisting in Moroccan forces, and, incidentally, historic foe of the Reguibat. Polisario objected to their identification not only because this was not a Western Saharan tribe but for lack of sheikhs.

King Hassan, in a personal message to the secretary-general, stressed that settling the question of the 'Saharan provinces' was of priority concern to his government and to him personally, a creative solution was needed for the identification of those from the three groups. The secretary-general, reporting to the Security Council that no proposals having been 'forthcoming from either party that would permit the resumption of identification of applicants from tribal groupings H41, H51 and J51/52'[2], suggested measures to salvage the plan: persons already identified but not found eligible would be allowed to appeal coincidental with identification of applicants from the contested groups who presented themselves individually; UNHCR would prepare for repatriation of refugees, with the referendum being rescheduled for December the following year.

When Kofi Annan visited the region in late 1998 the package was formally accepted by Polisario, it was March 1999 before Morocco, with certain amendments and a revised timetable, agreed in principle.[3] It was June before identification resumed; a protocol, meticulously phrased, gave both sides freedom to nominate whomever they wished to perform the function of sheikh, provided only he had reached the age of eighteen by December 1993, and advisers could assist, and concordant testimony of both sides' sheikhs was not invariably a sine qua non.[4] The appeals process would begin in mid-July – Morocco immediately filed some 79,000 appeals. Polisario was induced into taking part in what it considered a farce but a farce that would not be twisted to its detriment. What motivated Morocco was murkier, it might have been shrewd to halt the process with tens of thousands of 'well-qualified' applicants still to be identified by the commission, accused of bias by their press, and with Polisario unable to present recognised sheikhs. That would have permitted Morocco to argue that identification had not been completed, leaving it with a card undeclared and Polisario without the certainty it craved. Basri, entangled in his very public rhetoric, could have been hoist with his own petard, unable to retract or retreat, or he may have banked on Polisario refusing to complete, or become so tunnel-visioned that he still counted on manipulating the situation, and he would not have dared inform His Majesty of failure to deliver the outcome promised the king in his lifetime.

25

Non-ending

THE KING DIED IN JULY 1999. Crown Prince Mohammed succeeded as King Mohammed VI in an orderly transfer of power, there was no disruption. The young king enacted progressive measures, permitting greater freedom of expression, moving against corruption and restructuring the government. In September he relieved the ministry of interior of responsibility for Minurso, reassigning it to foreign affairs, and Azmi departed. In October the king dismissed Basri. Identification continued. The mystery remains why the Moroccans persisted in driving to the bitter end a process that would be to Morocco's disadvantage.

When a further part of the provisional voter list was released Morocco 'expressed surprise and dismay', questioned the impartiality and objectivity of identification commission members, and, immediately filed appeals to give 'all Saharans rejected by the Minurso Identification Commission ... the opportunity to restate their case'.[1] If anyone originating from the Sahara were denied the right to vote there would be no referendum. Appeals, lodged in conformity with the settlement plan, would ensure it being inconclusive. By 30 December all applicants had at long last been identified: of 195,589 persons identified, and including the disputed tribes, 86,412 were found eligible to vote, marginally exceeding the ten per cent increase on the census envisaged and matching my 1996 predictions.[2] A jubilant Polisario demanded the referendum, threatening a return to hostilities were this deferred.

The process was deadlocked, locked and bolted, without incentive for compromise. Morocco was obdurate in refusing to honour a procedure it dismissed as biased, and not only biased but incomplete, wielding appeals as foreseen in the plan – although it was unthinkable that the Security Council would mandate a repeat of the long and costly identification operation with an ultimate outcome unlikely to differ. Polisario, of course, saw no cause for appealing a convincing electoral roll and no justification for postponing the referendum. Polisario supporters had long aspired to this, it was what they most wanted, what they had not dared to expect, and now it was theirs, impatient for action they campaigned for immediate implementation.

Baker was asked to explore ways to address the situation. This was not the abyss he once envisaged inducing the parties to negotiate, it was a crest from which both peered ahead with blinding clarity. No creative ambiguity lent itself to compromise. Morocco, determined not to be coerced into any less advantageous deal, clung to the appeal provision fully aware that this would never be implemented. Polisario had the result it craved – the dog from whom the bone was not to be wrested. So both rejected alternatives, sticking to the plan for opposed and incompatible reasons.

An attempt was made to break the deadlock in early 2000. At two meetings in London, the parties faced each other for the first time since Houston. Neither gave ground: 'the meeting,' Baker reported, 'instead of resolving the problems, had in fact moved things backwards' as it had deepened the differences between the parties.[3] Experts gathered in July fared no better. In September, in Berlin, Baker presided personally over another encounter but failed to have them budge despite suggesting they explore ways to advance the appeals process while at the same time searching for a political solution.

Special representatives had a diminished political role, Dunbar had already resigned after little more than a year, to be followed by others, mostly American, none of whom stayed long. Baker's attention was diverted by American politics. It was late spring, following the hair's breadth victory of George W. Bush in the US presidential election, before Baker reverted to the confrontation over Western Sahara. Morocco, arguing that errors in implementation, with two-thirds of the Saharan population excluded from the referendum, invalidated the plan, was prepared to initiate a sincere and frank dialogue. Polisario consented to dialogue within the framework of the settlement plan.

Baker changed tack, he submitted, in annex to the secretary-general's Security Council report of 20 June 2001, a draft 'Framework agreement on the Status of Western Sahara', described as not unlike agreements used where a devolution of authority is granted to the inhabitants of a non-self-governing territory with the final status to be determined by referendum.[4] Morocco, reluctant though it vaguely professed to be, was willing to treat the proposal substantively, Polisario, barely controlling its anger, expressed total opposition to any solution ignoring its inalienable right to self-determination. In late August Baker invited Polisario and Algeria, with Mauritania as observer, to his ranch in Wyoming. Neither Polisario nor Algeria was open to considering the draft framework agreement seriously, for Polisario it merely paved the way for 'the precipitous integration of the Saharan Territory into Morocco'.[5]

In early 2002, Baker, after visiting the region, concluded that there was no real chance of the parties agreeing voluntarily. In tandem with Baker Secretary-General Kofi Annan took a radical decision, he presented to the Security Council four options from which to select one, and one only, to be imposed on the parties.[6] The first option was to resume implementation of the settlement plan; the second to accept the framework agreement, as revised by the personal envoy; the third for the personal envoy to explore possible division of the territory; the fourth would terminate Minurso. The Council, in a quandary, voted time for consideration by 'experts', but opinion was sharply divided, compromise impossible. The resolution eventually adopted gave Baker six months to develop a political solution, other than the earlier alternatives; nothing hinted that this be imposed on the parties without their consent – that was a mandate Baker had been unable to have Washington endorse. On 5 November 2002, the twenty-seventh anniversary of the Green March, in a speech to the nation, King Mohammed VI claimed increasing support internationally for a political solution respecting Moroccan sovereignty and territorial integrity, the king decreed this rendered the settlement plan referendum '*caduc, car inapplicable*' – lapsed, because not applicable.[7]

Baker presented the parties, in January 2003, with a draft 'Peace plan for self-determination of the people of Western Sahara' and invited comments. By mid-March, when comments were received, the Council had the Iraq war to contend with. It was May before Baker's proposal and the parties' comments could be considered. The Peace Plan was elaborated in greater detail than the 'Framework Agreement' with areas of competence spelled out.[8] It provided for a referendum of self-determination not less than four or more than five years after the plan's implementation in which would be entitled to vote those found eligible by Minurso, repatriated refugees and persons who had resided continually in Western Sahara since 30 December 1999. Pending the referendum powers would be vested in a Western Sahara Authority to be elected by those on the Minurso list and repatriated refugees. The secretary-general's interpretation would be binding in the event of any dispute. Neither side was overjoyed. In summarizing critical points the secretary-general thought Morocco objected principally to a choice between integration and independence without provision for a negotiated compromise; Polisario's main objection seemed to be that the Peace Plan was not the settlement plan.

The problem, he concluded, would not be solved without one or both of the parties doing something they were not otherwise prepared to do.[9] No one expected the Security Council acting to enforce compliance.

Polisario sprang a surprise, it accepted the Peace Plan, although Boukhari, the representative in New York, qualified this as not abandoning the 1991 settlement plan.[10] The Moroccans, appalled at the prospect of a Western Sahara Authority dominated by the Polisario leadership for at least four years, were surely counting on Polisario's rejection and had been outmanoeuvred. Concerted lobbying in and around the Security Council was needed to convince the Council to elbow aside the Peace Plan discreetly by adopting a resolution to 'assist the parties to achieve a just, lasting and mutually acceptable political solution, which will provide for the self-determination of the people of Western Sahara'.[11] The preamble specified that the Council was acting under chapter VI of the UN charter, thus excluding binding arbitration or enforcement. While in New York for the UN General Assembly King Mohammed met with President George W Bush and was reportedly assured that the US would not seek to impose a solution unacceptable to Morocco or have the Security Council do so. The Moroccan response to a terrorist attack in Casablanca on 16 May 2003 had helped demonstrate value to America. In 2004 Washington recognized the US-Morocco relationship by designating Morocco a major non-NATO ally, 'our appreciation for Morocco's steadfast support in the global war on terror'.[12] The same month the senate ratified a free trade agreement.

James Baker informed the secretary-general in June 2004 that he believed he had done all he could and tendered his resignation. An international statesman, after seven plus years, had abandoned the search for a solution; his departure left a vacuum. The US did not propose a successor despite Polisario lobbying for another eminent American, touting names like Bill Clinton and Colin Powell;[13] Washington was prepared to disengage. Combining personal envoy with special representative misfired, Polisario refused dealing with a well-qualified Peruvian, Alvaro de Soto, in the dual capacity and he was reassigned.

Only in July 2005 did the secretary-general appoint a personal envoy: Peter van Walsum, a Netherlands diplomat. By the time he came to brief the Security Council in January 2006 he had concluded there was no merit in presenting yet another plan that would be subject to the parties' voluntary acceptance, the UN had either to await a 'different political reality' or move to 'direct negotiations between the parties'. Direct negotiations 'without preconditions' might develop a compromise respecting both international legality and political reality,[14] talks, van Walsum was to say, 'shape their own consensuality'. With Security Council encouragement meetings were organized in 2007 and 2008 at Manhasset near New York, they were frosty, delivered nothing. Morocco refused any reference to independence, Polisario refused to exclude independence as an option. When, in August 2008, van Walsum declared in an interview that 'an independent Western Sahara is not an attainable goal' and coming to terms with reality would be in the Saharans best interest[15] Polisario withheld further dealing with him. His contract was allowed to lapse and an American diplomat, Christopher Ross, was appointed personal envoy. Little changed, despite Security Council calls to negotiate without preconditions, Morocco rejected any talk of independence and Polisario was unwilling to negotiate without mentioning independence.

Encouraged by Security Council interest in a 'political solution' Morocco had intimated readiness to develop a proposal for some devolution of governmental authority that was 'genuine, substantial and in keeping with international norms', but initial drafts were found wanting. In April 2007 Polisario submitted a proposal for a 'Mutually Acceptable Political Solution that Provides for the Self-Determination of the People of Western Sahara' reiterating acceptance of the Baker plan and expressing willingness to negotiate modalities leading to a referendum of self-determination with the options of independence, integration into Morocco and self-governance. The next day, 11 April, Morocco presented its 'Initiative for Negotiating an Autonomy Statute for the Sahara Region'. The US was quick to welcome the Moroccan proposal, characterizing it as 'serious and credible', language reflected in France's favourable reaction and later adopted by the Security Council.[16]

Ambassador Ross made occasional forays to the region, held Manhasset encounters, to little effect. Confident in an electoral roll based on the final list of eligible voters Polisario clung to independence as an option; Polisario saw no reason to give up, Morocco would never give in. For three years Polisario was unwilling even to talk. Morocco, comfortable with the response to its Autonomy Statute initiative and convinced that it would not be compelled to act against its interests, believed Minurso's electoral roll superseded. A new 'Moroccan Sahara' was in the making, this involved major investment in infrastructure, communications, services and, importantly, demography; the population grew and the population changed; settlers were encouraged. The proposed Autonomy Statute was enhanced through human rights measures, and, in 2011, announcement of Mohammed VI's revised constitution;[17]

regionalization, the granting of powers to the regions and away from the centre, received parliamentary approval.

Polisario, its supporters dispirited, faced losing the drive of its dynamic youthful leaders as they grew middle-aged, disillusioned. Morale in the camps suffered, after so many years of hope, disappointment, revived hope and repeated disappointment, it was increasingly hard to imagine a compromise being made politically acceptable. Sahrawis, throughout history accustomed to austerity and the deprivations of desert living, had qualities to endure, if only endurance sufficed. Morocco was prepared to wait. It went on investing in the territory it controlled where housing, schools, hospitals, water supplies and services alongside economic development were transforming Sahrawi life into a modern society, no longer nomadic desert tribes. Rabat, by stalling, exploiting alliances and diplomatic maneuvering had castrated a settlement plan that it long felt as an affront to its sovereignty. UN military observers continuing to monitor the cease-fire line helped provide an effective and economic defence against Polisario adventurism, Morocco accepted that price, but it was increasingly reluctant to accommodate the civilian component of Minurso as an embarrassing reminder of the call for a referendum.

Ban Ki-Moon, approaching his final year as UN secretary-general, proposed a visit to the region. Twice dates were put forward and agreed, twice they were cancelled by Ban, a third proposal was inconvenient to Morocco, the king would be travelling. Although this precluded being received in Rabat or Laayoune, Ban decided to go. In the camps he displayed a deference to the RASD flag that Morocco deemed inappropriate though this was nothing compared to what he said: he referred to Western Sahara as 'occupied' by the Moroccans. Rabat was outraged. Mass demonstrations followed – conservative estimates exceeded a million marchers - and the decision was announced to expel the civilian component of Minurso when Ban Ki-Moon not only failed to retract his words but criticized the demonstration.[18]

The Security Council faced a dilemma as it approached the annual renewal of Minurso's mandate. After a meeting, which was especially challenging and contentious,[19] the Council gave Morocco ninety days to reconsider but without threatening enforcement. Morocco, unalarmed, focused elsewhere. Having obtained the support of a majority of the organization's member states, twenty-eight out of fifty-four, in signing a proposal to withdraw the membership of SADR, Morocco signified its intention to return to the African Union. January following, 2017, to mark Morocco's readmission King Mohammed VI delivered an ambitious speech spelling out a vision for Africa and Morocco in

Africa. This was diplomatically reinforced by continent-wide state and official visits and treaties of cooperation. The development of fertilizer production greatly enhanced the value of Morocco's phosphate providing an export to rival hydrocarbons when Algeria's economy was in difficulty.

In March 2017 Christopher Ross resigned, which gratified Morocco. In April the new secretary-general, Antonio Guiterres, released a forceful report calling for a changed dynamic and spirit. Regional security concerns, terrorism, emigration, conditions in the camps made action imperative. The time had come to reach a solution to the conflict, the parties should negotiate without preconditions, explore means of self-determination, and Algeria and Mauritania should be involved.[20] The proposals received the Security Council's endorsement.[21]

Morocco's attempt to dislodge SADR to an extent revitalized Polisario. After years of trench warfare with only the occasional grenade lobbed across the divide the struggle grew in action and intensity. With the staunch backing of Algeria and South Africa Polisario was energetic in mobilizing support in its campaign for Africa's last colony to be decolonized through an act of self-determination in accordance with UN General Assembly resolutions, dismissing any alternative. Morocco, equally inflexible, insisted that there could be no alternative to a solution other than within the framework of Morocco's sovereignty over its Sahara and the Autonomy Initiative, as King Mohammed stated in a major speech commemorating the anniversary of the Green March.[22]

The secretary-general's new envoy, former president of Germany Horst Koehler, succeeded in organizing meetings attended by Algeria and Mauritania as well as Morocco and Polisario. The participation of Algeria, long demanded by Morocco, was significant and prospects were potentially improved by the demise of Algeria's president and the possibility of policy change. But in early 2019 South Africa co-opted twenty-seven countries, from the subregion plus Algeria, to express unflinching commitment to Polisario. Within a month Morocco welcomed thirty-eight countries to Marrakech to endorse the Moroccan position. Neither side hinted at compromise. In May 2019 Koehler resigned, ostensibly for health reasons. His departure bequeathed a situation in substance little changed. The Security Council took no new action.

By late 2020 a frustrated Polisario reinforced demonstrations near Guerguerat blocking traffic on the road leading into Mauritania and beyond. The blockage of commercial transport on the principal overland route into Africa aggravated Morocco just as it was developing trade throughout the continent. On 13 November Rabat reacted. The military were mobilized to disperse the demonstrators, which was effected successfully without loss of life. Polisario interpreted military action as violating the cease-fire agreement, which they thus considered lapsed. They embarked on a campaign of missile bombardment against Moroccan positions in the sandwall area.

Morocco, relieved at the opening of the road to business traffic and unphased by the bombardment, was further bolstered by outgoing President Trump's decision on 22 December to recognize Moroccan sovereignty over Western Sahara while formalizing the tripartite agreement between the US, Morocco and Israel. Despite objections from, for example, James Baker and John Bolton, the decision was not revoked by the subsequent Democrat administration.

Algeria, alongside unabated support in the AU and elsewhere for Polisario's commitment to a referendum of self-determination with the option of independence, pursued its active anti-Moroccan policy. The gas pipeline transiting Morocco to Europe was closed, as was airspace, and diplomatic relations were severed. Morocco meanwhile continued working to expand support and welcomed an impressive number of states in establishing a consular presence in the Saharan region, twenty before the end of 2021. Relations with the Gulf Cooperation Council and with Egypt strengthened and relations with the Federal Republic of Germany recovered following a temporary reversal.

In January 2022 the appointment by the secretary-general of the distinguished diplomat Staffan de Mistura as his personal envoy raised some hope that Security Council resolution 2602 strongly urging a mutually acceptable political solution based on compromise could be interpreted imaginatively. But de Mistura's tour of the region, where he visited Rabat, the Polisario camps, Algeria and Mauritania, seems only to have confirmed existing positions. Morocco remained willing to discuss a settlement in the framework of Moroccan sovereignty and the autonomy proposal recognized by the Security Council as serious and credible. Polisario, with Algeria's unflagging support, simply insisted on a referendum of self-determination with the option of independence.

Twenty-five years ago I had been successful in negotiating with both sides agreement to meet and debate a compromise solution. The rectangular coffee table always there during preliminary talks served to define the range for discussion. Off one end: independence – and I chopped that away, off the other: straightforward integration – and I chopped that away. Whatever remained on the table between those extremes, some degree of regional autonomy, could be considered. In 1996 constructive meetings took place in Geneva and Rabat with both Morocco and Algerian backed Polisario represented at the highest responsible level. Unfortunately, largely extraneous factors undermined a successful conclusion. And subsequent activity only served to entrench positions. At this time when nothing, short of radical political change, looks likely to permit progress it should not be forgotten that in living memory Morocco and Polisario, with Algeria's backing, have met to negotiate a compromise political solution.

Then in March 2022 Spain addressed a communiqué to King Mohammed expressing support for the political solution based on regional autonomy as endorsed by the Security Council.[24] Spain has a special role being the former colonial power with some residual administrative responsibility as well as the country with most geographical, historical and folk ties to the Mahgreb. Morocco was delighted, Polisario and Algeria outraged. Spain's alignment with the Security Council, the United States and Germany gives an important boost to hope for a negotiated political solution based on regional autonomy.

NOTES

The present memoir is a privileged insider account deliberately written in an informal style so as to reveal the motivations and conduct of the leading personalities involved. Describing in confidential detail how the most powerful acted explains why the UN settlement plan could not be implemented and why the conflict remains unresolved after all these years.

That was not possible in my official, more bureaucratic report published as *Western Sahara, Anatomy of a Stalemate?*. Quite different though this book is in both intent and style as well as in the significant parts of its content, it was, however, inevitable that some of the same source material be quoted and that something of my wording resurface in places, which I acknowledge. But this memoir is principally based, not on published documents or scholarly research, but on the meticulous notes that I wrote during or immediately after every meeting or event of significance. I endeavoured to record language verbatim and noted any revealing aspect of manner or expression.

I am greatly indebted to two colleagues, and friends, Louise Laheurte and Anna Theofilopoulou, who held key positions as Western Sahara desk officers at the UN in New York; they kept me comprehensively informed about everything relevant to Western Sahara. At a critical stage I also benefitted from briefing by a US State Department ally.

Prologue

1. Interview in *Jeune Afrique,* 7 March 2005, para 36.

Chapter 2

1 Bertrand Fessard de Foucault 'La question du Sahara espagnol' *Revue Francaise d'Etudes Politiques Africaines* 10, no.119, November 1975, 78. Cited in Tony Hodges, *Western Sahara: The Roots of a Desert War*, 85. See Erik Jensen, *Western Sahara: Anatomy of a Stalemate?* 13.
2 Spain conquered Mellila in 1497. Ceuta, taken by Portugal in 1415, came under the Spanish crown in 1556. Both remained Spanish possessions when Morocco achieved independence in 1956. By the Treaty of Fez and Tangier Statute, 1923, Tangier was administered by the major European powers until 1956.
3 Pronouncement at M'Hamid was included in a Moroccan memoire to the ICJ; see also Hodges, Roots, 96, n.7.
4 Hassan II, *La Memoire d'un Roi*, 85.
5 Ibid., 185.
6 Ibid., 187.
7 Ibid., 158-161 and personal communication (an invitee at the event).
8 Ibid., 171-2, see also Hodges, *Roots*, 177-8, and Perrault, *Notre ami le roi*, 170.

Chapter 3

1 See Jensen, *Anatomy*, 15
2 Report of UN Visiting Mission to Spanish Sahara, May-June 1975, UN General Assembly, thirtieth session, official records 1975, supplement 23, UN Doc. A/10023/Rev 1 (1975).See Jensen, *Anatomy*, 15.
3 Lewin, Andre, 'La mission de l'ONU' in Hassan II, *La Marche Verte*, 221-225.
4 Hassan II, *Memoire*, 188.
5 General Assembly Res. 3292 (13 December 1974).
6 International Court of Justice: Western Sahara, Advisory Opinion of 16 October 1975 (ICJ, The Hague, 1975). See Jensen, *Anatomy*, 16.
7 Thomas M. Franck 'The Stealing of the Sahara' in *American Journal of International Law* vol.70, no.4, October 1976, 711. Cited by Hodges, *Roots,* 225 n.4.
8 Hassan II, *Memoire,* 190.

9 See Jensen, *Anatomy*, 17.

10 Henry Kissinger 'declared in Madrid that "the United States will not allow another Angola on the East flank of the Atlantic Ocean."' Leo Kamil, *Fueling the Fire: US policy and the Western Sahara Conflict*, Trenton, NJ, The Red Sea Press, 1987, 10. See Jensen, *Anatomy*, 17.

11 Although the Madrid Accords of 14 November 1975 were secret, the declaration of principles as made public indicated that Spain would withdraw from Spanish Sahara by the end of February 1976, and in the meantime it would proceed forthwith to institute a temporary administration in which Morocco and Mauritania would participate in collaboration with the Djemaa Assembly (of chiefs). See Annex III to UN Doc S/11880 of 19 November 1975, cited by Hodges, *Roots*, 223. Jensen, *Anatomy*, 17.

12 UN General Assembly Res 3458 A (10 December 1976).

13 UN General Assembly Res 3458 B (10 December 1976). Jensen, *Anatomy*, 18.

14 Quoted in Anthony Pazzanita and Tony Hodges, *Historical Dictionary of Western Sahara*, Scarecrow, Metuchen NJ, 1994, 83. See Jensen, *Anatomy*, 17.

15 UN High Commissioner for Refugees, Programme of Humanitarian Assistance in the Tindouf Area, UN Doc. HCR/155/42/76 (1976). See Jensen, *Anatomy*, 18.

16 Olof Rydbeck's report was not published.

17 See Jensen, *Anatomy*, 18-19.

18 Hodges, *Roots*, 285, see 292, n.29, ref to *Sahara Libre*, no 75, February 20, 1979.

19 *Le Matin du Sahara*, February 10, 1982. See also Hodges, *Roots*, 314.

20 John Damis, *Conflict in Northwest Africa; The Western Sahara Dispute*, Hoover Institution Press, Stanford, California, 1983, 81-2. See Jensen, *Anatomy*, 22.

21 *Le Monde*, 28 – 29 June 1981, see Hodges, *Roots*, 311. Jensen, *Anatomy*, 22-23.

22 See Jensen, *Anatomy*, 23.

23 Report of the Secretary-General UN Doc. S/21360, 18 June 1990, para 1. Jensen, *Anatomy*, 25

24 Javier Perez de Cuellar, *Pilgrimage for Peace*, St Martin's Press, New York, 1997, 342-3. See Jensen, *Anatomy*, 26.

25 *Le Point*, 12 December 1988, and *New York Times*, 28 December 1988, cited Yahia H.Zoubir, 'Protracted Conflict and Failure to Achieve Prenegotiation in the Western Sahara Conflict' *Humboldt Journal of Social Relations* 20, no 2 (1994), 25. Compare Jensen, *Anatomy*, 26.

26 Zoubir, *Protracted Conflict*, 27. See Jensen, *Anatomy*, 26.

27 *Agence France Press* 16 January 1989, cited Zoubir, *Protracted Conflict*, 28. See Jensen, *Anatomy*, 26.

28 *Le Nouvel Observateur*, 12-18 January 1989, see Zoubir, *Protracted Conflict*, 28. See Jensen, *Anatomy*, 26.

29 Marrack Goulding, *Peacemonger*, John Murray, London, 2002, 203-4. See Jensen, *Anatomy*, 29.

30 Report of the Secretary-General UN Doc. S/21360, 18 June 1990.

31 Morocco Press Agency (MAP) press release, referenced *Maroc/Onu/Sahara*, 19 October 1990. See Jensen, *Anatomy*, 30-31.

32 Frente Polisario Office at the United Nations, New York, press release of 26 November 1990. Jensen, ibid.

33 Goulding, *Peacemonger*, 212. See Jensen, *Anatomy*, 31.

34 Perez de Cuellar, *Pilgrimage*, 352. See Jensen, *Anatomy*, 31.

35 Report of the Secretary-General UN Doc. S/22464, 19 April 1991.

36 Security Council Resolution 690 (1991) of 29 April 1991. Jensen, *Anatomy*, 33.

37 Report of the Secretary-General UN Doc. S/23299, 19 December 1991, para 3.

38 Ibid. para 8. See Jensen, *Anatomy*, 34.

39 'After he retired, Perez de Cuellar was reportedly appointed to the board of a Moroccan-owned holding firm, Omnium Nord Africa, and the international press accused him of malfeasance.' Jaret Chopra, 'A Chance for Peace in Western Sahara', *Survival* 39, no 3 (1997), 54. Cited Jensen, *Anatomy*, 34.

40 Report of the Secretary-General UN Doc. S/23299, Annex, para 15 *et passim*.

41 John Bolton, *Resolving the Western Sahara Conflict*, transcript of the Congressional Defense and Foreign Policy Forum, Washington, DC, March 1998, 3-4.

42 Ibid. See Jensen, *Anatomy*, 37.

43 Security Council Resolution 725 (1991) 31 December 1991.
44 See Jensen, *Anatomy*, 38.
45 Report of the Secretary-General UN Doc. S/25170, 26 January 1993, para 33.
46 Security Council Resolution 809 (1993), 2 March 1993.

Chapter 4

1 Comment made to me personally.
2 See Jensen, *Anatomy*, 11.
3 See Jensen, *Anatomy*, 10.
4 See Jensen, *Anatomy*, 11.

Chapter 5

1 See Jensen, *Anatomy*, 43, where the meeting-room issue is described.

Chapter 6

1 Quoted Jensen, *Anatomy*, 51.
2 See Jensen, *Anatomy*, 56.
3 See Jensen, *Anatomy*, 44.

Chapter 7

1 Report of the Secretary-General UN Doc. S/1994/283, 10 March 1994, paras 24-26.
2 Security Council Resolution 907 (1994), 29 March 1994, see op. para 4.

Chapter 8

1 Security Council Presidential Statement, 29 July 1994.

Chapter 10

1 Also quoted in Jensen, *Anatomy*, 63-64.
2 Compare Jensen, *Anatomy*, 64.

Chapter 14

1 Personal communication (State Department source).
2 Goulding reporting to me.

Chapter 15

1 Personal communication.
2 Ibid.

Chapter 17

1 Personal communication.

Chapter 18

1 Personal communication
2 Analogy similarly described in Jensen, *Anatomy*, 78.

Chapter 20

1 Report from Tindouf.
2 Ibid.
3 Personal communication.

Chapter 21

1 Personal communication
2 Report from Tindouf
3 Personal communication (State Department source).
4 Ibid.

5 Personal communication.
6 Ibid.
7 Snoussi addressing the General Assembly Fourth Committee, October 1996; see Morocco's official statement to Security Council of 25 November 1996 (UN Doc. S/1996/973) urging the Council to refrain from mentioning contacts ('contacts with a part of the Saharan population and our lost sons with the aim of inducing them to return to the motherland') since not part of the Settlement Plan.
8 Sir Crispin Tickell responding to press queries outside Security Council.
9 Report from Tindouf.
10 Personal communications.
11 Sahrawi National Radio, as reported from Tindouf.
12 Goulemine and Tan-Tan, both places of some size, are situated in southern Morocco. Although inhabited by predominantly Saharan tribes these are generally sympathetic to Morocco and are not 'Western Saharans', unlike those living around Smara.

Chapter 22

1 Personal communication (State Department source).
2 Basri interview, *Jeune Afrique*, 7 March 2005, para 37.
3 UN Doc S/1997/358, 5 May 1997, para 3. Quoted Jensen, *Anatomy*, 82.
4 Personal communications (US, UK sources).

Chapter 23

1 As monitored.
2 Polisario broadcast as reported from Tindouf.

Chapter 24

1 'submerged by the Bakerine tide' , see similar language in Jensen, *Anatomy*, 85.
2 Report of the Secretary-General UN Doc. S/1998/849, 11 September 1998, para 4. See Jensen, *Anatomy*, 87. Note error in census category number: H51 should read H61.
3 Report of the Secretary-General UN Doc. S/1999/307, 22 March para.
4 See Jensen, *Anatomy*, 88.
5 See also Jensen, *Anatomy*, 88.

Chapter 25

1 Report of the Secretary-General UN Doc. S/2000/131, 17 February 2000, para 5. See Jensen, *Anatomy*, 89.
2 Report of the Secretary-General UN Doc. S/2001/148, 20 February 2001, para 8. See Jensen, *Anatomy*, 90.
3 Report of the Secretary-General UN Doc. S/2000/683, 12 July 2000, para 27. See Jensen, *Anatomy*, 93
4 Report of the Secretary- General UN Doc. S/2001/613, 20 June 2001, Annex. See Jensen, *Anatomy*, 96.
5 Report of the Secretary-General UN Doc. S/2002/41, 10 January 2002, Annex I, 8. See Jensen, *Anatomy*, 96.
6 Report of the Secretary-General UN Doc. S/2002/178, 19 February 2002, paras 48-51.See Jensen, *Anatomy*, 97-98.
7 *Le Matin*, 6 November 2002. See Jensen, *Anatomy*, 100.
8 Report of the Secretary-General UN Doc. S/2003/565, 23 May 2003, Annex II. See Jensen, *Anatomy*, 100-101.
9 Ibid., paras 51-54.
10 Frente Polisario Office at the United Nations, New York, press release, 11 July 2003. See Jensen, *Anatomy*, 102.
11 Security Council Resolution 1495 (2003), 31 July 2003, S/RES/1495 (2003) see Preambular para 4. See Jensen, *Anatomy*, 102.

12 BBC News and World Service online, June 4, 2004, cited Stephen Zunes and Jacob Mundy, *Western Sahara: War, Nationalism and Conflict Irresolution*, Syracuse University Press, Syracuse, 2010, 238-9.
13 Zunes and Mundy, *War, Nationalism*, 240. See Jensen, *Anatomy*, 108.
14 Report of the Secretary-General UN Doc. S/2006/249, 19 April 2006, paras 32 and 34. See Jensen, *Anatomy*, 109.
15 *El Pais*, 8 August 2008. See Jensen, *Anatomy*, 111.
16 *Agence France Presse*, 11 April 2007. Morocco's efforts characterized as 'serious and credible', see Report of the Secretary-General UN Doc. S/2007/202 of 13 April 2007 and Security Council Resolution 1754 S/RES/1754 (2007) of 30 April 2007. See Jensen, *Anatomy*, 111.
17 Security Council Resolution 1979 (2011), 27 April 2011, welcomed measures enacted by Morocco with respect to Human Rights, etc. See Jensen, *Anatomy*, 115.
18 Moroccan march protesting Ban Ki-Moon statement in Polisario camps, see *The Associated Press*, 13 March 2016, *Le Monde*, 17 and 18 March 2016, expulsion of UN personnel and reaction in New York, see *Daily Maverick*, 24 March 2016, *Sahara Press Service* and *Morocco World News*, 20 April 2016.
19 Security Council meeting was described as challenging and contentious (by the US ambassador), and the resolution, S/RES/2285(2016) of 29 April 2016, was not adopted by consensus. See *Sahara Press Service* and *Morocco World News*, 28 and 29 April 2016.
20 Report of the newly appointed Secretary-General, Antonio Guterres, UN Doc. S/2017/307, 10 April 2017.
21 Security Council Resolution S/RES/2351(2017) 28 April 2017.
22 Mohamed VI address to Nation at Anniversary of Green March, published *Morocco World News*, 6 November 2017.
23 Quoted *Morocco World News*, 22 May 2020.
24 Morocco World News 18 and 20 March 2022

Bibliography of works referred to and related publications

Adebajo, Adekeye. *Selling out the Sahara: The tragic tale of the UN referendum.* Ithaca: Cornell University Institute for African Development, 2002.

Albright, Madeleine. *Madam secretary.* London: Macmillan, 2003.

Bahaijoub, Ali. *Western Sahara conflict: historical, regional and international dimensions.* London: North-South Books, 2010.

Balta, Paul, and Claudine Rulleau. *Le grand Maghreb: des indépendances à l'an 2000.* Paris: La Découverte, 1990.

Barbier, Maurice. *Le conflit du Sahara Occidental.* Paris, L'Harmattan, 1982.

Berramdane, Abdelkhaleq. *Le Sahara Occidental: Enjeu maghrébin.* Paris, Karthala,1992.

Bolton, John. "Resolving the Western Sahara Conflict." Transcript of the Congressional Defense and Foreign Policy Forum, Washington, DC, 1998.

Boutros-Ghali, Boutros. *Unvanquished, a U.S.-U.N. Saga.* New York, Random House, 1999.

Chopra, Jarat. "A chance for peace in Western Sahara." *Survival* 39, no. 3 (1997): 51-65.

Damis, John. *Conflict in Northwest Africa: The Western Sahara Dispute.* Stanford, Hoover Institution Press, 1983.

Dunbar, Charles. "Saharan Stasis: Status and Future Prospects of the Western Sahara Conflict." *The Middle East Journal* 4 (2000): 522-545.

Durch, William J. "Building on sand: UN Peacekeeping in the Western Sahara." *International Security* 17, no. 4 (1993): 151-171.

Durch, William. "The United Nations Mission for the Referendum in Western Sahara." In *The Evolution of UN Peacekeeping,* ed. William J. Durch (New York, St Martin's Press,1993), pp. 406-433.

Fessard de Foucault, Bertrand. "La question du Sahara espagnol." *Revue française d'études politiques africaines* 10, no. 119 (1975): 74-106.

Franck, Thomas M., 1976. "The Stealing of the Sahara." *American Journal of International Law, 70* no. 4 (1976), pp.694-721.

Froberville, Martine de. *Sahara Occidental: la confiance perdue.* Paris: L'Harmattan,1996.

Gaudio, Attilio. *Les populations du Sahara Occidental: Histoire, vie et culture.* Paris, Karthala,1993.

Goulding, Marrack. *Peacemonger.* London: John Murray, 2002.

Hannay, David. *Cyprus: The Search for a Solution.* London: IB Tauris, 2005.

Hassan II. *La mémoire d'un roi: Entretiens avec Eric Laurent.* Paris: Plon, 1993.

Hodges, Tony. *Western Sahara: The Roots of a Desert War,* Westport CT: Lawrence Hill, 1983.

---------*The Western Saharans.* No. 40. Minority Rights Group, 1984.

Jensen, Erik. *Western Sahara: Anatomy of a Stalemate?* Boulder and London: Lynne Reinner, 2012.

Kamil, Leo. *Fueling the Fire: US Policy and the Western Sahara Conflict.* Trenton, NJ: Red Sea, 1987.

Maxwell, Gavin. *Lords of the Atlas.* London: Eland, 2004

Mercer, John. *Spanish Sahara.* London: Allen and Unwin, 1976

--------- *The Sahrawis of Western Sahara.* London: Minority Rights Group, 1979.

Pazzanita, Anthony G. *Western Sahara.* Oxford: Clio, 1996.

Pazzanita, Anthony, and Tony Hodges. *Historical Dictionary of Western Sahara.* London: Scarecrow Press, 1994.

Perez de Cuellar, Javier. *Pilgrimage for peace: A Secretary-General's memoir.* New York, St Martin's Press, 1997.

Perrault, Gilles. *Notre ami le roi.* Paris: Gallimard, 1990.

Rézette, Robert. *The Western Sahara and the frontiers of Morocco.* Nouvelles éditions latines, 1975.

Shelley, Toby. *Endgame in the Western Sahara: what future for Africa's last colony? London:* Zed Books, 2004.

Smith de Cherif, Teresa K. "Western Sahara: a Moroccan-style election?" Review of African Political Economy (1993): 99-105.

Spector, Samuel J. "Western Sahara and the self-determination debate." *Middle East Quarterly* (2009).

Theofilopoulou, Anna. *The United Nations and Western Sahara: a never-ending affair* (Vol. 166). United States Institute of Peace.

UN General Assembly. *Report of the U.N. Visiting Mission to Spanish Sahara, May-June 1975.* Thirtieth session, Official Records, Supplement 23, UN Doc. A/10023 Rev. 1, 1975.

UN General Assembly resolutions referenced by resolution number followed by date.

UN High Commissioner for Refugees, Programme of Humanitarian Assistance in the Tindouf Area. UN Doc. HCR/155/42/76, 1976.

UN Security Council resolutions referenced by resolution number with year, followed by date.

UN Security Council documents including Secretary-General's reports to the Council referenced by UN Document number with prefix S, followed by date.

Willis, Michael J. "Conclusion: the dynamics of reform in Morocco."Mediterranean Politics 14.2 (2009: 229-237).

---------- Politics and Power in the Maghreb: Algeria, Tunisia and Morocco form independence to the Arab spring.

Zartman, I. William. *Ripe for resolution: Conflict and intervention in Africa.* New York: Oxford University Press, 1989.

Zoubir, Yahia H. "Protracted conflict and failure to achieve prenegotiation in the Western Sahara conflict." Humboldt Journal of Social Relations 20, 2 (1994: 1-44).

Zoubir, Yahia H. and Daniel Volman, eds. *International Dimensions of the Western Sahara Conflict.* Westport, CT: Prager, 1993.

Zunes, Stephen and Jacob Mundy. *Western Sahara: War, nationalism, and conflict irresolution.* Syracuse: Syracuse University Press, 2010.

Index